WarCraft

LEGENDS

VOLUME TWO

HAMBURG // LONDON // LOS ANGELES // TOKYO

WARCRAFT

LEGENDS

VOLUME TWO

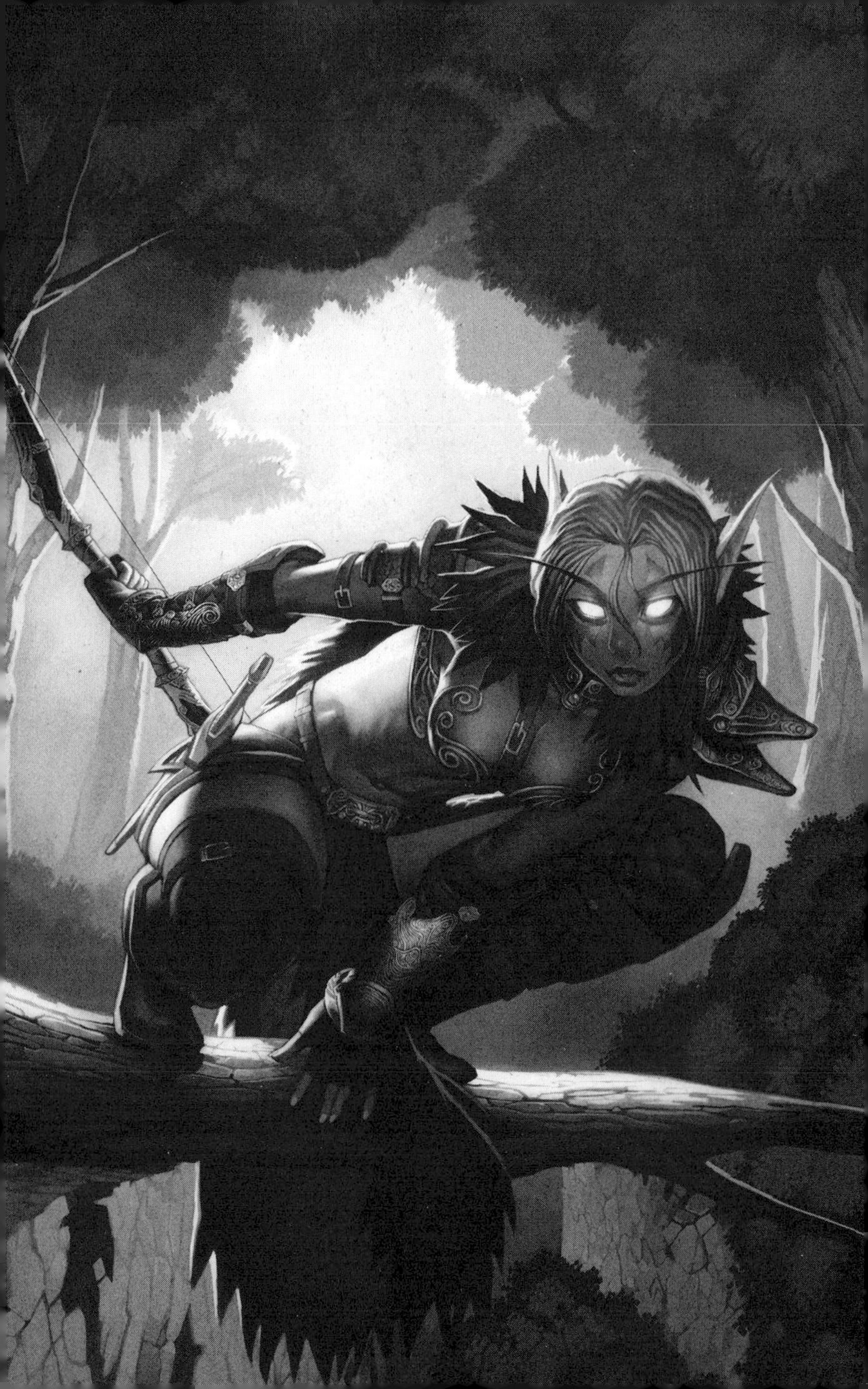

Warcraft: Legends Vol. 2

Contributing Editor - Hyun Joo Kim
Layout and Lettering - Michael Paolilli
Creative Consultant - Michael Paolilli
Graphic Designer - James Lee
Cover Artist - UDON with Saejin Oh

Editor - Troy Lewter
Pre-Production Supervisor - Vicente Rivera, Jr.
Print-Production Specialist - Lucas Rivera
Managing Editor - Vy Nguyen
Senior Designer - Louis Csontos
Senior Designer - James Lee
Associate Publisher - Marco F. Pavia
President and C.O.O. - John Parker
C.E.O. and Chief Creative Officer - Stu Levy

BLIZZARD ENTERTAINMENT

Senior Vice President, Creative Development - Chris Metzen
Director, Creative Development - Jeff Donais
Lead Developer, Licensed Products - Shawn Carnes
Publishing Lead, Creative Development - Rob Tokar
Story Consultation and Development - Micky Neilson
Art Director - Glenn Rane
Director, Global Business
Development and Licensing - Cory Jones
Associate Licensing Manager - Jason Bischoff
Additional Development - Samwise Didier, Evelyn Fredericksen,
Ben Brode, Sean Wang, Bob Richardson

A 🎮 TOKYOPOP Manga

TOKYOPOP and 🎮 are trademarks or registered trademarks of TOKYOPOP Inc.

TOKYOPOP Inc.
5900 Wilshire Blvd. Suite 2000
Los Angeles, CA 90036

E-mail: info@TOKYOPOP.com
Come visit us online at www.TOKYOPOP.com

ISBN: 978-1-4278-0828-8

First TOKYOPOP printing: November 2008
10 9 8 7 6 5 4
Printed in the USA

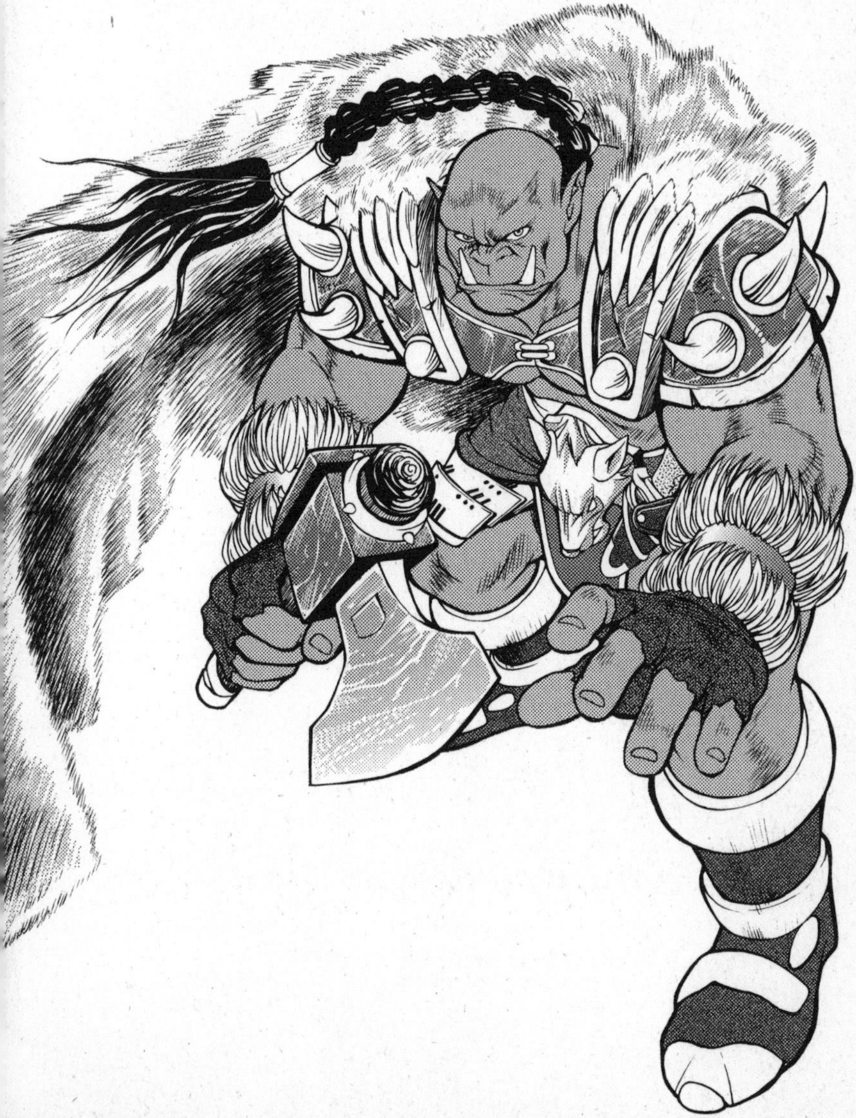

LEGENDS
VOLUME TWO

FEAR

WRITTEN BY RICHARD A. KNAAK

ART BY JAE-HWAN KIM

EDITOR: TROY LEWTER
CONTRIBUTING EDITOR: HYUN JOO KIM
LETTERER: MICHAEL PAOLILLI

STORY SO FAR

The undead walk the lands of Azeroth as rotting nightmares, creatures that are vicious and unyielding in their brutality. They are broken into two factions--the Forsaken (led by the Dark Lady Sylvanas Windrunner) and the Scourge (commanded by the Dark Lord of the Dead, the Lich King). For the living in Azeroth, to be born again undead is to be damned for all eternity.

Trag Highmountain, the courageous tauren who sacrificed his life in *Warcraft: Shadows of Ice,* finds himself reborn as one of the undead. However, Trag's form of undeath is unlike any other, as his mind struggles against the carnal bloodlust. His thoughts are clouded with visions of a foreboding place of ice and snow, his ears filled with the rancid whispers of the Lich King's urges to kill...

In his desperate search to understand the reasons and ramifications of his unnatural state, Trag sought out the tauren shaman Sulamm in hopes that he could restore his life. Sulamm agreed to help him, and together they journeyed to the Henge of the Earth Mother. Once there, Sulamm and Trag fell into a trance that was to return Trag back to his living state.

But alas, Sulamm's tongue was forked, as he betrayed Trag to Ornamm and his tauren kinsmen. Helpless and unaware in his trance, they carried Trag to a pit of fire and thrust him into it. With flames licking at his body, Trag's mysterious power enabled him to overcome the shaman's trance, a feat that should not have been possible. Trag leapt out of the pit, fighting his way through his would-be executioners and to freedom.

Trag returned to Sulamm, the one who betrayed him, his hands hungering for the shaman's neck...only to find Sulamm unable to awaken from his trance, as Trag's sudden burst of power imprisoned his mind for seemingly all eternity. Though Sulamm's fate was sealed, Trag's wasn't, as the search for the truth behind his state has just begun...

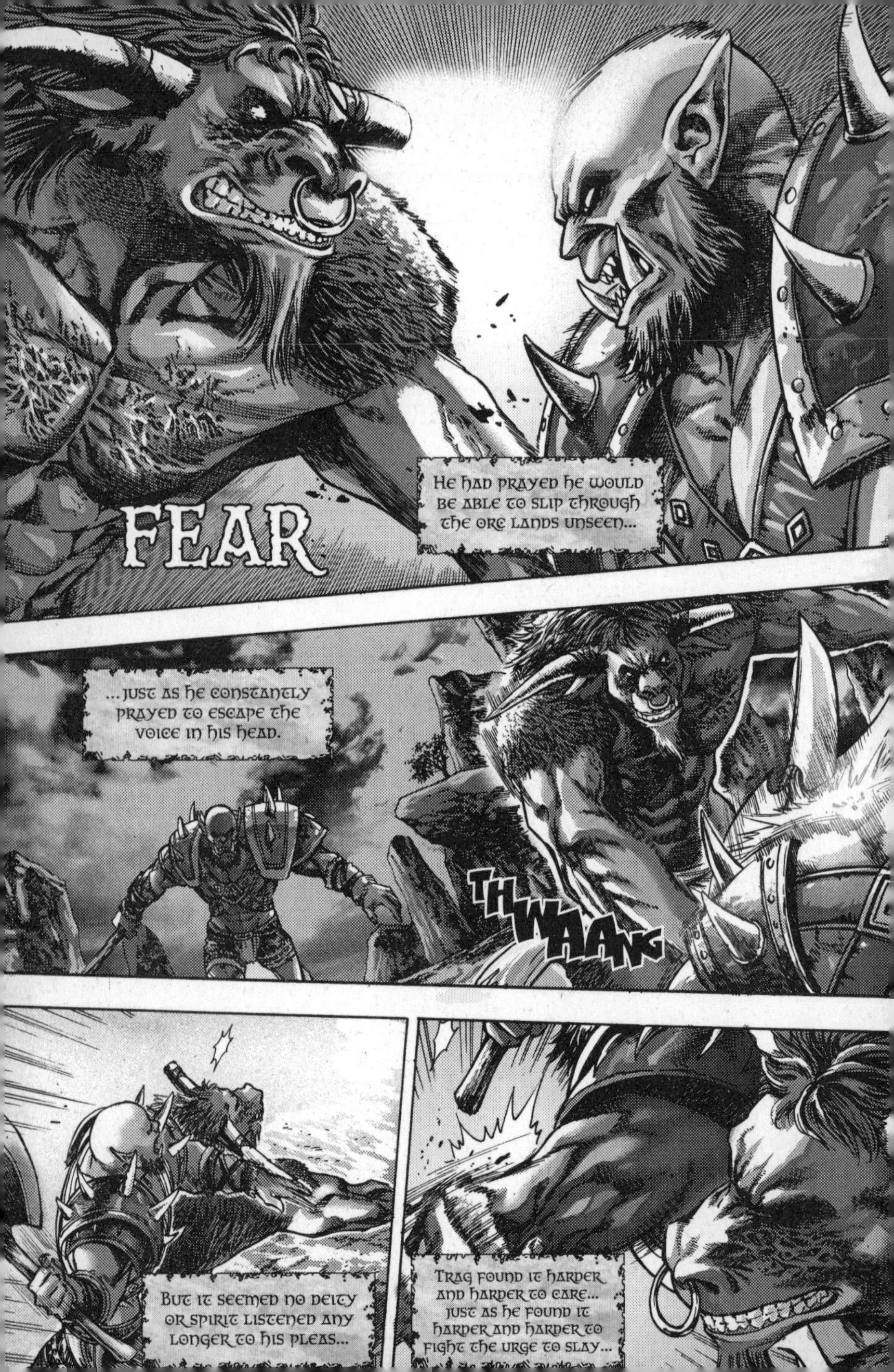
FEAR
He had prayed he would be able to slip through the orc lands unseen...
...just as he constantly prayed to escape the voice in his head.
THWAANG
But it seemed no deity or spirit listened any longer to his pleas...
Trag found it harder and harder to care... just as he found it harder and harder to fight the urge to slay...

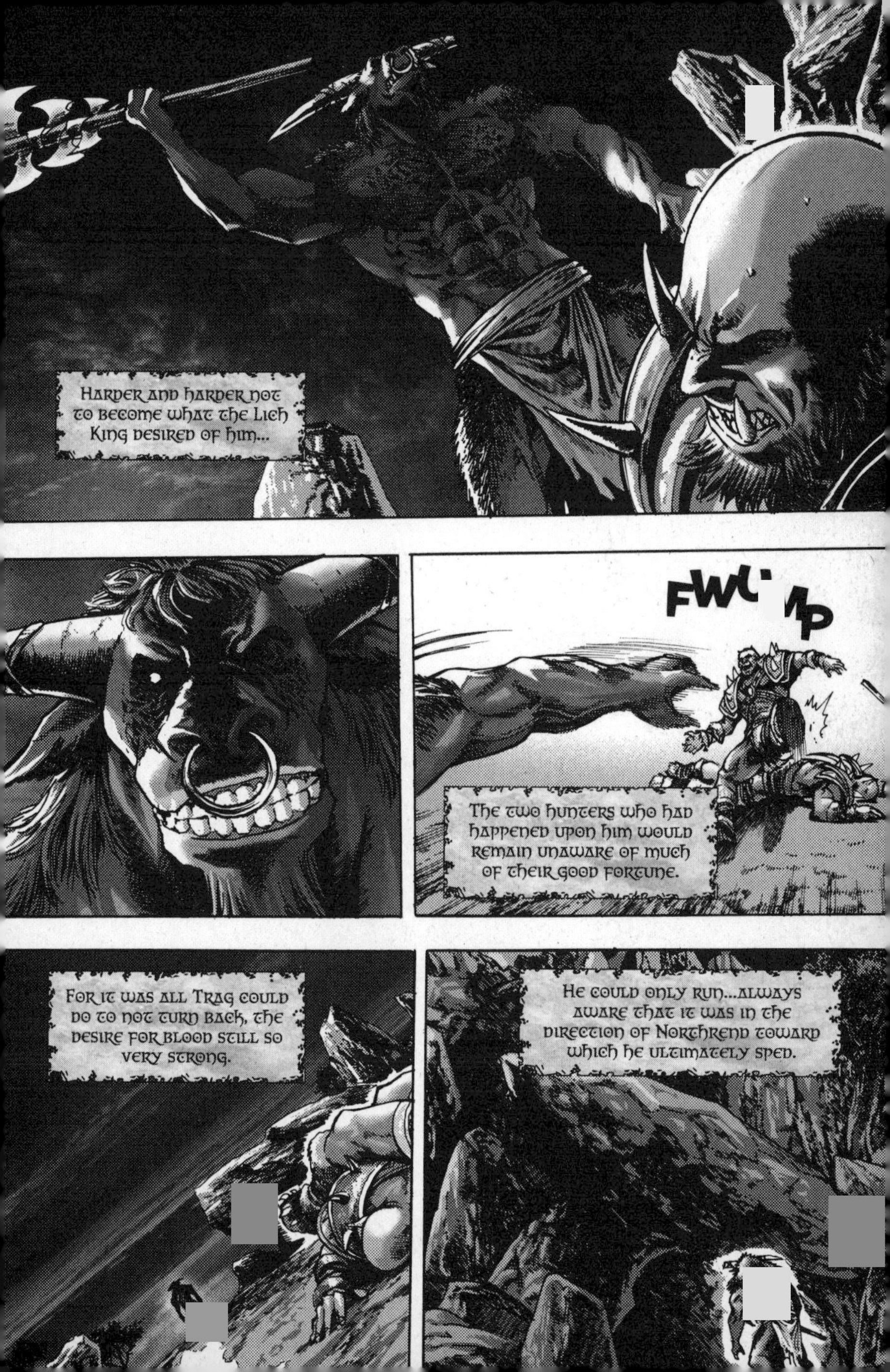
Harder and harder not to become what the Lich King desired of him...
FWUMP
The two hunters who had happened upon him would remain unaware of much of their good fortune.
For it was all Trag could do to not turn back, the desire for blood still so very strong.
He could only run...always aware that it was in the direction of Northrend toward which he ultimately sped.

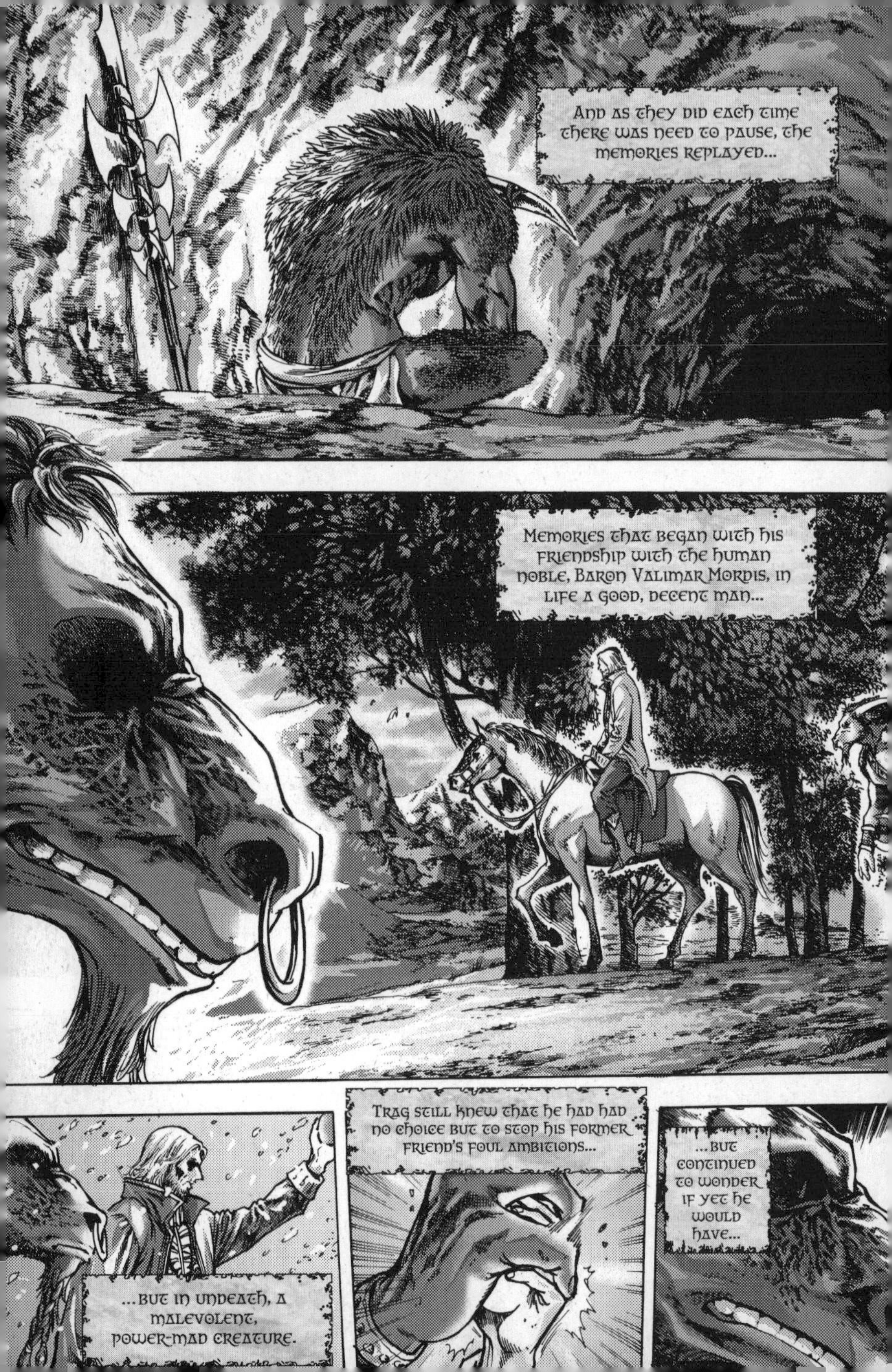
And as they did each time there was need to pause, the memories replayed...
Memories that began with his friendship with the human noble, Baron Valimar Mordis, in life a good, decent man...
...but in undeath, a malevolent, power-mad creature.
Trag still knew that he had had no choice but to stop his former friend's foul ambitions...
...but continued to wonder if yet he would have...

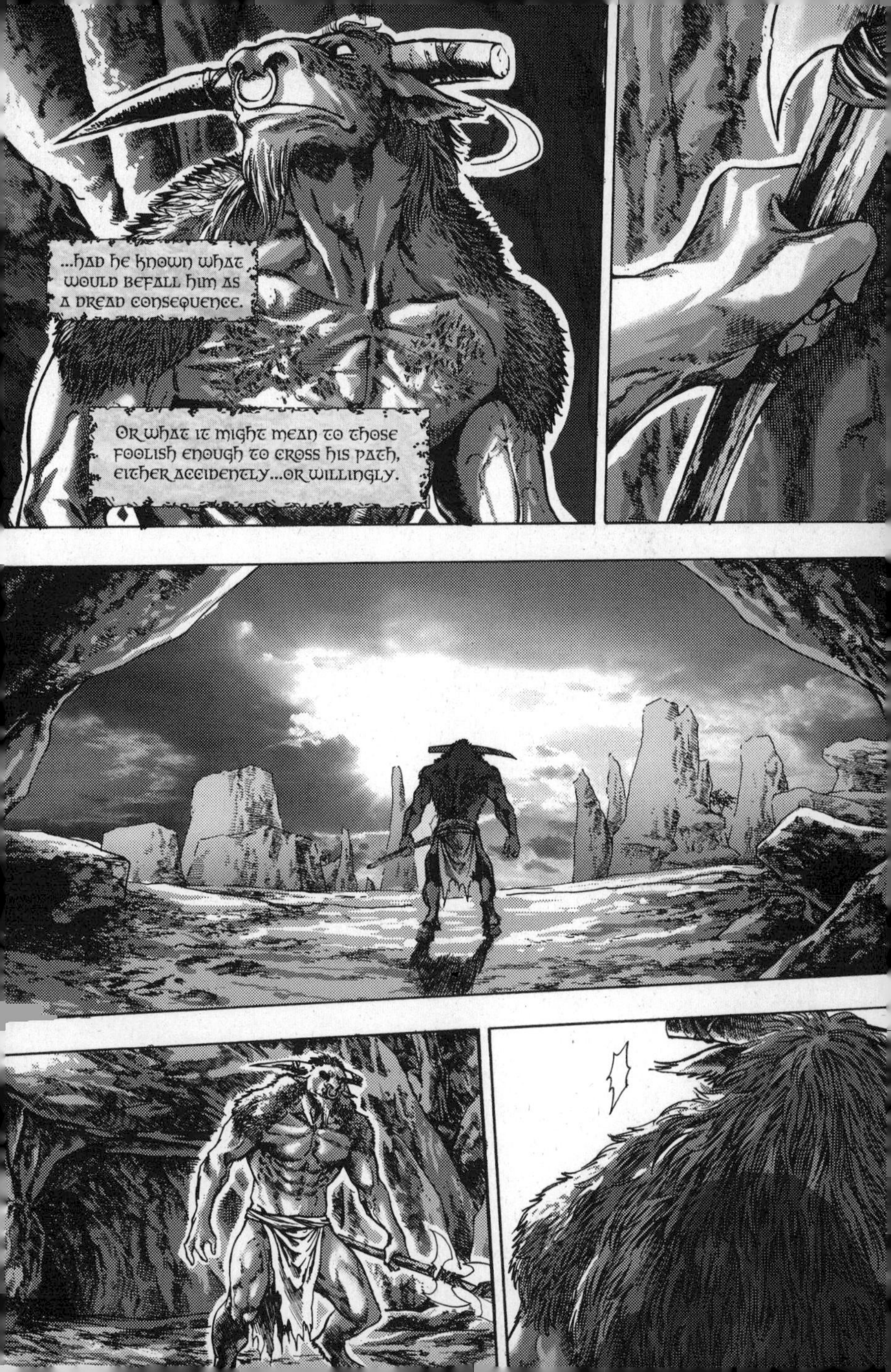
...had he known what would befall him as a dread consequence.
Or what it might mean to those foolish enough to cross his path, either accidently...or willingly.

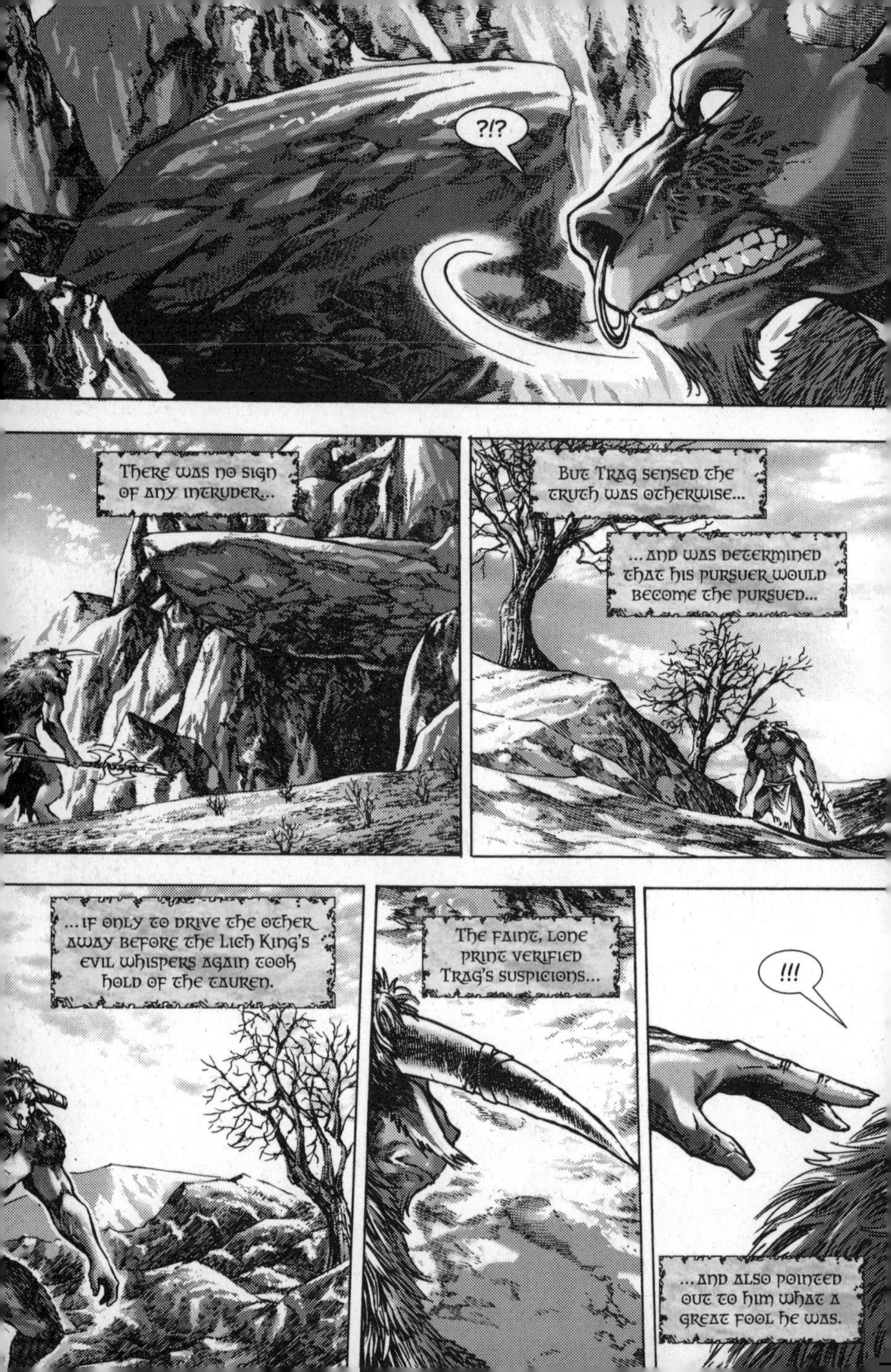
?!?
There was no sign of any intruder...
But Trag sensed the truth was otherwise...
...and was determined that his pursuer would become the pursued...
...if only to drive the other away before the Lich King's evil whispers again took hold of the tauren.
The faint, lone print verified Trag's suspicions...
!!!
...and also pointed out to him what a great fool he was.

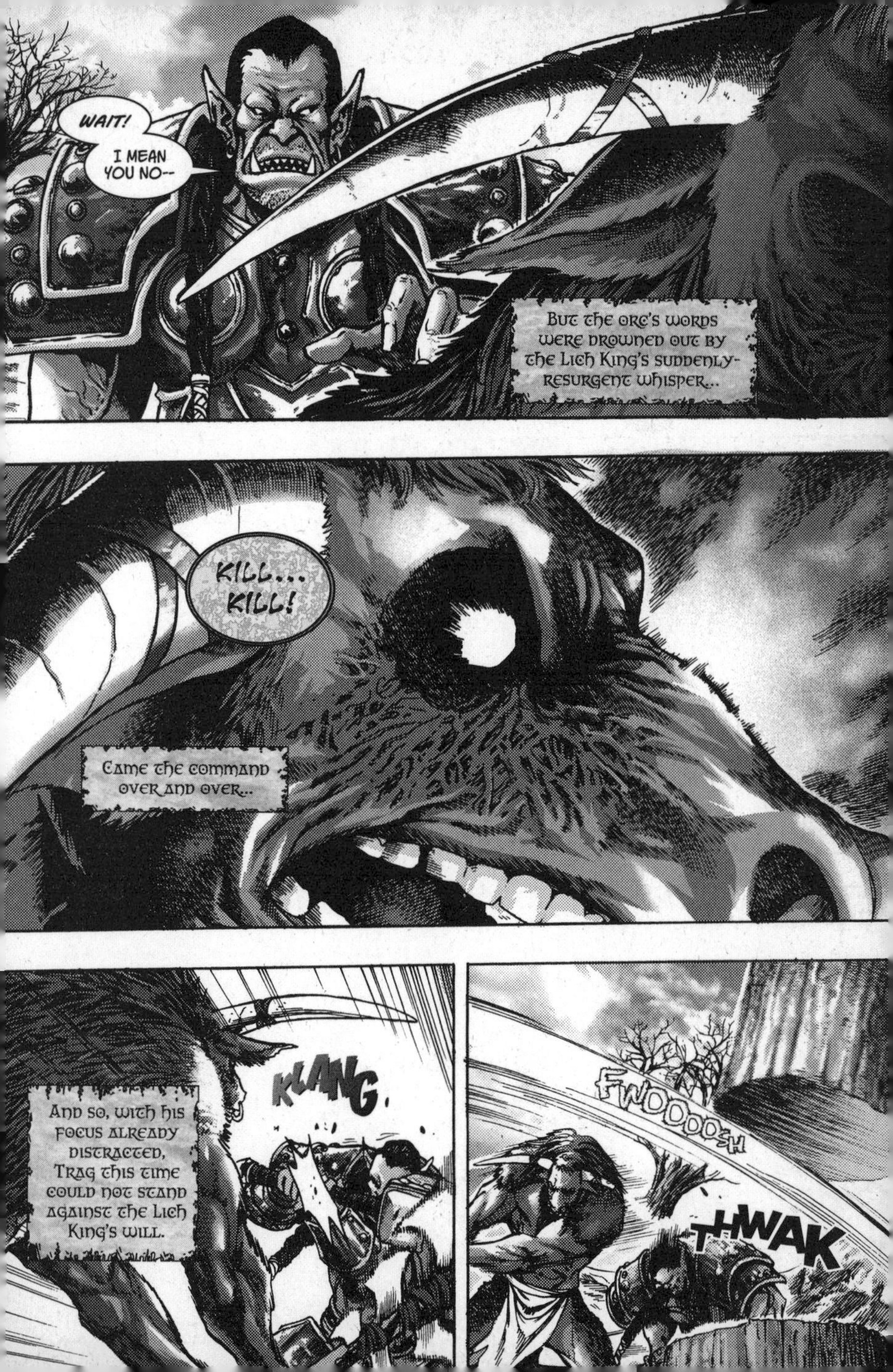
WAIT!
I MEAN YOU NO--
But the orc's words were drowned out by the Lich King's suddenly-resurgent whisper...
KILL... KILL!
Came the command over and over...
And so, with his focus already distracted, Trag this time could not stand against the Lich King's will.
KLANG
FWOOOOOSH
THWAK

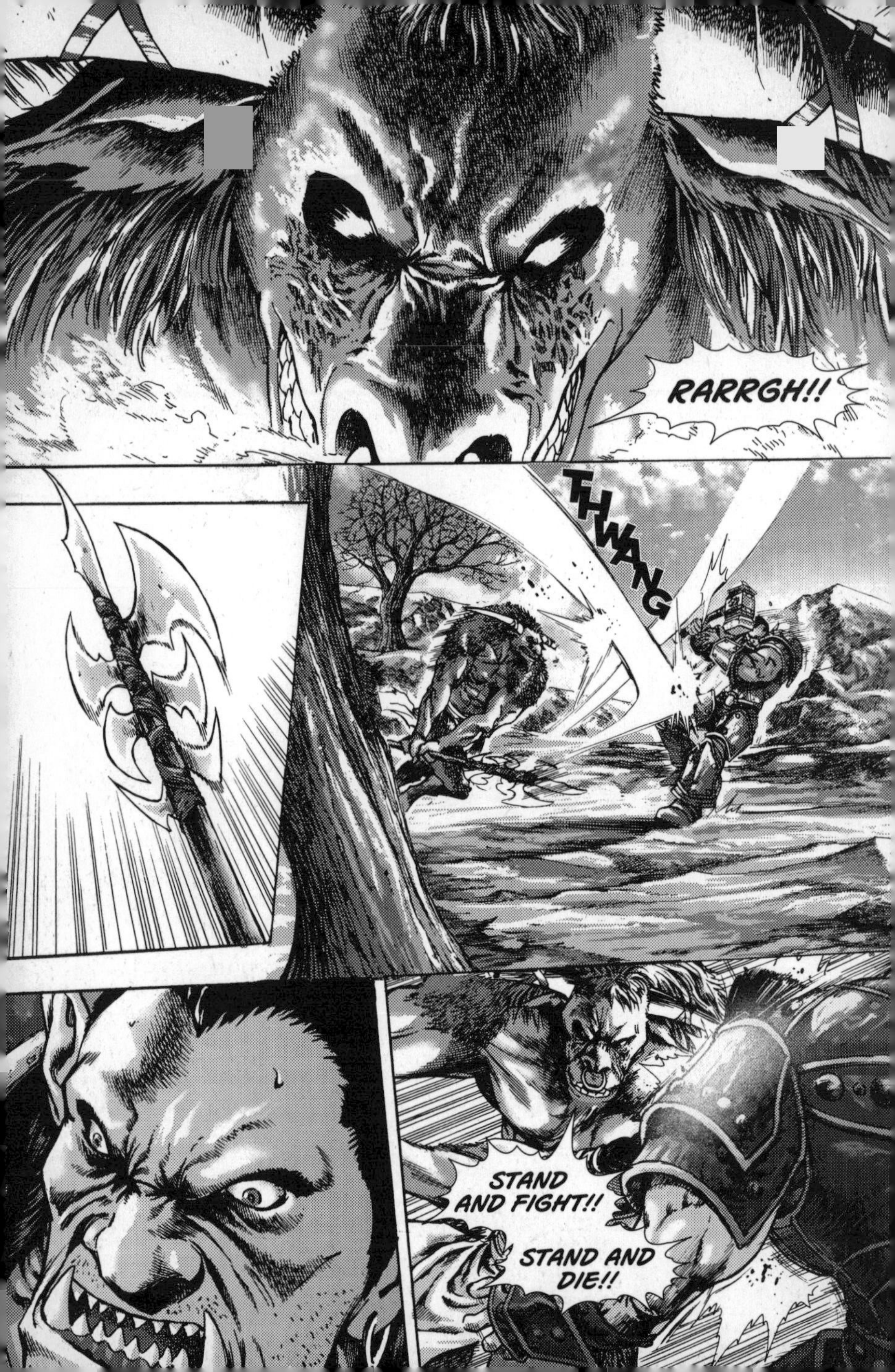
RARRGH!!
THWANG
STAND AND FIGHT!!
STAND AND DIE!!

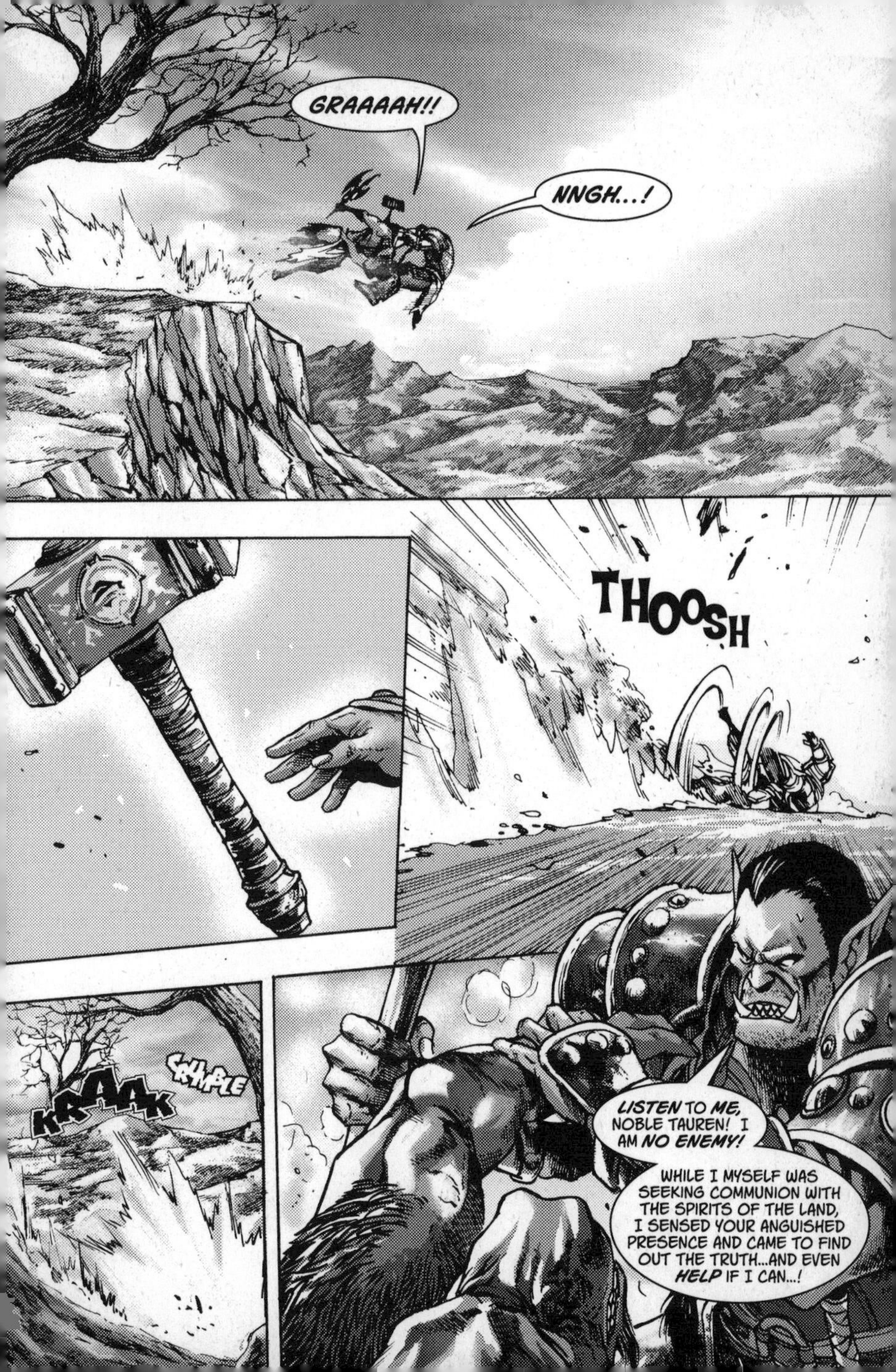
GRAAAAH!!
NNGH...!
THOOSH
KRAAAK
CRUMBLE
LISTEN TO ME, NOBLE TAUREN! I AM NO ENEMY!
WHILE I MYSELF WAS SEEKING COMMUNION WITH THE SPIRITS OF THE LAND, I SENSED YOUR ANGUISHED PRESENCE AND CAME TO FIND OUT THE TRUTH...AND EVEN HELP IF I CAN...!

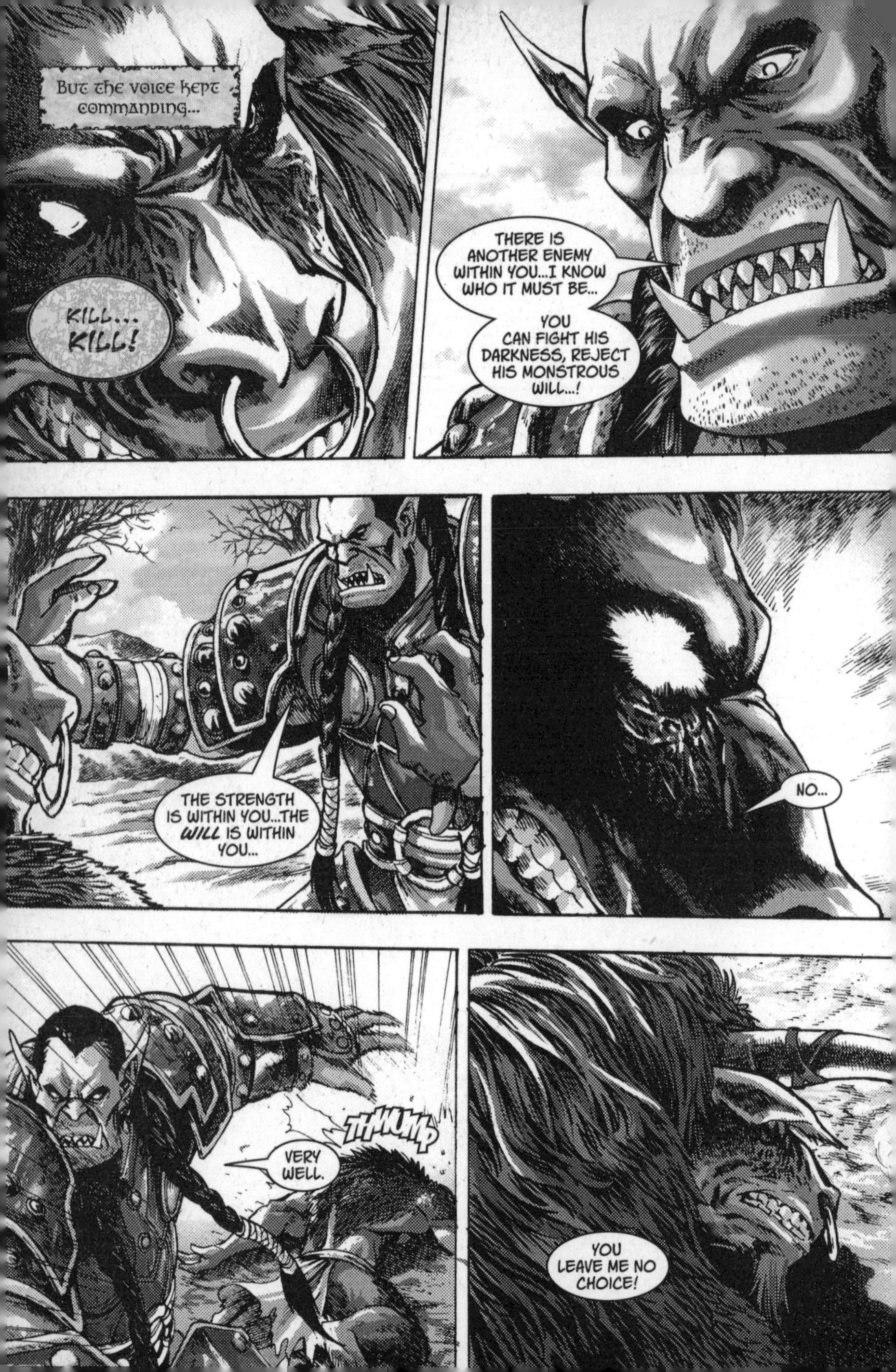

But the voice kept commanding...
KILL... KILL!
THERE IS ANOTHER ENEMY WITHIN YOU...I KNOW WHO IT MUST BE...
YOU CAN FIGHT HIS DARKNESS, REJECT HIS MONSTROUS WILL...!
THE STRENGTH IS WITHIN YOU...THE WILL IS WITHIN YOU...
NO...
THWUMP
VERY WELL.
YOU LEAVE ME NO CHOICE!

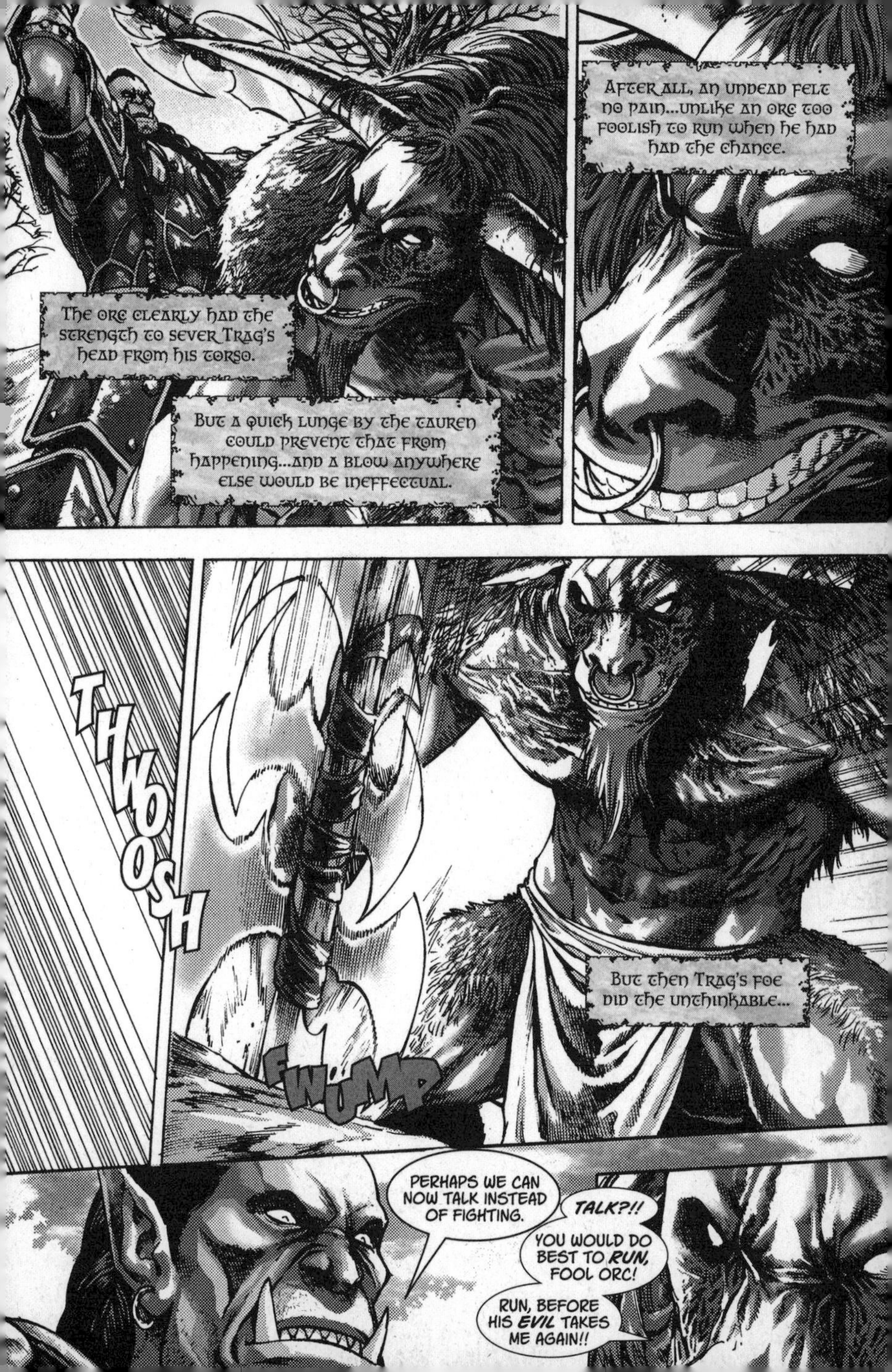

The orc clearly had the strength to sever Trag's head from his torso.
But a quick lunge by the tauren could prevent that from happening...and a blow anywhere else would be ineffectual.
After all, an undead felt no pain...unlike an orc too foolish to run when he had had the chance.
THWOOSH
But then Trag's foe did the unthinkable...
FWUMP
PERHAPS WE CAN NOW TALK INSTEAD OF FIGHTING.
TALK?!!
YOU WOULD DO BEST TO RUN, FOOL ORC!
RUN, BEFORE HIS EVIL TAKES ME AGAIN!!

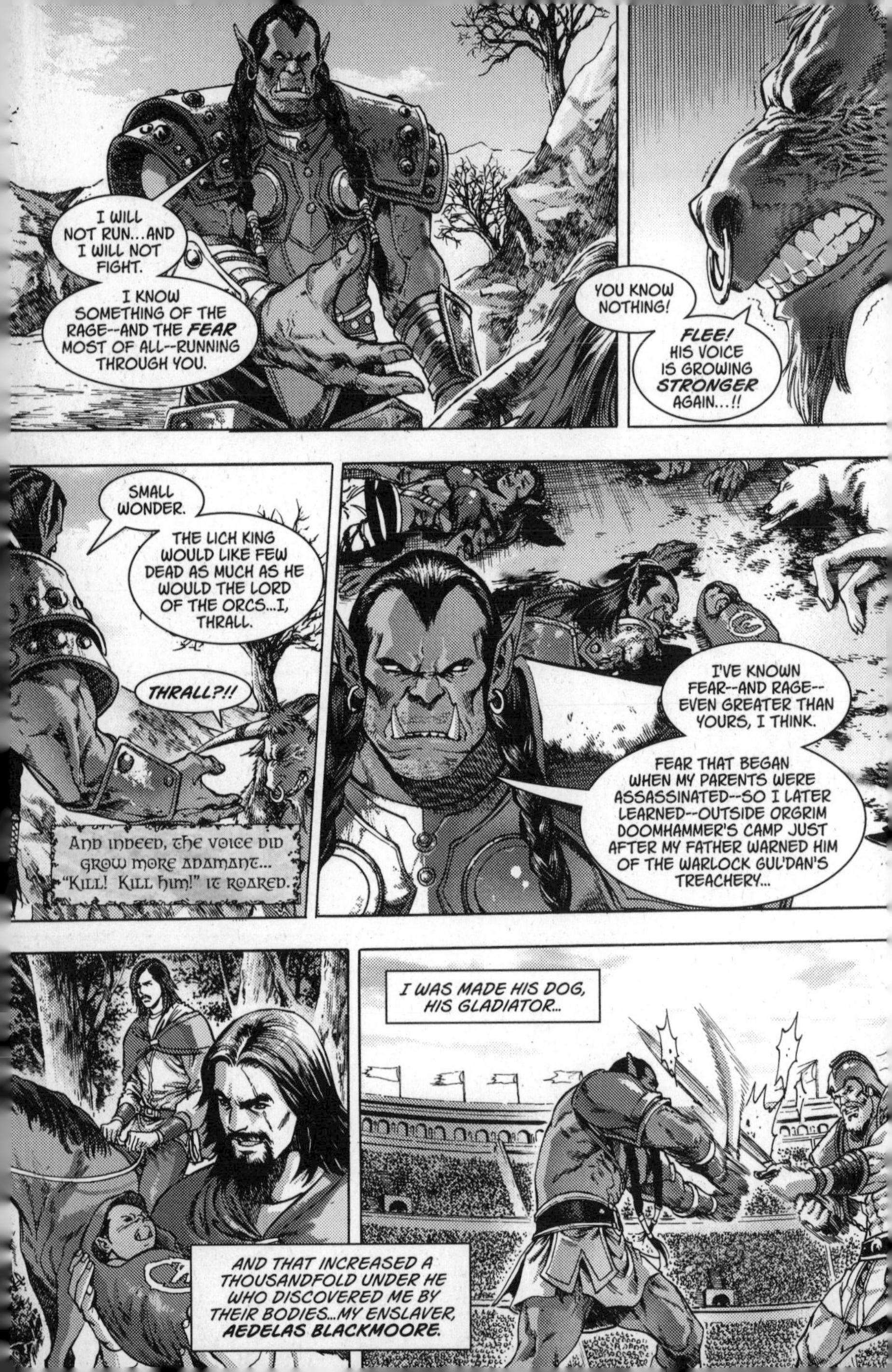
I WILL NOT RUN...AND I WILL NOT FIGHT.
I KNOW SOMETHING OF THE RAGE--AND THE *FEAR* MOST OF ALL--RUNNING THROUGH YOU.
YOU KNOW NOTHING!
FLEE! HIS VOICE IS GROWING *STRONGER* AGAIN...!!
SMALL WONDER.
THE LICH KING WOULD LIKE FEW DEAD AS MUCH AS HE WOULD THE LORD OF THE ORCS...I, THRALL.
THRALL?!!
And indeed, the voice did grow more adamant... "Kill! Kill him!" it roared.
I'VE KNOWN FEAR--AND RAGE--EVEN GREATER THAN YOURS, I THINK.
FEAR THAT BEGAN WHEN MY PARENTS WERE ASSASSINATED--SO I LATER LEARNED--OUTSIDE ORGRIM DOOMHAMMER'S CAMP JUST AFTER MY FATHER WARNED HIM OF THE WARLOCK GUL'DAN'S TREACHERY...
AND THAT INCREASED A THOUSANDFOLD UNDER HE WHO DISCOVERED ME BY THEIR BODIES...MY ENSLAVER, **AEDELAS BLACKMOORE.**
I WAS MADE HIS DOG, HIS GLADIATOR...

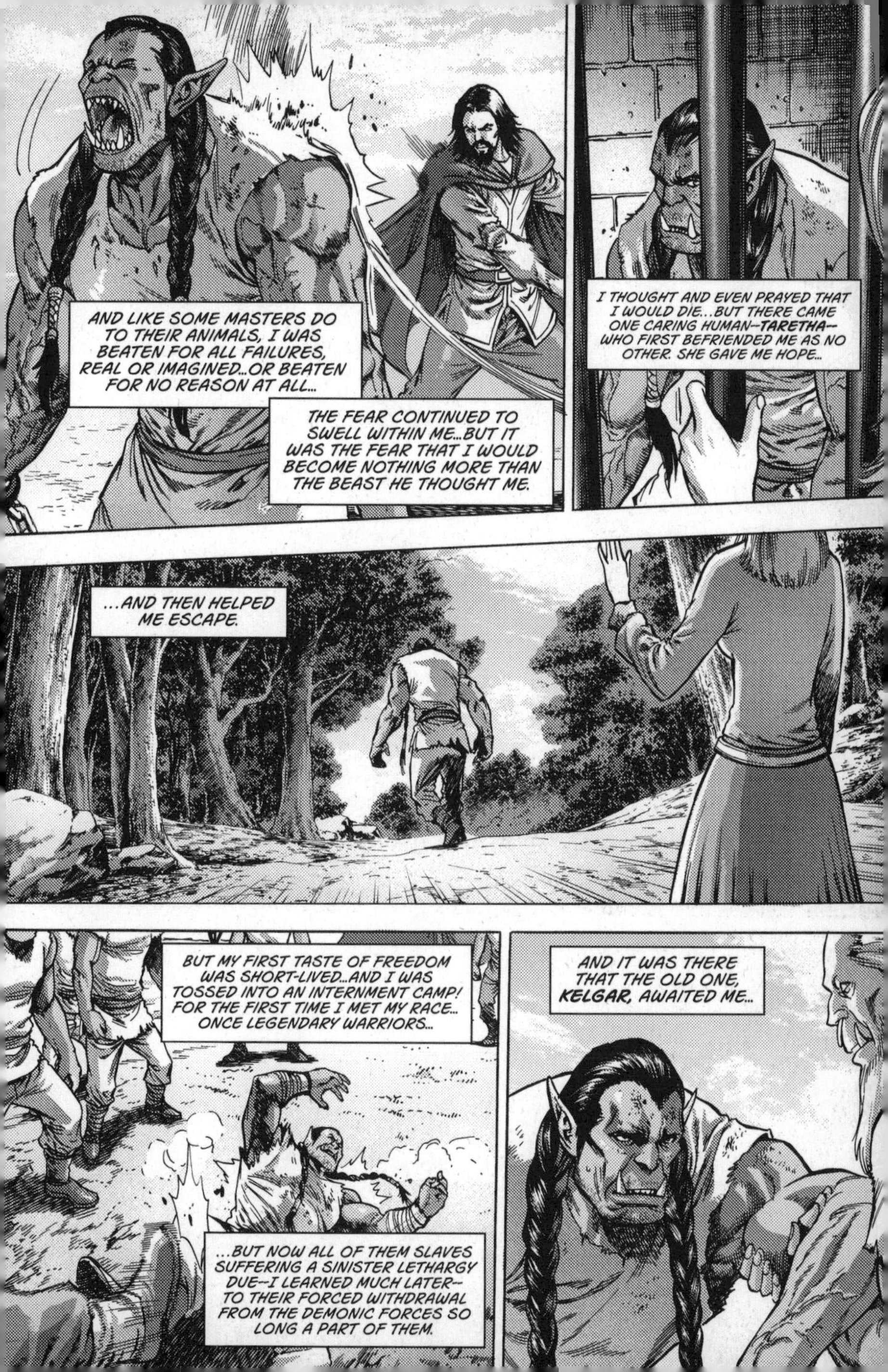
AND LIKE SOME MASTERS DO TO THEIR ANIMALS, I WAS BEATEN FOR ALL FAILURES, REAL OR IMAGINED...OR BEATEN FOR NO REASON AT ALL...
THE FEAR CONTINUED TO SWELL WITHIN ME...BUT IT WAS THE FEAR THAT I WOULD BECOME NOTHING MORE THAN THE BEAST HE THOUGHT ME.
I THOUGHT AND EVEN PRAYED THAT I WOULD DIE...BUT THERE CAME ONE CARING HUMAN--TARETHA--WHO FIRST BEFRIENDED ME AS NO OTHER. SHE GAVE ME HOPE...
...AND THEN HELPED ME ESCAPE.
BUT MY FIRST TASTE OF FREEDOM WAS SHORT-LIVED...AND I WAS TOSSED INTO AN INTERNMENT CAMP! FOR THE FIRST TIME I MET MY RACE... ONCE LEGENDARY WARRIORS...
...BUT NOW ALL OF THEM SLAVES SUFFERING A SINISTER LETHARGY DUE--I LEARNED MUCH LATER--TO THEIR FORCED WITHDRAWAL FROM THE DEMONIC FORCES SO LONG A PART OF THEM.
AND IT WAS THERE THAT THE OLD ONE, KELGAR, AWAITED ME...

FROM KELGAR I LEARNED OF A LONE LEADER WHO DID NOT SHARE THE UNSETTLING LETHARGY I SAW ALL AROUND, WHO STILL CHAMPIONED THE OLD WAYS, THE WAYS OF THE SHAMAN...

GROM HELLSCREAM.

HE WAS A WARRIOR SEEKING TO SAVE MY KIND...

AND SO, WHEN I MANAGED ESCAPE AGAIN, BLACKMOORE'S SOLDIERS BEHIND ME...

...I FOUND GROM HELLSCREAM, WHO STILL EACH DAY FOUGHT BACK THE LETHARGY. HE NOT ONLY WELCOMED A LONE OUTCAST...

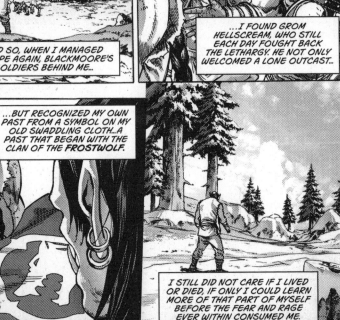

...BUT RECOGNIZED MY OWN PAST FROM A SYMBOL ON MY OLD SWADDLING CLOTH...A PAST THAT BEGAN WITH THE CLAN OF THE FROSTWOLF.

I STILL DID NOT CARE IF I LIVED OR DIED, IF ONLY I COULD LEARN MORE OF THAT PART OF MYSELF BEFORE THE FEAR AND RAGE EVER WITHIN CONSUMED ME.

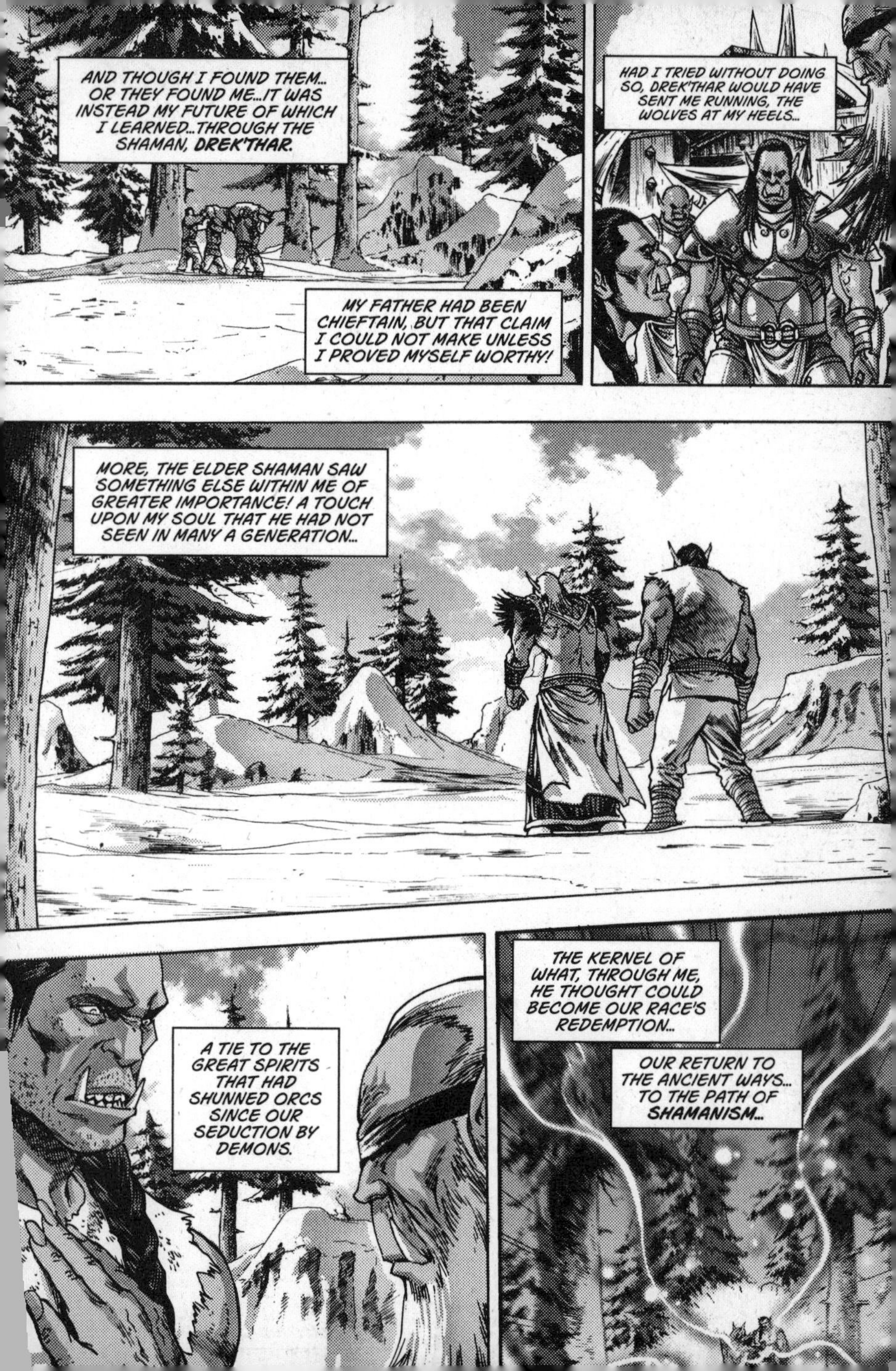
AND THOUGH I FOUND THEM... OR THEY FOUND ME...IT WAS INSTEAD MY FUTURE OF WHICH I LEARNED...THROUGH THE SHAMAN, DREK'THAR.
MY FATHER HAD BEEN CHIEFTAIN, BUT THAT CLAIM I COULD NOT MAKE UNLESS I PROVED MYSELF WORTHY!
HAD I TRIED WITHOUT DOING SO, DREK'THAR WOULD HAVE SENT ME RUNNING, THE WOLVES AT MY HEELS...
MORE, THE ELDER SHAMAN SAW SOMETHING ELSE WITHIN ME OF GREATER IMPORTANCE! A TOUCH UPON MY SOUL THAT HE HAD NOT SEEN IN MANY A GENERATION...
A TIE TO THE GREAT SPIRITS THAT HAD SHUNNED ORCS SINCE OUR SEDUCTION BY DEMONS.
THE KERNEL OF WHAT, THROUGH ME, HE THOUGHT COULD BECOME OUR RACE'S REDEMPTION...
OUR RETURN TO THE ANCIENT WAYS... TO THE PATH OF SHAMANISM...

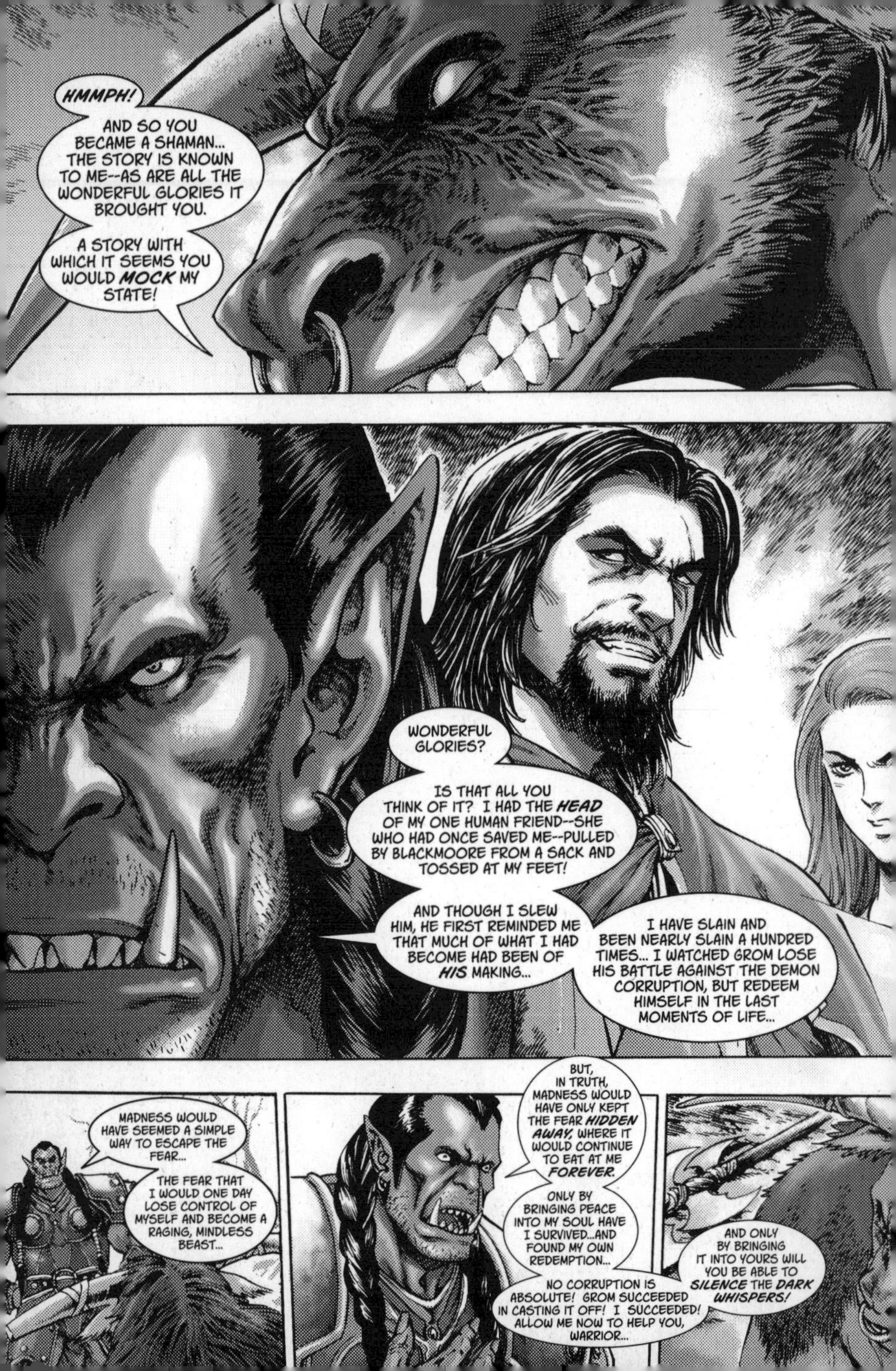
HMMPH!
AND SO YOU BECAME A SHAMAN... THE STORY IS KNOWN TO ME--AS ARE ALL THE WONDERFUL GLORIES IT BROUGHT YOU.
A STORY WITH WHICH IT SEEMS YOU WOULD MOCK MY STATE!
WONDERFUL GLORIES?
IS THAT ALL YOU THINK OF IT? I HAD THE HEAD OF MY ONE HUMAN FRIEND--SHE WHO HAD ONCE SAVED ME--PULLED BY BLACKMOORE FROM A SACK AND TOSSED AT MY FEET!
AND THOUGH I SLEW HIM, HE FIRST REMINDED ME THAT MUCH OF WHAT I HAD BECOME HAD BEEN OF HIS MAKING...
I HAVE SLAIN AND BEEN NEARLY SLAIN A HUNDRED TIMES... I WATCHED GROM LOSE HIS BATTLE AGAINST THE DEMON CORRUPTION, BUT REDEEM HIMSELF IN THE LAST MOMENTS OF LIFE...
MADNESS WOULD HAVE SEEMED A SIMPLE WAY TO ESCAPE THE FEAR...
THE FEAR THAT I WOULD ONE DAY LOSE CONTROL OF MYSELF AND BECOME A RAGING, MINDLESS BEAST...
BUT, IN TRUTH, MADNESS WOULD HAVE ONLY KEPT THE FEAR HIDDEN AWAY, WHERE IT WOULD CONTINUE TO EAT AT ME FOREVER.
ONLY BY BRINGING PEACE INTO MY SOUL HAVE I SURVIVED...AND FOUND MY OWN REDEMPTION...
NO CORRUPTION IS ABSOLUTE! GROM SUCCEEDED IN CASTING IT OFF! I SUCCEEDED! ALLOW ME NOW TO HELP YOU, WARRIOR...
AND ONLY BY BRINGING IT INTO YOURS WILL YOU BE ABLE TO SILENCE THE DARK WHISPERS!

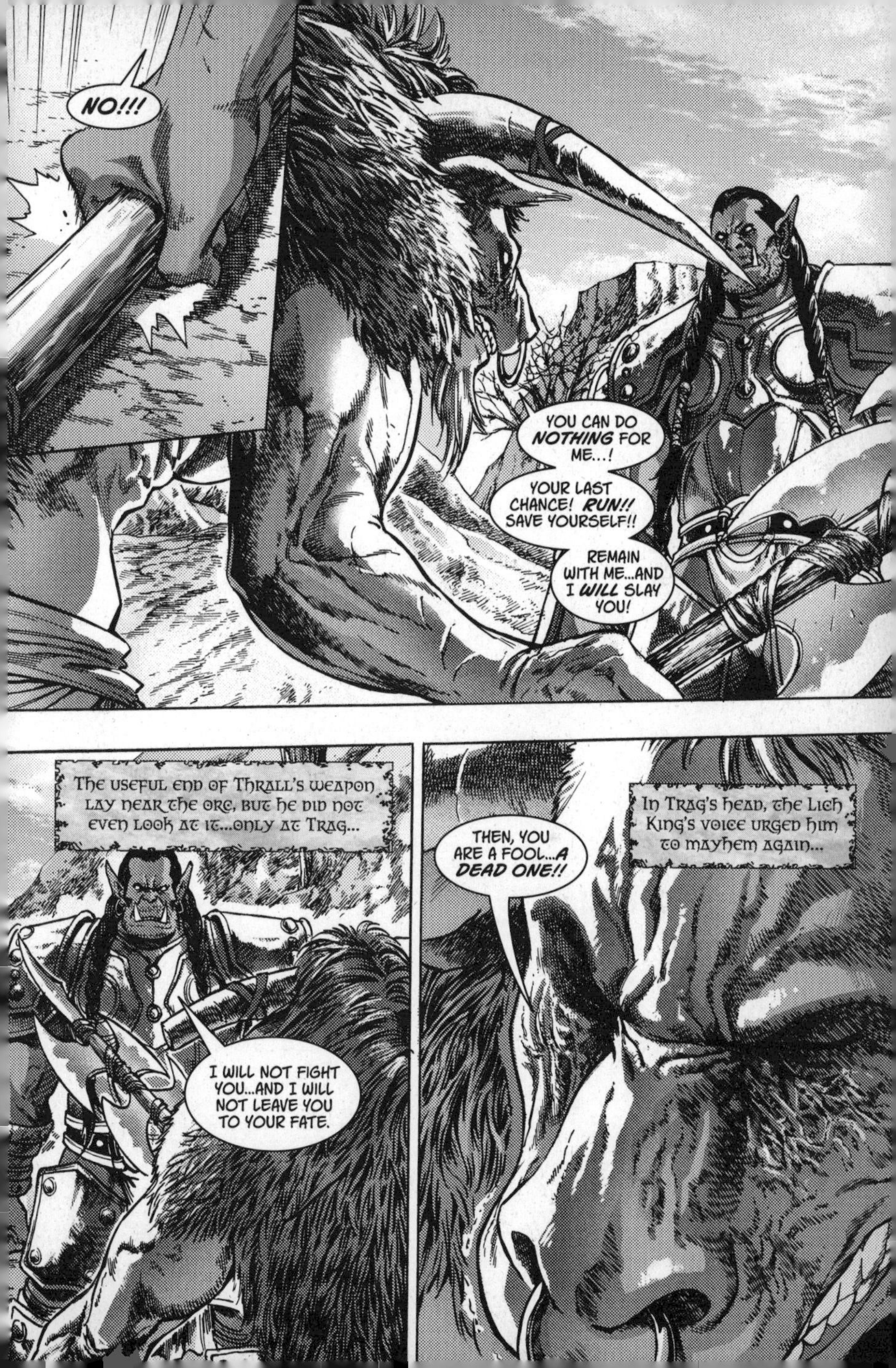

NO!!!
YOU CAN DO NOTHING FOR ME...!
YOUR LAST CHANCE! RUN!! SAVE YOURSELF!!
REMAIN WITH ME...AND I WILL SLAY YOU!
The useful end of Thrall's weapon lay near the orc, but he did not even look at it...only at Trag...
I WILL NOT FIGHT YOU...AND I WILL NOT LEAVE YOU TO YOUR FATE.
In Trag's head, the Lich King's voice urged him to mayhem again...
THEN, YOU ARE A FOOL...A DEAD ONE!!

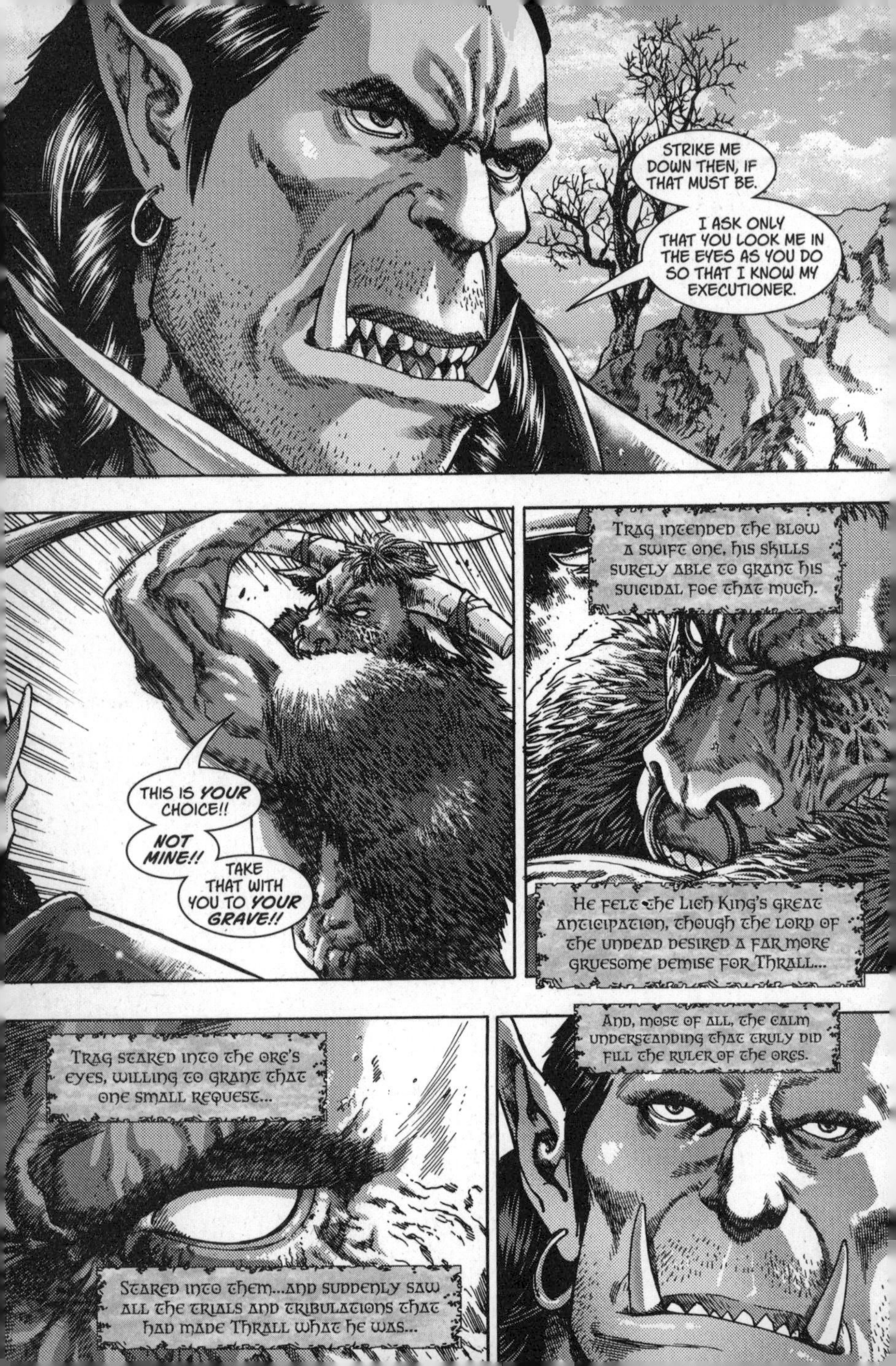
STRIKE ME DOWN THEN, IF THAT MUST BE.
I ASK ONLY THAT YOU LOOK ME IN THE EYES AS YOU DO SO THAT I KNOW MY EXECUTIONER.
THIS IS YOUR CHOICE!!
NOT MINE!!
TAKE THAT WITH YOU TO YOUR GRAVE!!
Trag intended the blow a swift one, his skills surely able to grant his suicidal foe that much.
He felt the Lich King's great anticipation, though the lord of the undead desired a far more gruesome demise for Thrall...
Trag stared into the orc's eyes, willing to grant that one small request...
Stared into them...and suddenly saw all the trials and tribulations that had made Thrall what he was...
And, most of all, the calm understanding that truly did fill the ruler of the orcs.

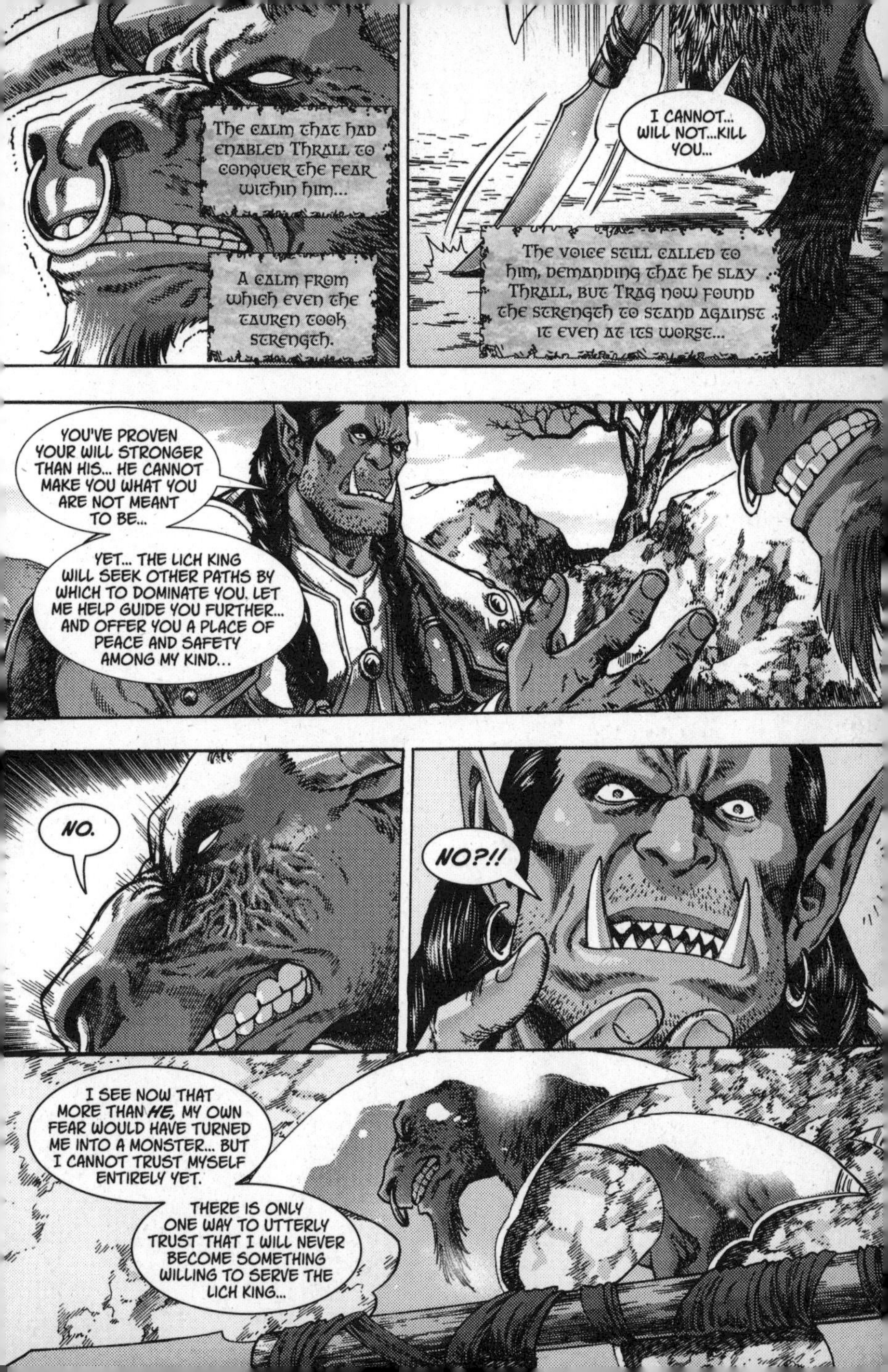
The calm that had enabled Thrall to conquer the fear within him...
A calm from which even the tauren took strength.
I CANNOT... WILL NOT...KILL YOU...
The voice still called to him, demanding that he slay Thrall, but Trag now found the strength to stand against it even at its worst...
YOU'VE PROVEN YOUR WILL STRONGER THAN HIS... HE CANNOT MAKE YOU WHAT YOU ARE NOT MEANT TO BE...
YET... THE LICH KING WILL SEEK OTHER PATHS BY WHICH TO DOMINATE YOU. LET ME HELP GUIDE YOU FURTHER... AND OFFER YOU A PLACE OF PEACE AND SAFETY AMONG MY KIND...
NO.
NO?!!
I SEE NOW THAT MORE THAN HE, MY OWN FEAR WOULD HAVE TURNED ME INTO A MONSTER... BUT I CANNOT TRUST MYSELF ENTIRELY YET.
THERE IS ONLY ONE WAY TO UTTERLY TRUST THAT I WILL NEVER BECOME SOMETHING WILLING TO SERVE THE LICH KING...

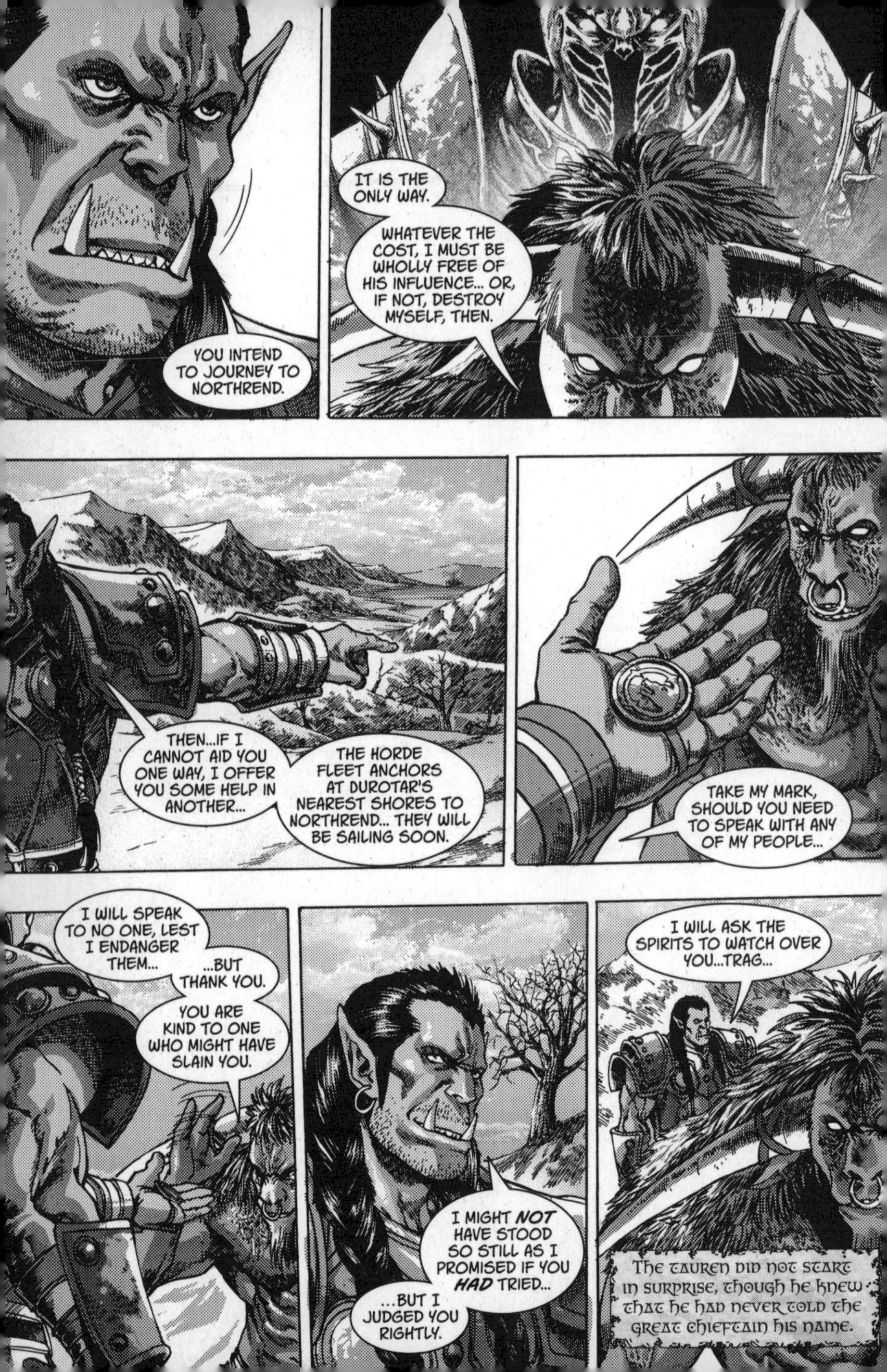
YOU INTEND TO JOURNEY TO NORTHREND.
IT IS THE ONLY WAY.
WHATEVER THE COST, I MUST BE WHOLLY FREE OF HIS INFLUENCE... OR, IF NOT, DESTROY MYSELF, THEN.
THEN...IF I CANNOT AID YOU ONE WAY, I OFFER YOU SOME HELP IN ANOTHER...
THE HORDE FLEET ANCHORS AT DUROTAR'S NEAREST SHORES TO NORTHREND... THEY WILL BE SAILING SOON.
TAKE MY MARK, SHOULD YOU NEED TO SPEAK WITH ANY OF MY PEOPLE...
I WILL SPEAK TO NO ONE, LEST I ENDANGER THEM...
...BUT THANK YOU.
YOU ARE KIND TO ONE WHO MIGHT HAVE SLAIN YOU.
I MIGHT **NOT** HAVE STOOD SO STILL AS I PROMISED IF YOU **HAD** TRIED...
...BUT I JUDGED YOU RIGHTLY.
I WILL ASK THE SPIRITS TO WATCH OVER YOU...TRAG...
The tauren did not start in surprise, though he knew that he had never told the great chieftain his name.

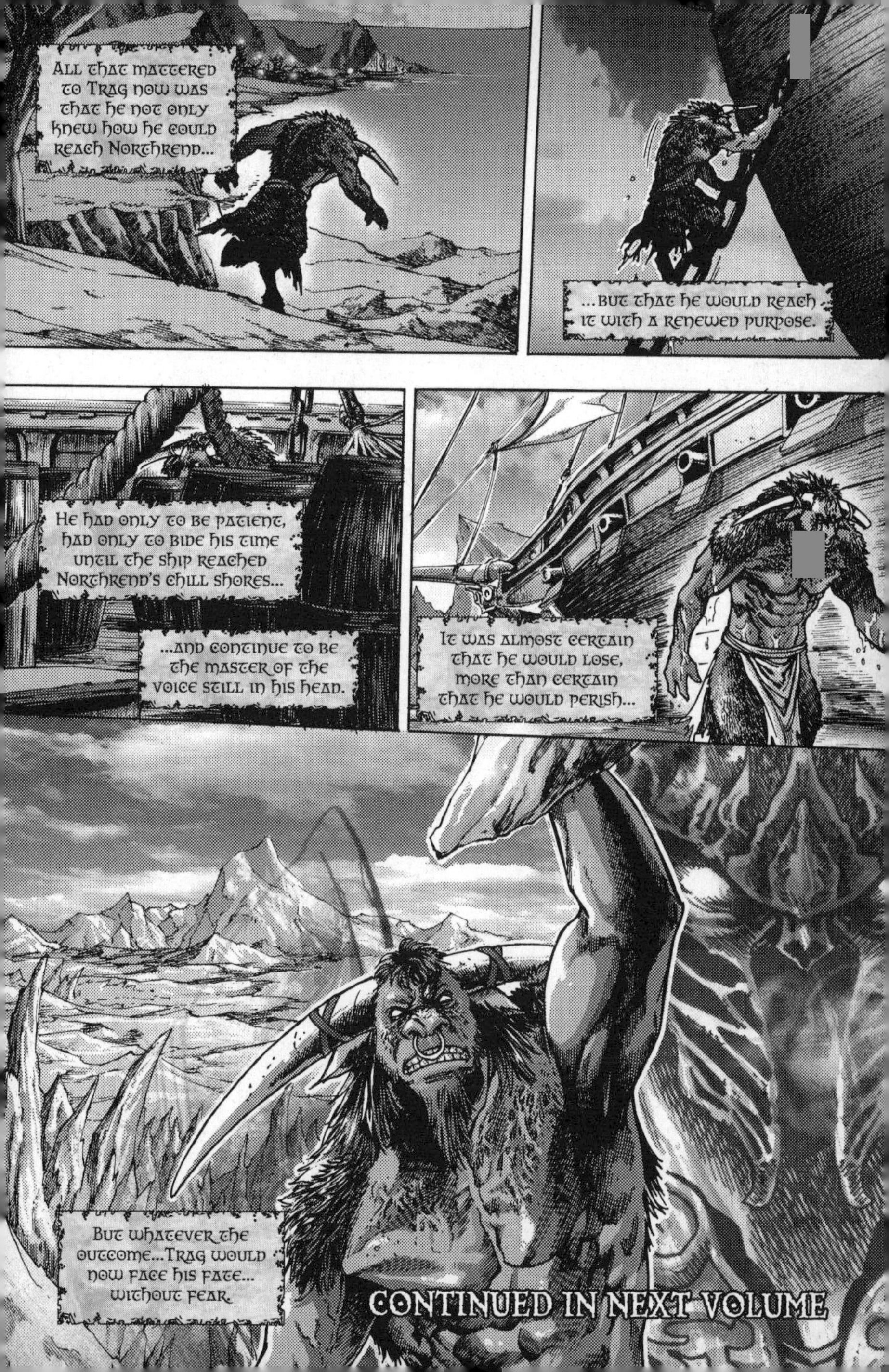
All that mattered to Trag now was that he not only knew how he could reach Northrend...
...but that he would reach it with a renewed purpose.
He had only to be patient, had only to bide his time until the ship reached Northrend's chill shores...
...and continue to be the master of the voice still in his head.
It was almost certain that he would lose, more than certain that he would perish...
But whatever the outcome...Trag would now face his fate... without fear.
CONTINUED IN NEXT VOLUME

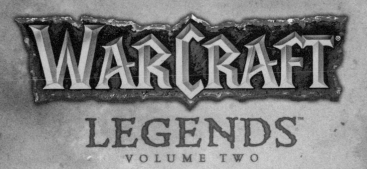

WARCRAFT®

LEGENDS™

VOLUME TWO

WARRIOR: DIVIDED

WRITTEN BY GRACE RANDOLPH

PENCILS BY ERIE
BACKGROUNDS BY LINCE
LAYOUTS & CHARACTER DESIGNS
BY YOUNG-OH KIM
INKS BY ERIE & LINCE
TONES BY LINCY CHAN

Editor: Troy Lewter
Contributing Editors: Hyun Joo Kim & Tim Beedle
Retouch Artist & Letterer: Michael Paolilli

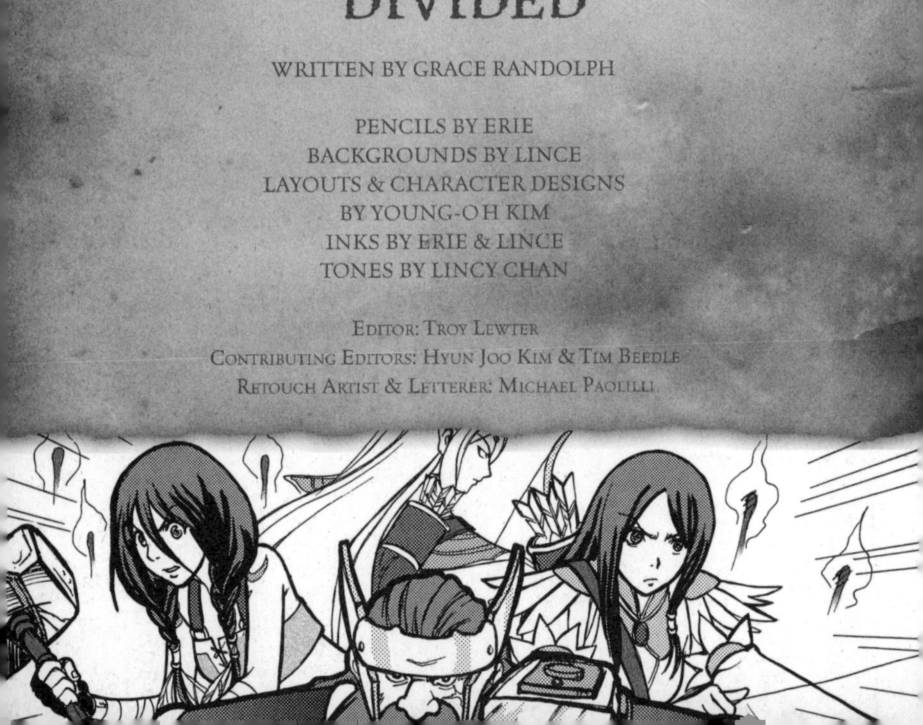

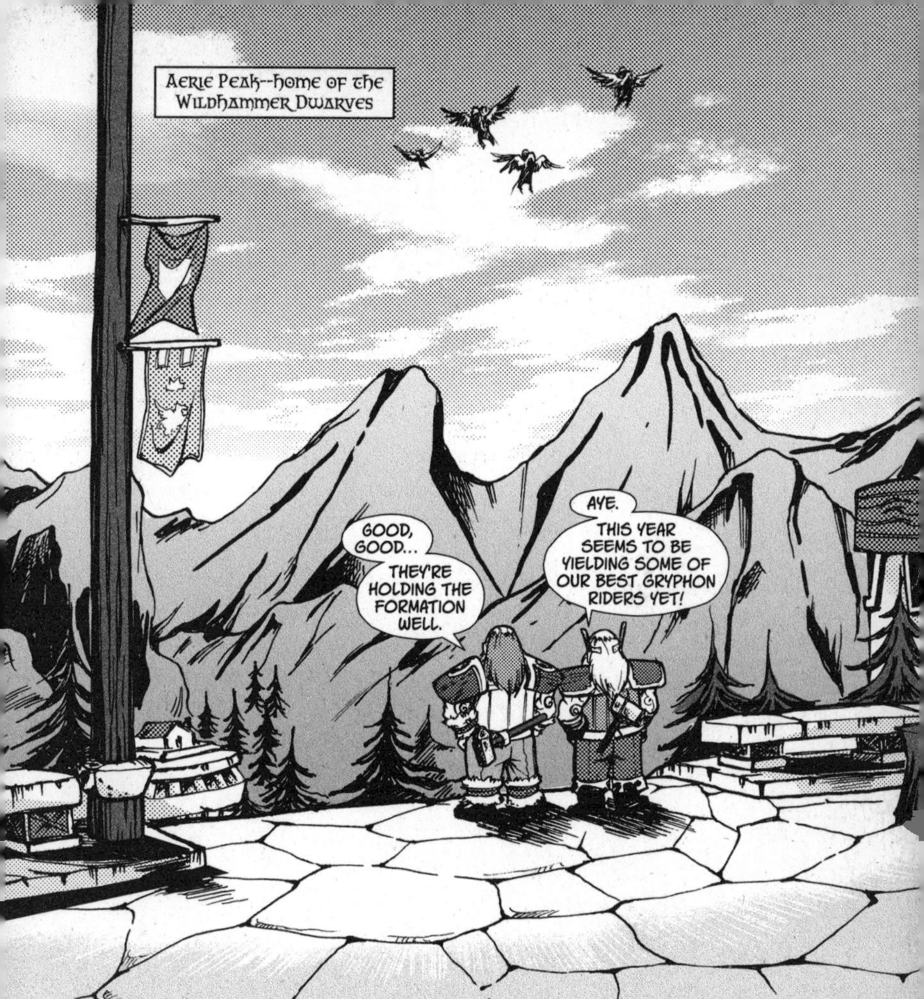
Aerie Peak--home of the Wildhammer Dwarves
Good, good...
They're holding the formation well.
Aye.
This year seems to be yielding some of our best gryphon riders yet!
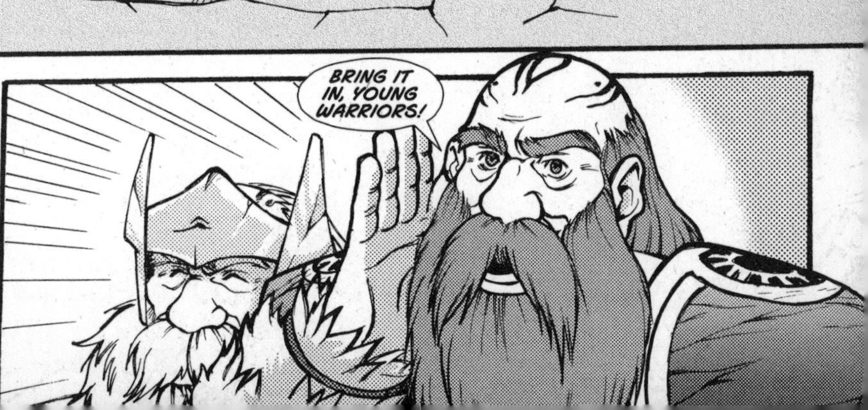
Bring it in, young warriors!

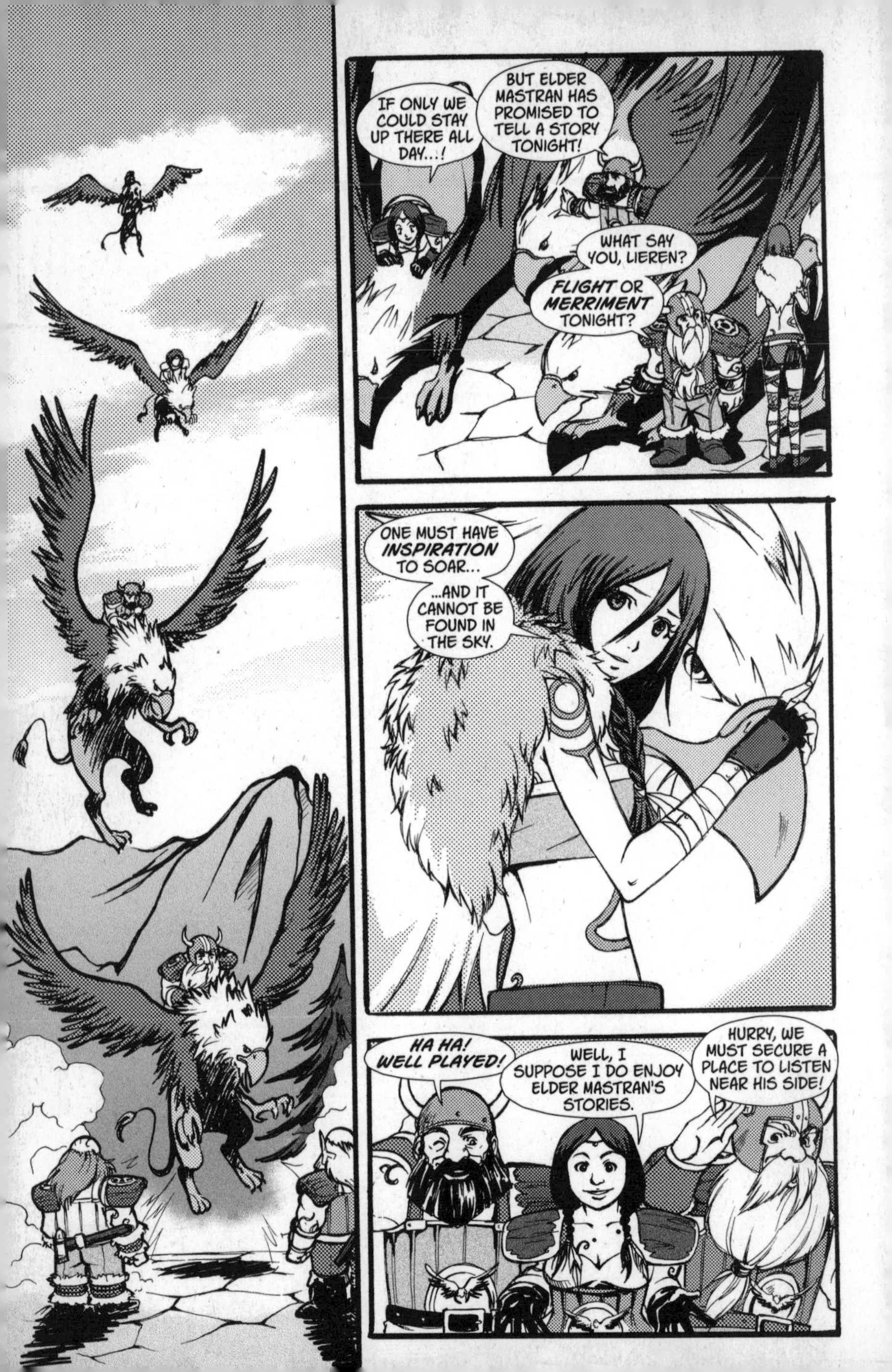
IF ONLY WE COULD STAY UP THERE ALL DAY...!
BUT ELDER MASTRAN HAS PROMISED TO TELL A STORY TONIGHT!
WHAT SAY YOU, LIEREN?
FLIGHT OR MERRIMENT TONIGHT?
ONE MUST HAVE INSPIRATION TO SOAR...
...AND IT CANNOT BE FOUND IN THE SKY.
HA HA! WELL PLAYED!
WELL, I SUPPOSE I DO ENJOY ELDER MASTRAN'S STORIES.
HURRY, WE MUST SECURE A PLACE TO LISTEN NEAR HIS SIDE!

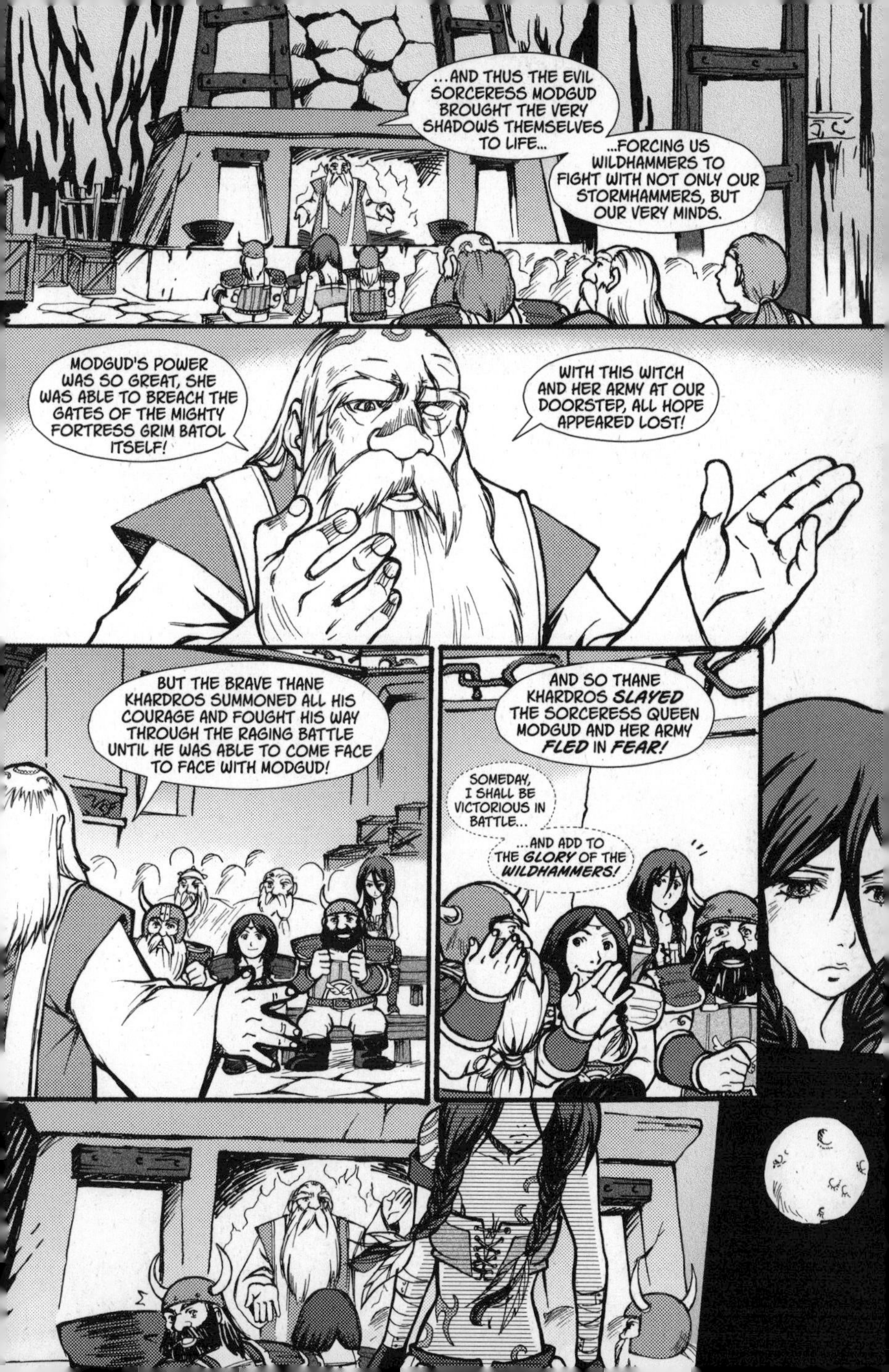
...AND THUS THE EVIL SORCERESS MODGUD BROUGHT THE VERY SHADOWS THEMSELVES TO LIFE...
...FORCING US WILDHAMMERS TO FIGHT WITH NOT ONLY OUR STORMHAMMERS, BUT OUR VERY MINDS.
MODGUD'S POWER WAS SO GREAT, SHE WAS ABLE TO BREACH THE GATES OF THE MIGHTY FORTRESS GRIM BATOL ITSELF!
WITH THIS WITCH AND HER ARMY AT OUR DOORSTEP, ALL HOPE APPEARED LOST!
BUT THE BRAVE THANE KHARDROS SUMMONED ALL HIS COURAGE AND FOUGHT HIS WAY THROUGH THE RAGING BATTLE UNTIL HE WAS ABLE TO COME FACE TO FACE WITH MODGUD!
AND SO THANE KHARDROS *SLAYED* THE SORCERESS QUEEN MODGUD AND HER ARMY *FLED* IN *FEAR!*
SOMEDAY, I SHALL BE VICTORIOUS IN BATTLE...
...AND ADD TO THE *GLORY* OF THE *WILDHAMMERS!*

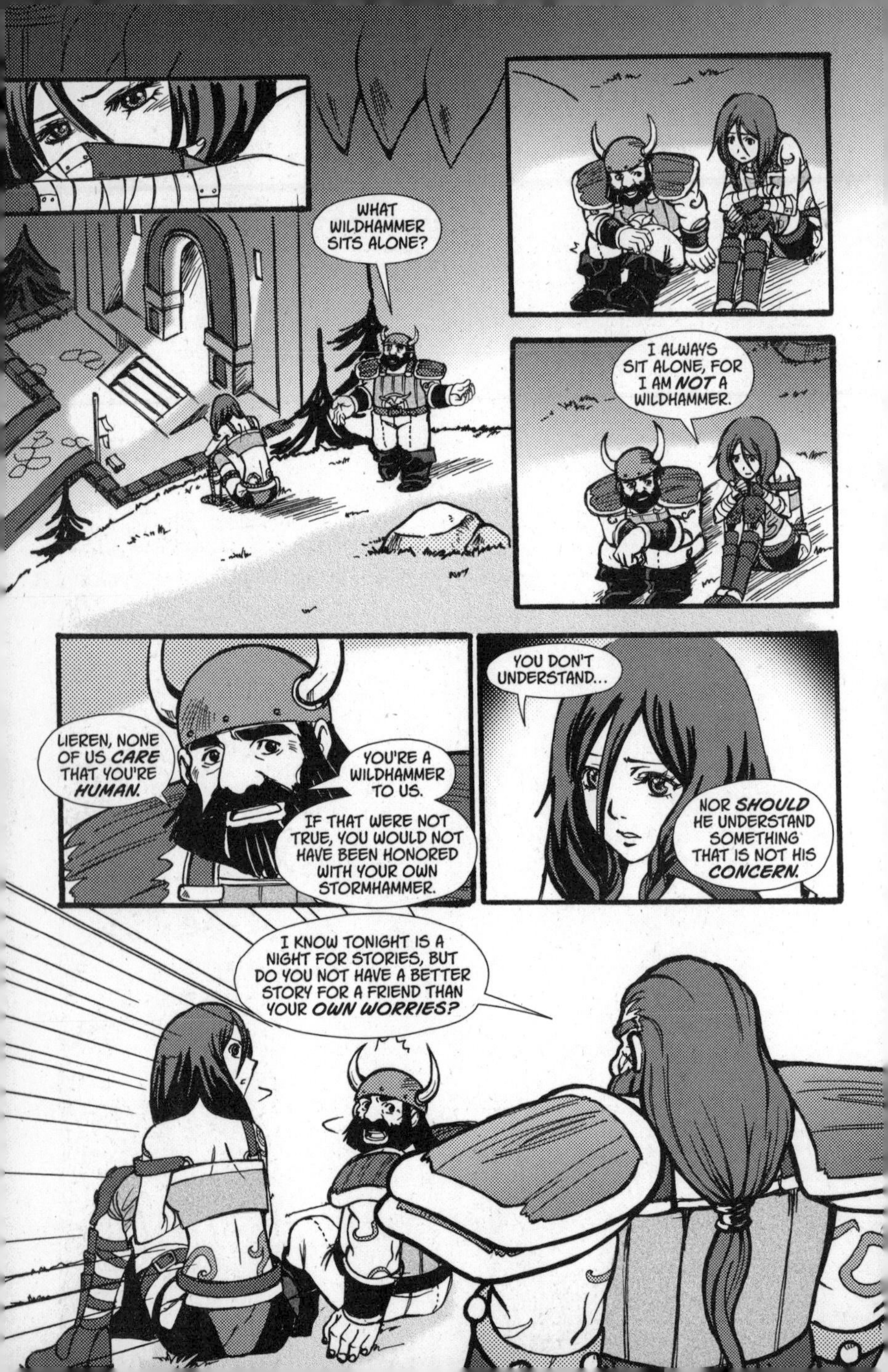
WHAT WILDHAMMER SITS ALONE?
I ALWAYS SIT ALONE, FOR I AM *NOT* A WILDHAMMER.
LIEREN, NONE OF US *CARE* THAT YOU'RE *HUMAN.*
YOU'RE A WILDHAMMER TO US.
IF THAT WERE NOT TRUE, YOU WOULD NOT HAVE BEEN HONORED WITH YOUR OWN STORMHAMMER.
YOU DON'T UNDERSTAND...
NOR *SHOULD* HE UNDERSTAND SOMETHING THAT IS NOT HIS *CONCERN.*
I KNOW TONIGHT IS A NIGHT FOR STORIES, BUT DO YOU NOT HAVE A BETTER STORY FOR A FRIEND THAN YOUR *OWN WORRIES?*

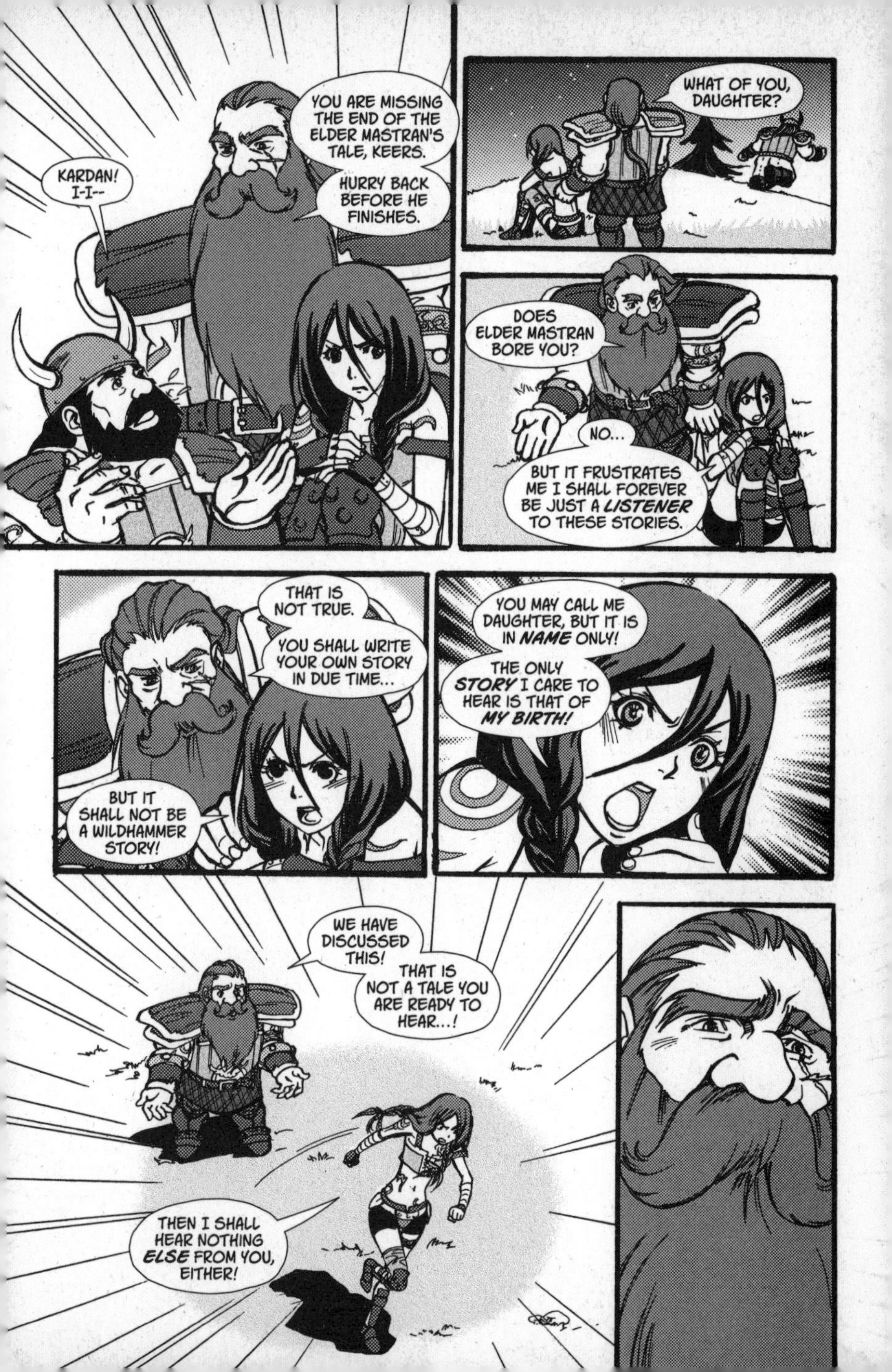
KARDAN! I-I--
YOU ARE MISSING THE END OF THE ELDER MASTRAN'S TALE, KEERS.
HURRY BACK BEFORE HE FINISHES.
WHAT OF YOU, DAUGHTER?
DOES ELDER MASTRAN BORE YOU?
NO...
BUT IT FRUSTRATES ME I SHALL FOREVER BE JUST A LISTENER TO THESE STORIES.
THAT IS NOT TRUE.
YOU SHALL WRITE YOUR OWN STORY IN DUE TIME...
BUT IT SHALL NOT BE A WILDHAMMER STORY!
YOU MAY CALL ME DAUGHTER, BUT IT IS IN NAME ONLY!
THE ONLY STORY I CARE TO HEAR IS THAT OF MY BIRTH!
WE HAVE DISCUSSED THIS!
THAT IS NOT A TALE YOU ARE READY TO HEAR...!
THEN I SHALL HEAR NOTHING ELSE FROM YOU, EITHER!

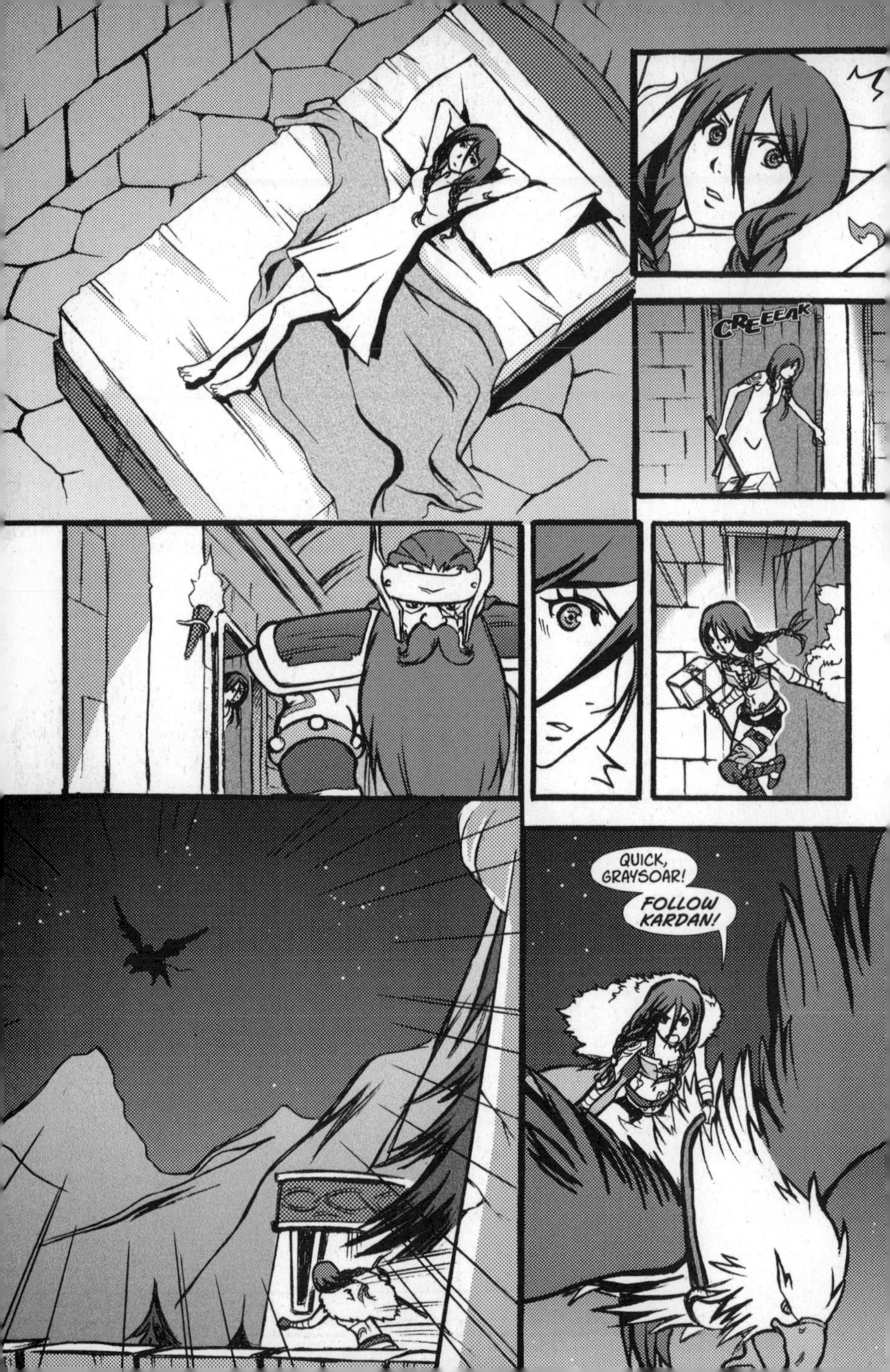
CREEEAK
QUICK, GRAYSOAR!
FOLLOW KARDAN!

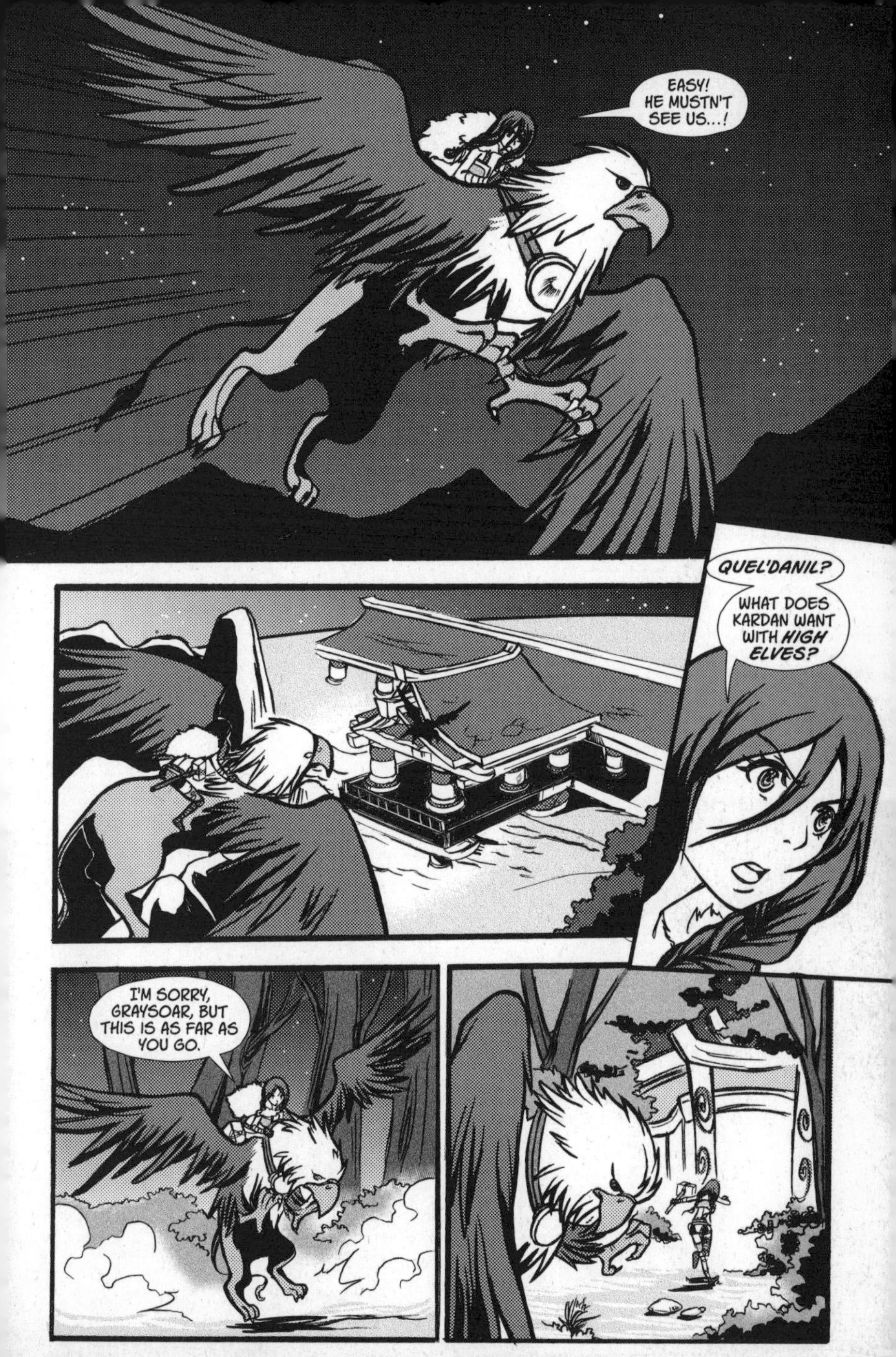
EASY! HE MUSTN'T SEE US...!
QUEL'DANIL?
WHAT DOES KARDAN WANT WITH HIGH ELVES?
I'M SORRY, GRAYSOAR, BUT THIS IS AS FAR AS YOU GO.

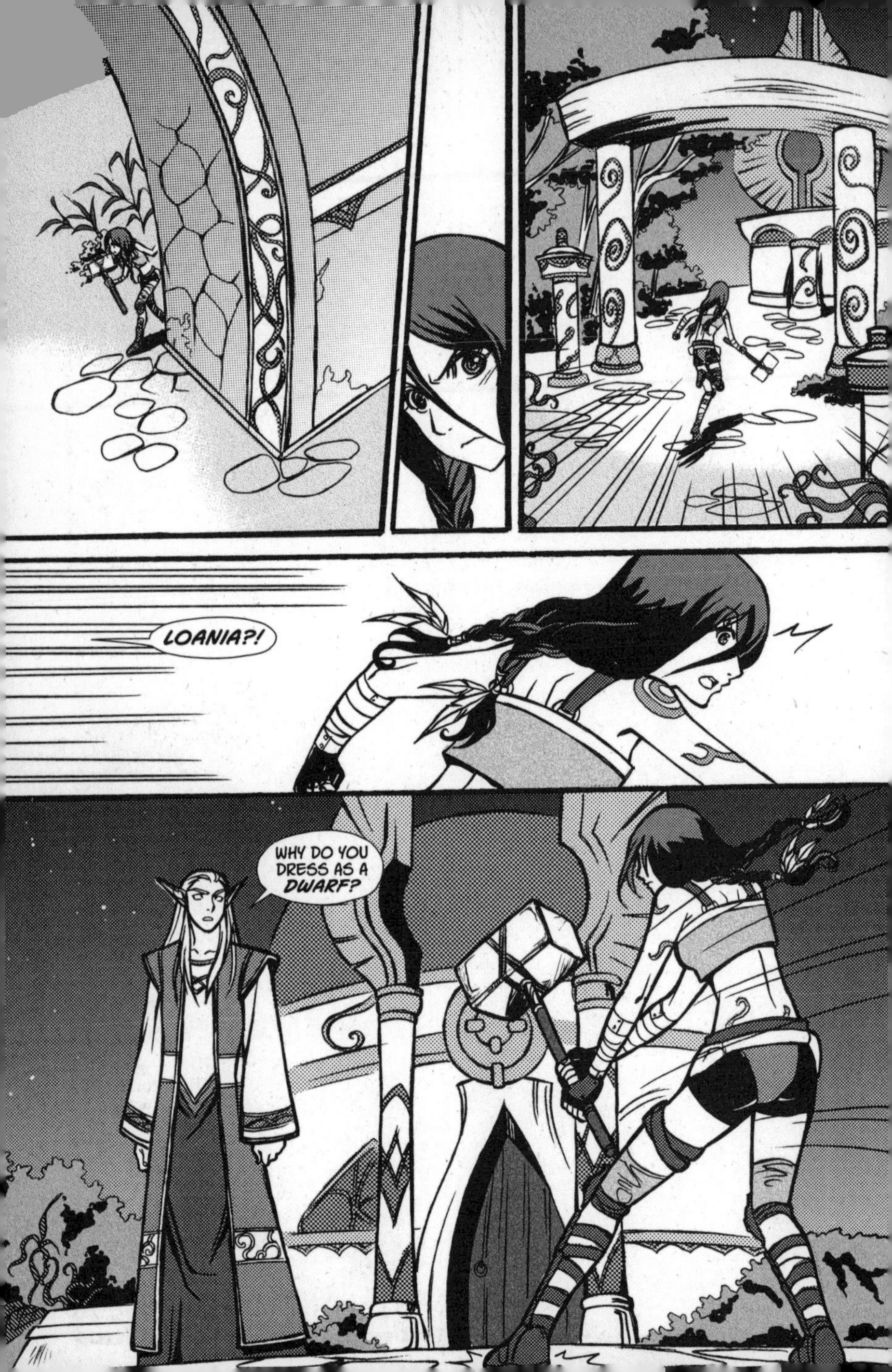
LOANIA?!
WHY DO YOU DRESS AS A DWARF?

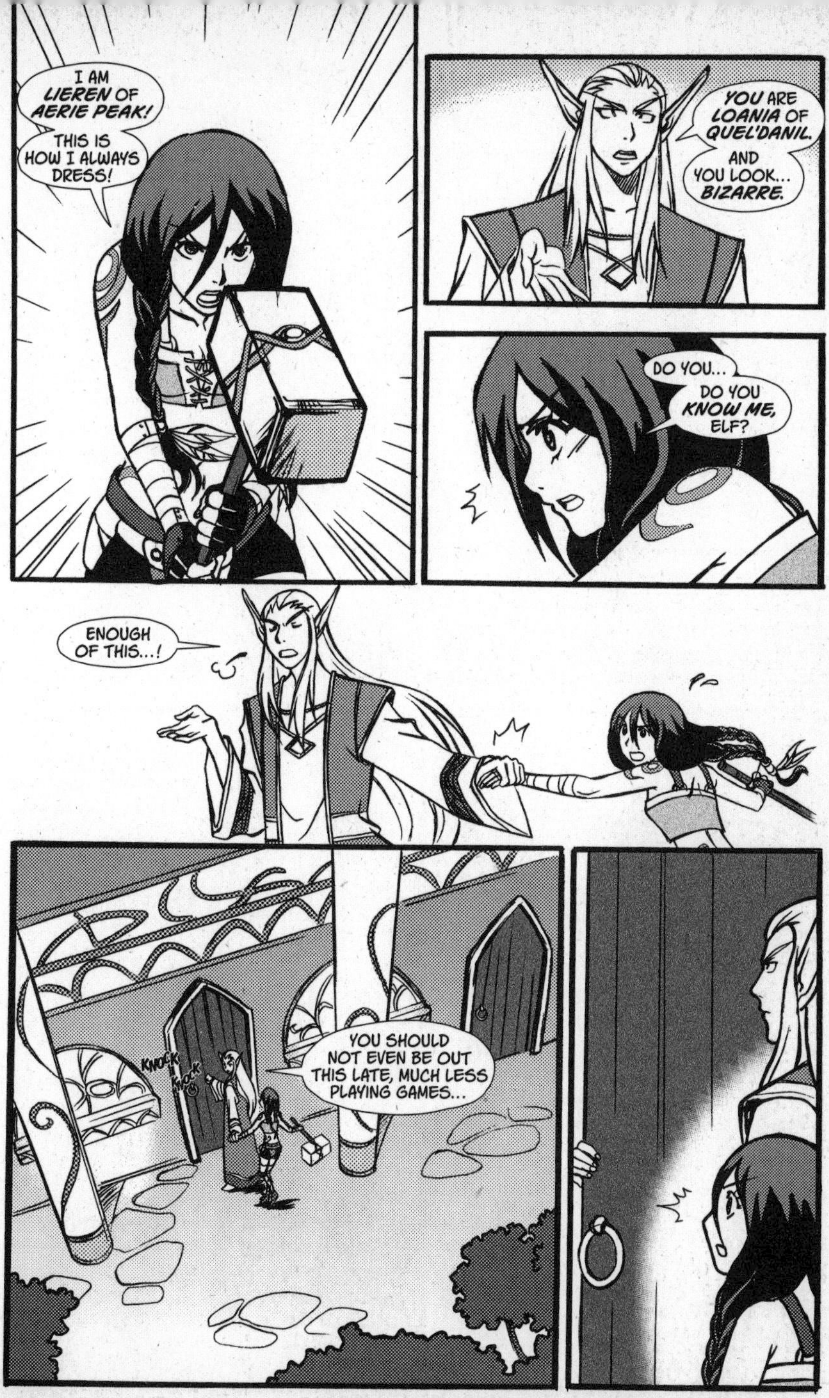
I AM *LIEREN* OF *AERIE PEAK!*
THIS IS HOW I ALWAYS DRESS!
YOU ARE *LOANIA* OF *QUEL'DANIL.*
AND YOU LOOK... *BIZARRE.*
DO YOU... DO YOU *KNOW ME,* ELF?
ENOUGH OF THIS...!
KNOCK KNOCK
YOU SHOULD NOT EVEN BE OUT THIS LATE, MUCH LESS PLAYING GAMES...

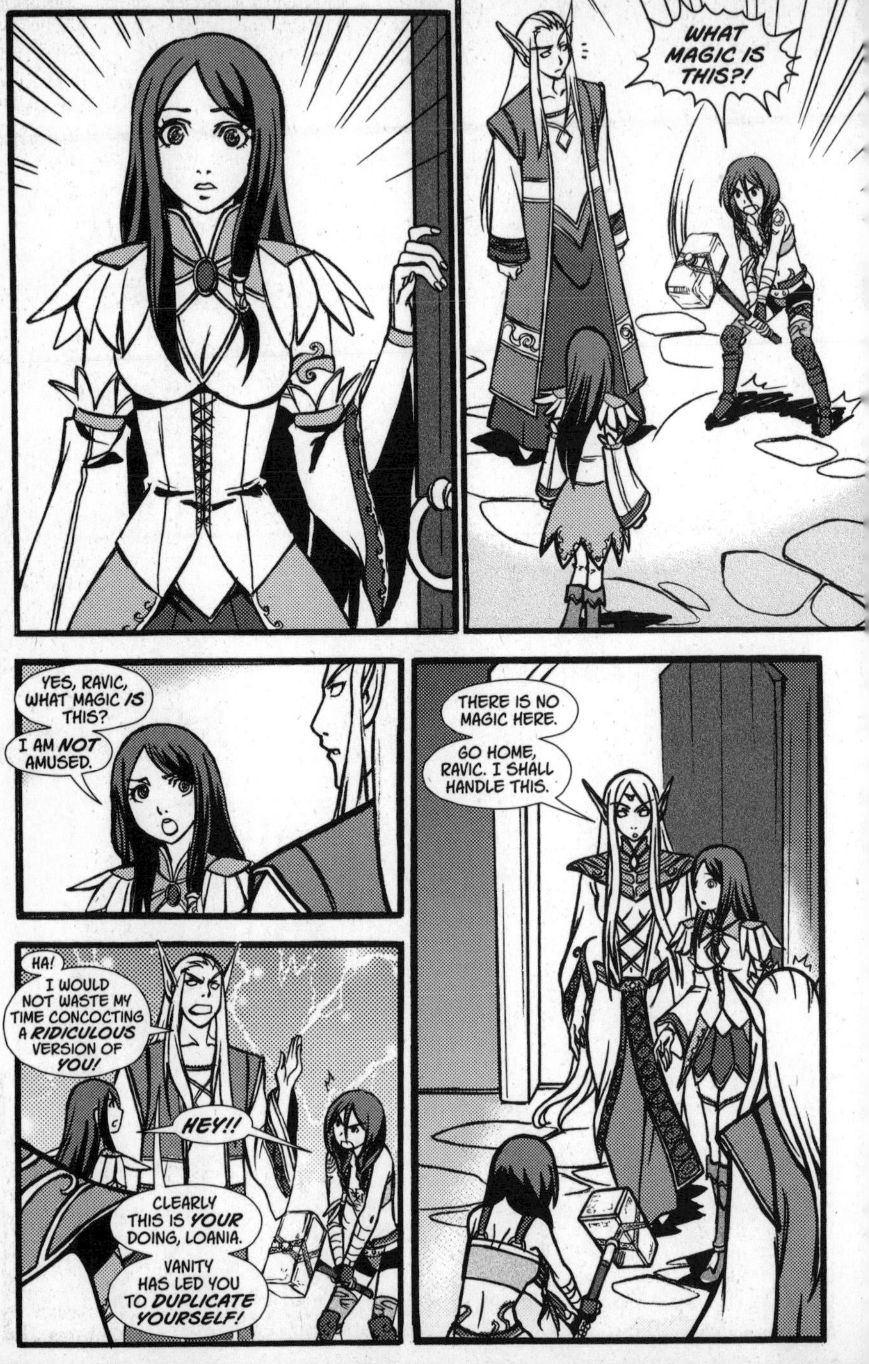
WHAT MAGIC IS THIS?!
YES, RAVIC, WHAT MAGIC IS THIS?
I AM NOT AMUSED.
THERE IS NO MAGIC HERE.
GO HOME, RAVIC. I SHALL HANDLE THIS.
HA!
I WOULD NOT WASTE MY TIME CONCOCTING A RIDICULOUS VERSION OF YOU!
HEY!!
CLEARLY THIS IS YOUR DOING, LOANIA.
VANITY HAS LED YOU TO DUPLICATE YOURSELF!

PLEASE, COME INSIDE.

I AM NOT AS EASILY CONVINCED AS HE!

WHAT *BUT* MAGIC COULD MOCK ME AS DOES *THAT?!*

HOW DO YOU *COME* TO THIS *DOOR*, LIEREN?!

AND BE TRUTHFUL!

WHY?! YOU DO NOT BESTOW THE *TRUTH* UPON *ME!!*

YOU DO NOT-- THAT IS UNFAIR! I--

NO. IT IS *I* WHO IS UNFAIR.

COME INSIDE, YOUNG ONE... THE TIME HAS COME TO HEAR *YOUR* STORY.

SO IF THIS *THING* IS NOT A PRODUCT OF MAGIC...

...THEN WHAT BE IT?

HER NAME IS *LOANIA.*

AND I HAVE RAISED HER...

...JUST AS KARDAN HAS RAISED *YOU.*

YOU ARE *TWINS.*

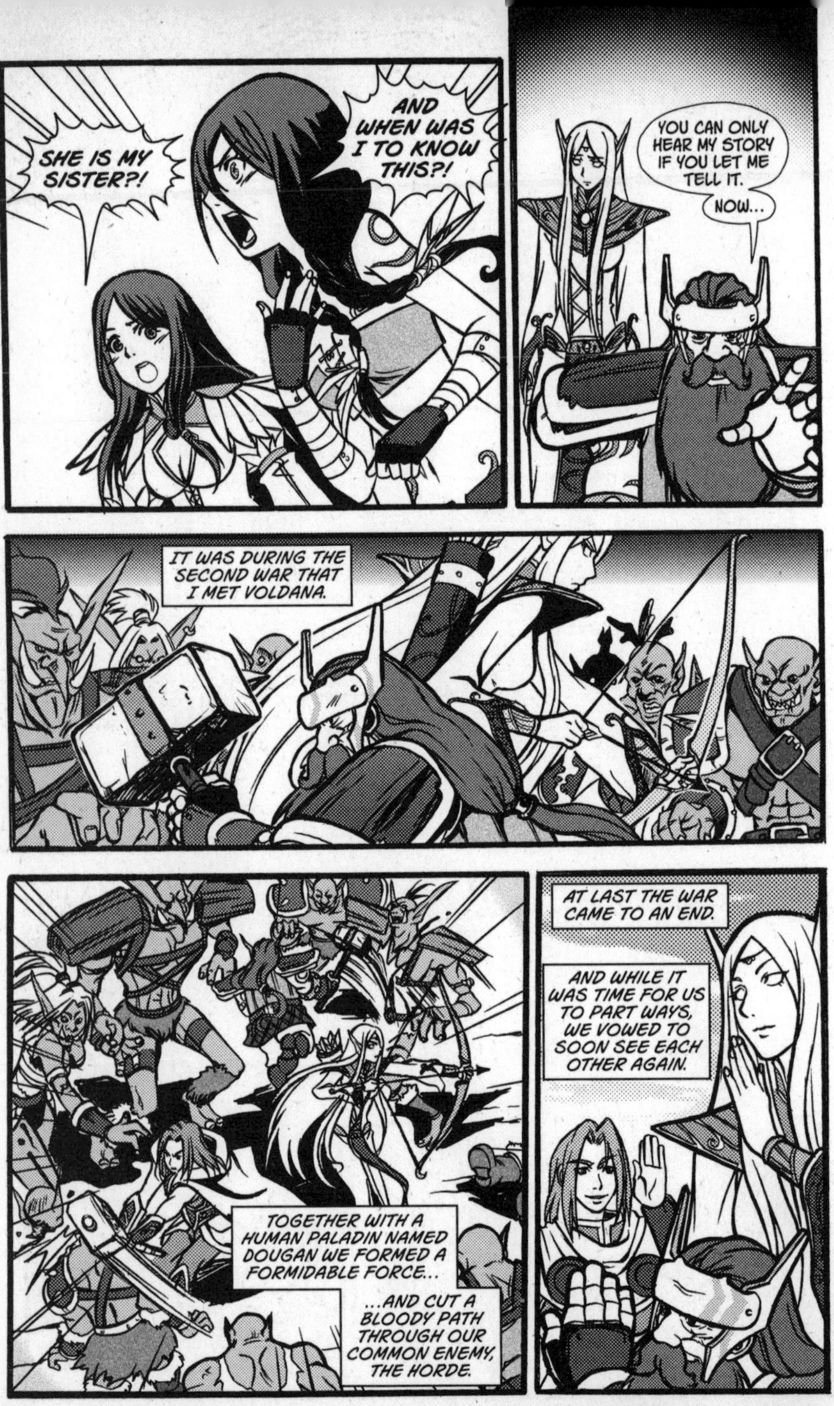
SHE IS MY SISTER?!
AND WHEN WAS I TO KNOW THIS?!
YOU CAN ONLY HEAR MY STORY IF YOU LET ME TELL IT.
NOW...
IT WAS DURING THE SECOND WAR THAT I MET VOLDANA.
TOGETHER WITH A HUMAN PALADIN NAMED DOUGAN WE FORMED A FORMIDABLE FORCE...
...AND CUT A BLOODY PATH THROUGH OUR COMMON ENEMY, THE HORDE.
AT LAST THE WAR CAME TO AN END.
AND WHILE IT WAS TIME FOR US TO PART WAYS, WE VOWED TO SOON SEE EACH OTHER AGAIN.

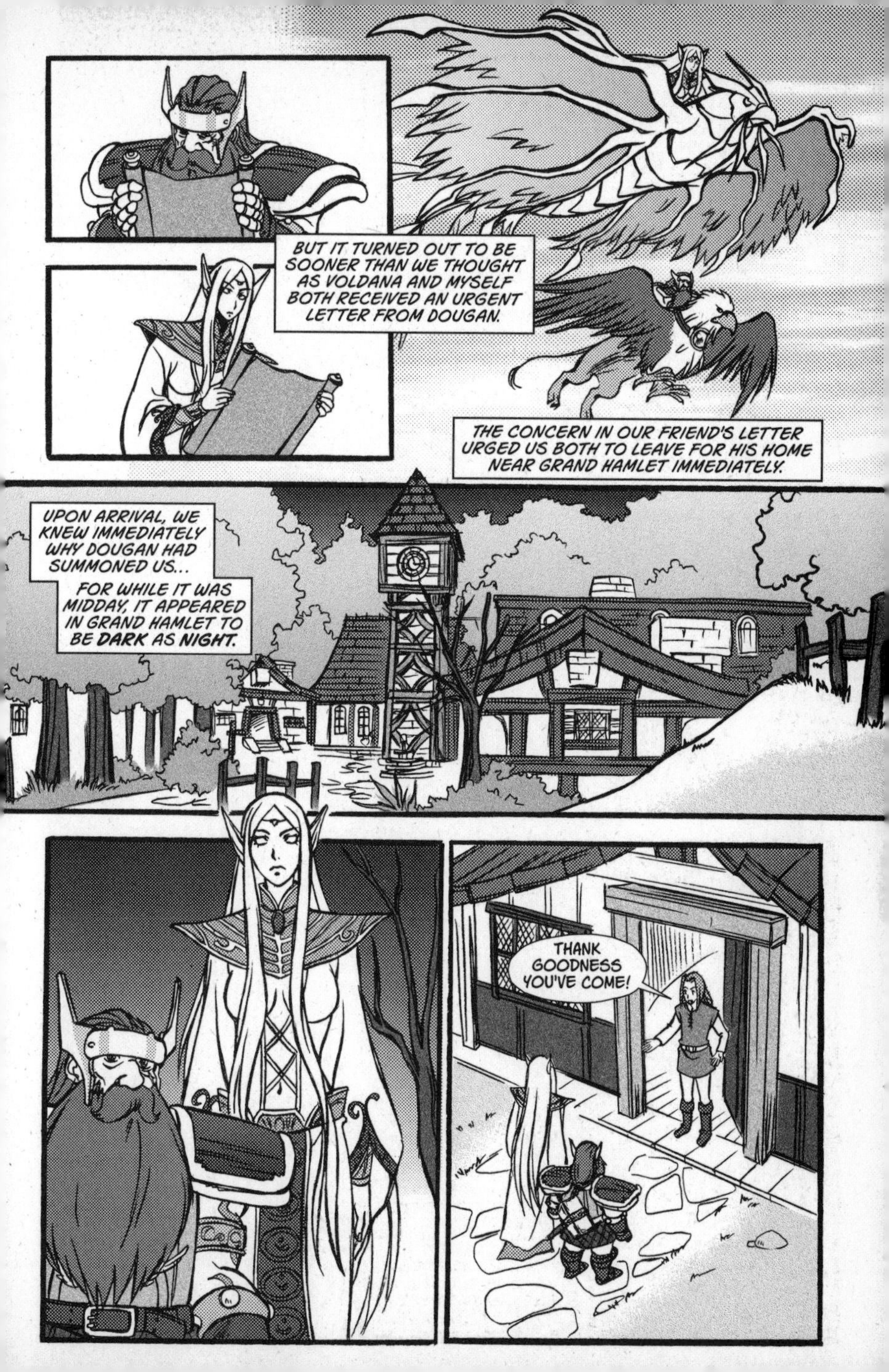
BUT IT TURNED OUT TO BE SOONER THAN WE THOUGHT AS VOLDANA AND MYSELF BOTH RECEIVED AN URGENT LETTER FROM DOUGAN.
THE CONCERN IN OUR FRIEND'S LETTER URGED US BOTH TO LEAVE FOR HIS HOME NEAR GRAND HAMLET IMMEDIATELY.
UPON ARRIVAL, WE KNEW IMMEDIATELY WHY DOUGAN HAD SUMMONED US...
FOR WHILE IT WAS MIDDAY, IT APPEARED IN GRAND HAMLET TO BE DARK AS NIGHT.
THANK GOODNESS YOU'VE COME!

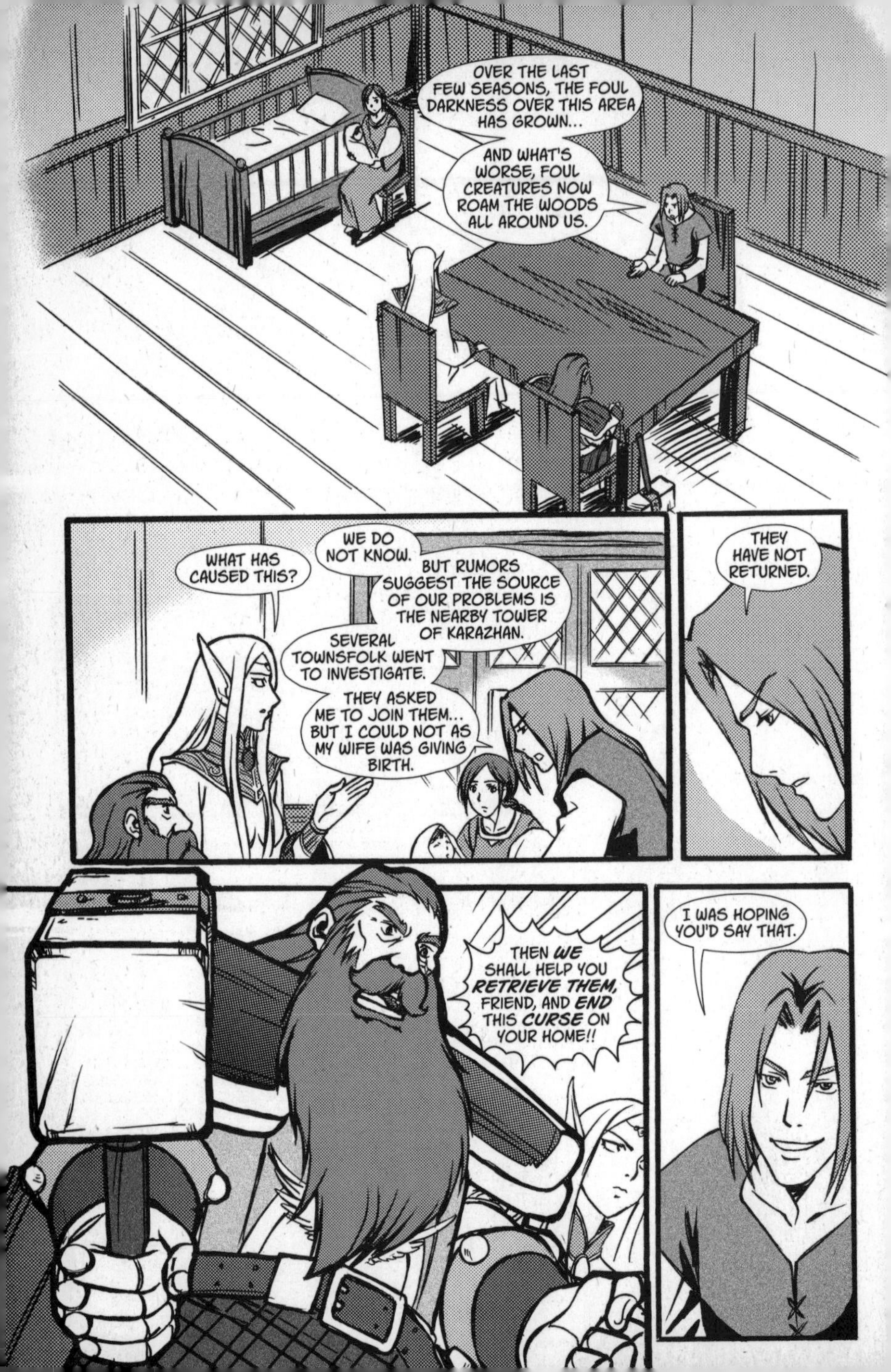
OVER THE LAST FEW SEASONS, THE FOUL DARKNESS OVER THIS AREA HAS GROWN...
AND WHAT'S WORSE, FOUL CREATURES NOW ROAM THE WOODS ALL AROUND US.
WHAT HAS CAUSED THIS?
WE DO NOT KNOW.
BUT RUMORS SUGGEST THE SOURCE OF OUR PROBLEMS IS THE NEARBY TOWER OF KARAZHAN.
SEVERAL TOWNSFOLK WENT TO INVESTIGATE.
THEY ASKED ME TO JOIN THEM... BUT I COULD NOT AS MY WIFE WAS GIVING BIRTH.
THEY HAVE NOT RETURNED.
THEN ***WE*** SHALL HELP YOU ***RETRIEVE THEM,*** FRIEND, AND ***END*** THIS ***CURSE*** ON YOUR HOME!!
I WAS HOPING YOU'D SAY THAT.

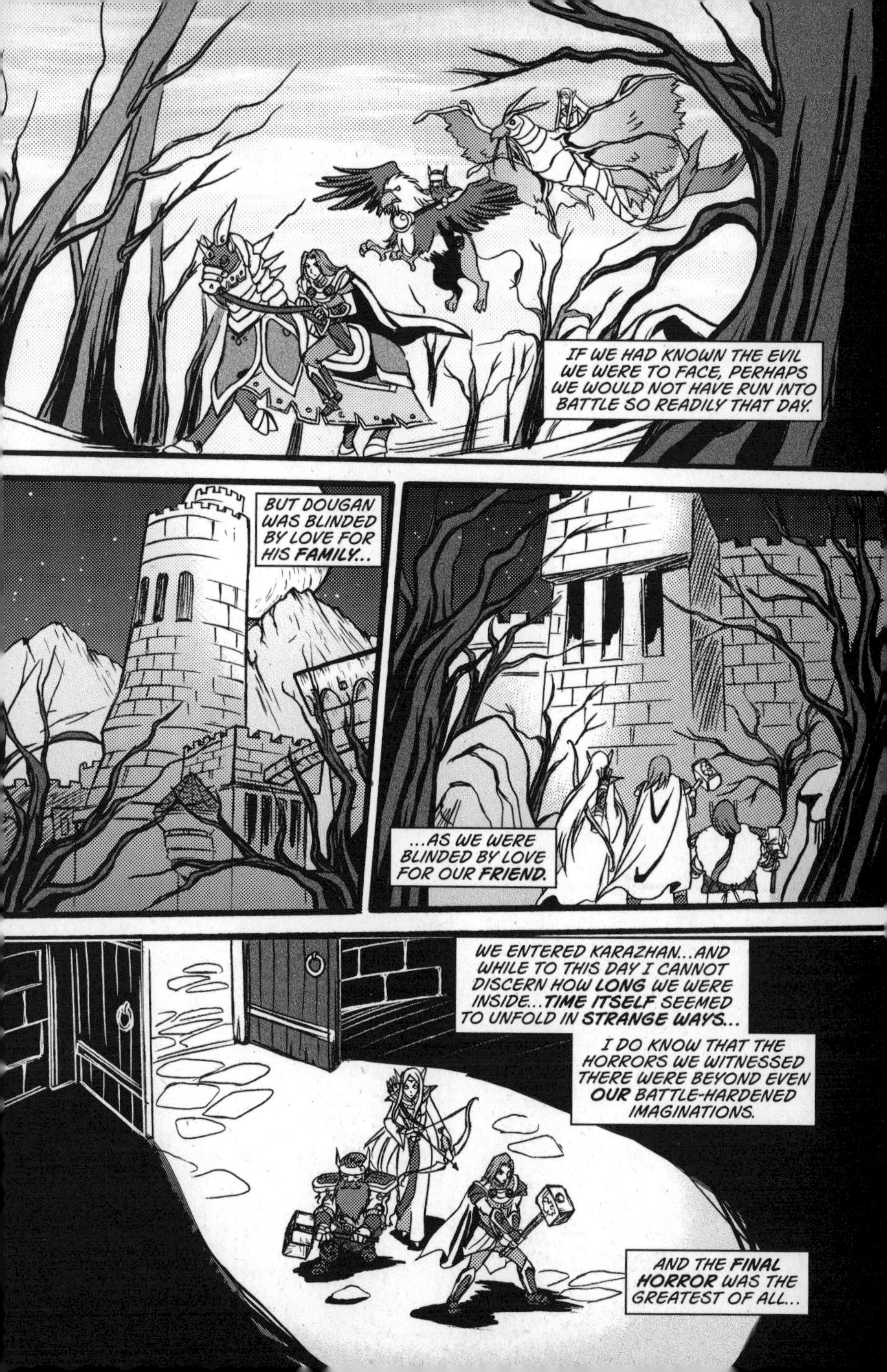
IF WE HAD KNOWN THE EVIL WE WERE TO FACE, PERHAPS WE WOULD NOT HAVE RUN INTO BATTLE SO READILY THAT DAY.
BUT DOUGAN WAS BLINDED BY LOVE FOR HIS **FAMILY**...
...AS WE WERE BLINDED BY LOVE FOR OUR **FRIEND**.
WE ENTERED KARAZHAN...AND WHILE TO THIS DAY I CANNOT DISCERN HOW **LONG** WE WERE INSIDE...**TIME ITSELF** SEEMED TO UNFOLD IN **STRANGE WAYS**...
I DO KNOW THAT THE HORRORS WE WITNESSED THERE WERE BEYOND EVEN **OUR** BATTLE-HARDENED IMAGINATIONS.
AND THE **FINAL HORROR** WAS THE GREATEST OF ALL...

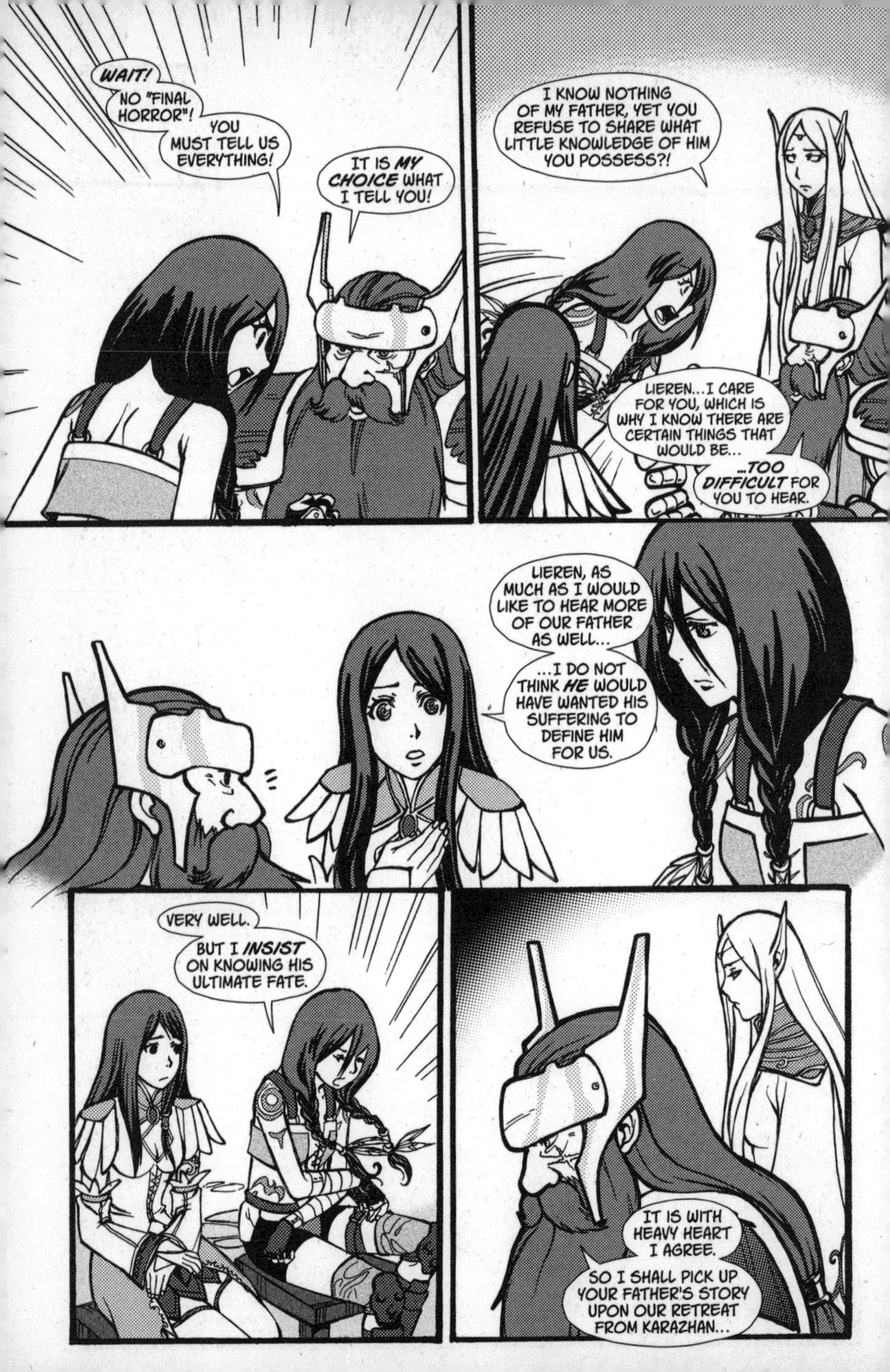
WAIT!
NO "FINAL HORROR"!
YOU MUST TELL US EVERYTHING!
IT IS MY CHOICE WHAT I TELL YOU!
I KNOW NOTHING OF MY FATHER, YET YOU REFUSE TO SHARE WHAT LITTLE KNOWLEDGE OF HIM YOU POSSESS?!
LIEREN...I CARE FOR YOU, WHICH IS WHY I KNOW THERE ARE CERTAIN THINGS THAT WOULD BE...
...TOO DIFFICULT FOR YOU TO HEAR.
LIEREN, AS MUCH AS I WOULD LIKE TO HEAR MORE OF OUR FATHER AS WELL...
...I DO NOT THINK HE WOULD HAVE WANTED HIS SUFFERING TO DEFINE HIM FOR US.
VERY WELL.
BUT I INSIST ON KNOWING HIS ULTIMATE FATE.
IT IS WITH HEAVY HEART I AGREE.
SO I SHALL PICK UP YOUR FATHER'S STORY UPON OUR RETREAT FROM KARAZHAN...

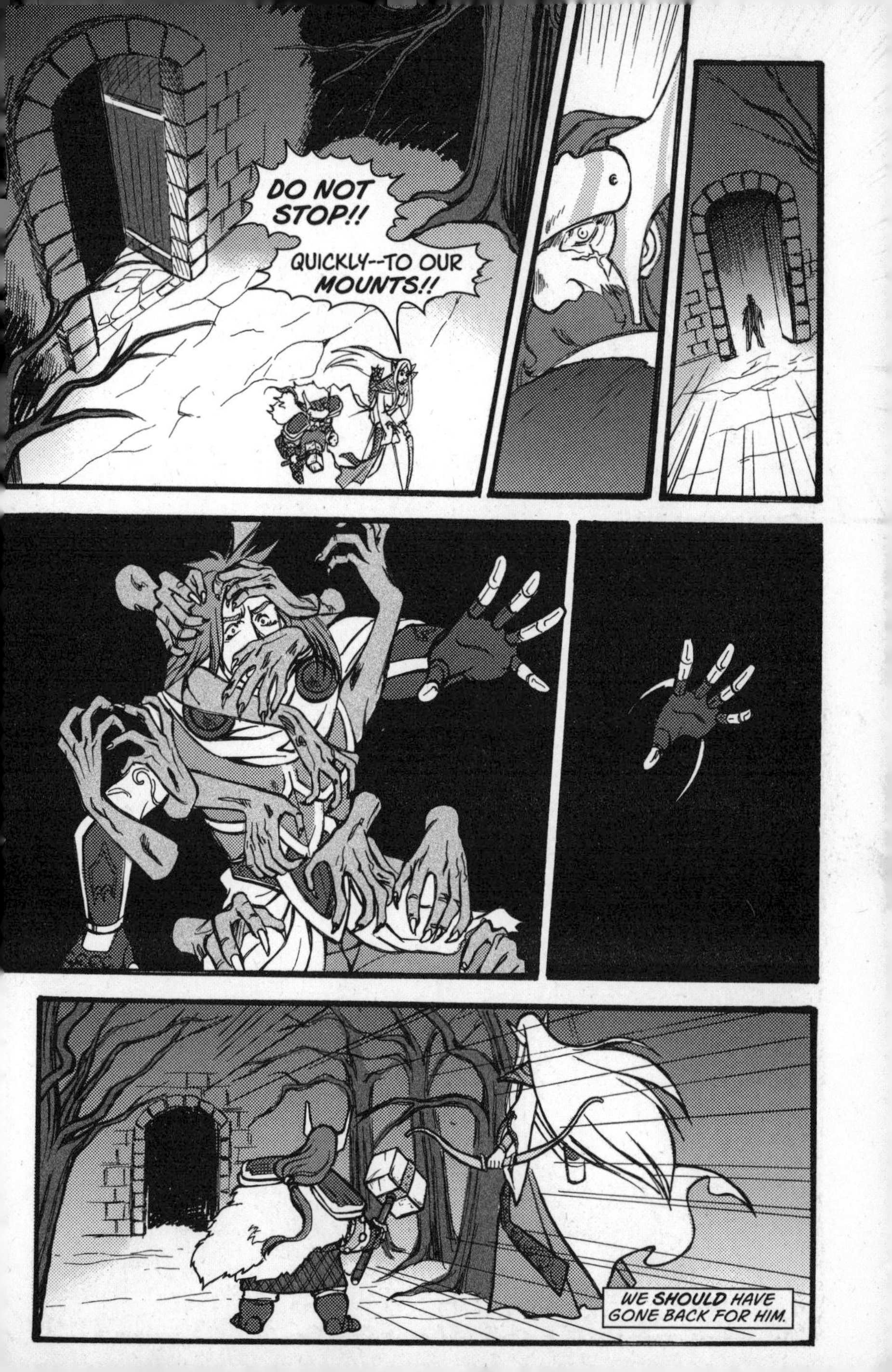
DO NOT STOP!!
QUICKLY--TO OUR MOUNTS!!
WE SHOULD HAVE GONE BACK FOR HIM.

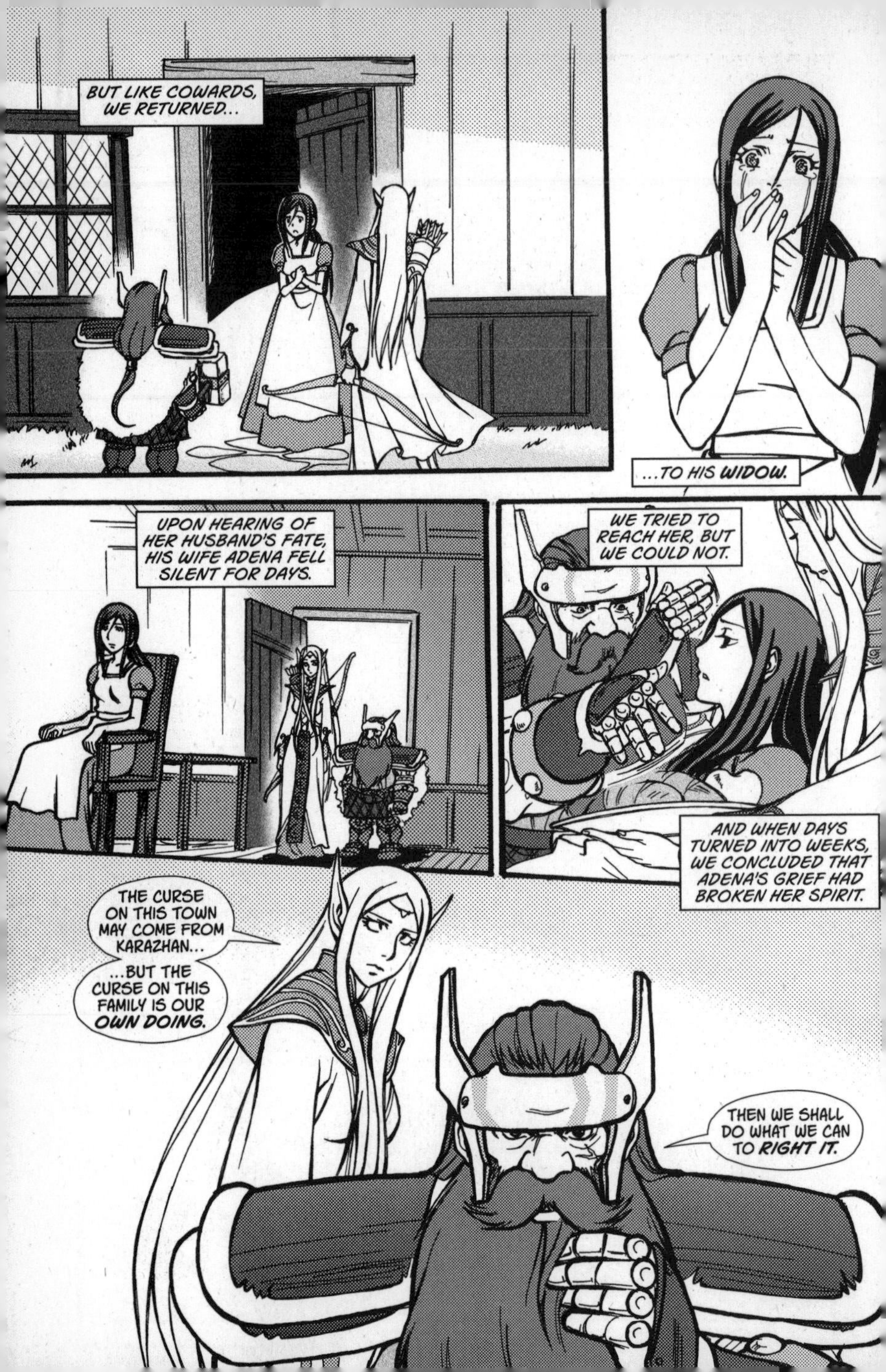
BUT LIKE COWARDS, WE RETURNED...
...TO HIS WIDOW.
UPON HEARING OF HER HUSBAND'S FATE, HIS WIFE ADENA FELL SILENT FOR DAYS.
WE TRIED TO REACH HER, BUT WE COULD NOT.
AND WHEN DAYS TURNED INTO WEEKS, WE CONCLUDED THAT ADENA'S GRIEF HAD BROKEN HER SPIRIT.
THE CURSE ON THIS TOWN MAY COME FROM KARAZHAN...
...BUT THE CURSE ON THIS FAMILY IS OUR OWN DOING.
THEN WE SHALL DO WHAT WE CAN TO RIGHT IT.

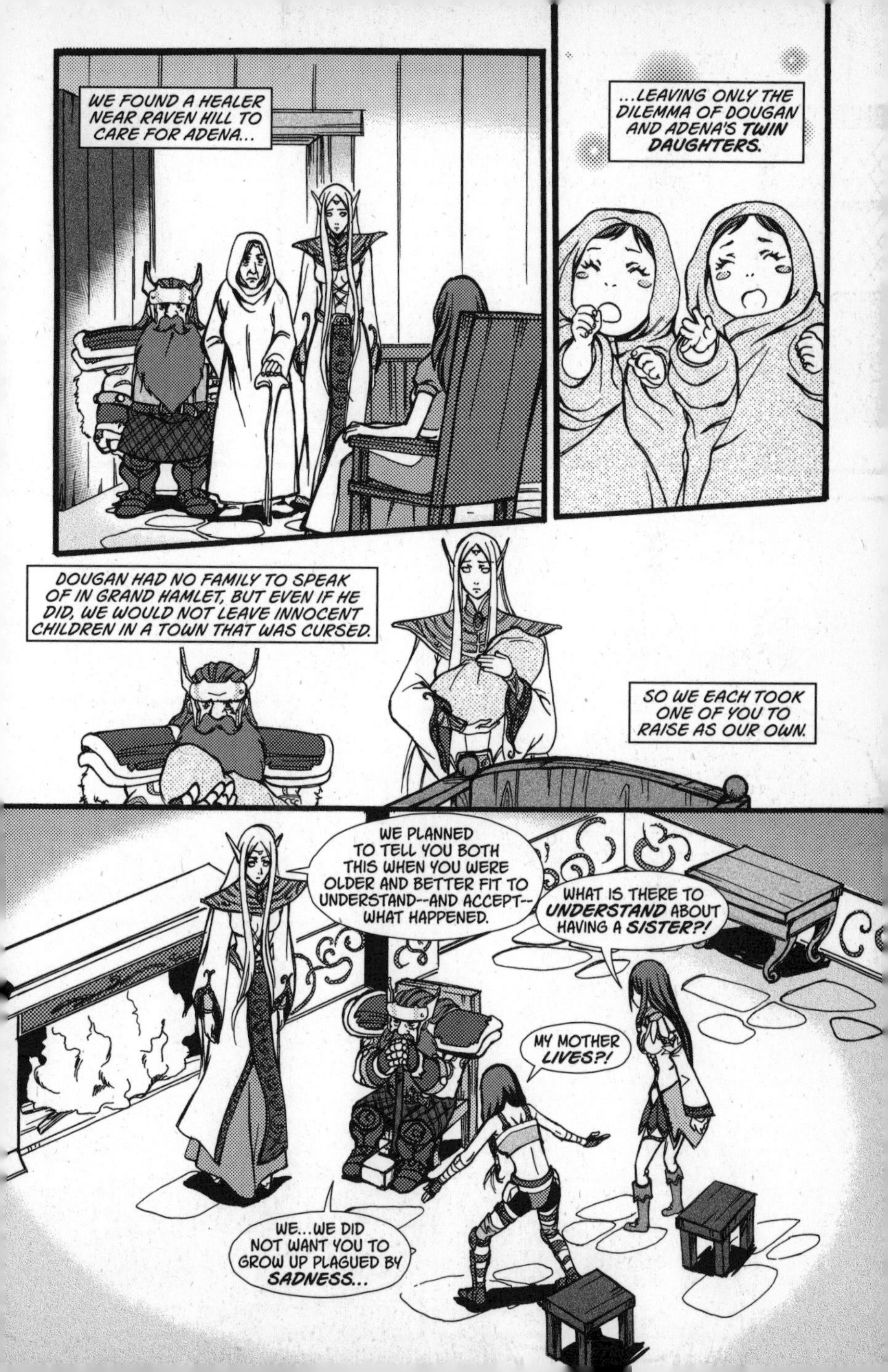
WE FOUND A HEALER NEAR RAVEN HILL TO CARE FOR ADENA...
...LEAVING ONLY THE DILEMMA OF DOUGAN AND ADENA'S TWIN DAUGHTERS.
DOUGAN HAD NO FAMILY TO SPEAK OF IN GRAND HAMLET, BUT EVEN IF HE DID, WE WOULD NOT LEAVE INNOCENT CHILDREN IN A TOWN THAT WAS CURSED.
SO WE EACH TOOK ONE OF YOU TO RAISE AS OUR OWN.
WE PLANNED TO TELL YOU BOTH THIS WHEN YOU WERE OLDER AND BETTER FIT TO UNDERSTAND--AND ACCEPT--WHAT HAPPENED.
WHAT IS THERE TO UNDERSTAND ABOUT HAVING A SISTER?!
MY MOTHER LIVES?!
WE...WE DID NOT WANT YOU TO GROW UP PLAGUED BY SADNESS...

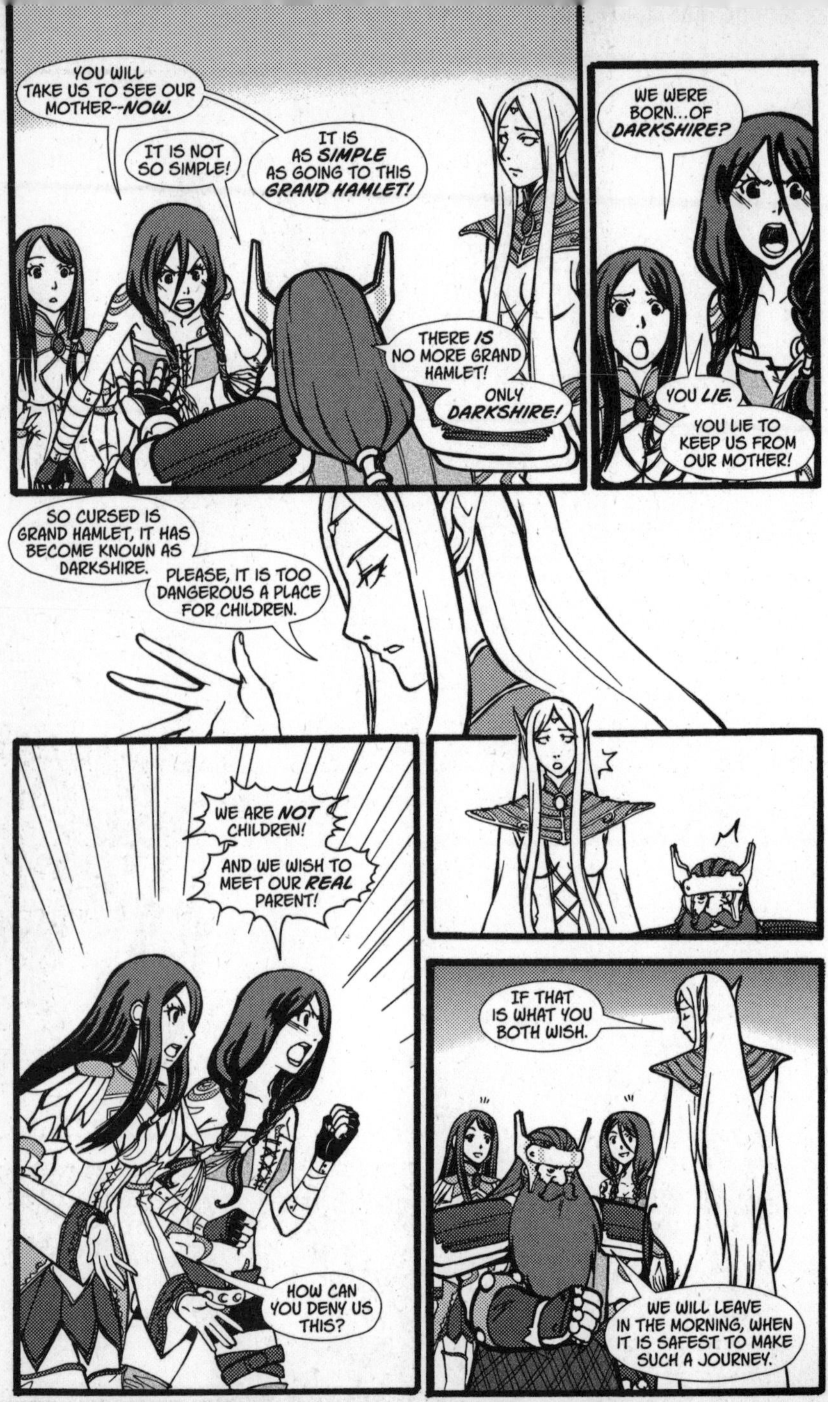
YOU WILL TAKE US TO SEE OUR MOTHER--NOW.
IT IS NOT SO SIMPLE!
IT IS AS SIMPLE AS GOING TO THIS GRAND HAMLET!
THERE IS NO MORE GRAND HAMLET!
ONLY DARKSHIRE!
WE WERE BORN...OF DARKSHIRE?
YOU LIE.
YOU LIE TO KEEP US FROM OUR MOTHER!
SO CURSED IS GRAND HAMLET, IT HAS BECOME KNOWN AS DARKSHIRE.
PLEASE, IT IS TOO DANGEROUS A PLACE FOR CHILDREN.
WE ARE NOT CHILDREN!
AND WE WISH TO MEET OUR REAL PARENT!
HOW CAN YOU DENY US THIS?
IF THAT IS WHAT YOU BOTH WISH.
WE WILL LEAVE IN THE MORNING, WHEN IT IS SAFEST TO MAKE SUCH A JOURNEY.

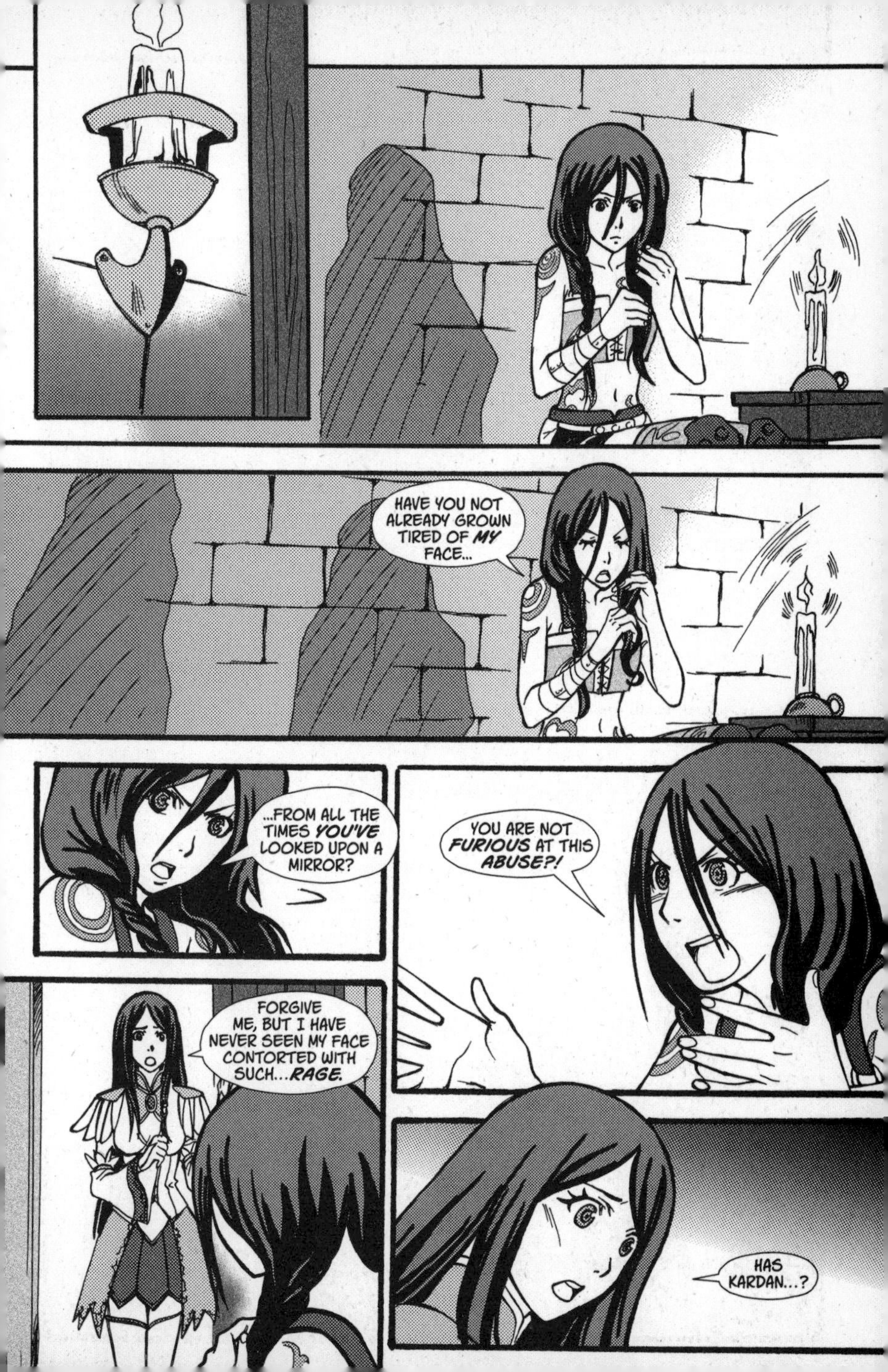

HAVE YOU NOT ALREADY GROWN TIRED OF *MY* FACE...
...FROM ALL THE TIMES *YOU'VE* LOOKED UPON A MIRROR?
YOU ARE NOT *FURIOUS* AT THIS *ABUSE?!*
FORGIVE ME, BUT I HAVE NEVER SEEN MY FACE CONTORTED WITH SUCH...*RAGE.*
HAS KARDAN...?

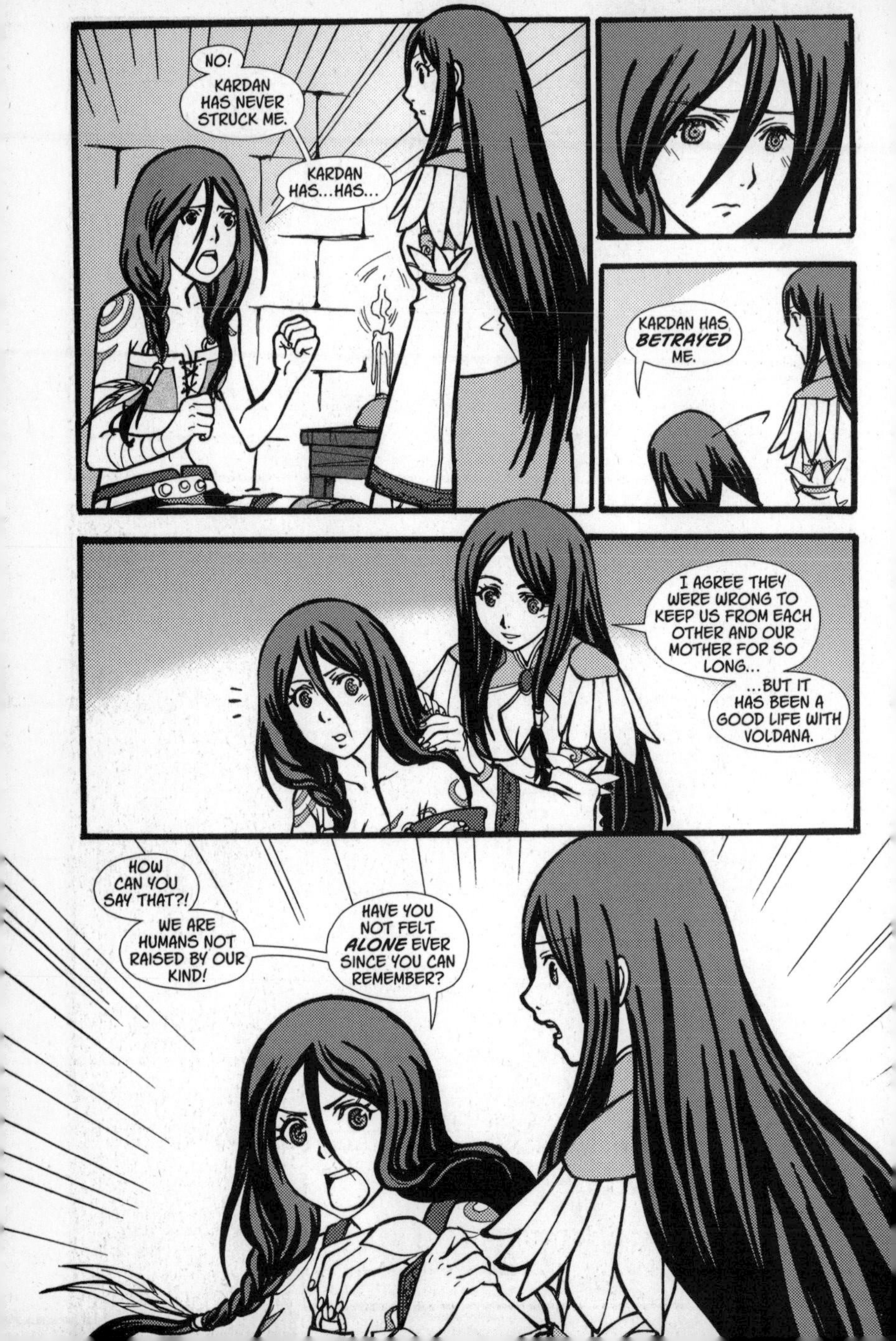
NO! KARDAN HAS NEVER STRUCK ME.
KARDAN HAS...HAS...
KARDAN HAS **BETRAYED** ME.
I AGREE THEY WERE WRONG TO KEEP US FROM EACH OTHER AND OUR MOTHER FOR SO LONG...
...BUT IT HAS BEEN A GOOD LIFE WITH VOLDANA.
HOW CAN YOU SAY THAT?!
WE ARE HUMANS NOT RAISED BY OUR KIND!
HAVE YOU NOT FELT **ALONE** EVER SINCE YOU CAN REMEMBER?

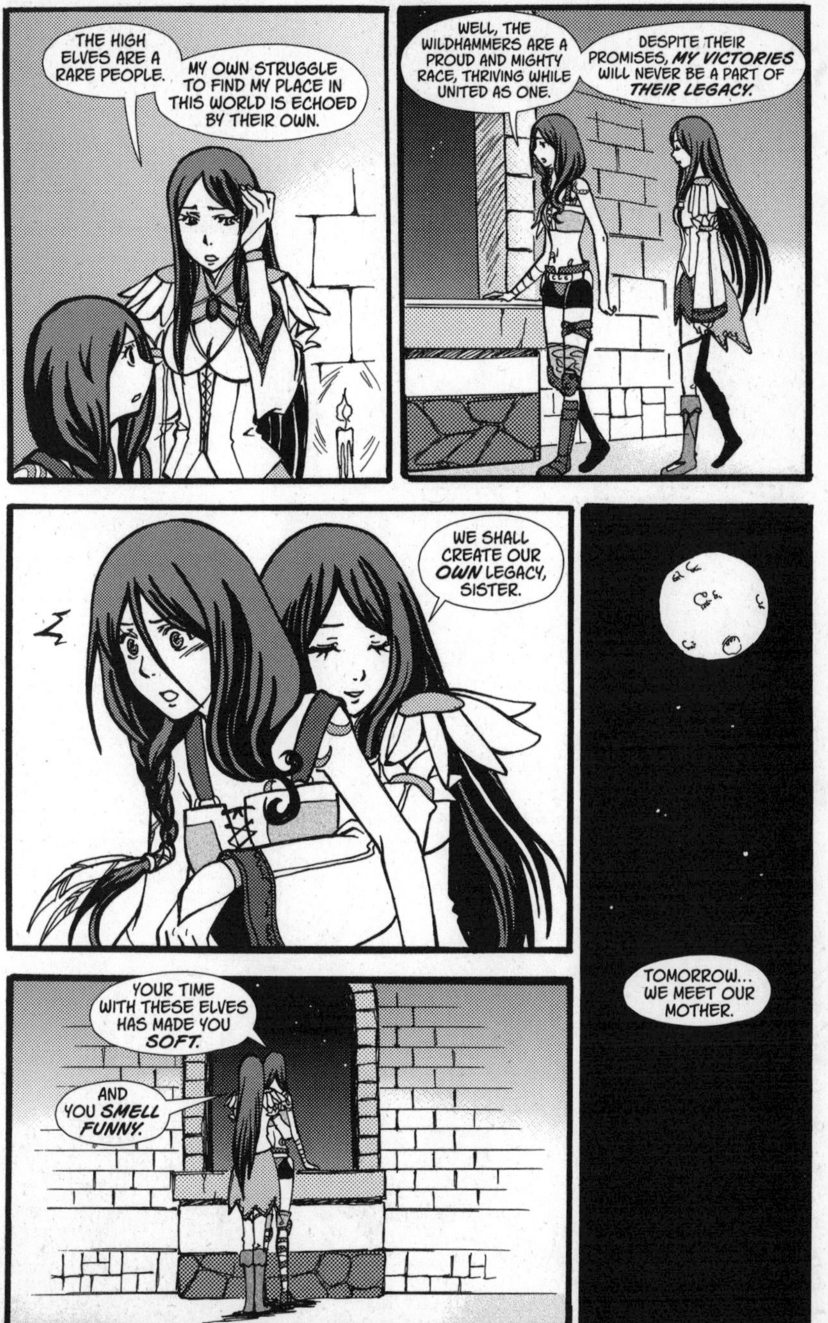
THE HIGH ELVES ARE A RARE PEOPLE.
MY OWN STRUGGLE TO FIND MY PLACE IN THIS WORLD IS ECHOED BY THEIR OWN.
WELL, THE WILDHAMMERS ARE A PROUD AND MIGHTY RACE, THRIVING WHILE UNITED AS ONE.
DESPITE THEIR PROMISES, MY VICTORIES WILL NEVER BE A PART OF THEIR LEGACY.
WE SHALL CREATE OUR OWN LEGACY, SISTER.
YOUR TIME WITH THESE ELVES HAS MADE YOU SOFT.
AND YOU SMELL FUNNY.
TOMORROW... WE MEET OUR MOTHER.

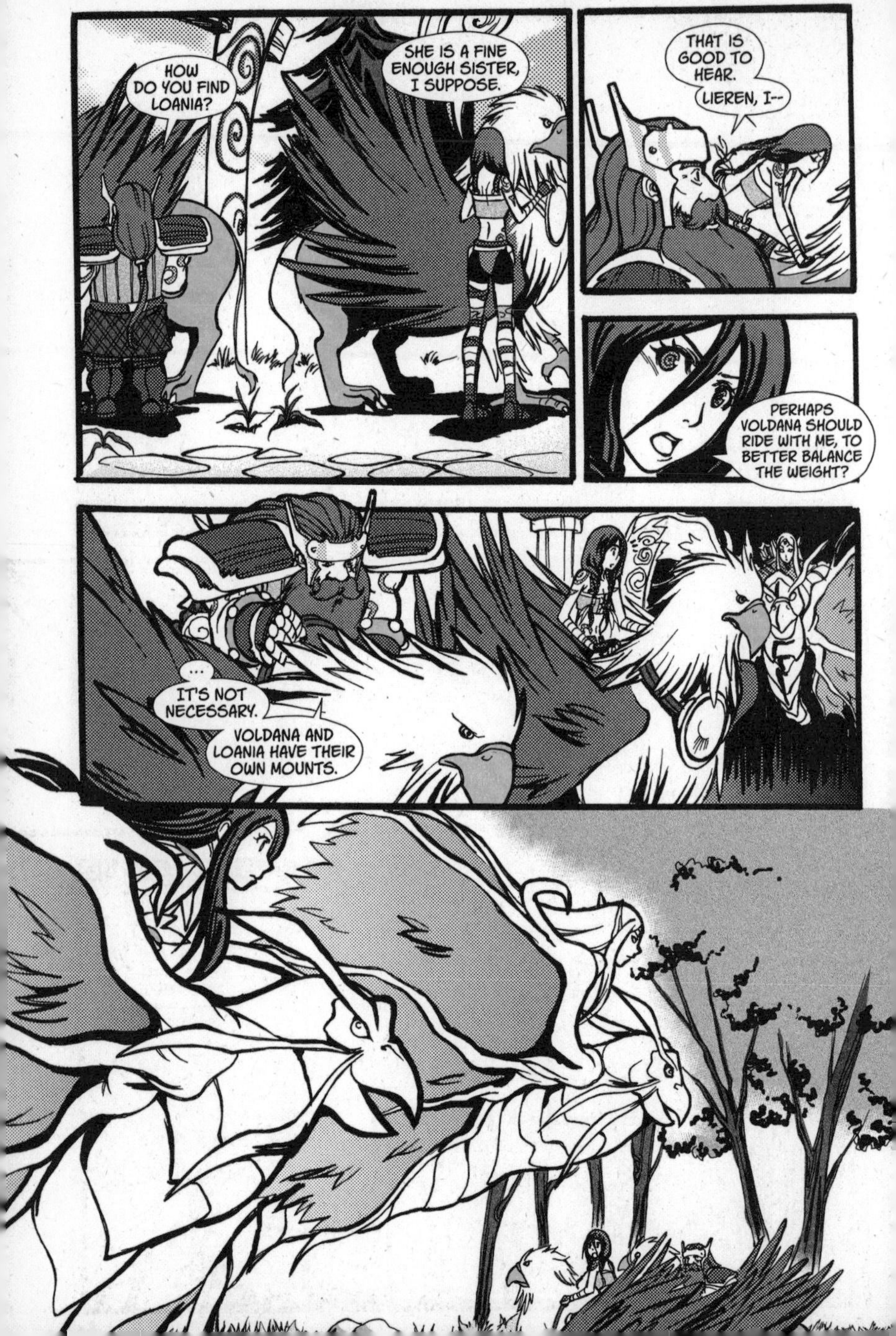
HOW DO YOU FIND LOANIA?
SHE IS A FINE ENOUGH SISTER, I SUPPOSE.
THAT IS GOOD TO HEAR.
LIEREN, I--
PERHAPS VOLDANA SHOULD RIDE WITH ME, TO BETTER BALANCE THE WEIGHT?
...
IT'S NOT NECESSARY.
VOLDANA AND LOANIA HAVE THEIR OWN MOUNTS.

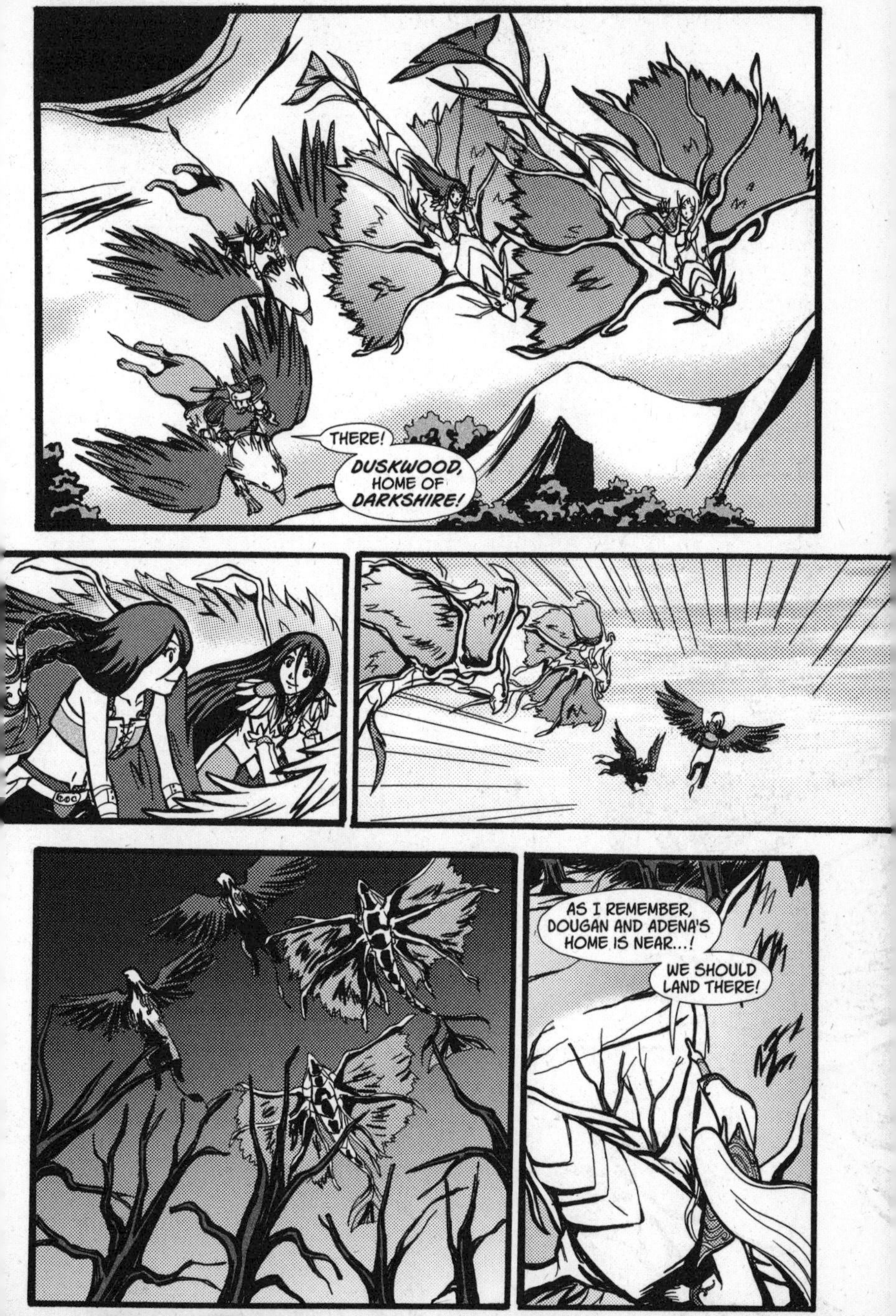
THERE!
DUSKWOOD, HOME OF DARKSHIRE!
AS I REMEMBER, DOUGAN AND ADENA'S HOME IS NEAR...!
WE SHOULD LAND THERE!

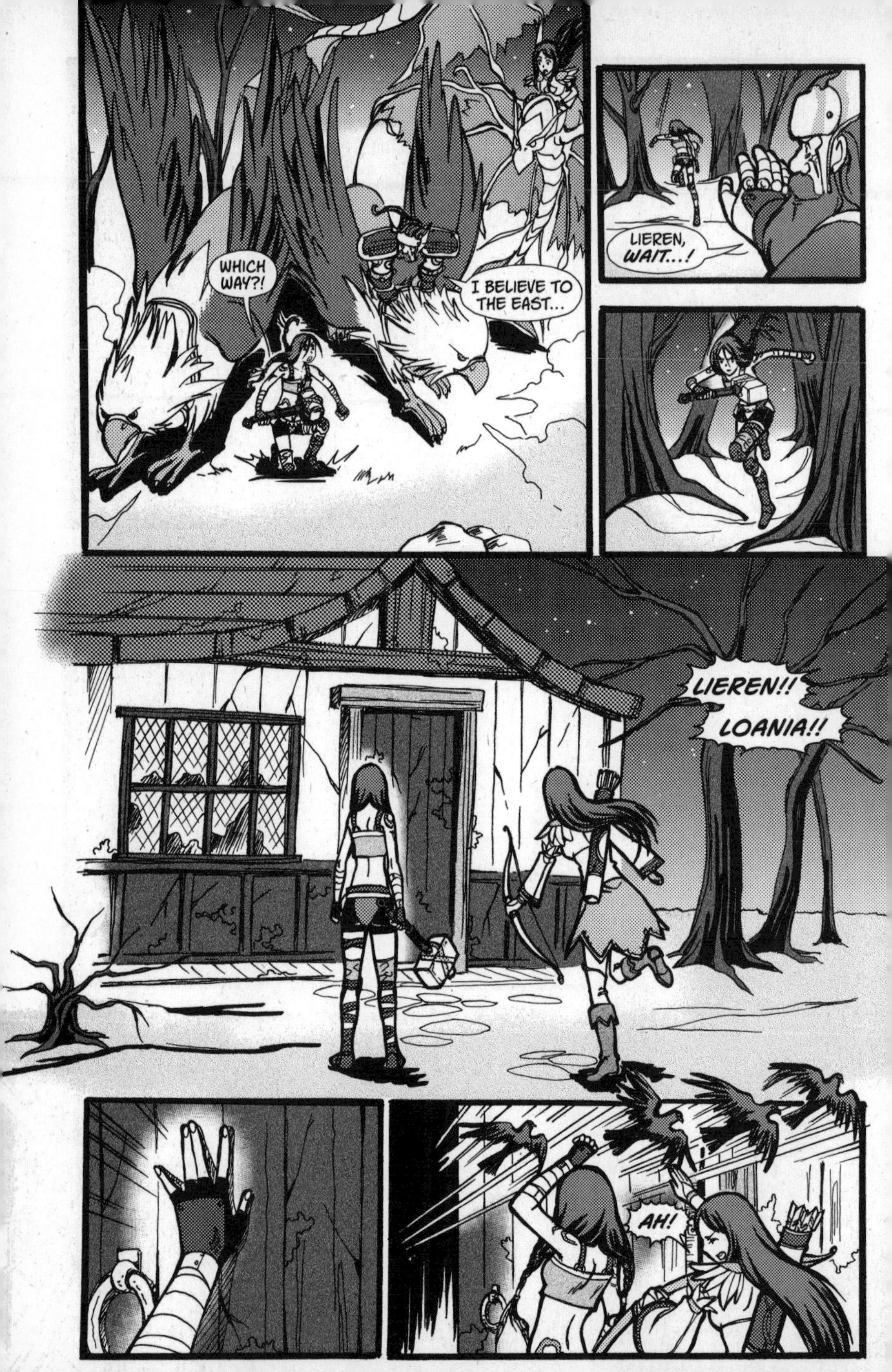
WHICH WAY?!
I BELIEVE TO THE EAST...
LIEREN, WAIT...!
LIEREN!!
LOANIA!!
AH!

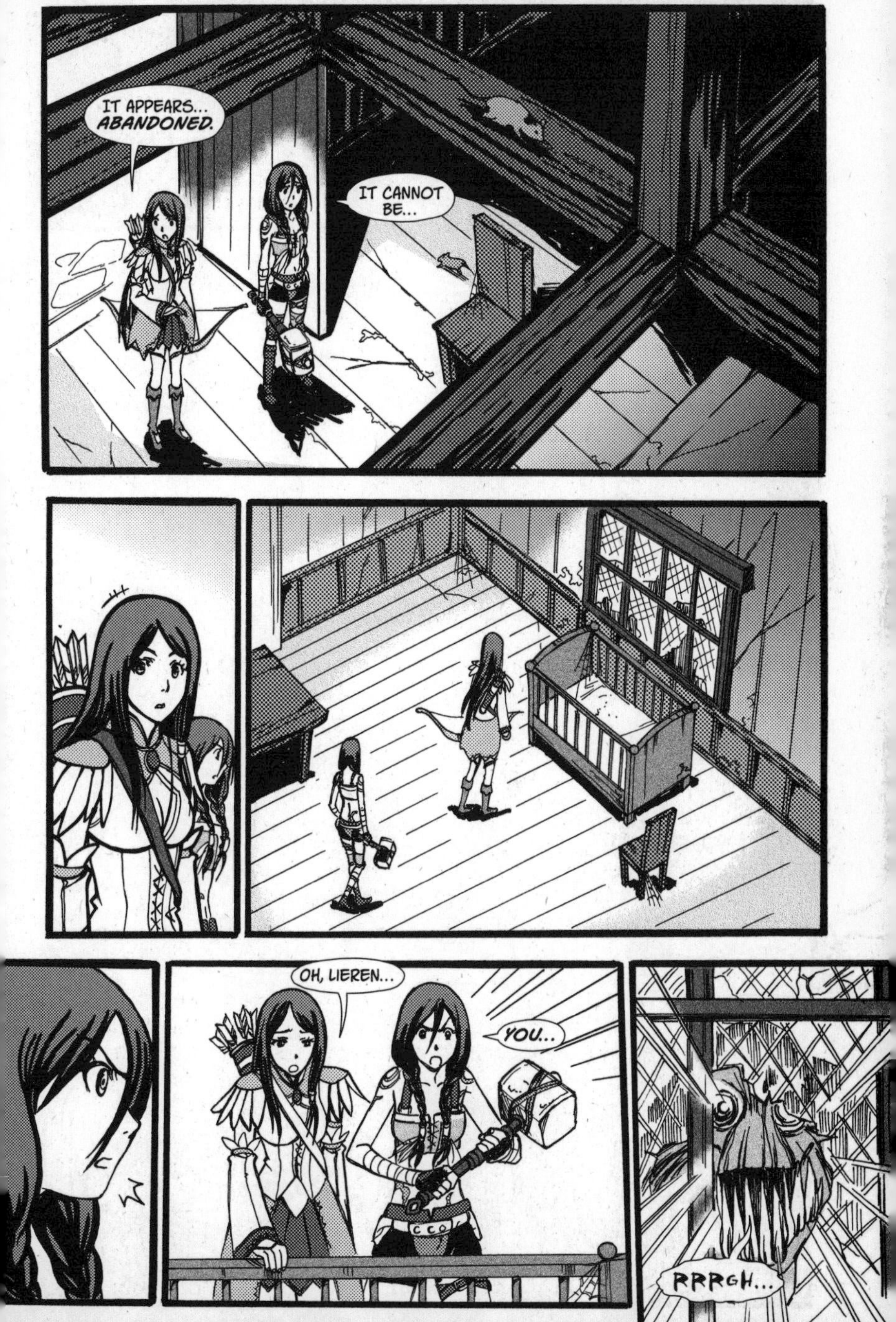
IT APPEARS... ABANDONED.
IT CANNOT BE...
OH, LIEREN...
YOU...
RRRGH...

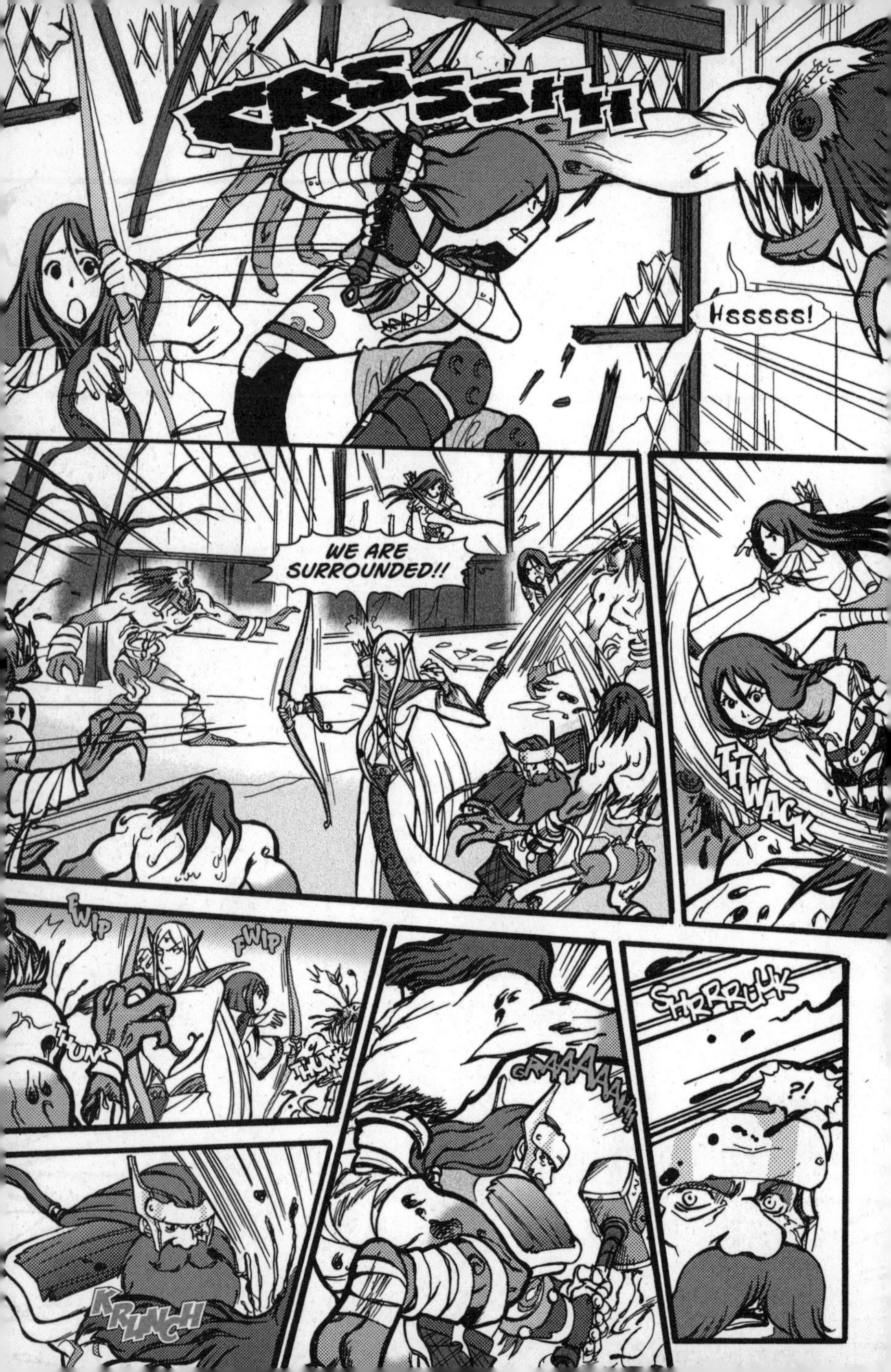
CRSSHH
Hsssss!
WE ARE SURROUNDED!!
THWACK
FWIP
FWIP
THUNK
THUNK
KRUNCH
GRAAAAAAW
SHRRUK
?!

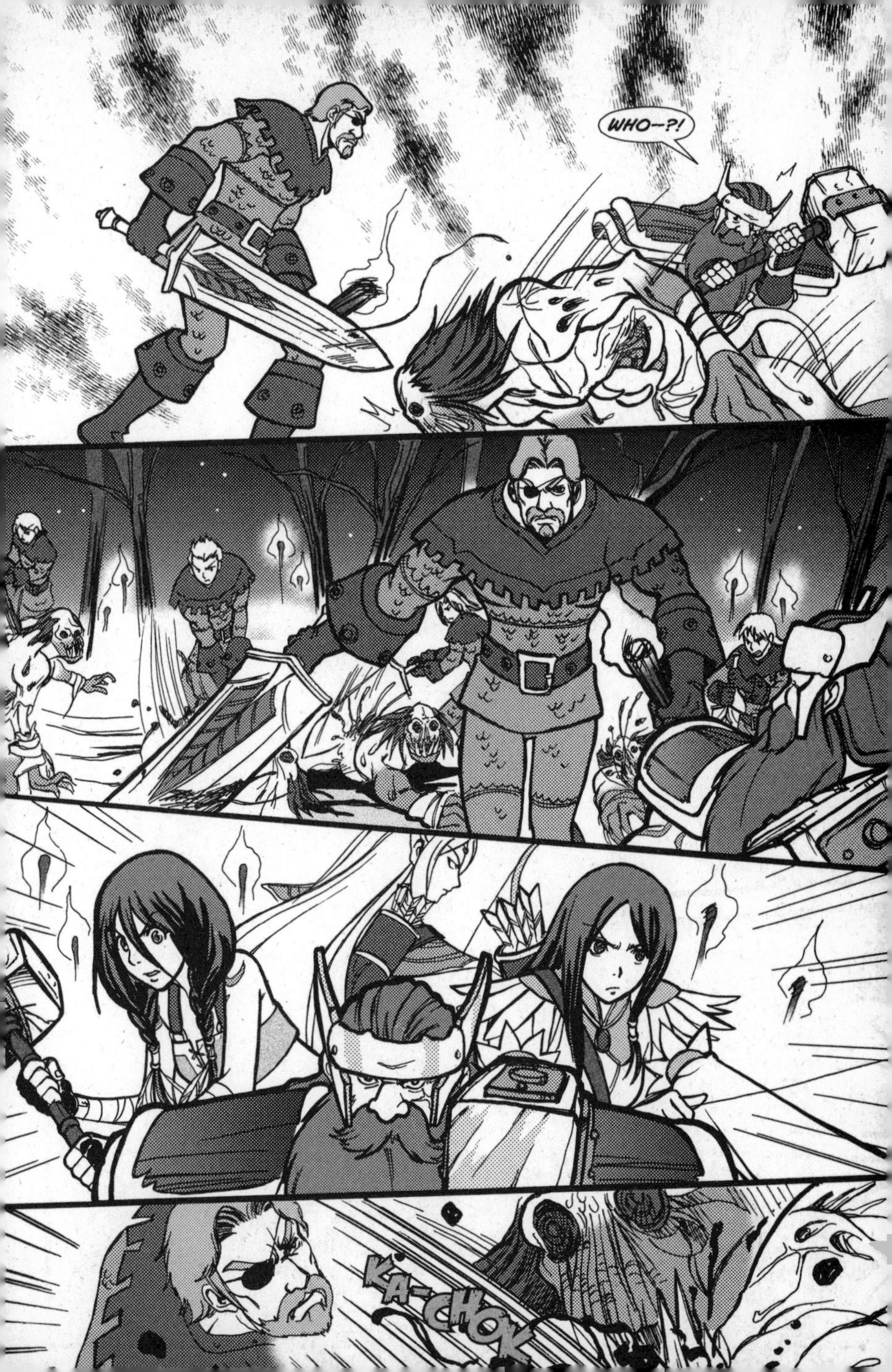
WHO--?!
KA-CHOK

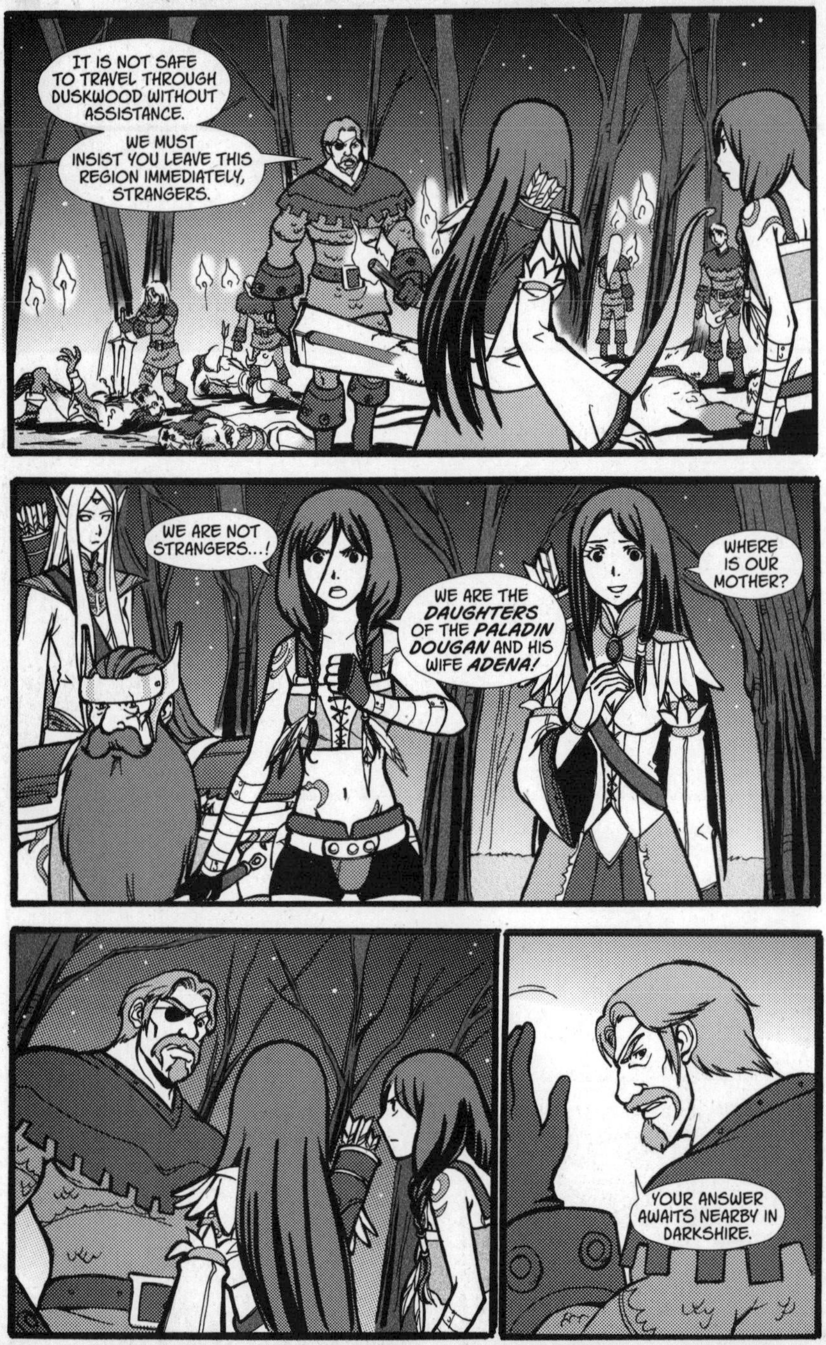
IT IS NOT SAFE TO TRAVEL THROUGH DUSKWOOD WITHOUT ASSISTANCE.
WE MUST INSIST YOU LEAVE THIS REGION IMMEDIATELY, STRANGERS.
WE ARE NOT STRANGERS...!
WE ARE THE DAUGHTERS OF THE PALADIN DOUGAN AND HIS WIFE ADENA!
WHERE IS OUR MOTHER?
YOUR ANSWER AWAITS NEARBY IN DARKSHIRE.

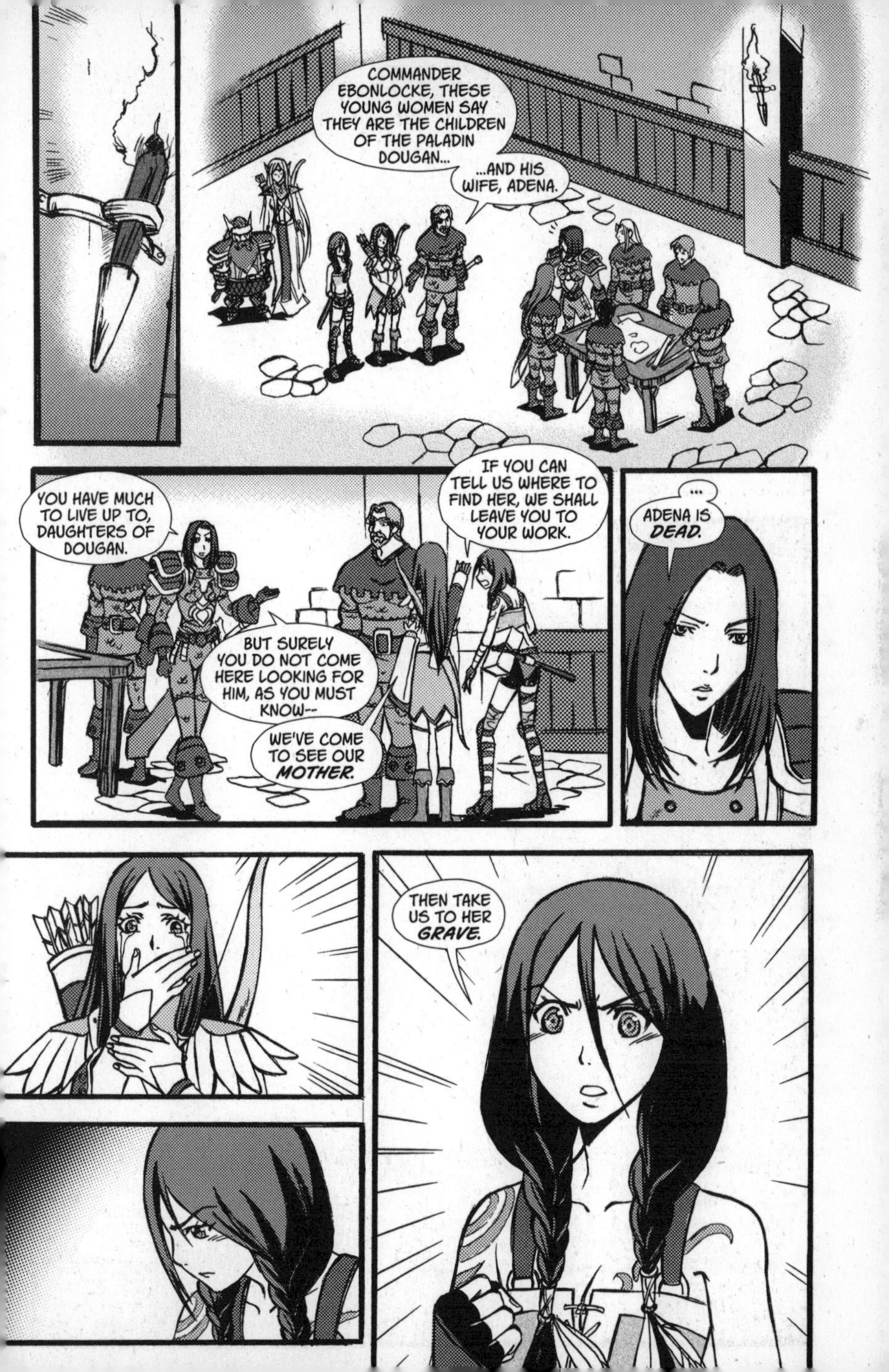
COMMANDER EBONLOCKE, THESE YOUNG WOMEN SAY THEY ARE THE CHILDREN OF THE PALADIN DOUGAN...
...AND HIS WIFE, ADENA.
YOU HAVE MUCH TO LIVE UP TO, DAUGHTERS OF DOUGAN.
BUT SURELY YOU DO NOT COME HERE LOOKING FOR HIM, AS YOU MUST KNOW--
IF YOU CAN TELL US WHERE TO FIND HER, WE SHALL LEAVE YOU TO YOUR WORK.
WE'VE COME TO SEE OUR MOTHER.
...
ADENA IS DEAD.
THEN TAKE US TO HER GRAVE.

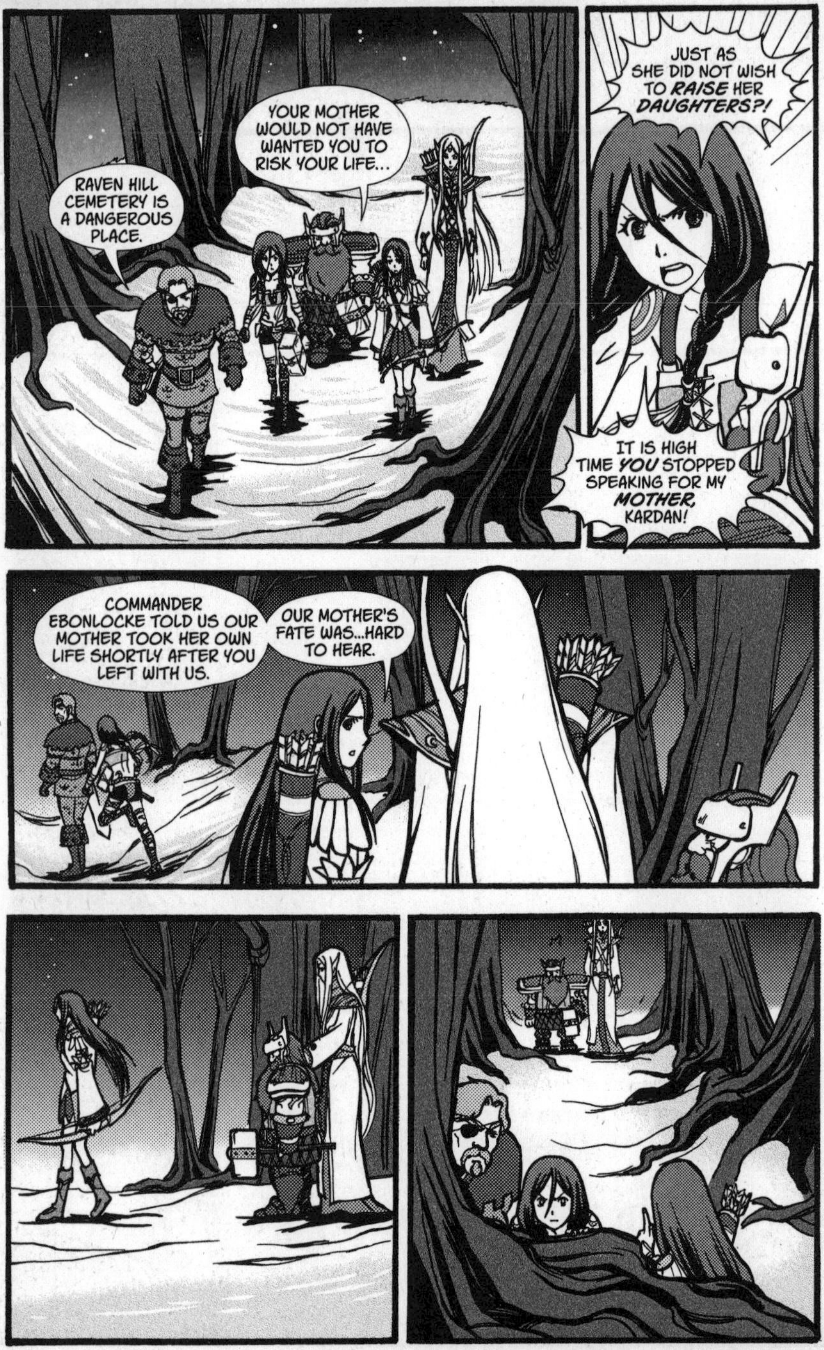
RAVEN HILL CEMETERY IS A DANGEROUS PLACE.
YOUR MOTHER WOULD NOT HAVE WANTED YOU TO RISK YOUR LIFE...
JUST AS SHE DID NOT WISH TO RAISE HER DAUGHTERS?!
IT IS HIGH TIME YOU STOPPED SPEAKING FOR MY MOTHER, KARDAN!
COMMANDER EBONLOCKE TOLD US OUR MOTHER TOOK HER OWN LIFE SHORTLY AFTER YOU LEFT WITH US.
OUR MOTHER'S FATE WAS...HARD TO HEAR.

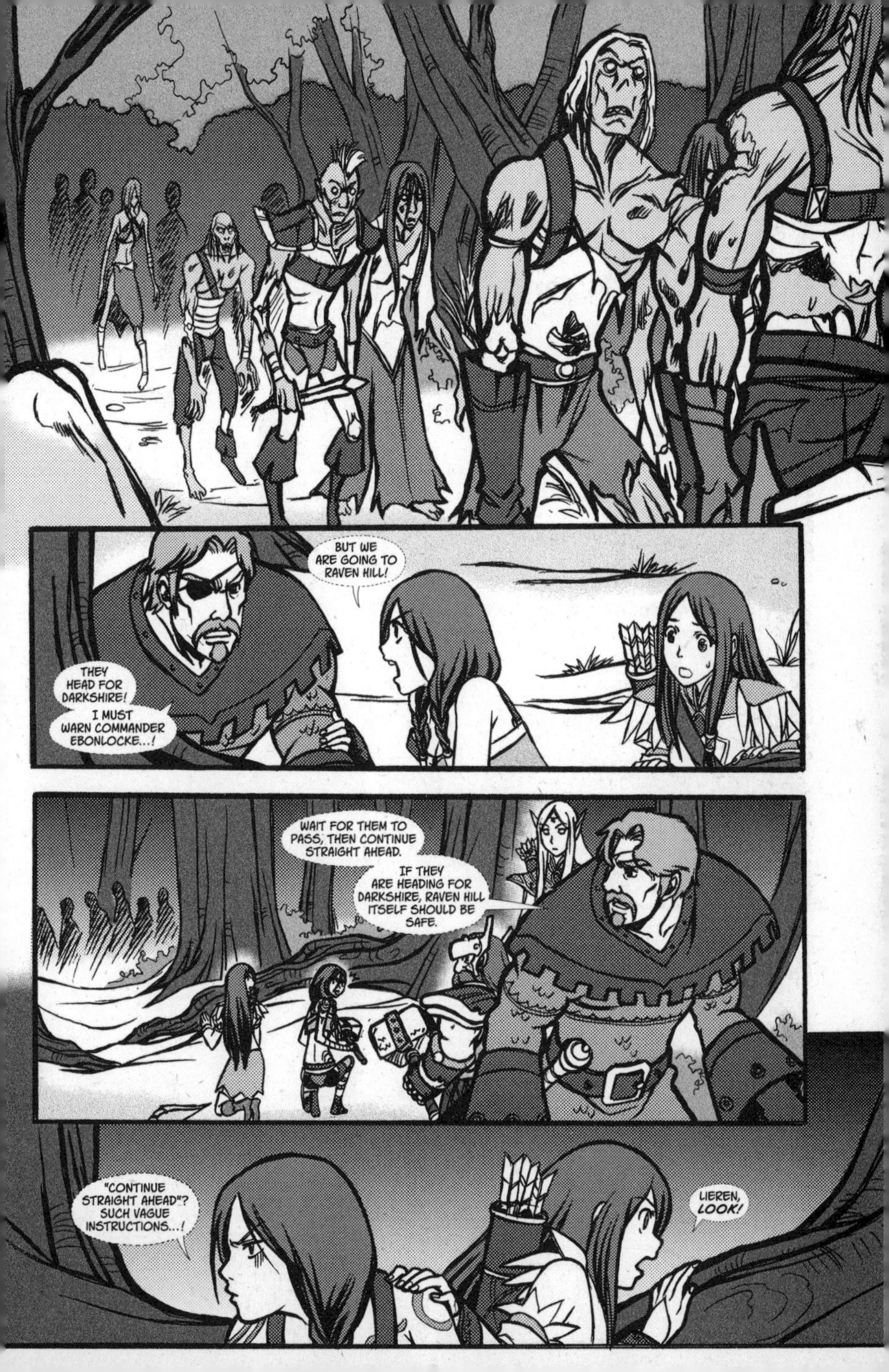
BUT WE ARE GOING TO RAVEN HILL!
THEY HEAD FOR DARKSHIRE!
I MUST WARN COMMANDER EBONLOCKE...!
WAIT FOR THEM TO PASS, THEN CONTINUE STRAIGHT AHEAD.
IF THEY ARE HEADING FOR DARKSHIRE, RAVEN HILL ITSELF SHOULD BE SAFE.
"CONTINUE STRAIGHT AHEAD"? SUCH VAGUE INSTRUCTIONS...!
LIEREN, LOOK!

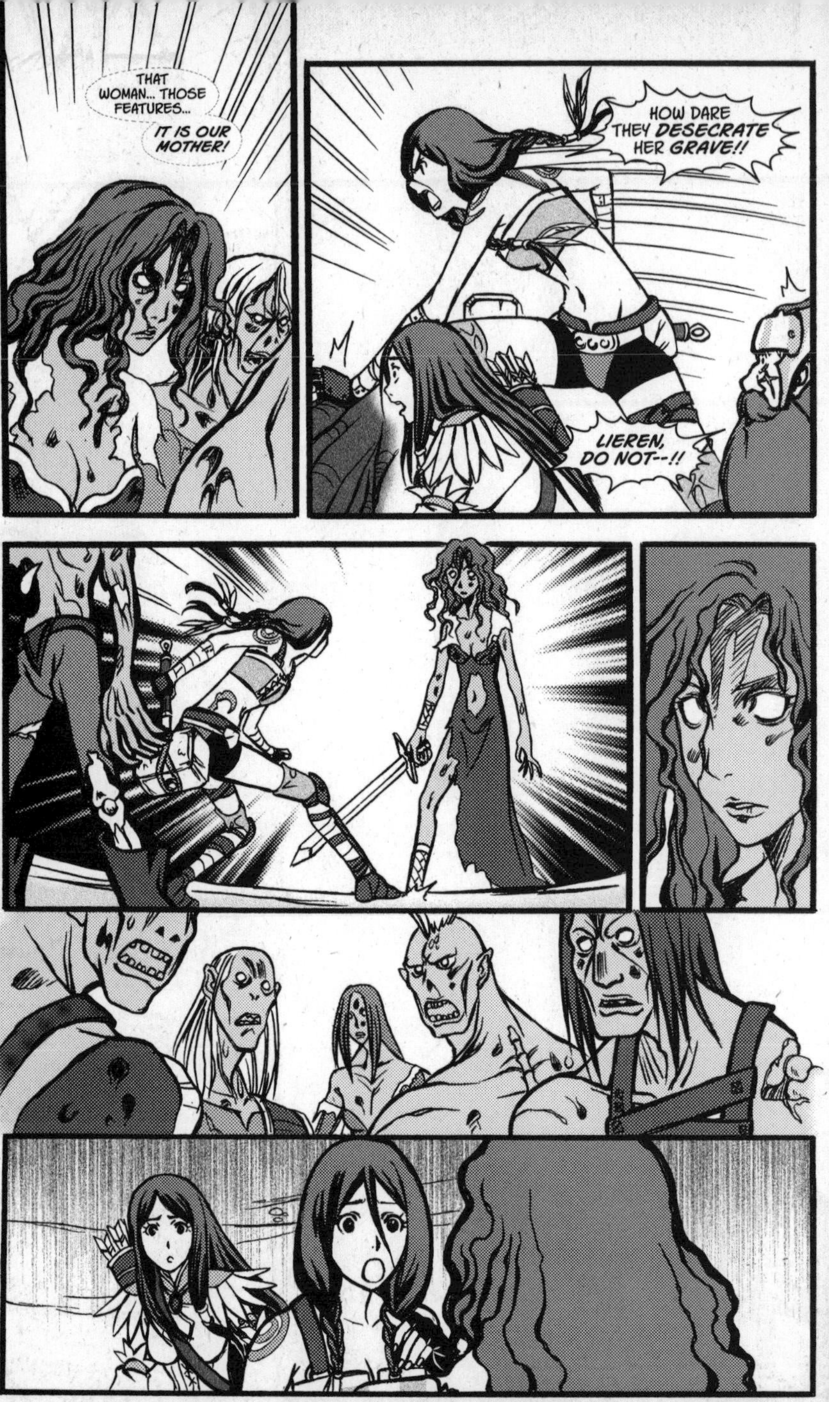
THAT WOMAN... THOSE FEATURES...
IT IS OUR MOTHER!
HOW DARE THEY DESECRATE HER GRAVE!!
LIEREN, DO NOT--!!

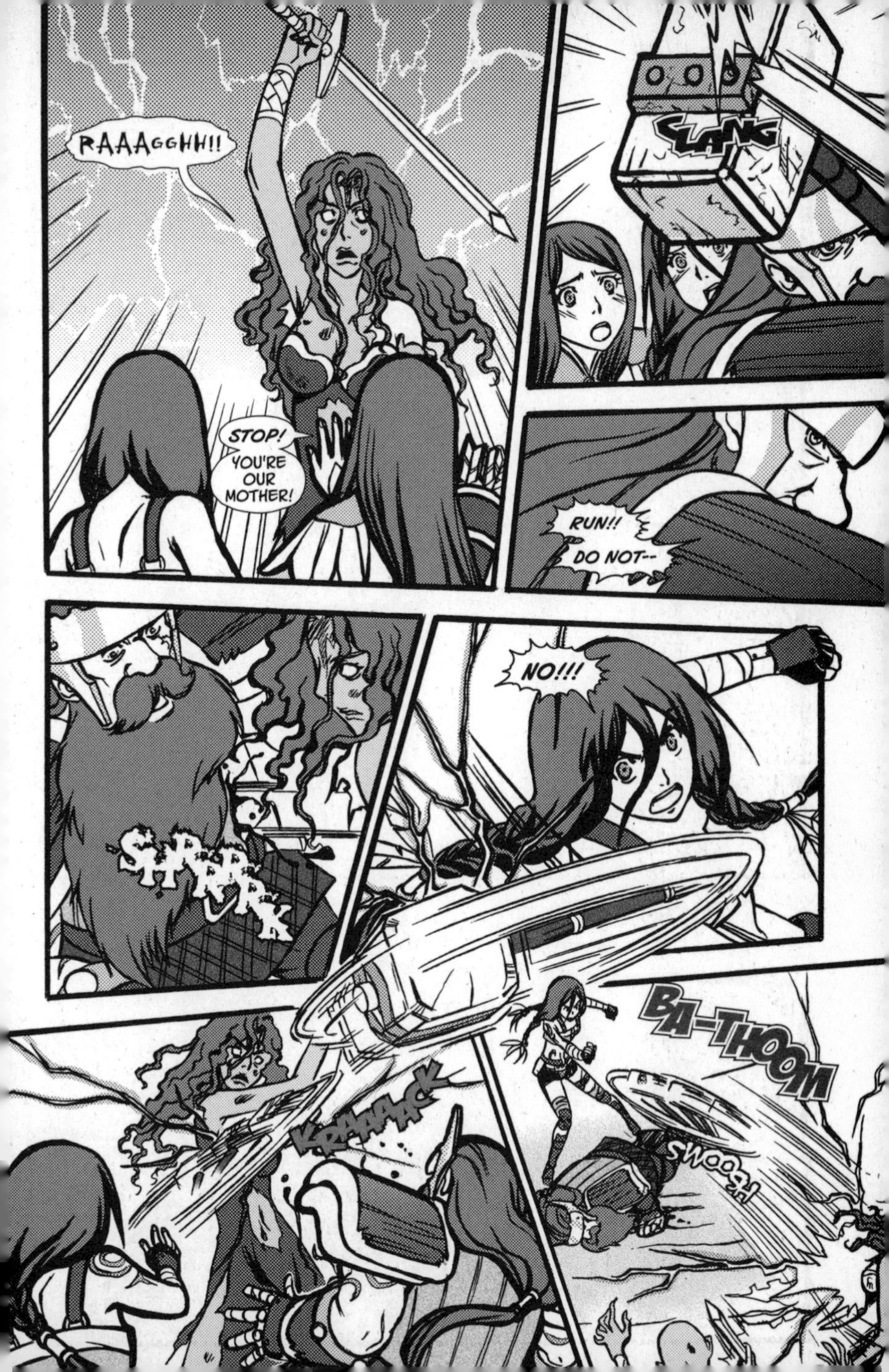
RAAAGGHH!!
STOP! YOU'RE OUR MOTHER!
CLANG
RUN!! DO NOT--
SHRRRK
NO!!!
KRAAAACK
BA-THOOM
SWOOSH

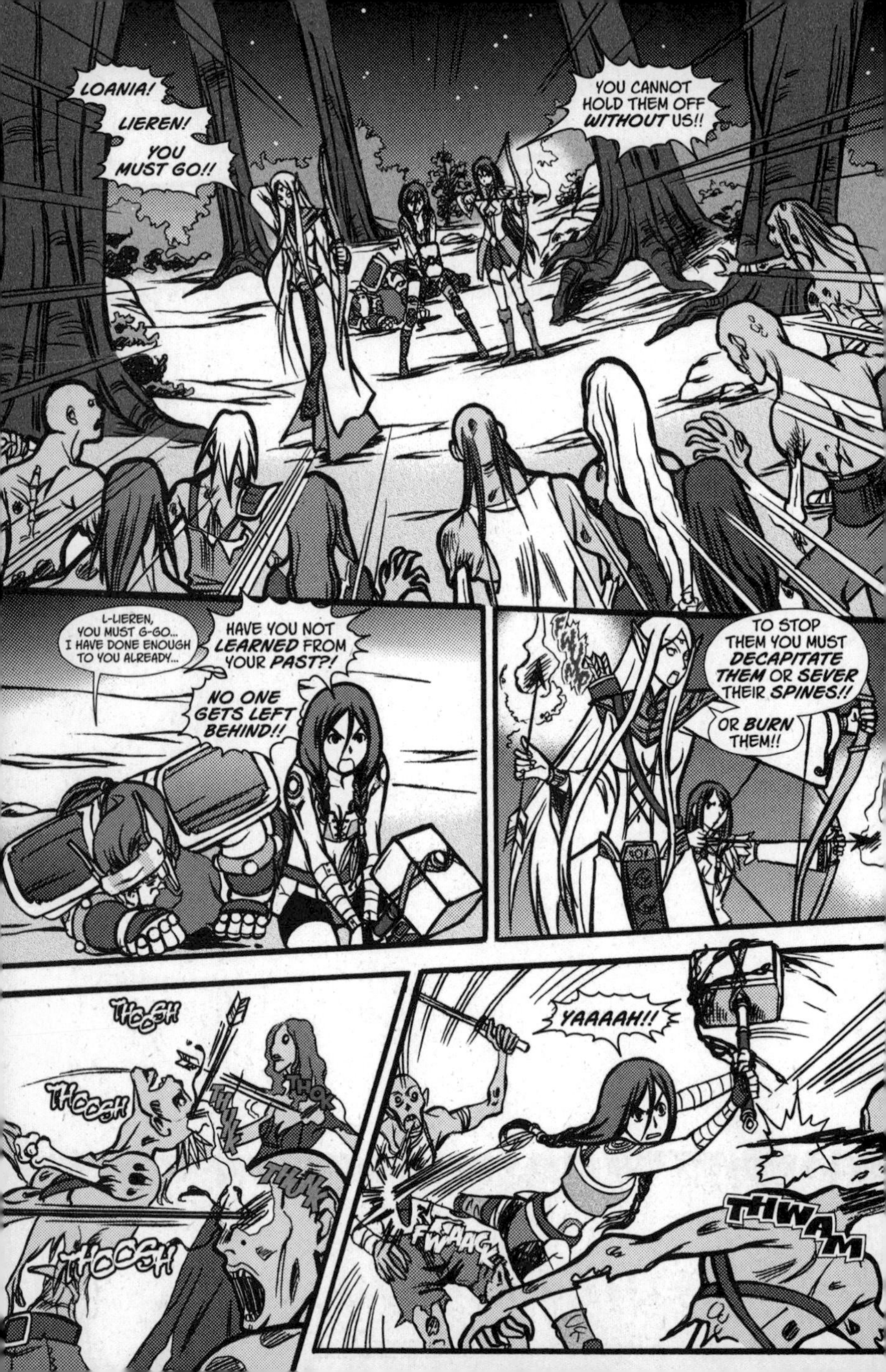
LOANIA!
LIEREN!
YOU MUST GO!!
YOU CANNOT HOLD THEM OFF WITHOUT US!!
L-LIEREN, YOU MUST G-GO... I HAVE DONE ENOUGH TO YOU ALREADY...
HAVE YOU NOT LEARNED FROM YOUR PAST?!
NO ONE GETS LEFT BEHIND!!
TO STOP THEM YOU MUST DECAPITATE THEM OR SEVER THEIR SPINES!!
OR BURN THEM!!
THOOSH
THOOSH
THUNK
THUNK
THUNK
THOOSH
YAAAAH!!
FWAACK
THWAM

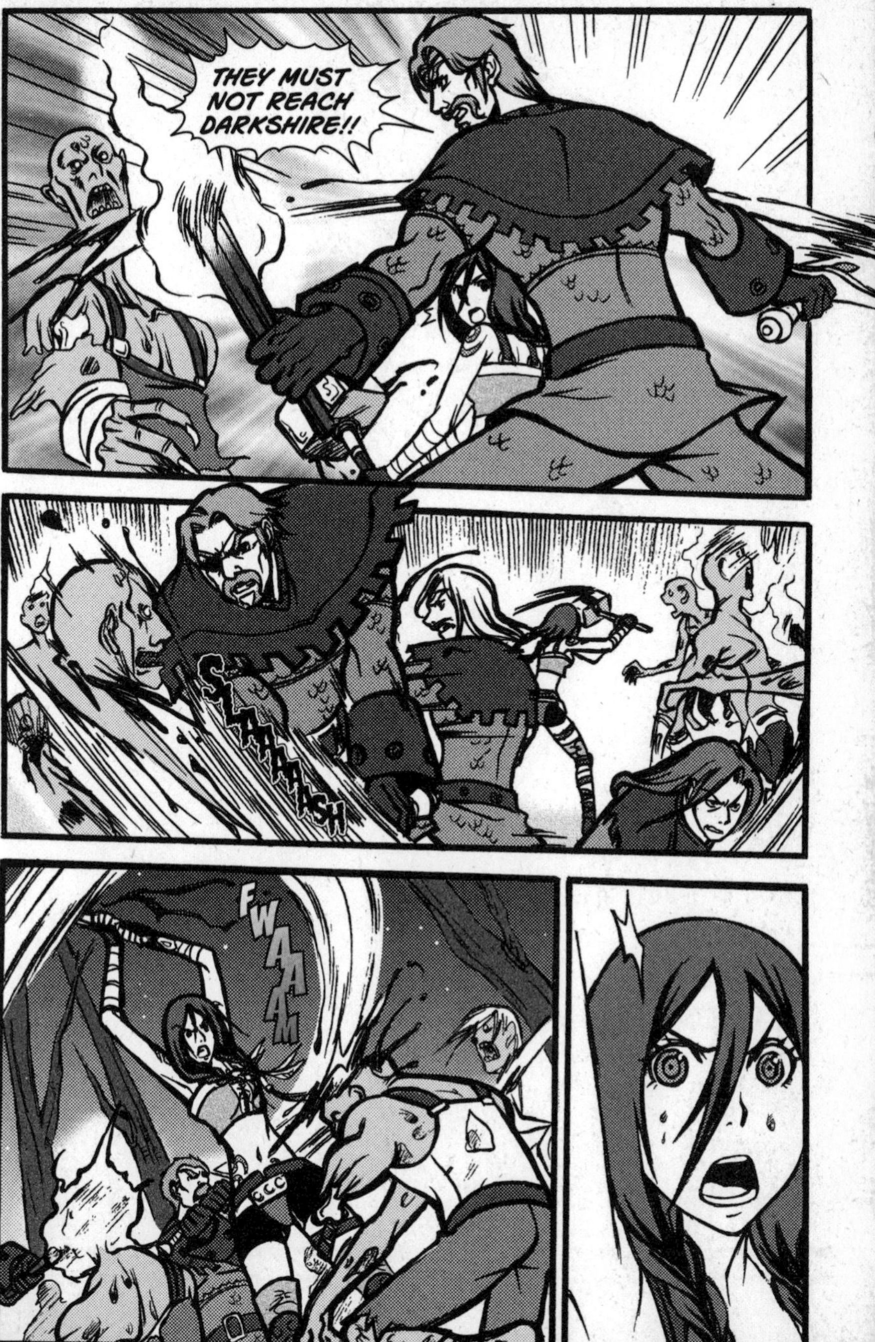
THEY MUST NOT REACH DARKSHIRE!!
SLAAAAAASH
FWAAAM

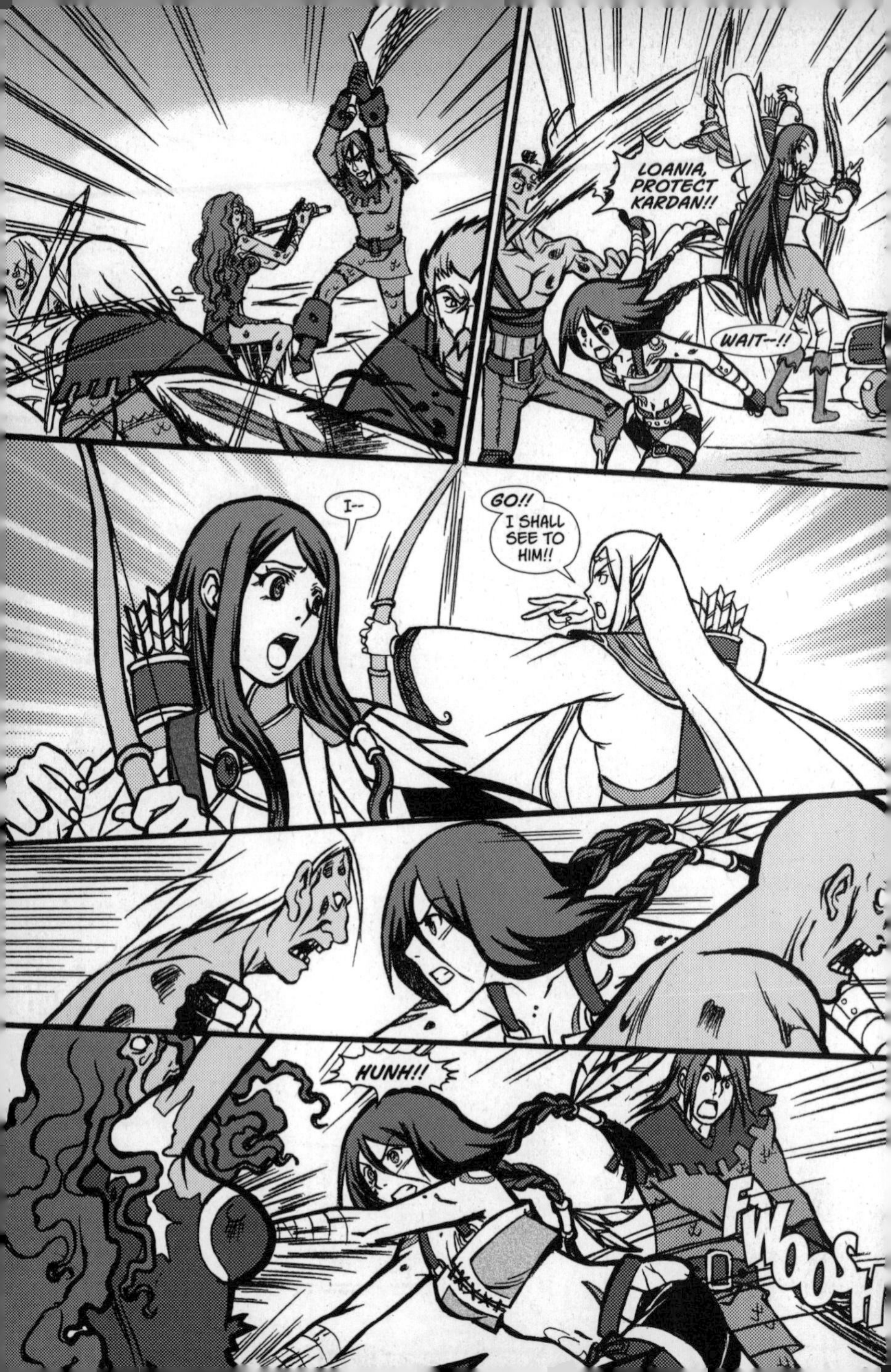
LOANIA, PROTECT KARDAN!!
WAIT--!!
I--
GO!! I SHALL SEE TO HIM!!
HUNH!!
FWOOSH

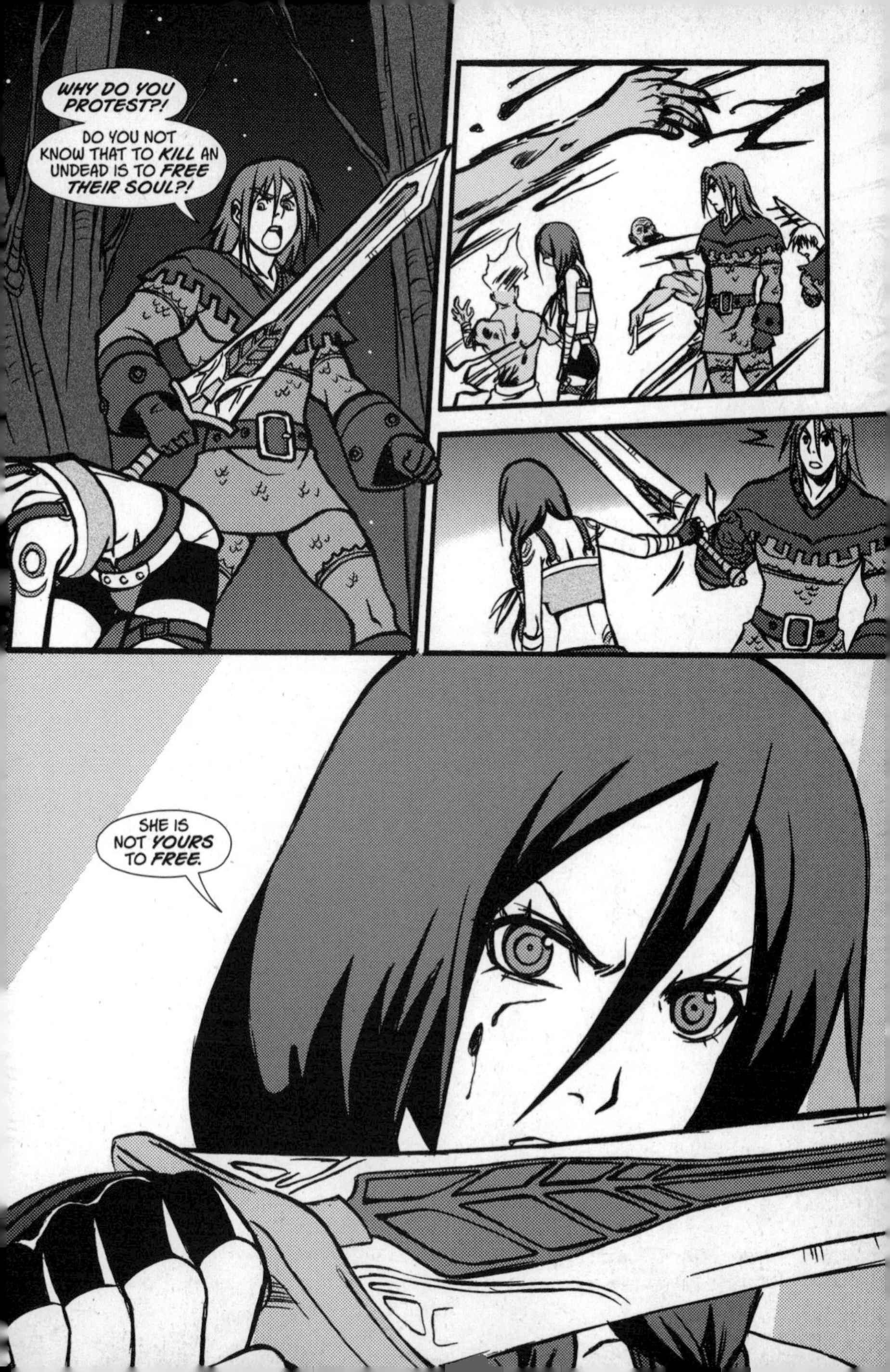
WHY DO YOU PROTEST?!
DO YOU NOT KNOW THAT TO KILL AN UNDEAD IS TO FREE THEIR SOUL?!
SHE IS NOT YOURS TO FREE.

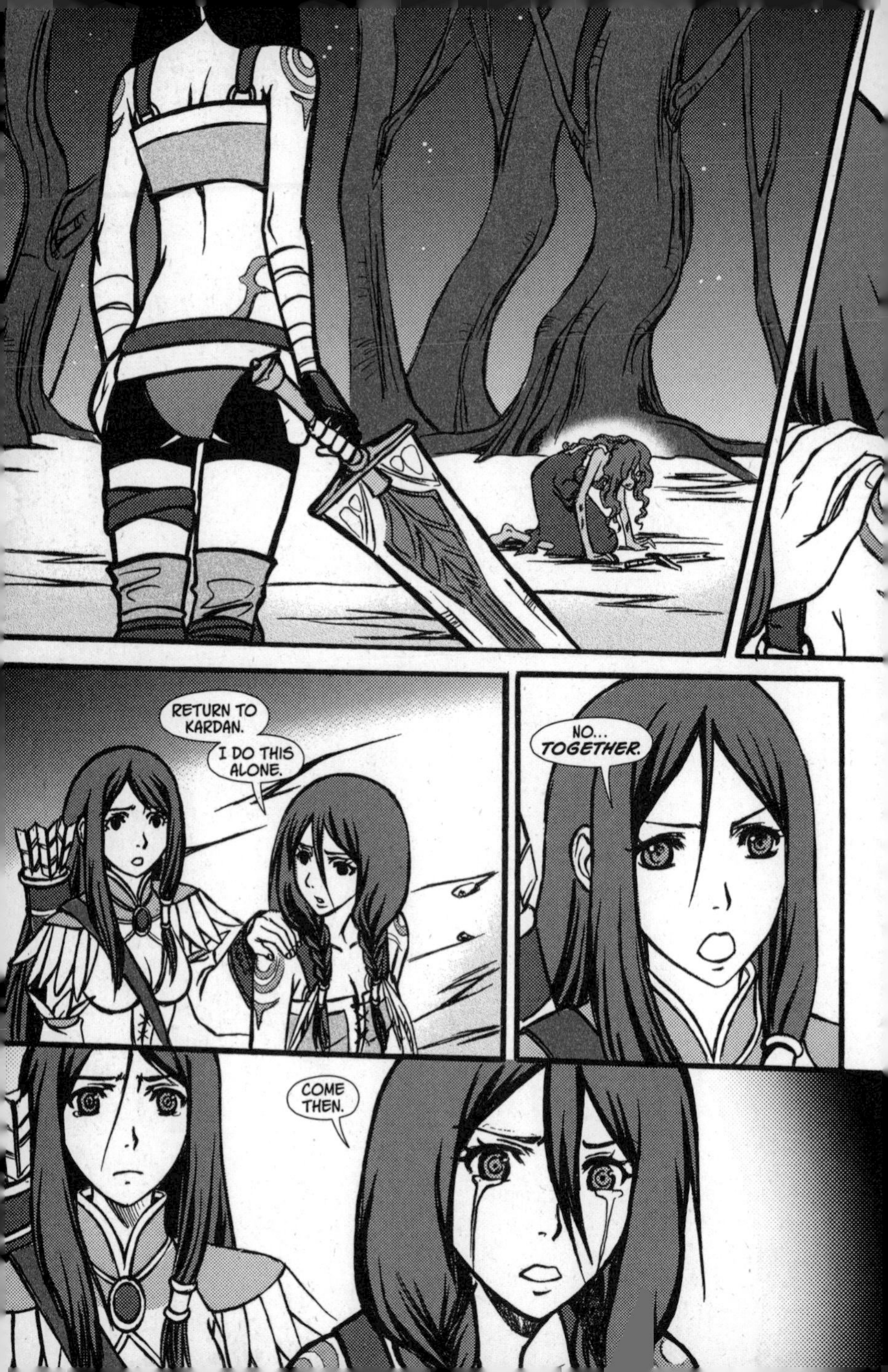
RETURN TO KARDAN.
I DO THIS ALONE.
NO... TOGETHER.
COME THEN.

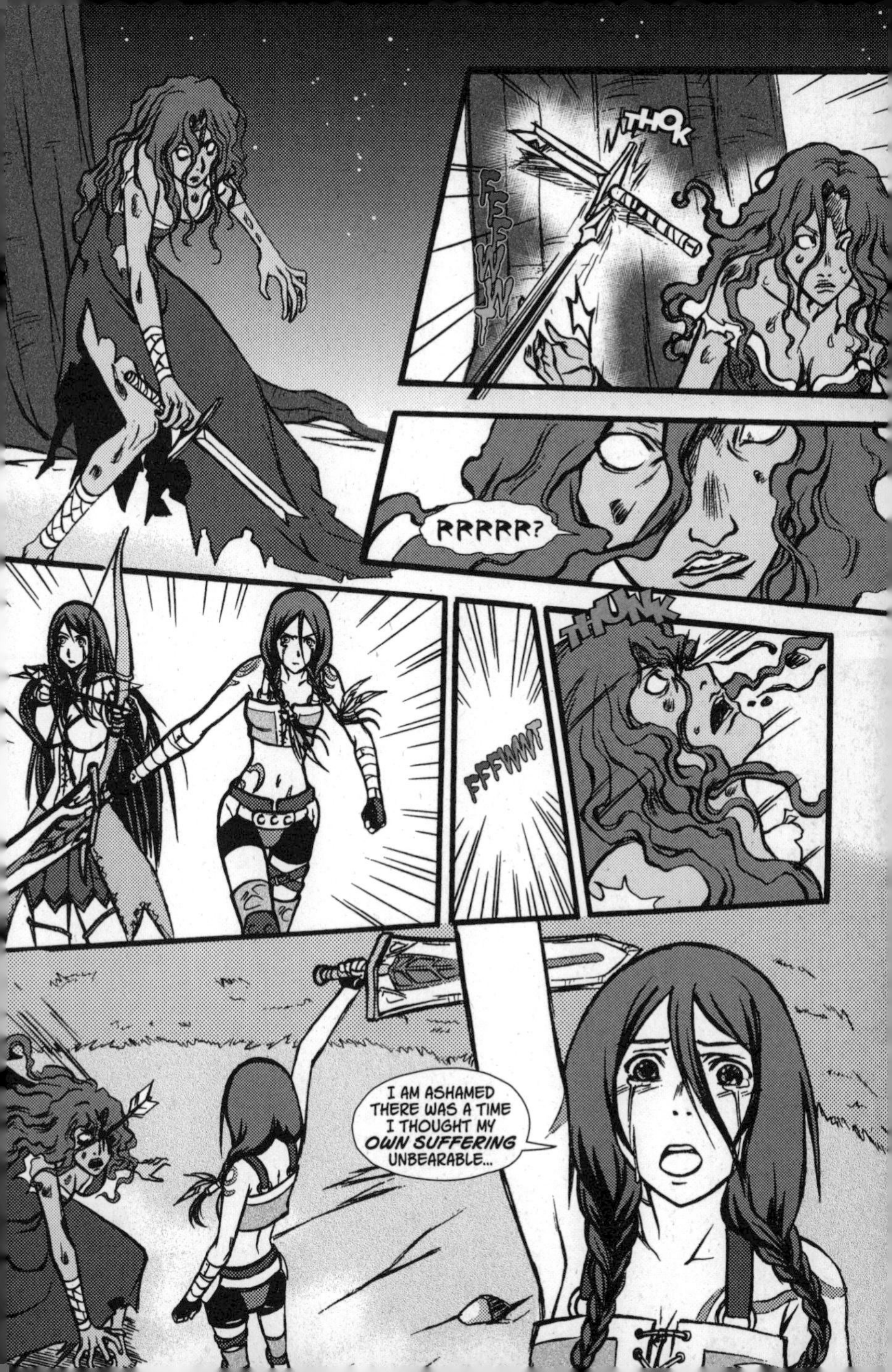
THOK
FFFWWT
RRRRR?
FFFWWNT
THUNK
I AM ASHAMED THERE WAS A TIME I THOUGHT MY ***OWN SUFFERING*** UNBEARABLE...

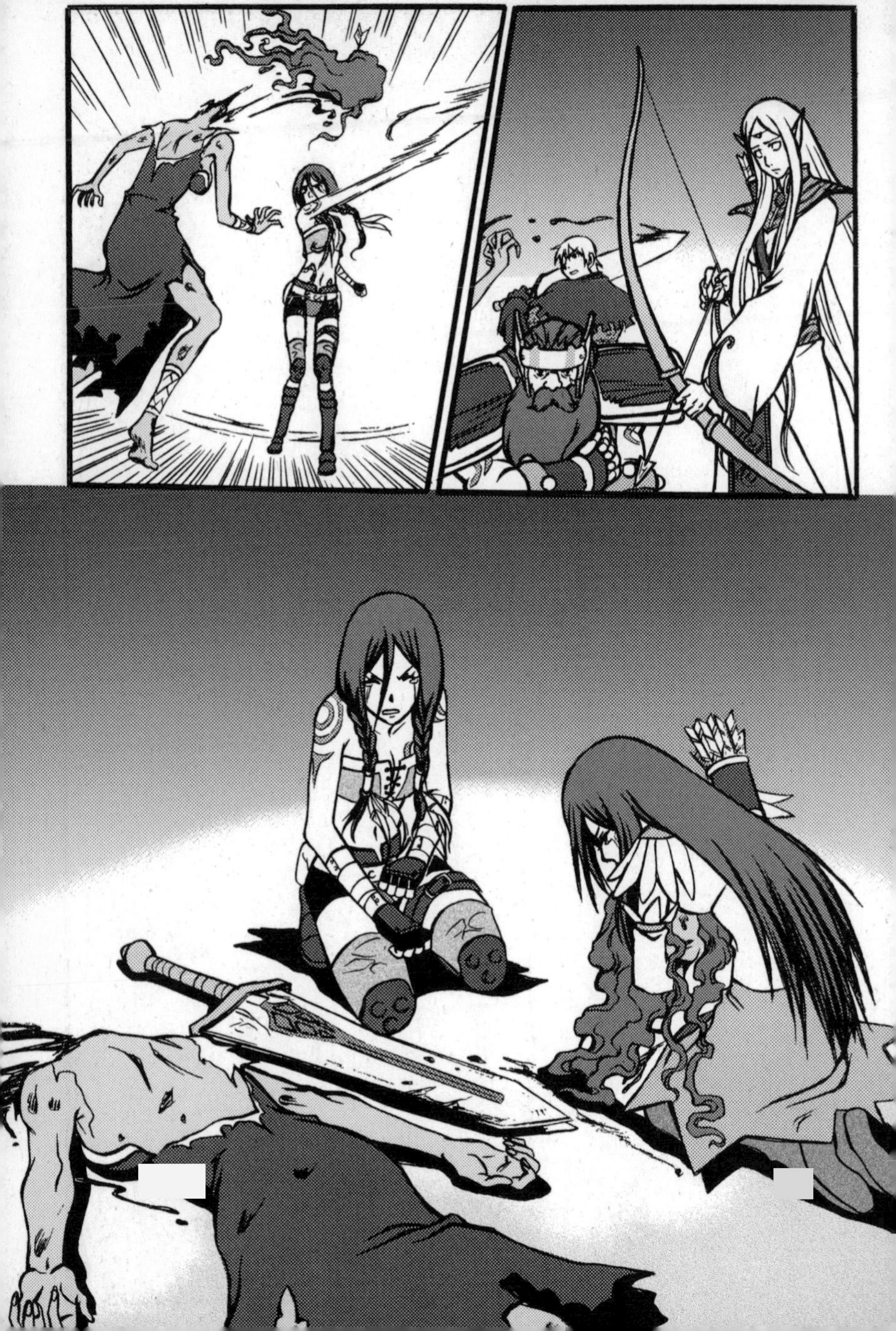

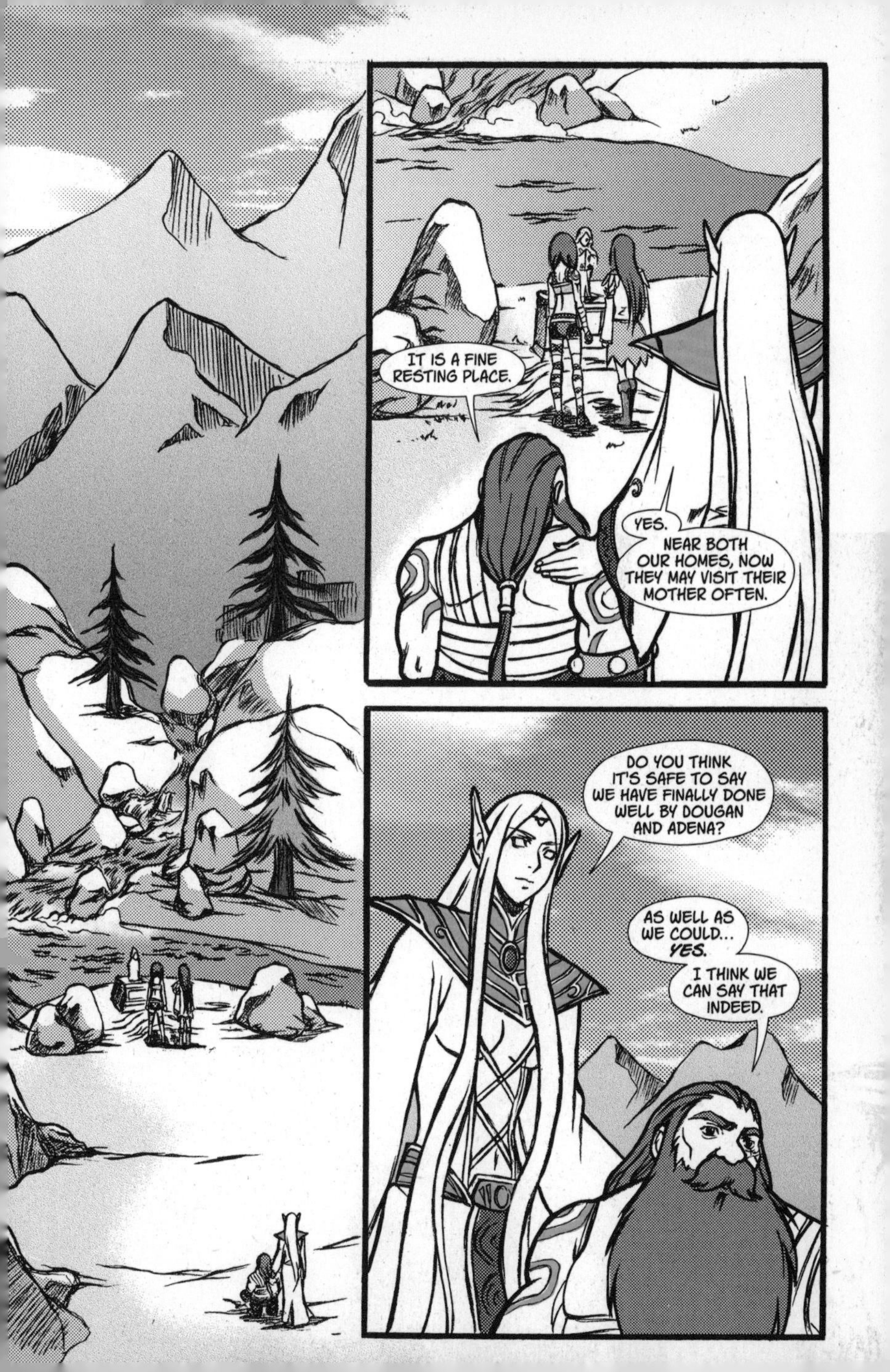
IT IS A FINE RESTING PLACE.
YES.
NEAR BOTH OUR HOMES, NOW THEY MAY VISIT THEIR MOTHER OFTEN.
DO YOU THINK IT'S SAFE TO SAY WE HAVE FINALLY DONE WELL BY DOUGAN AND ADENA?
AS WELL AS WE COULD... *YES.*
I THINK WE CAN SAY THAT INDEED.

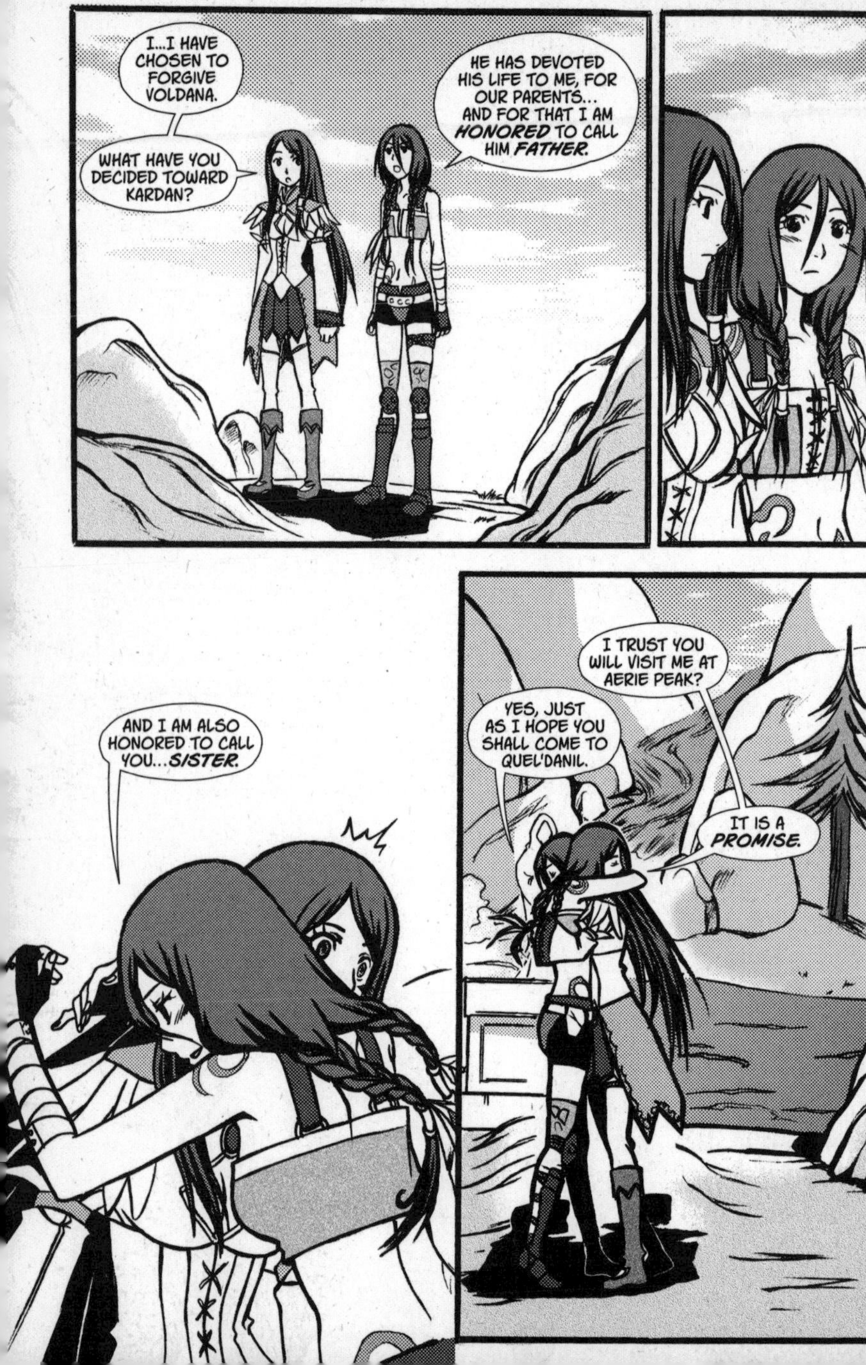
I...I HAVE CHOSEN TO FORGIVE VOLDANA.
WHAT HAVE YOU DECIDED TOWARD KARDAN?
HE HAS DEVOTED HIS LIFE TO ME, FOR OUR PARENTS... AND FOR THAT I AM HONORED TO CALL HIM FATHER.
AND I AM ALSO HONORED TO CALL YOU...SISTER.
I TRUST YOU WILL VISIT ME AT AERIE PEAK?
YES, JUST AS I HOPE YOU SHALL COME TO QUEL'DANIL.
IT IS A PROMISE.

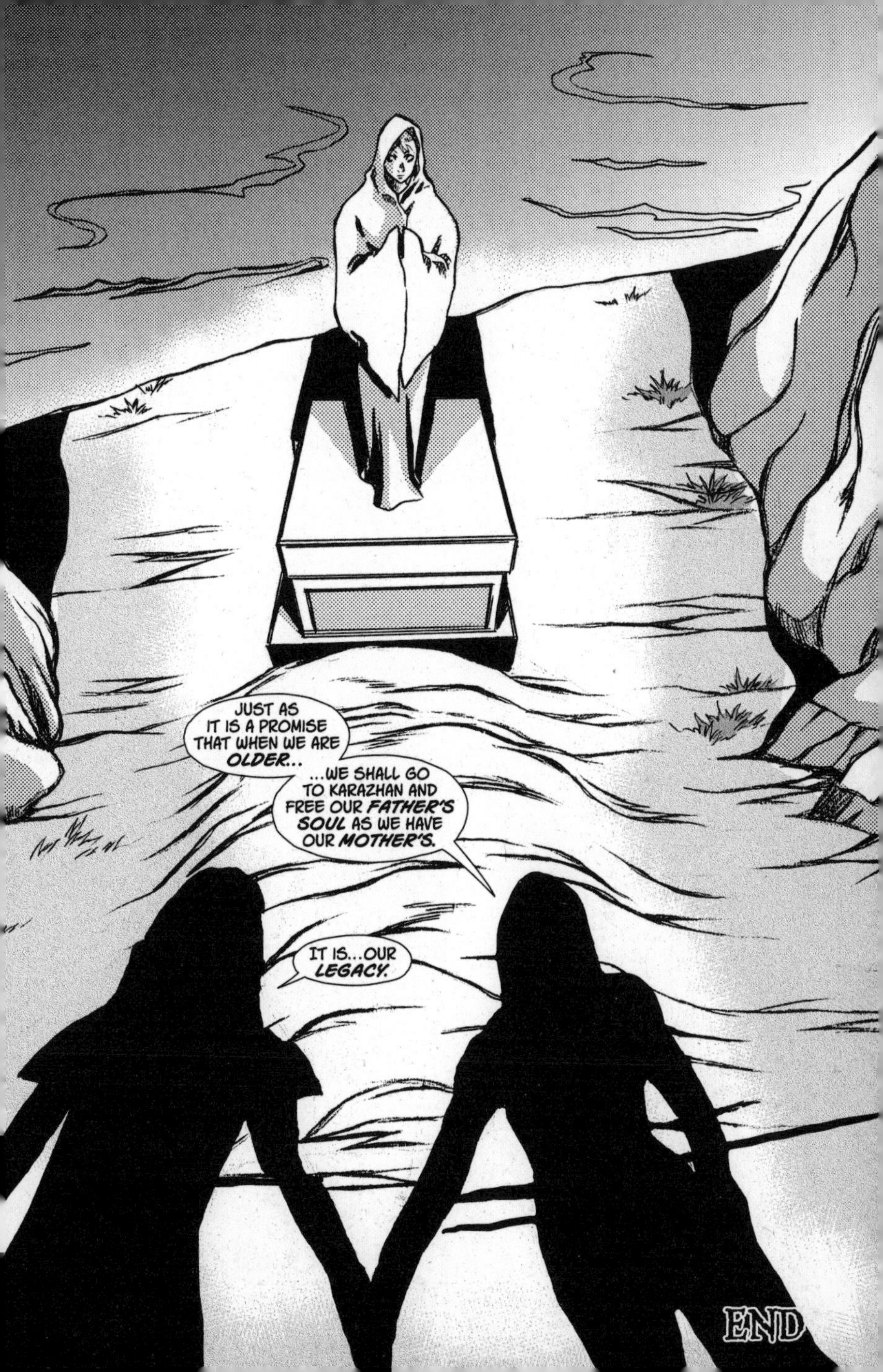
JUST AS IT IS A PROMISE THAT WHEN WE ARE OLDER...
...WE SHALL GO TO KARAZHAN AND FREE OUR FATHER'S SOUL AS WE HAVE OUR MOTHER'S.
IT IS...OUR LEGACY.
END

WARCRAFT

LEGENDS
VOLUME TWO

MILES TO GO

WRITTEN BY DAN JOLLEY

PENCILS & INKS BY ELISA KWON
TONES BY MARLON ILAGAN

EDITOR: TROY LEWTER
LETTERER: MICHAEL PAOLILLI

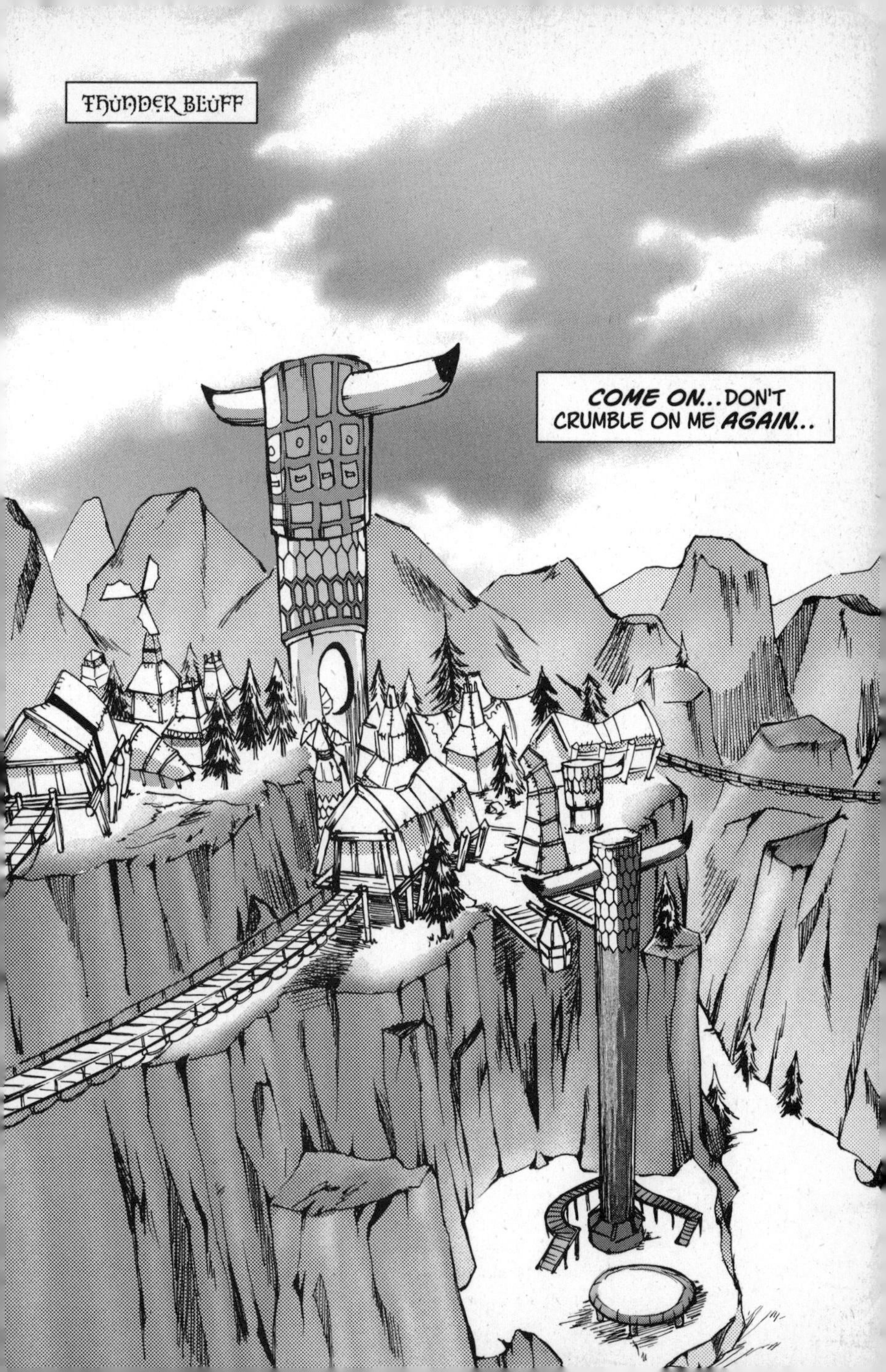
THUNDER BLUFF
COME ON...DON'T CRUMBLE ON ME AGAIN...

ALL RIGHT... GOT THE BLINDWEED.

NOW IF I CAN JUST GET THE KHADGAR'S WHISKER TO COOPERATE...

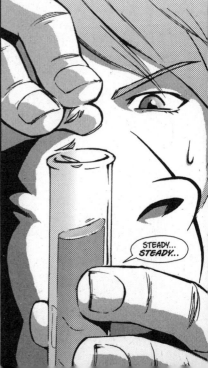

STEADY... STEADY...

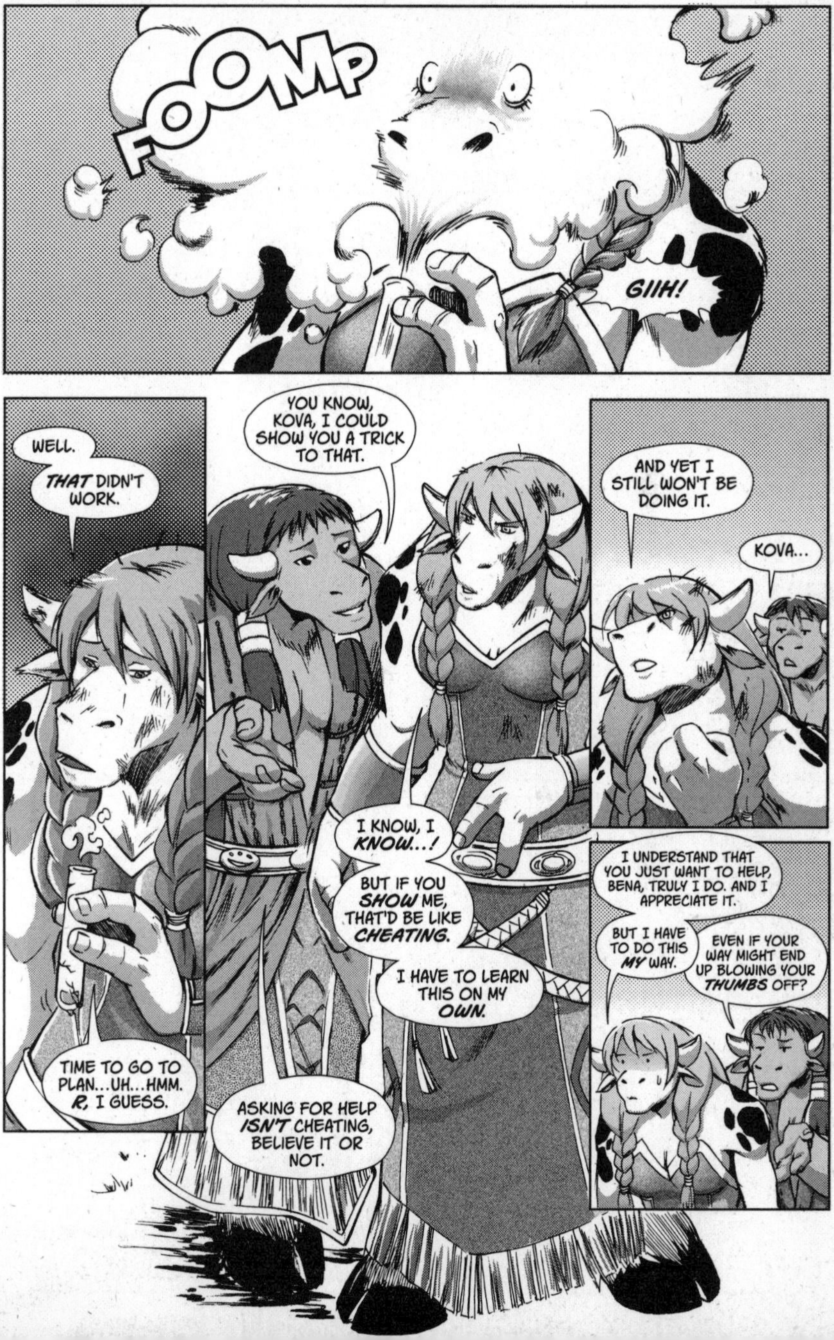
FOOMP
GIIH!
WELL.
THAT DIDN'T WORK.
TIME TO GO TO PLAN...UH...HMM. R, I GUESS.
YOU KNOW, KOVA, I COULD SHOW YOU A TRICK TO THAT.
I KNOW, I KNOW...!
BUT IF YOU SHOW ME, THAT'D BE LIKE CHEATING.
I HAVE TO LEARN THIS ON MY OWN.
ASKING FOR HELP ISN'T CHEATING, BELIEVE IT OR NOT.
AND YET I STILL WON'T BE DOING IT.
KOVA...
I UNDERSTAND THAT YOU JUST WANT TO HELP, BENA, TRULY I DO. AND I APPRECIATE IT.
BUT I HAVE TO DO THIS MY WAY.
EVEN IF YOUR WAY MIGHT END UP BLOWING YOUR THUMBS OFF?

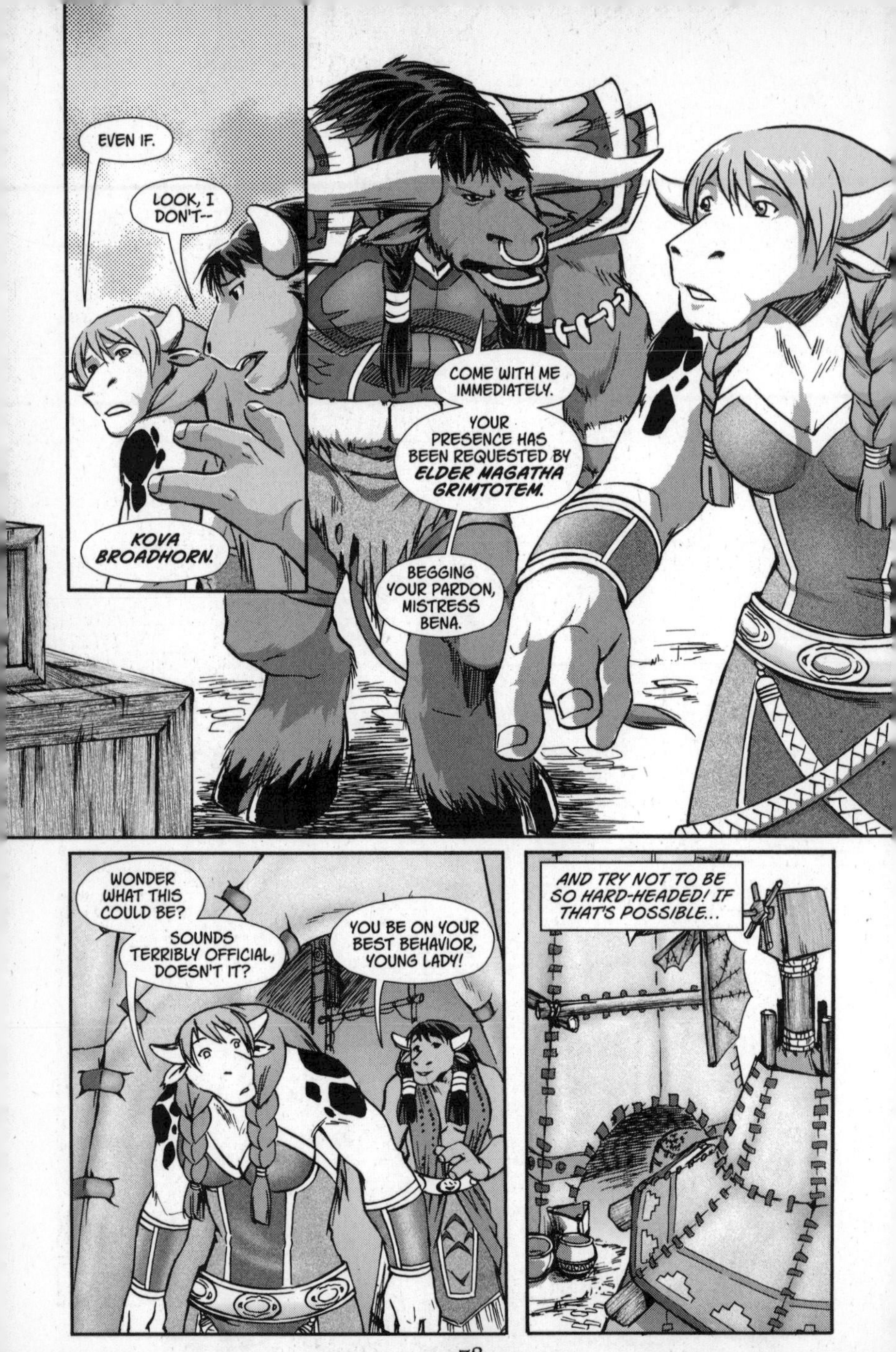
EVEN IF.
LOOK, I DON'T--
KOVA BROADHORN.
COME WITH ME IMMEDIATELY.
YOUR PRESENCE HAS BEEN REQUESTED BY ELDER MAGATHA GRIMTOTEM.
BEGGING YOUR PARDON, MISTRESS BENA.
WONDER WHAT THIS COULD BE?
SOUNDS TERRIBLY OFFICIAL, DOESN'T IT?
YOU BE ON YOUR BEST BEHAVIOR, YOUNG LADY!
AND TRY NOT TO BE SO HARD-HEADED! IF THAT'S POSSIBLE...

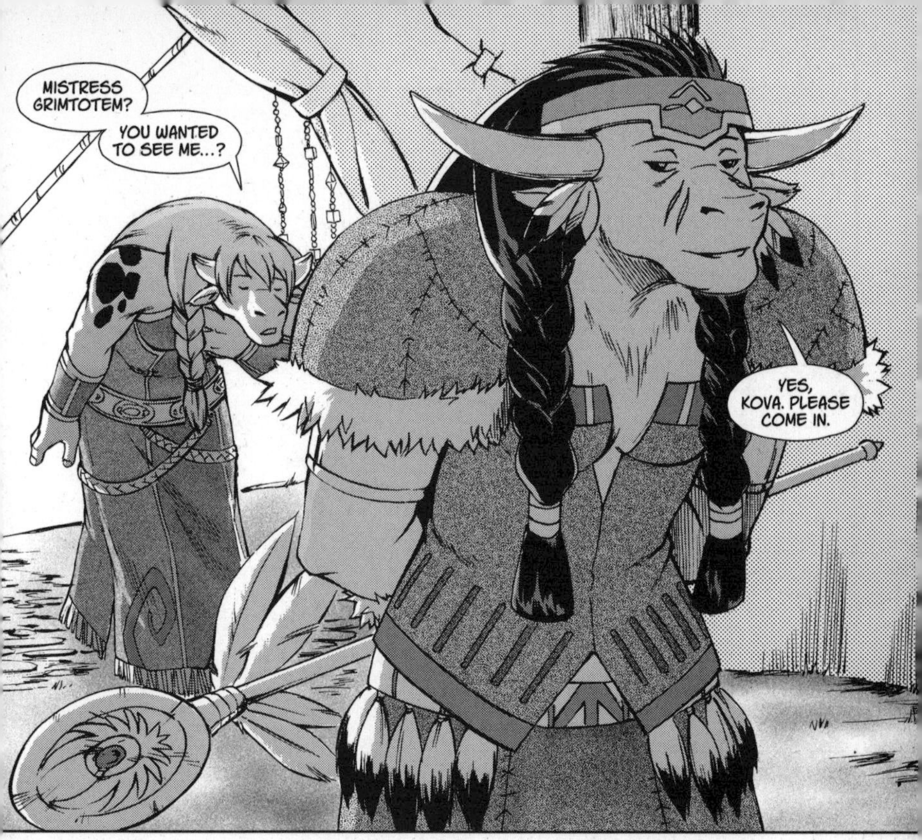
MISTRESS GRIMTOTEM?
YOU WANTED TO SEE ME...?
YES, KOVA. PLEASE COME IN.
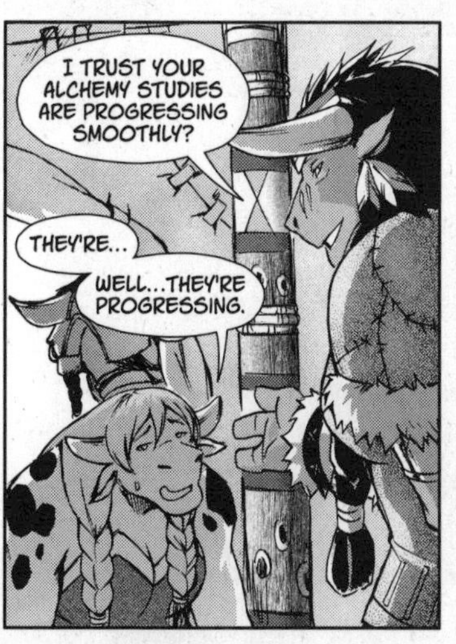
I TRUST YOUR ALCHEMY STUDIES ARE PROGRESSING SMOOTHLY?
THEY'RE...
WELL...THEY'RE PROGRESSING.
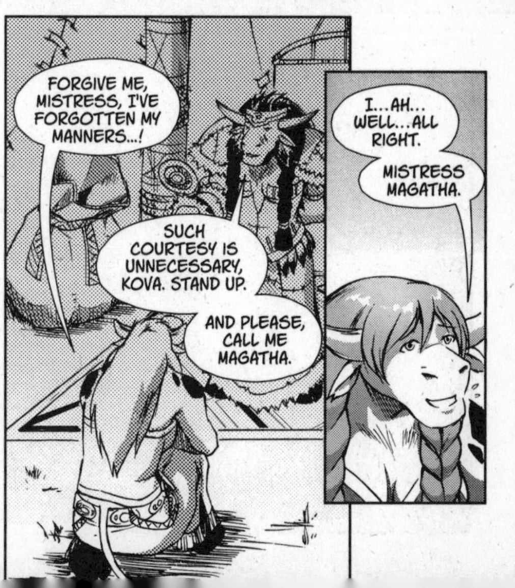
FORGIVE ME, MISTRESS, I'VE FORGOTTEN MY MANNERS...!
SUCH COURTESY IS UNNECESSARY, KOVA. STAND UP.
AND PLEASE, CALL ME MAGATHA.
I...AH... WELL...ALL RIGHT.
MISTRESS MAGATHA.

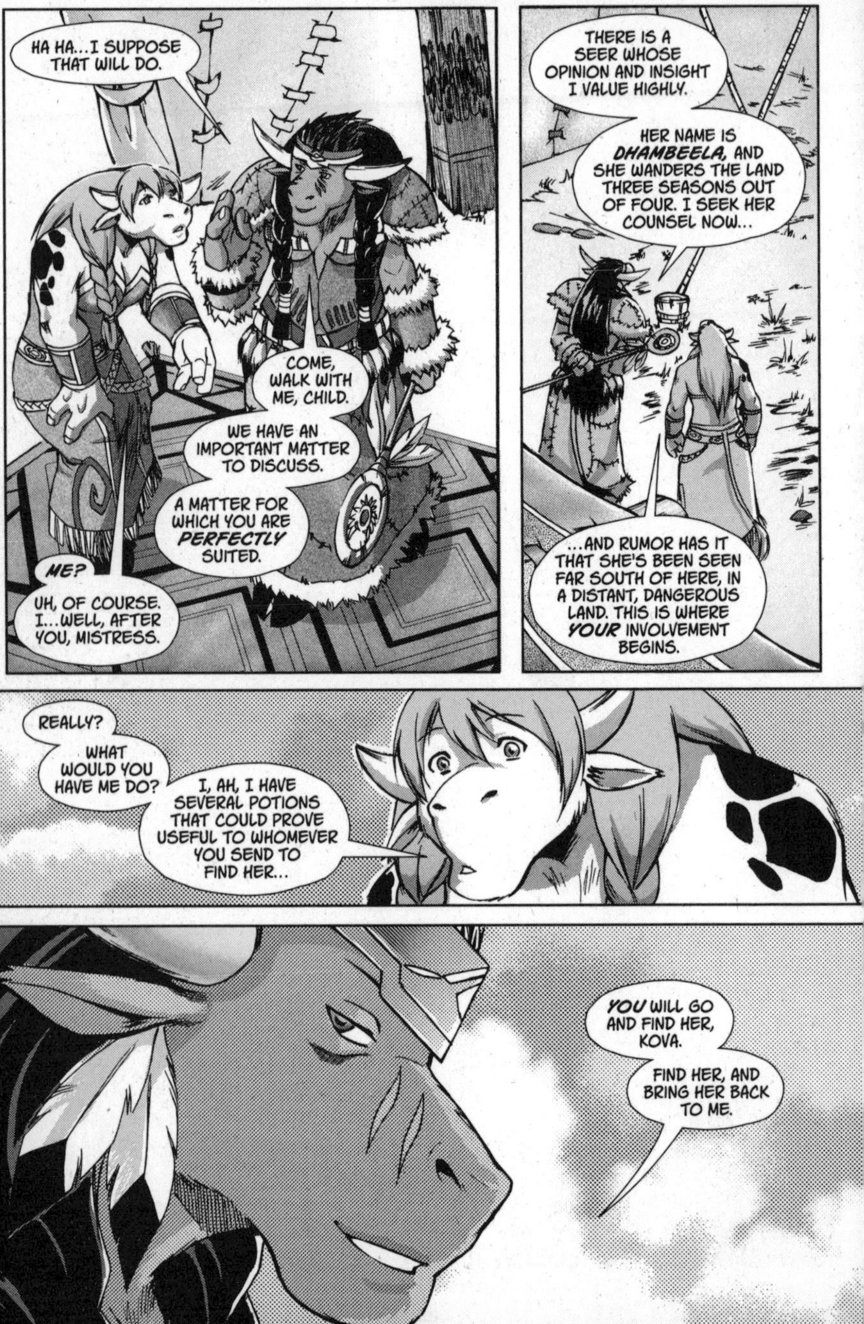
HA HA...I SUPPOSE THAT WILL DO.
COME, WALK WITH ME, CHILD.
WE HAVE AN IMPORTANT MATTER TO DISCUSS.
A MATTER FOR WHICH YOU ARE PERFECTLY SUITED.
ME?
UH, OF COURSE. I...WELL, AFTER YOU, MISTRESS.
THERE IS A SEER WHOSE OPINION AND INSIGHT I VALUE HIGHLY.
HER NAME IS DHAMBEELA, AND SHE WANDERS THE LAND THREE SEASONS OUT OF FOUR. I SEEK HER COUNSEL NOW...
...AND RUMOR HAS IT THAT SHE'S BEEN SEEN FAR SOUTH OF HERE, IN A DISTANT, DANGEROUS LAND. THIS IS WHERE YOUR INVOLVEMENT BEGINS.
REALLY?
WHAT WOULD YOU HAVE ME DO?
I, AH, I HAVE SEVERAL POTIONS THAT COULD PROVE USEFUL TO WHOMEVER YOU SEND TO FIND HER...
YOU WILL GO AND FIND HER, KOVA.
FIND HER, AND BRING HER BACK TO ME.

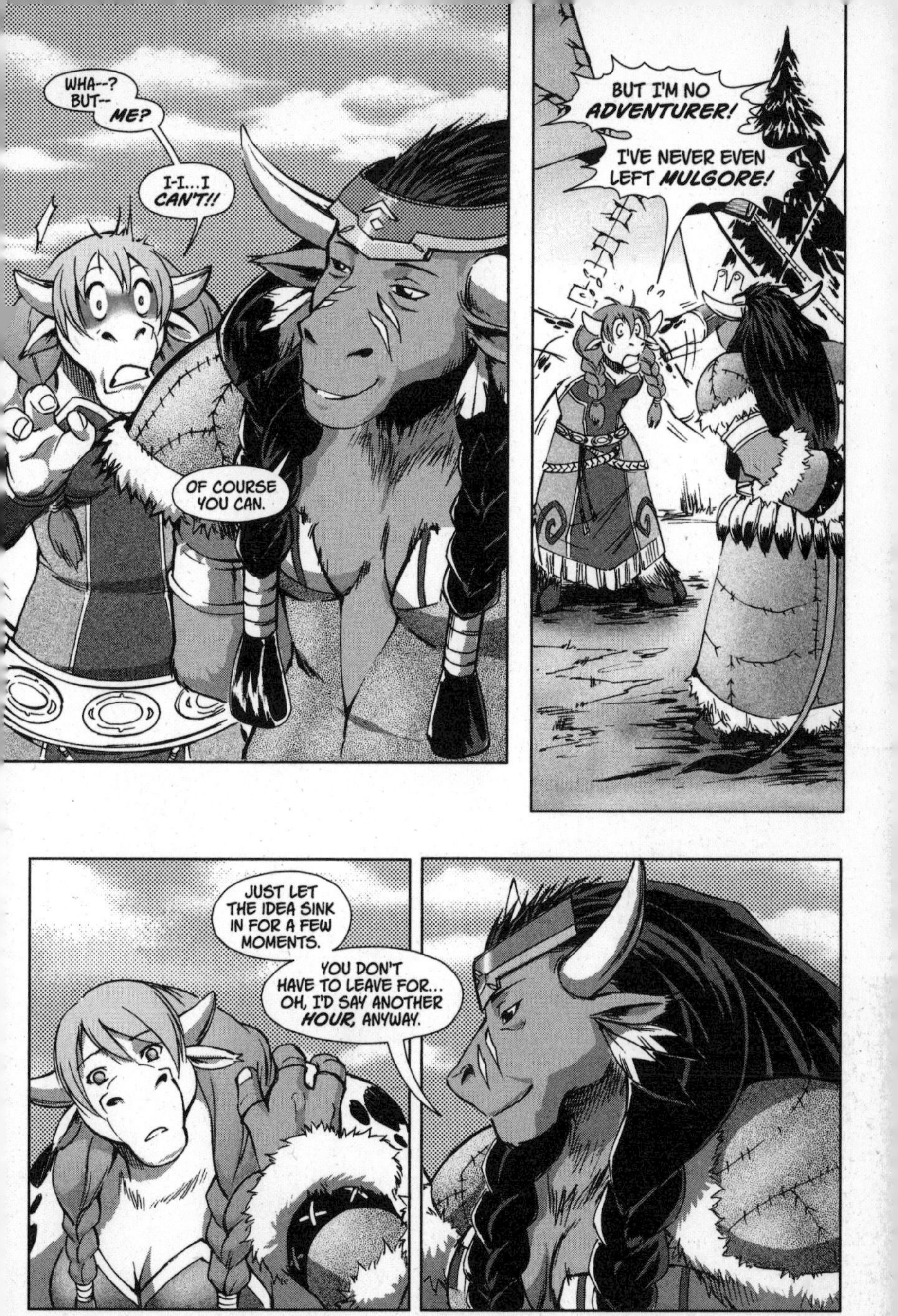
WHA--? BUT-- ME?
I-I...I CAN'T!!
OF COURSE YOU CAN.
BUT I'M NO ADVENTURER!
I'VE NEVER EVEN LEFT MULGORE!
JUST LET THE IDEA SINK IN FOR A FEW MOMENTS.
YOU DON'T HAVE TO LEAVE FOR... OH, I'D SAY ANOTHER HOUR, ANYWAY.

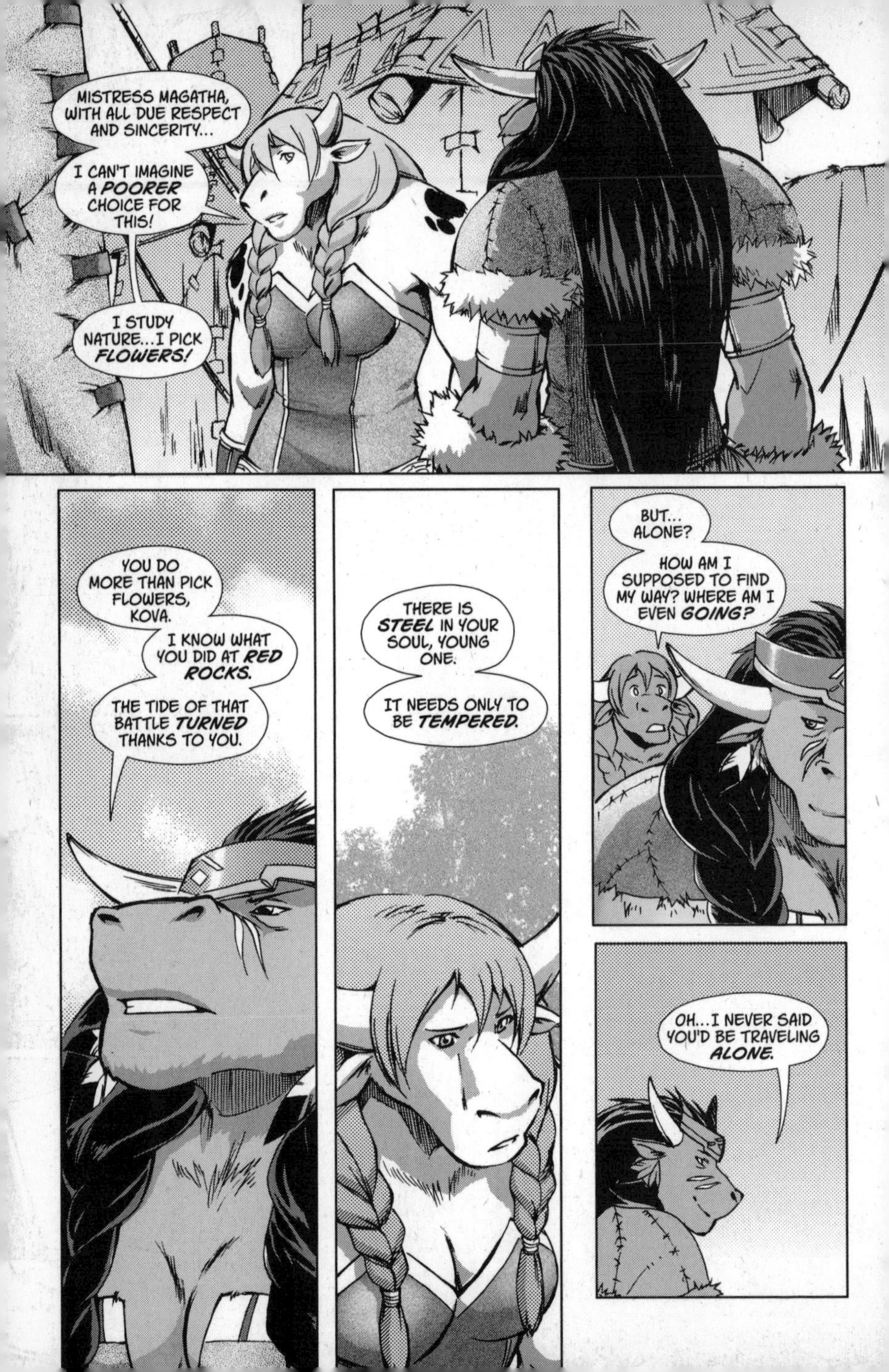
MISTRESS MAGATHA, WITH ALL DUE RESPECT AND SINCERITY...
I CAN'T IMAGINE A *POORER* CHOICE FOR THIS!
I STUDY NATURE...I PICK *FLOWERS!*
YOU DO MORE THAN PICK FLOWERS, KOVA.
I KNOW WHAT YOU DID AT *RED ROCKS.*
THE TIDE OF THAT BATTLE *TURNED* THANKS TO YOU.
THERE IS *STEEL* IN YOUR SOUL, YOUNG ONE.
IT NEEDS ONLY TO BE *TEMPERED.*
BUT... ALONE?
HOW AM I SUPPOSED TO FIND MY WAY? WHERE AM I EVEN *GOING?*
OH...I NEVER SAID YOU'D BE TRAVELING *ALONE.*

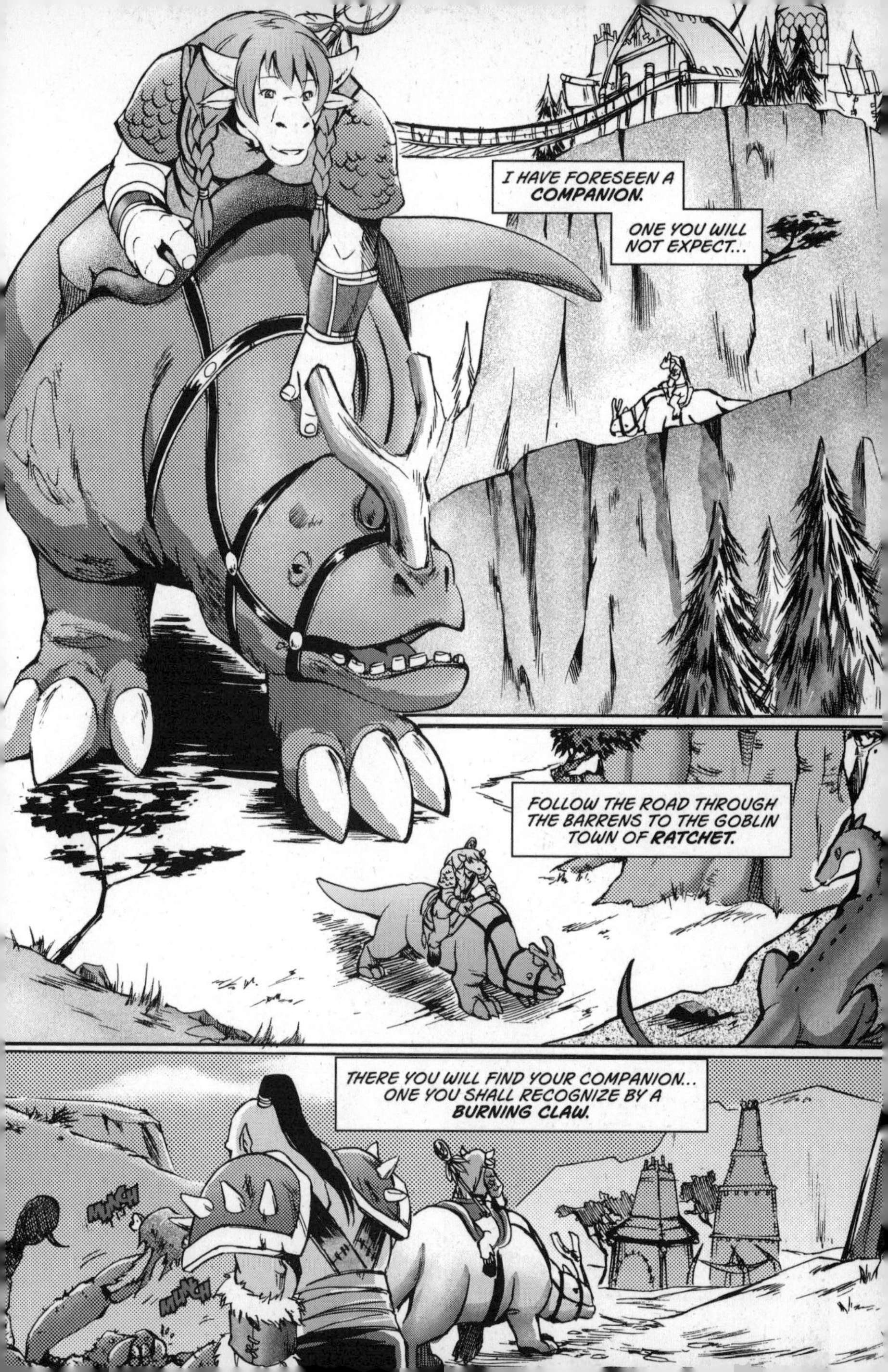
I HAVE FORESEEN A **COMPANION.**
ONE YOU WILL NOT EXPECT...
FOLLOW THE ROAD THROUGH THE BARRENS TO THE GOBLIN TOWN OF **RATCHET.**
THERE YOU WILL FIND YOUR COMPANION... ONE YOU SHALL RECOGNIZE BY A **BURNING CLAW.**
MUNCH
MUNCH

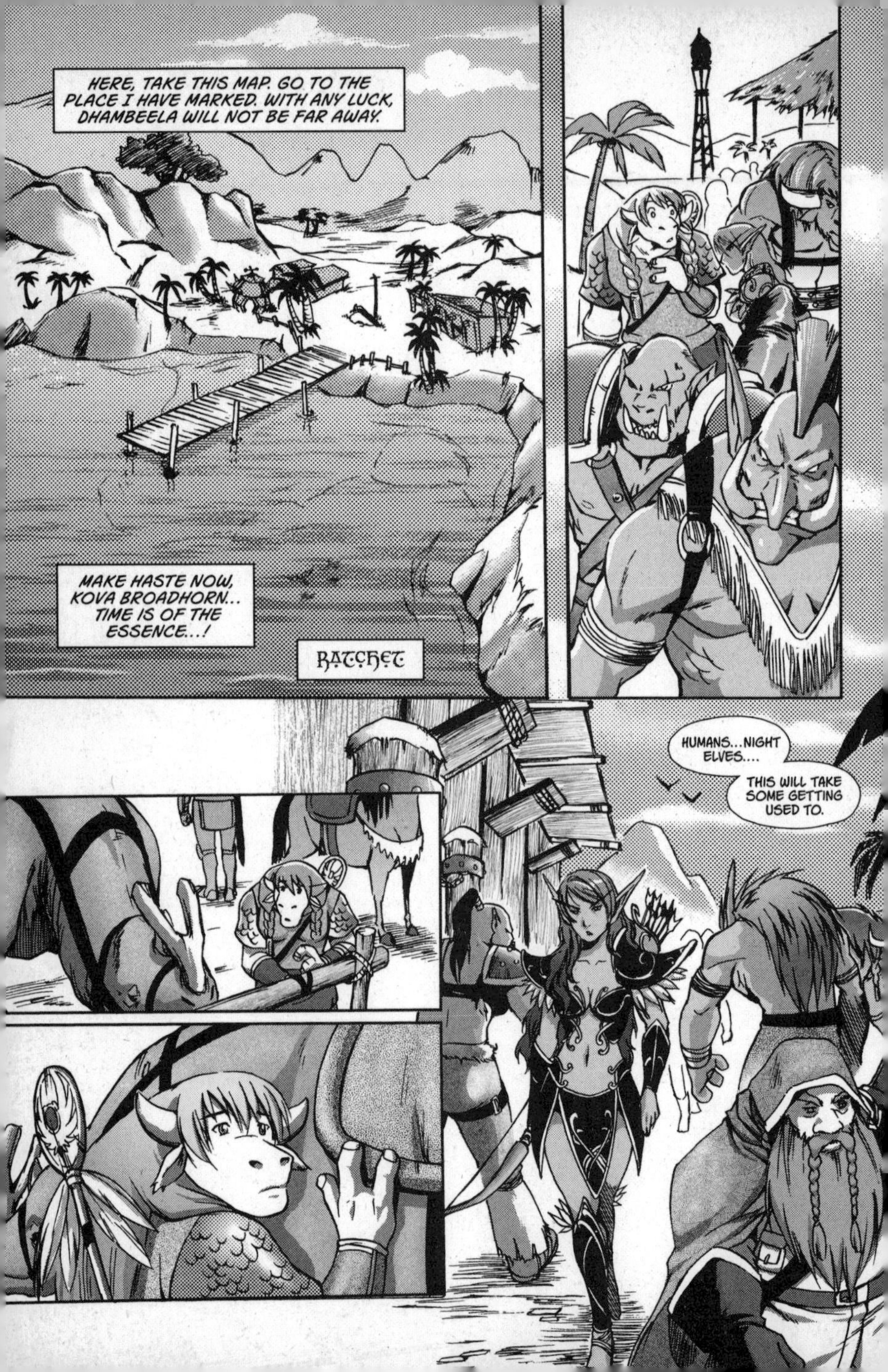
HERE, TAKE THIS MAP. GO TO THE PLACE I HAVE MARKED. WITH ANY LUCK, DHAMBEELA WILL NOT BE FAR AWAY.
MAKE HASTE NOW, KOVA BROADHORN... TIME IS OF THE ESSENCE...!
RATCHET
HUMANS...NIGHT ELVES....
THIS WILL TAKE SOME GETTING USED TO.

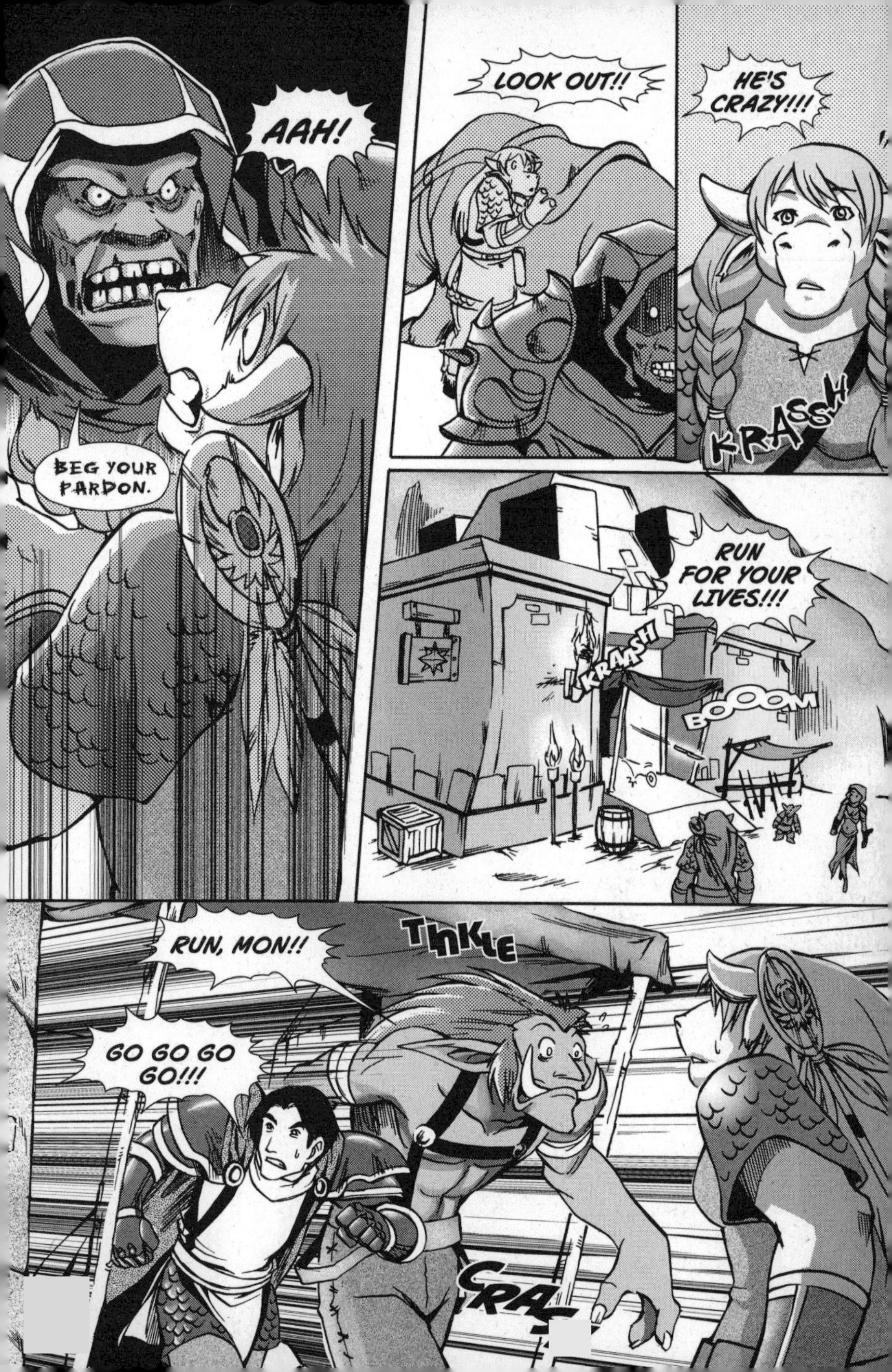
AAH!
BEG YOUR PARDON.
LOOK OUT!!
HE'S CRAZY!!!
KRASSH
RUN FOR YOUR LIVES!!!
KRAASH
BOOOM
RUN, MON!!
TINKLE
GO GO GO GO!!!
CRAS

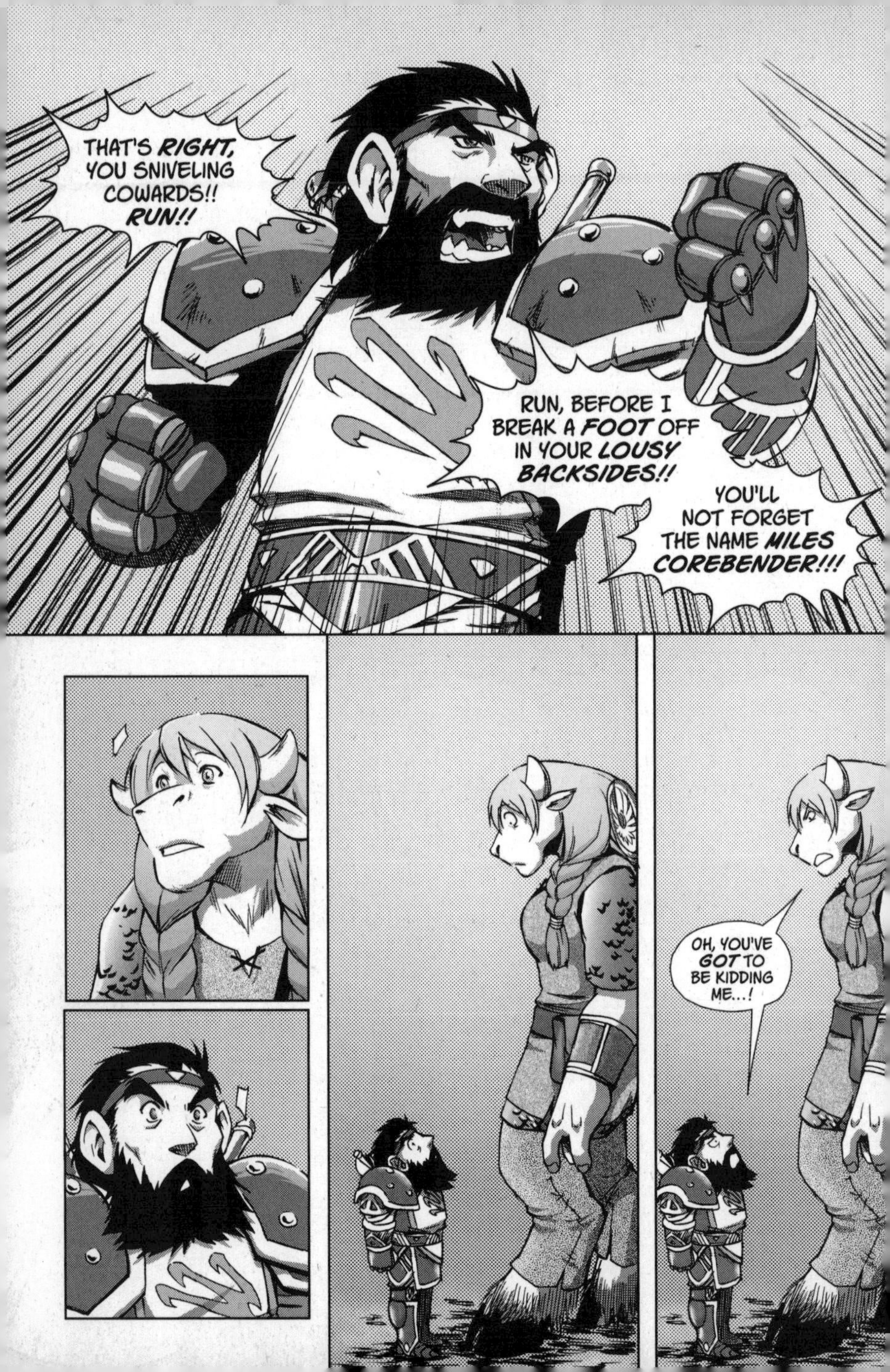
THAT'S RIGHT, YOU SNIVELING COWARDS!! RUN!!
RUN, BEFORE I BREAK A FOOT OFF IN YOUR LOUSY BACKSIDES!!
YOU'LL NOT FORGET THE NAME MILES COREBENDER!!!
OH, YOU'VE GOT TO BE KIDDING ME...!

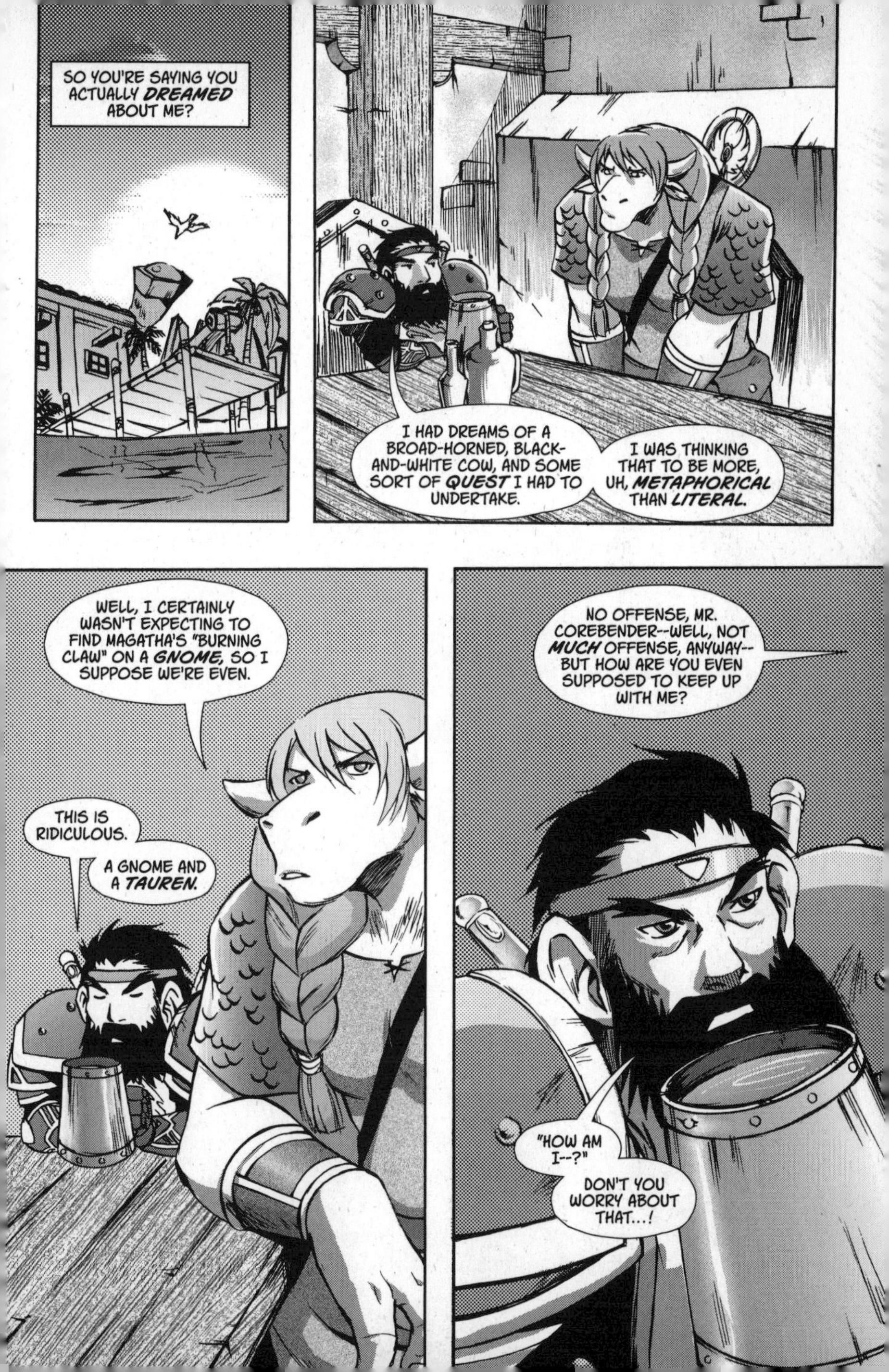
SO YOU'RE SAYING YOU ACTUALLY DREAMED ABOUT ME?
I HAD DREAMS OF A BROAD-HORNED, BLACK-AND-WHITE COW, AND SOME SORT OF QUEST I HAD TO UNDERTAKE.
I WAS THINKING THAT TO BE MORE, UH, METAPHORICAL THAN LITERAL.
WELL, I CERTAINLY WASN'T EXPECTING TO FIND MAGATHA'S "BURNING CLAW" ON A GNOME, SO I SUPPOSE WE'RE EVEN.
THIS IS RIDICULOUS.
A GNOME AND A TAUREN.
NO OFFENSE, MR. COREBENDER--WELL, NOT MUCH OFFENSE, ANYWAY--BUT HOW ARE YOU EVEN SUPPOSED TO KEEP UP WITH ME?
"HOW AM I--?"
DON'T YOU WORRY ABOUT THAT...!

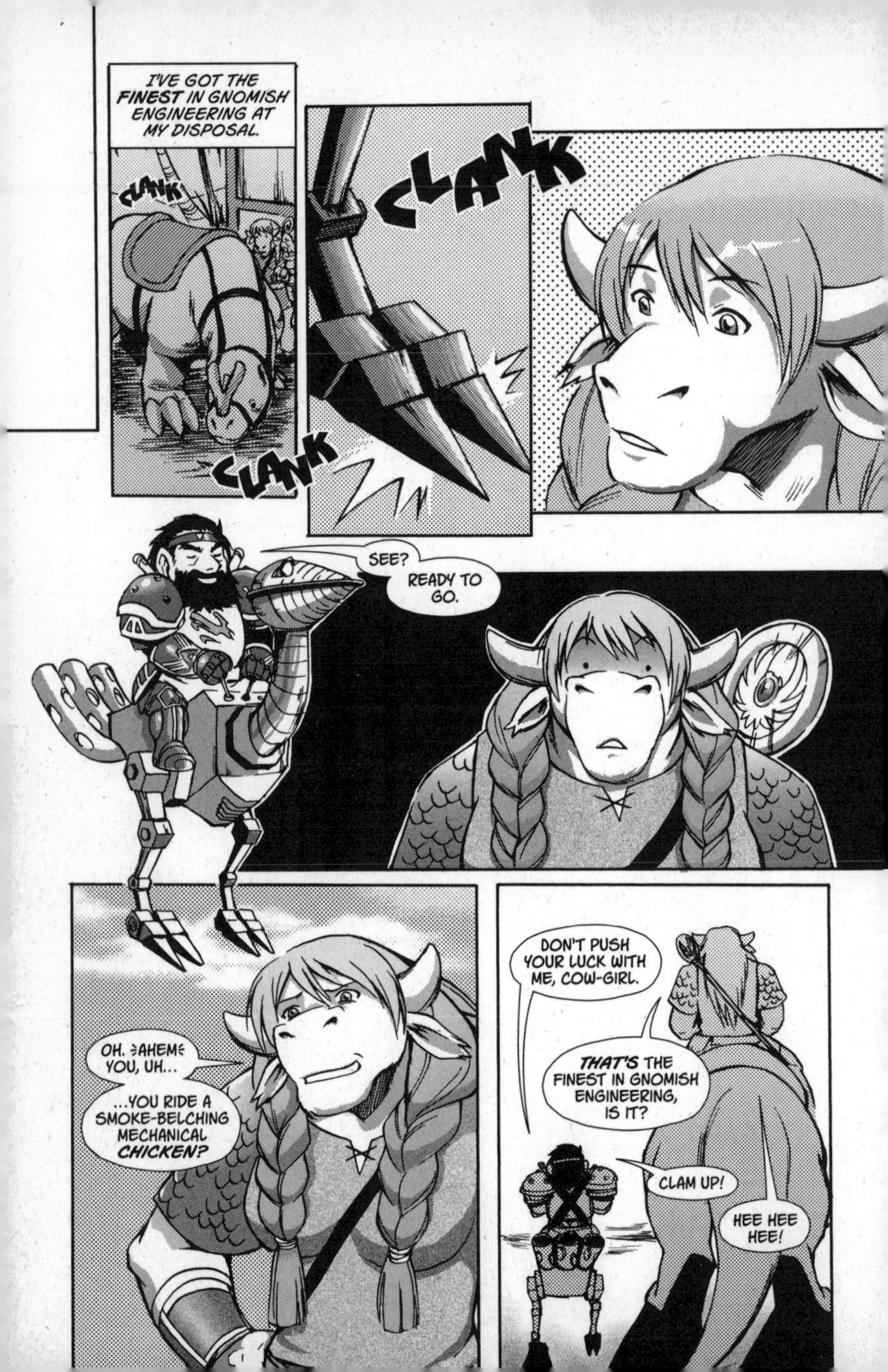
I'VE GOT THE FINEST IN GNOMISH ENGINEERING AT MY DISPOSAL.
CLANK
CLANK
CLANK
CLANK
SEE? READY TO GO.
OH. ≷AHEM≶ YOU, UH...
...YOU RIDE A SMOKE-BELCHING MECHANICAL CHICKEN?
DON'T PUSH YOUR LUCK WITH ME, COW-GIRL.
THAT'S THE FINEST IN GNOMISH ENGINEERING, IS IT?
CLAM UP!
HEE HEE HEE!

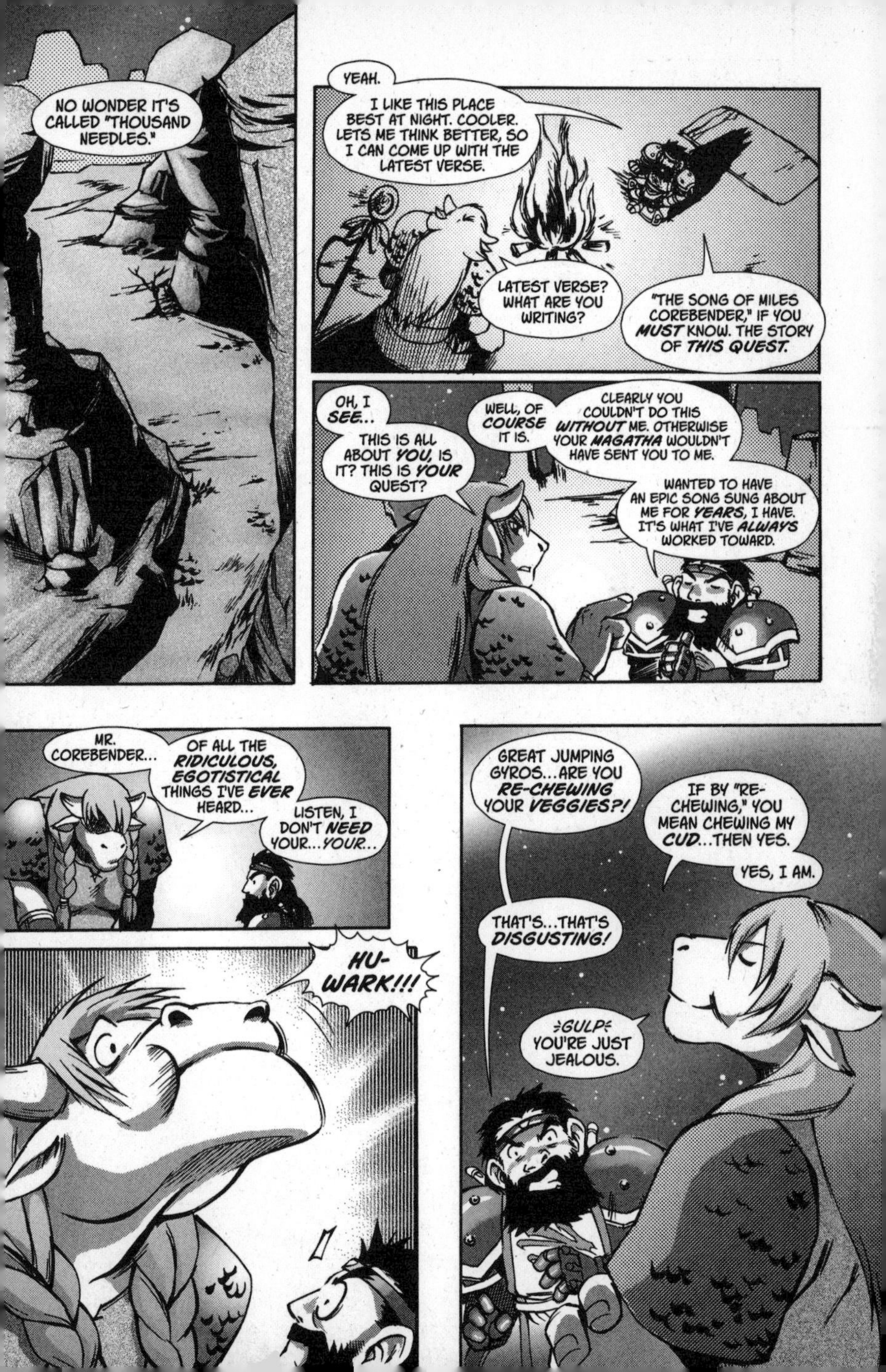
NO WONDER IT'S CALLED "THOUSAND NEEDLES."
YEAH.
I LIKE THIS PLACE BEST AT NIGHT. COOLER. LETS ME THINK BETTER, SO I CAN COME UP WITH THE LATEST VERSE.
LATEST VERSE? WHAT ARE YOU WRITING?
"THE SONG OF MILES COREBENDER," IF YOU MUST KNOW. THE STORY OF THIS QUEST.
OH, I SEE...
THIS IS ALL ABOUT YOU, IS IT? THIS IS YOUR QUEST?
WELL, OF COURSE IT IS.
CLEARLY YOU COULDN'T DO THIS WITHOUT ME. OTHERWISE YOUR MAGATHA WOULDN'T HAVE SENT YOU TO ME.
WANTED TO HAVE AN EPIC SONG SUNG ABOUT ME FOR YEARS, I HAVE. IT'S WHAT I'VE ALWAYS WORKED TOWARD.
MR. COREBENDER...
OF ALL THE RIDICULOUS, EGOTISTICAL THINGS I'VE EVER HEARD...
LISTEN, I DON'T NEED YOUR...YOUR...
HU-WARK!!!
GREAT JUMPING GYROS...ARE YOU RE-CHEWING YOUR VEGGIES?!
IF BY "RE-CHEWING," YOU MEAN CHEWING MY CUD...THEN YES.
YES, I AM.
THAT'S...THAT'S DISGUSTING!
GULP
YOU'RE JUST JEALOUS.

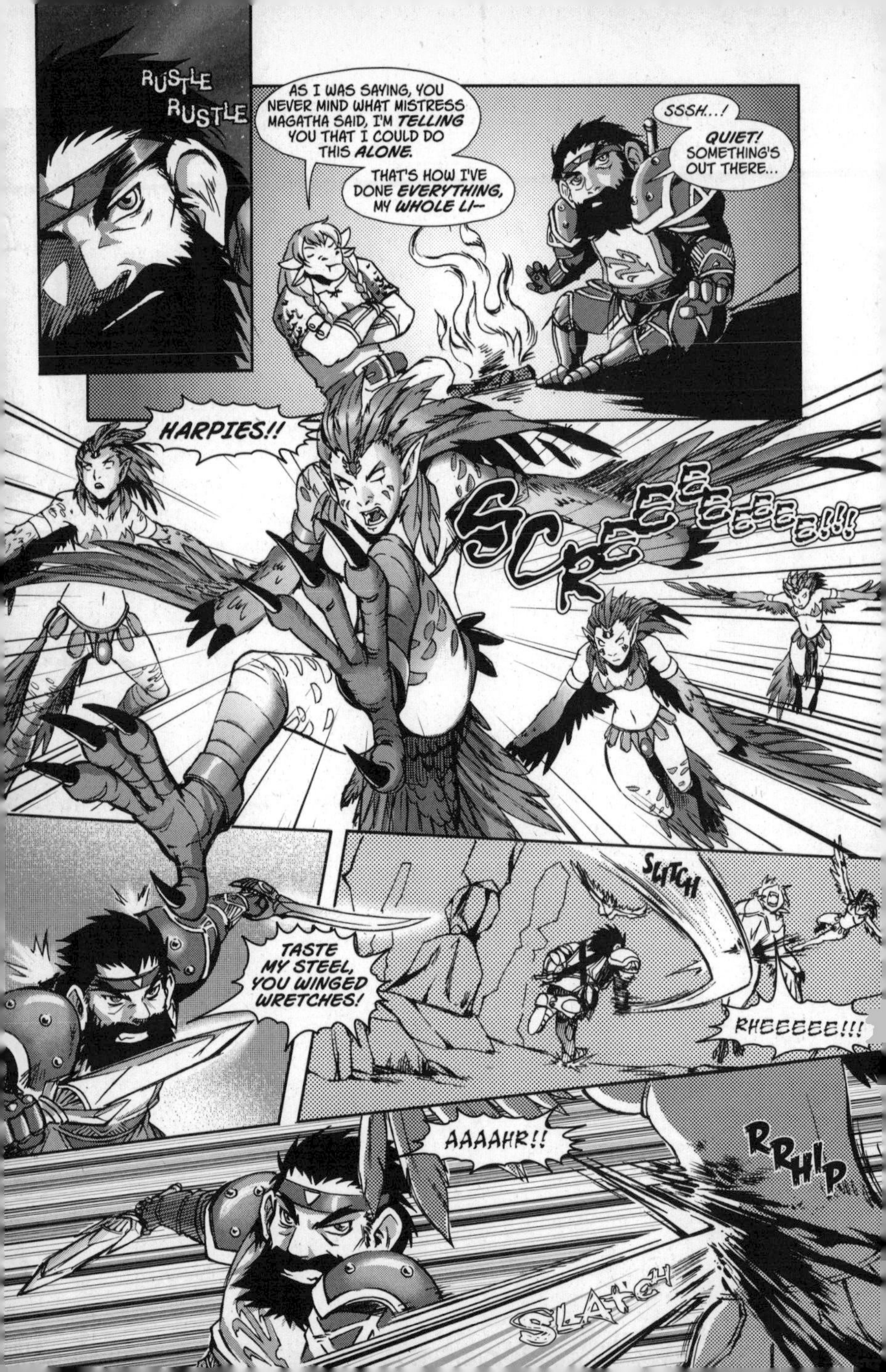
RUSTLE RUSTLE
AS I WAS SAYING, YOU NEVER MIND WHAT MISTRESS MAGATHA SAID, I'M TELLING YOU THAT I COULD DO THIS ALONE.
THAT'S HOW I'VE DONE EVERYTHING, MY WHOLE LI--
SSSH...!
QUIET! SOMETHING'S OUT THERE...
HARPIES!!
SCREEEEEEEEEE!!!
TASTE MY STEEL, YOU WINGED WRETCHES!
SLITCH
RHEEEEE!!!
AAAAHR!!
RRHIP
SLATCH

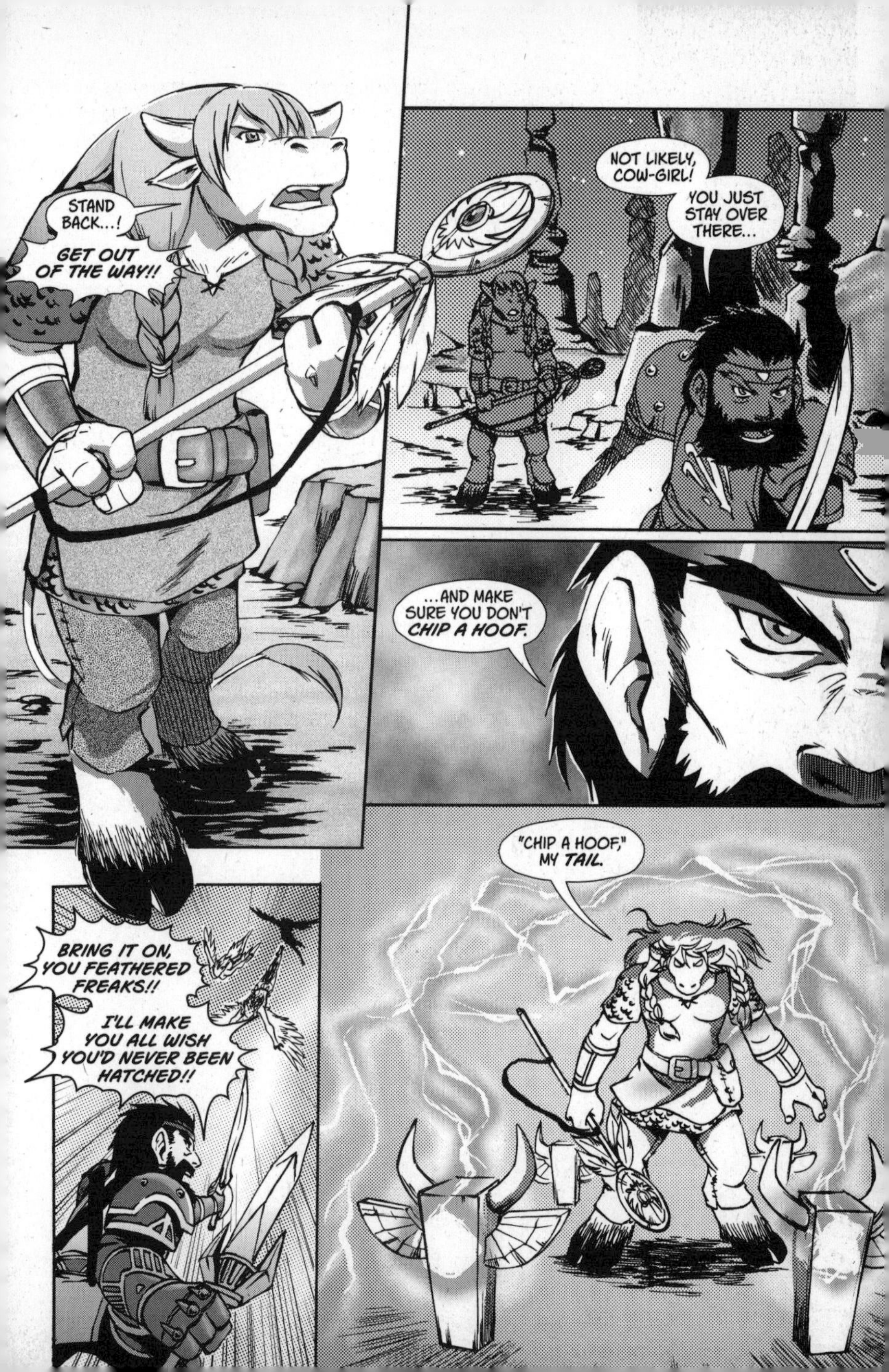
STAND BACK...!
GET OUT OF THE WAY!!
NOT LIKELY, COW-GIRL!
YOU JUST STAY OVER THERE...
...AND MAKE SURE YOU DON'T CHIP A HOOF.
BRING IT ON, YOU FEATHERED FREAKS!!
I'LL MAKE YOU ALL WISH YOU'D NEVER BEEN HATCHED!!
"CHIP A HOOF," MY TAIL.

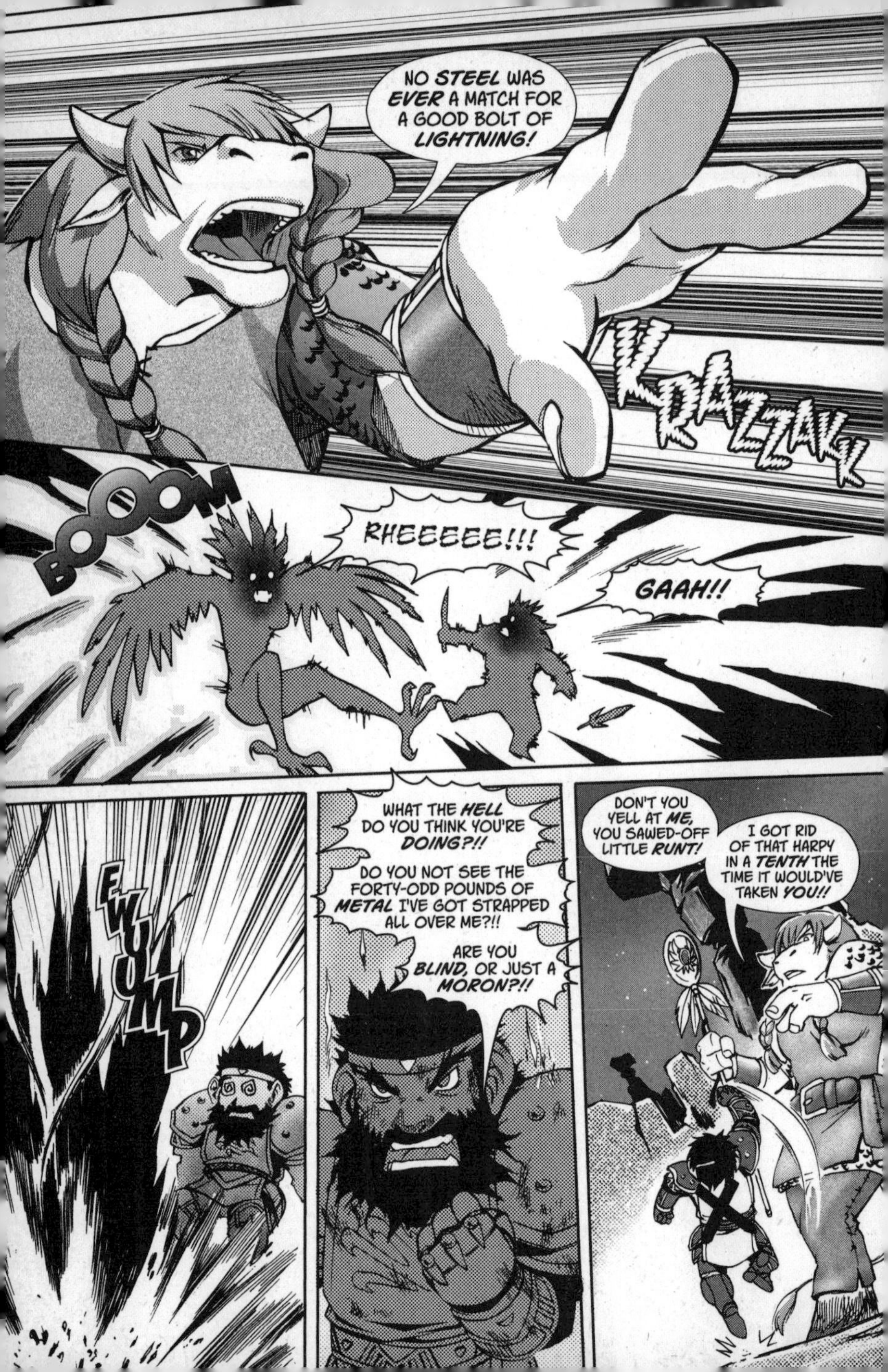
NO STEEL WAS EVER A MATCH FOR A GOOD BOLT OF LIGHTNING!
KRAZZAKK
BOOOOM
RHEEEEEE!!!
GAAH!!
FWUUMP
WHAT THE HELL DO YOU THINK YOU'RE DOING?!!
DO YOU NOT SEE THE FORTY-ODD POUNDS OF METAL I'VE GOT STRAPPED ALL OVER ME?!!
ARE YOU BLIND, OR JUST A MORON?!!
DON'T YOU YELL AT ME, YOU SAWED-OFF LITTLE RUNT!
I GOT RID OF THAT HARPY IN A TENTH THE TIME IT WOULD'VE TAKEN YOU!!

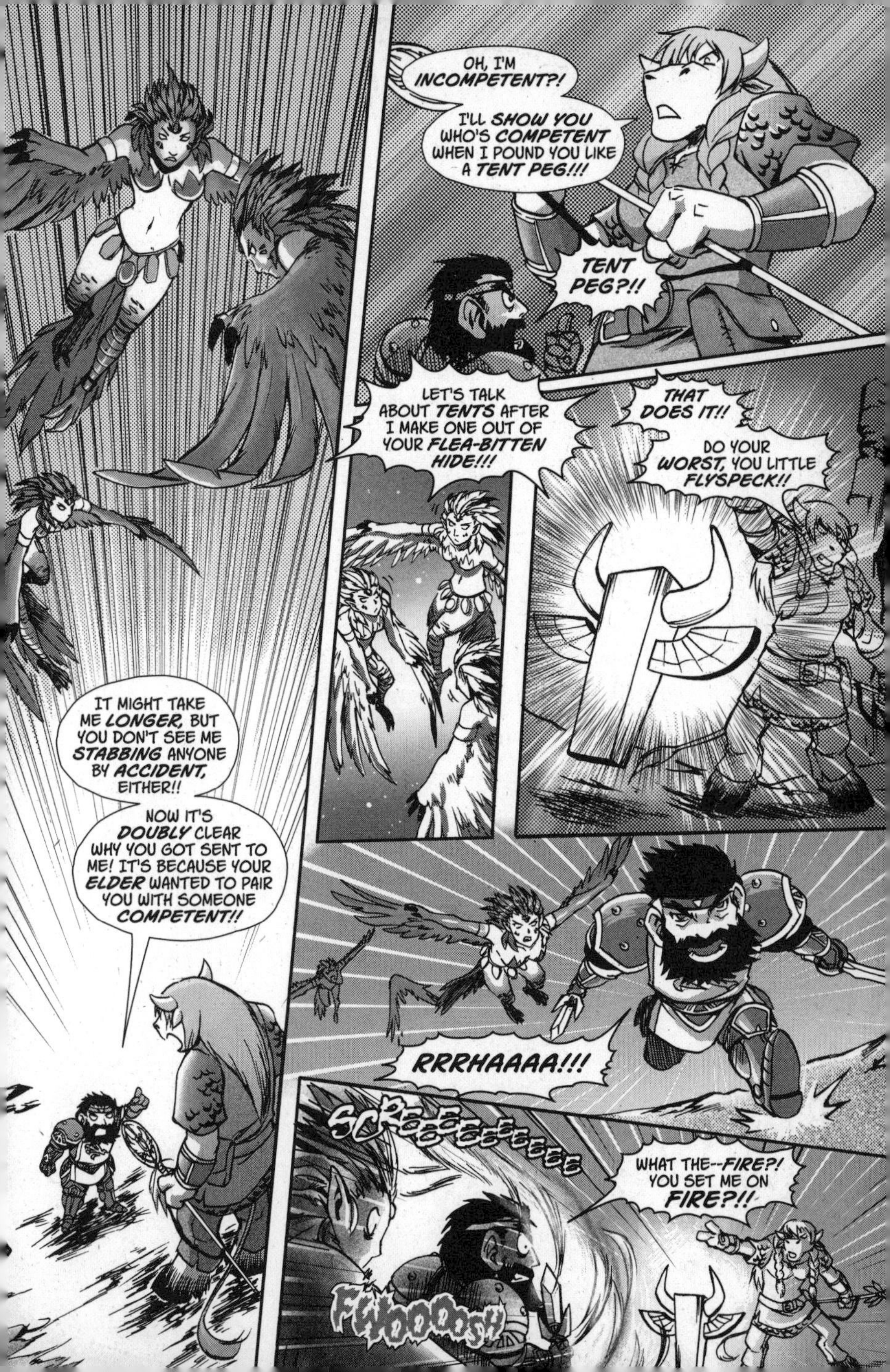
IT MIGHT TAKE ME LONGER, BUT YOU DON'T SEE ME STABBING ANYONE BY ACCIDENT, EITHER!!
NOW IT'S DOUBLY CLEAR WHY YOU GOT SENT TO ME! IT'S BECAUSE YOUR ELDER WANTED TO PAIR YOU WITH SOMEONE COMPETENT!!
OH, I'M INCOMPETENT?!
I'LL SHOW YOU WHO'S COMPETENT WHEN I POUND YOU LIKE A TENT PEG!!!
TENT PEG?!!
LET'S TALK ABOUT TENTS AFTER I MAKE ONE OUT OF YOUR FLEA-BITTEN HIDE!!!
THAT DOES IT!!
DO YOUR WORST, YOU LITTLE FLYSPECK!!
RRRHAAAA!!!
SCREEEEEEEEEEEEEE
WHAT THE--FIRE?! YOU SET ME ON FIRE?!!
FWOOOOSH

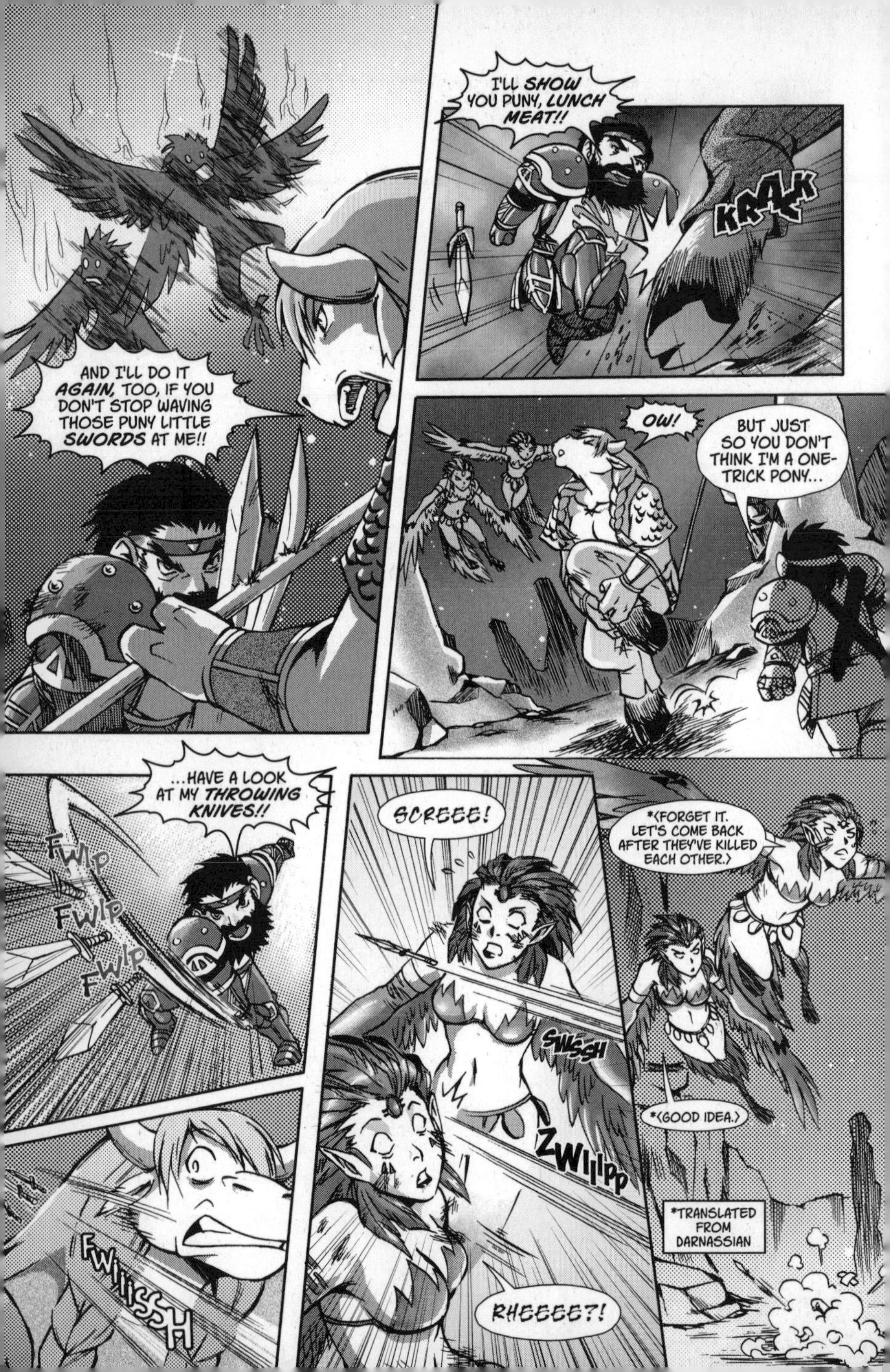
AND I'LL DO IT AGAIN, TOO, IF YOU DON'T STOP WAVING THOSE PUNY LITTLE SWORDS AT ME!!
I'LL SHOW YOU PUNY, LUNCH MEAT!!
KRAAK
OW!
BUT JUST SO YOU DON'T THINK I'M A ONE-TRICK PONY...
...HAVE A LOOK AT MY THROWING KNIVES!!
FWIP
FWIP
FWIP
FWIIISSH
SCREEEE!
SWISSH
ZWIIIPP
RHEEEE?!
*<FORGET IT. LET'S COME BACK AFTER THEY'VE KILLED EACH OTHER.>
*<GOOD IDEA.>
*TRANSLATED FROM DARNASSIAN

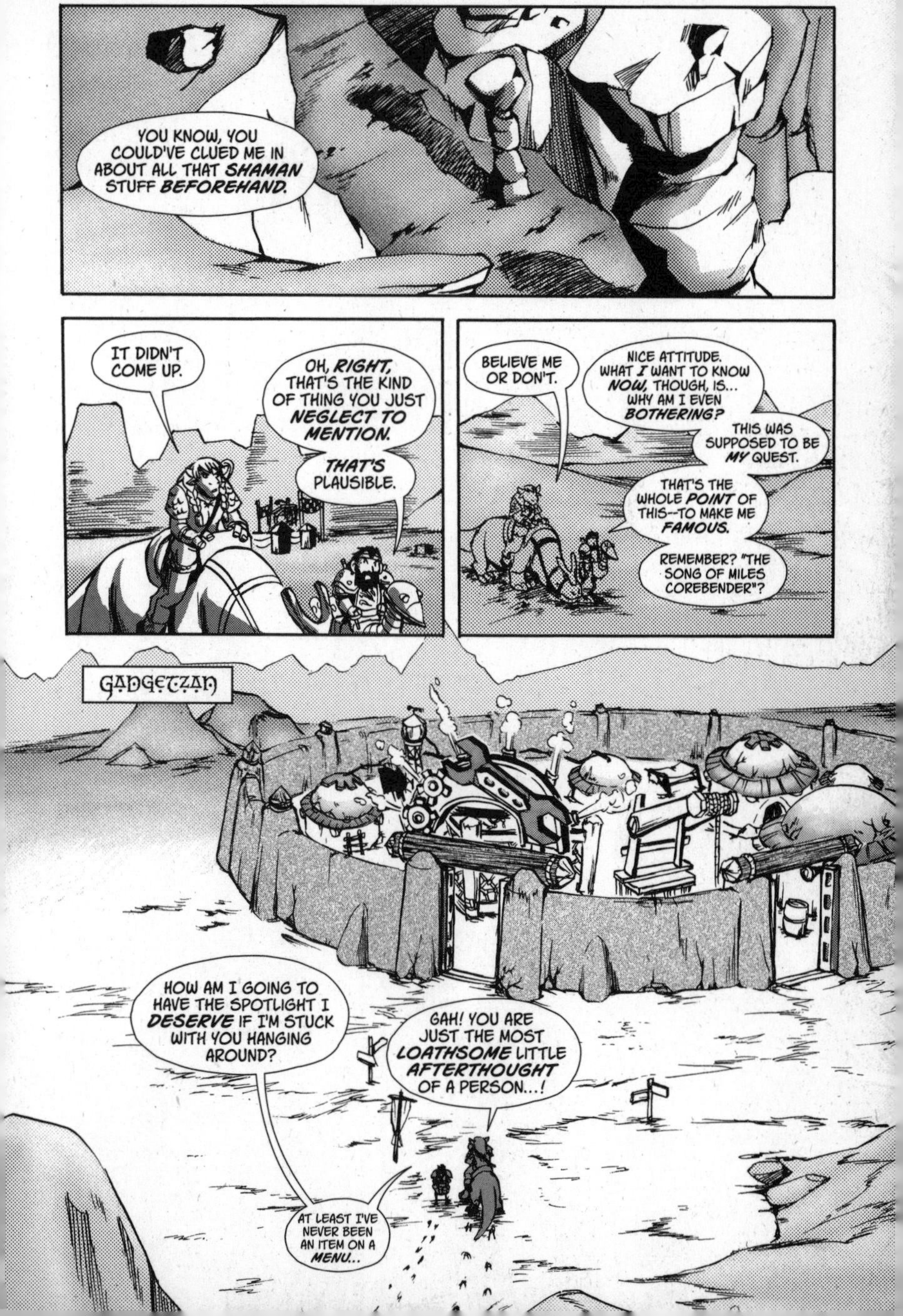
YOU KNOW, YOU COULD'VE CLUED ME IN ABOUT ALL THAT SHAMAN STUFF BEFOREHAND.
IT DIDN'T COME UP.
OH, RIGHT, THAT'S THE KIND OF THING YOU JUST NEGLECT TO MENTION.
THAT'S PLAUSIBLE.
BELIEVE ME OR DON'T.
NICE ATTITUDE. WHAT I WANT TO KNOW NOW, THOUGH, IS... WHY AM I EVEN BOTHERING?
THIS WAS SUPPOSED TO BE MY QUEST.
THAT'S THE WHOLE POINT OF THIS--TO MAKE ME FAMOUS.
REMEMBER? "THE SONG OF MILES COREBENDER"?
GADGETZAN
HOW AM I GOING TO HAVE THE SPOTLIGHT I DESERVE IF I'M STUCK WITH YOU HANGING AROUND?
GAH! YOU ARE JUST THE MOST LOATHSOME LITTLE AFTERTHOUGHT OF A PERSON...!
AT LEAST I'VE NEVER BEEN AN ITEM ON A MENU...

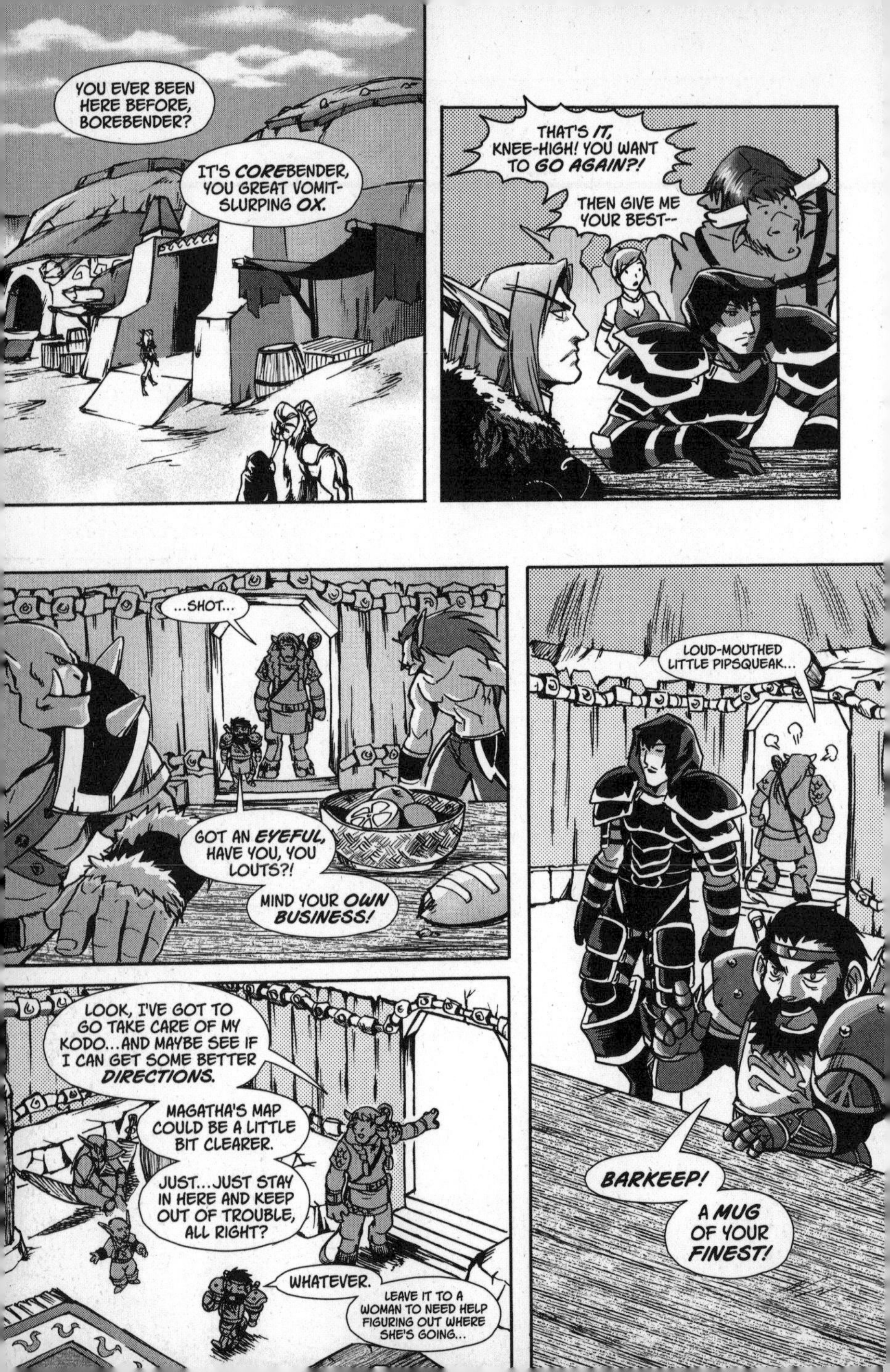
YOU EVER BEEN HERE BEFORE, BOREBENDER?
IT'S COREBENDER, YOU GREAT VOMIT-SLURPING OX.
THAT'S IT, KNEE-HIGH! YOU WANT TO GO AGAIN?!
THEN GIVE ME YOUR BEST--
...SHOT...
GOT AN EYEFUL, HAVE YOU, YOU LOUTS?!
MIND YOUR OWN BUSINESS!
LOOK, I'VE GOT TO GO TAKE CARE OF MY KODO...AND MAYBE SEE IF I CAN GET SOME BETTER DIRECTIONS.
MAGATHA'S MAP COULD BE A LITTLE BIT CLEARER.
JUST...JUST STAY IN HERE AND KEEP OUT OF TROUBLE, ALL RIGHT?
WHATEVER.
LEAVE IT TO A WOMAN TO NEED HELP FIGURING OUT WHERE SHE'S GOING...
LOUD-MOUTHED LITTLE PIPSQUEAK...
BARKEEP!
A MUG OF YOUR FINEST!

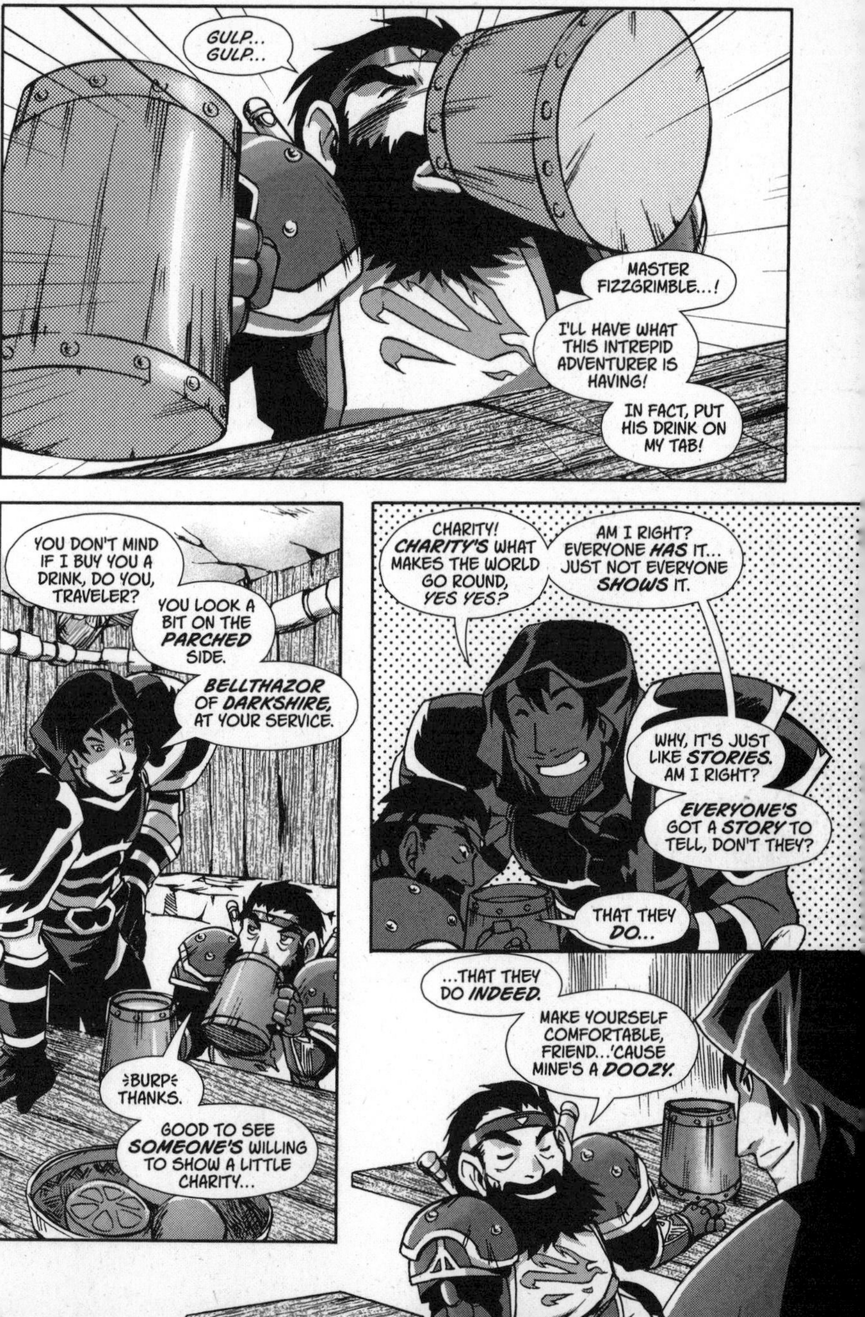
GULP... GULP...
MASTER FIZZGRIMBLE...!
I'LL HAVE WHAT THIS INTREPID ADVENTURER IS HAVING!
IN FACT, PUT HIS DRINK ON MY TAB!
YOU DON'T MIND IF I BUY YOU A DRINK, DO YOU, TRAVELER?
YOU LOOK A BIT ON THE PARCHED SIDE.
BELLTHAZOR OF DARKSHIRE, AT YOUR SERVICE.
BURP THANKS.
GOOD TO SEE SOMEONE'S WILLING TO SHOW A LITTLE CHARITY...
CHARITY! CHARITY'S WHAT MAKES THE WORLD GO ROUND, YES YES?
AM I RIGHT? EVERYONE HAS IT... JUST NOT EVERYONE SHOWS IT.
WHY, IT'S JUST LIKE STORIES. AM I RIGHT?
EVERYONE'S GOT A STORY TO TELL, DON'T THEY?
THAT THEY DO...
...THAT THEY DO INDEED.
MAKE YOURSELF COMFORTABLE, FRIEND...'CAUSE MINE'S A DOOZY.

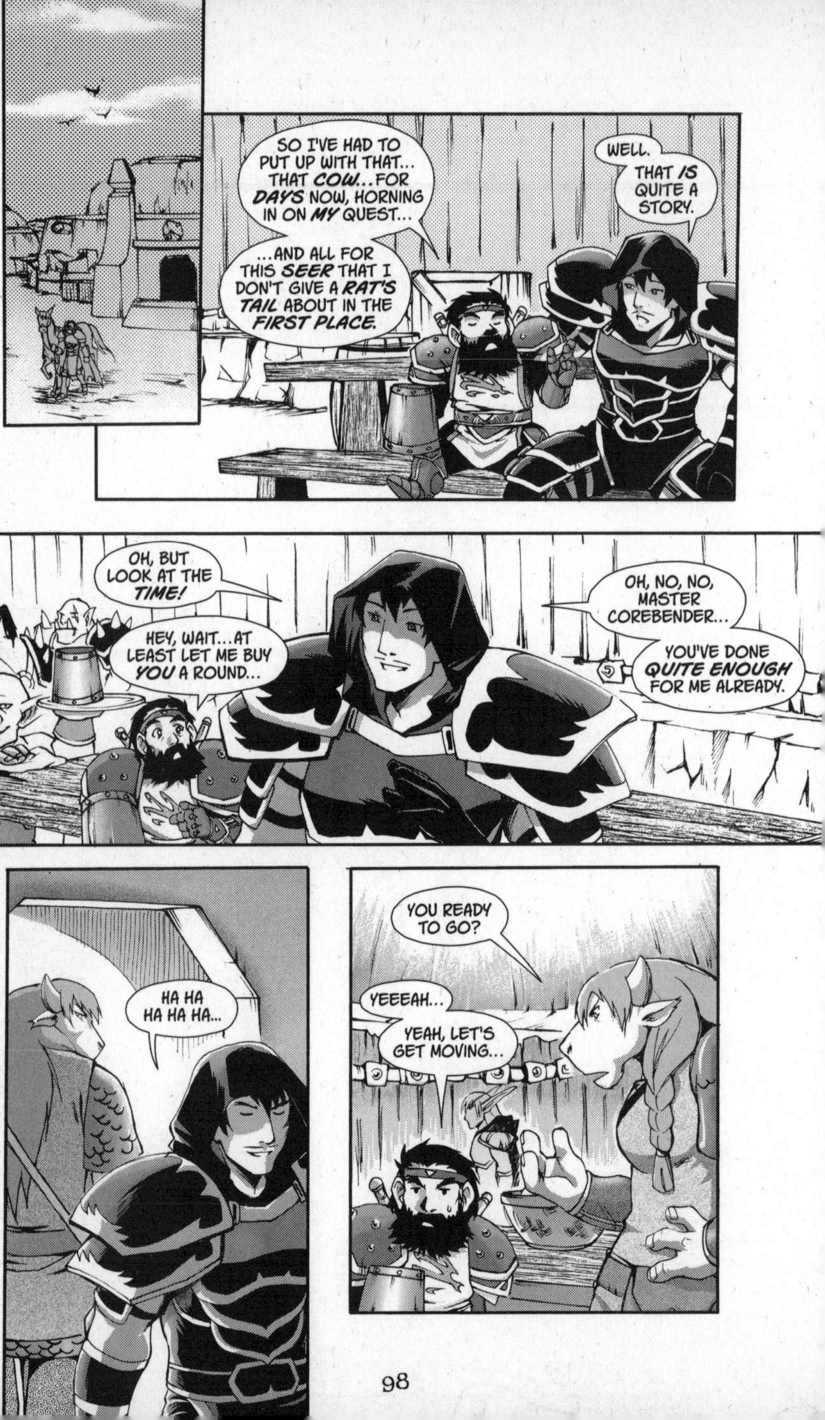
SO I'VE HAD TO PUT UP WITH THAT... THAT COW...FOR DAYS NOW, HORNING IN ON MY QUEST...
...AND ALL FOR THIS SEER THAT I DON'T GIVE A RAT'S TAIL ABOUT IN THE FIRST PLACE.
WELL.
THAT IS QUITE A STORY.
OH, BUT LOOK AT THE TIME!
HEY, WAIT...AT LEAST LET ME BUY YOU A ROUND...
OH, NO, NO, MASTER COREBENDER...
YOU'VE DONE QUITE ENOUGH FOR ME ALREADY.
HA HA HA HA HA...
YOU READY TO GO?
YEEEAH...
YEAH, LET'S GET MOVING...

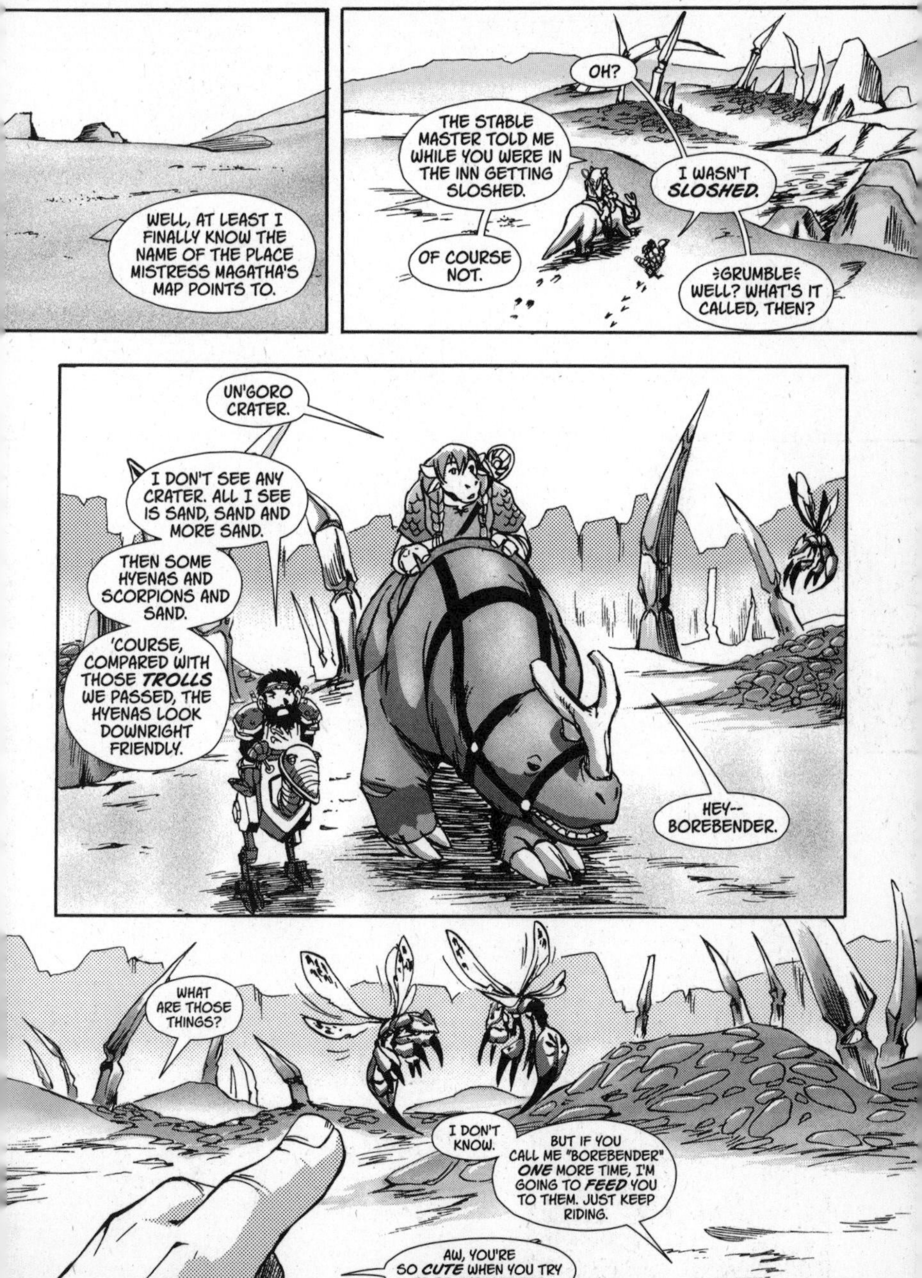
WELL, AT LEAST I FINALLY KNOW THE NAME OF THE PLACE MISTRESS MAGATHA'S MAP POINTS TO.
OH?
THE STABLE MASTER TOLD ME WHILE YOU WERE IN THE INN GETTING SLOSHED.
I WASN'T ***SLOSHED.***
OF COURSE NOT.
≶GRUMBLE≶ WELL? WHAT'S IT CALLED, THEN?
UN'GORO CRATER.
I DON'T SEE ANY CRATER. ALL I SEE IS SAND, SAND AND MORE SAND.
THEN SOME HYENAS AND SCORPIONS AND SAND.
'COURSE, COMPARED WITH THOSE ***TROLLS*** WE PASSED, THE HYENAS LOOK DOWNRIGHT FRIENDLY.
HEY-- BOREBENDER.
WHAT ARE THOSE THINGS?
I DON'T KNOW.
BUT IF YOU CALL ME "BOREBENDER" ***ONE*** MORE TIME, I'M GOING TO ***FEED*** YOU TO THEM. JUST KEEP RIDING.
AW, YOU'RE SO ***CUTE*** WHEN YOU TRY TO BE THREATENING.

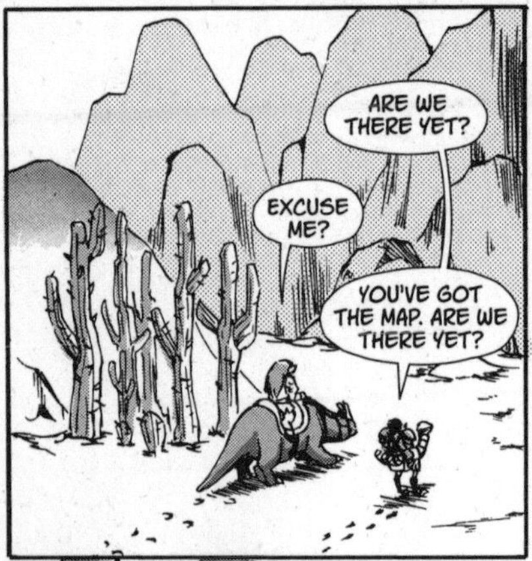
ARE WE THERE YET?
EXCUSE ME?
YOU'VE GOT THE MAP. ARE WE THERE YET?

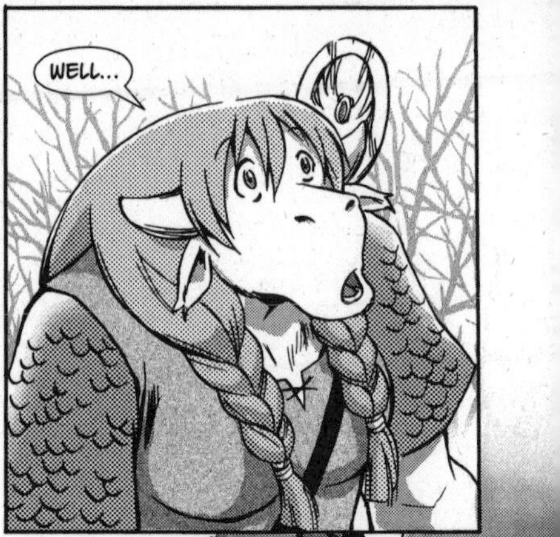
WELL...

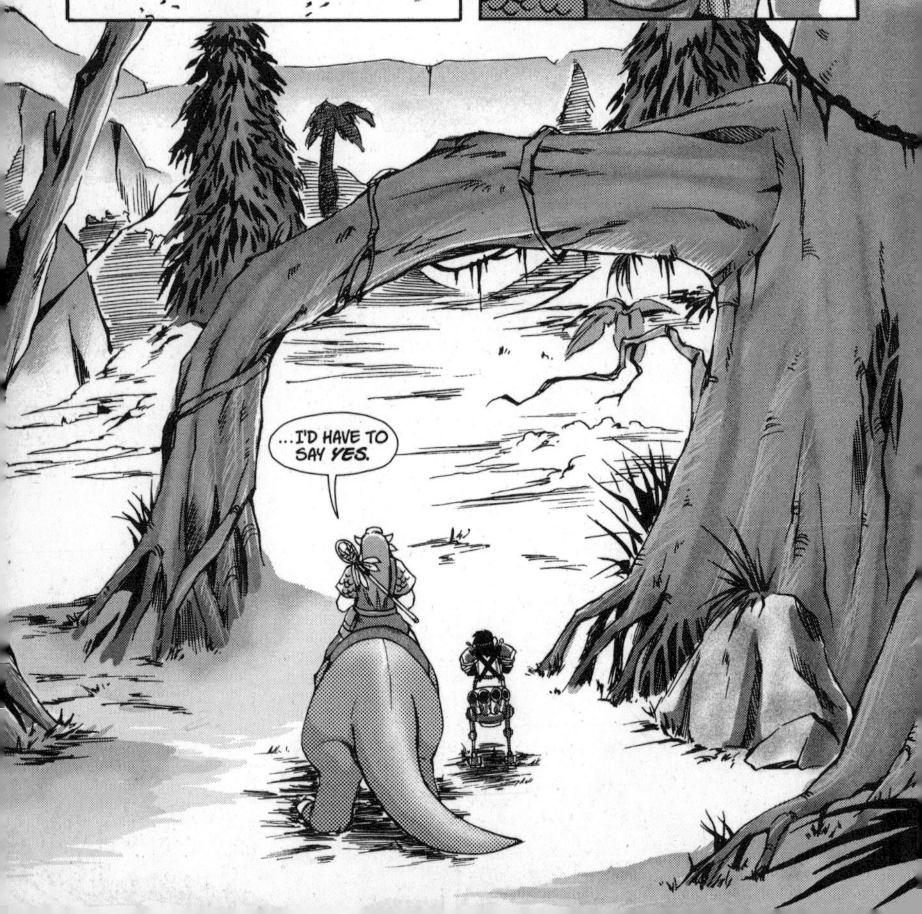
...I'D HAVE TO SAY *YES*.

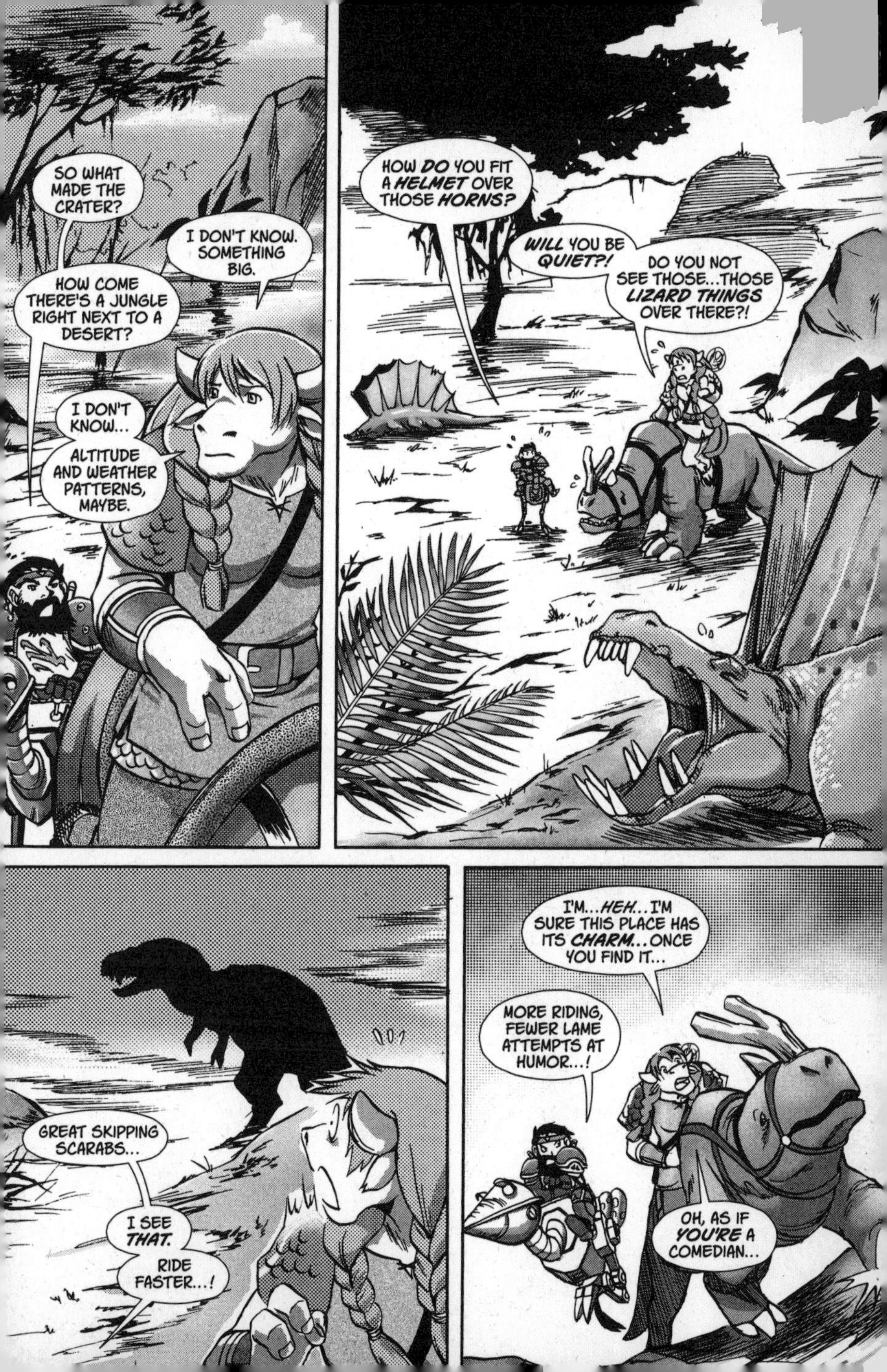
SO WHAT MADE THE CRATER?
I DON'T KNOW. SOMETHING BIG.
HOW COME THERE'S A JUNGLE RIGHT NEXT TO A DESERT?
I DON'T KNOW...
ALTITUDE AND WEATHER PATTERNS, MAYBE.
HOW *DO* YOU FIT A *HELMET* OVER THOSE *HORNS?*
WILL YOU BE *QUIET?!*
DO YOU NOT SEE THOSE...THOSE *LIZARD THINGS* OVER THERE?!
GREAT SKIPPING SCARABS...
I SEE *THAT.*
RIDE FASTER...!
I'M...*HEH*...I'M SURE THIS PLACE HAS ITS *CHARM*...ONCE YOU FIND IT...
MORE RIDING, FEWER LAME ATTEMPTS AT HUMOR...!
OH, AS IF *YOU'RE* A COMEDIAN...

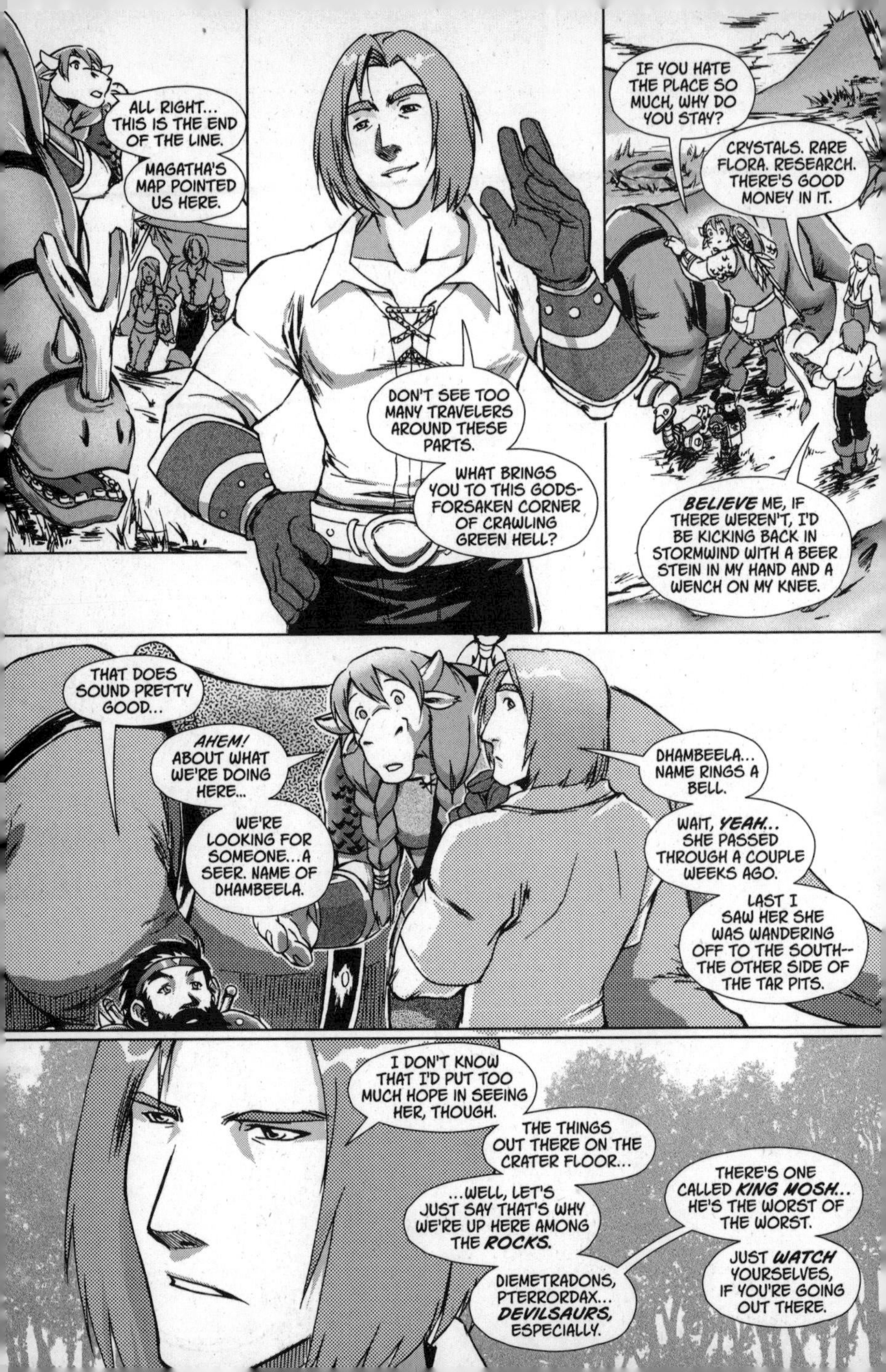
ALL RIGHT... THIS IS THE END OF THE LINE.
MAGATHA'S MAP POINTED US HERE.
DON'T SEE TOO MANY TRAVELERS AROUND THESE PARTS.
WHAT BRINGS YOU TO THIS GODS-FORSAKEN CORNER OF CRAWLING GREEN HELL?
IF YOU HATE THE PLACE SO MUCH, WHY DO YOU STAY?
CRYSTALS. RARE FLORA. RESEARCH. THERE'S GOOD MONEY IN IT.
BELIEVE ME, IF THERE WEREN'T, I'D BE KICKING BACK IN STORMWIND WITH A BEER STEIN IN MY HAND AND A WENCH ON MY KNEE.
THAT DOES SOUND PRETTY GOOD...
AHEM! ABOUT WHAT WE'RE DOING HERE...
WE'RE LOOKING FOR SOMEONE...A SEER. NAME OF DHAMBEELA.
DHAMBEELA... NAME RINGS A BELL.
WAIT, YEAH... SHE PASSED THROUGH A COUPLE WEEKS AGO.
LAST I SAW HER SHE WAS WANDERING OFF TO THE SOUTH-- THE OTHER SIDE OF THE TAR PITS.
I DON'T KNOW THAT I'D PUT TOO MUCH HOPE IN SEEING HER, THOUGH.
THE THINGS OUT THERE ON THE CRATER FLOOR...
...WELL, LET'S JUST SAY THAT'S WHY WE'RE UP HERE AMONG THE ROCKS.
DIEMETRADONS, PTERRORDAX... DEVILSAURS, ESPECIALLY.
THERE'S ONE CALLED KING MOSH... HE'S THE WORST OF THE WORST.
JUST WATCH YOURSELVES, IF YOU'RE GOING OUT THERE.

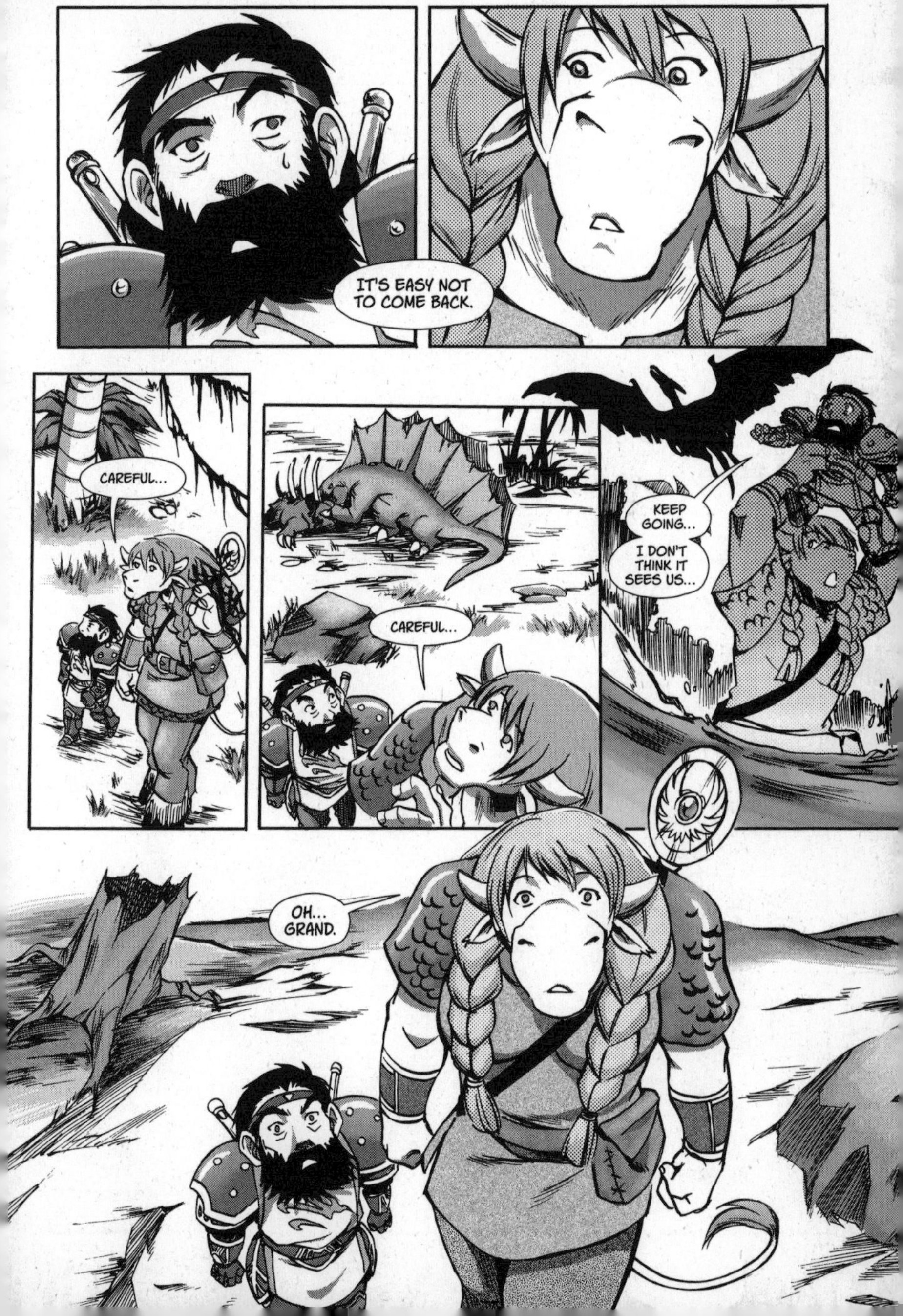
IT'S EASY NOT TO COME BACK.
CAREFUL...
CAREFUL...
KEEP GOING...
I DON'T THINK IT SEES US...
OH... GRAND.

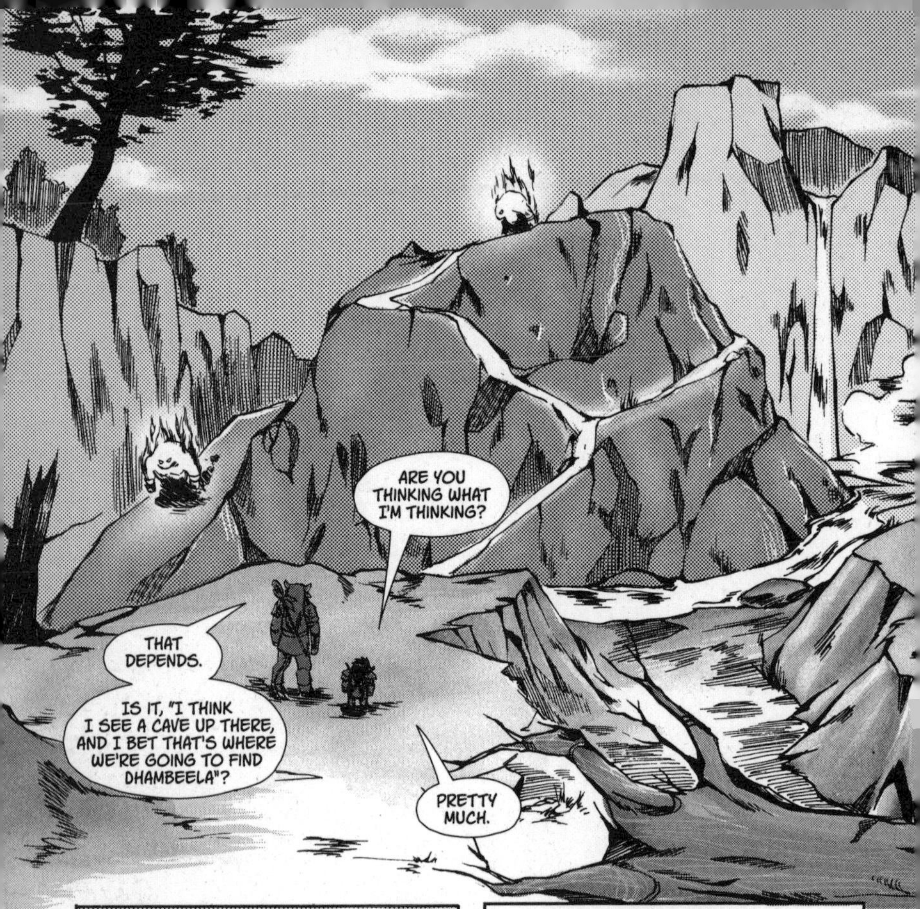
ARE YOU THINKING WHAT I'M THINKING?
THAT DEPENDS.
IS IT, "I THINK I SEE A CAVE UP THERE, AND I BET THAT'S WHERE WE'RE GOING TO FIND DHAMBEELA"?
PRETTY MUCH.
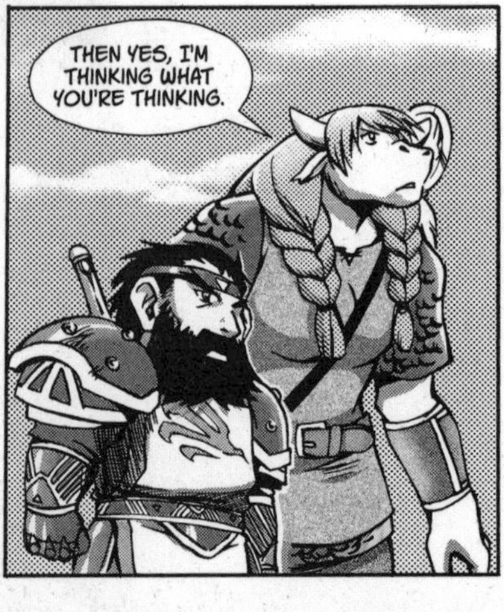
THEN YES, I'M THINKING WHAT YOU'RE THINKING.
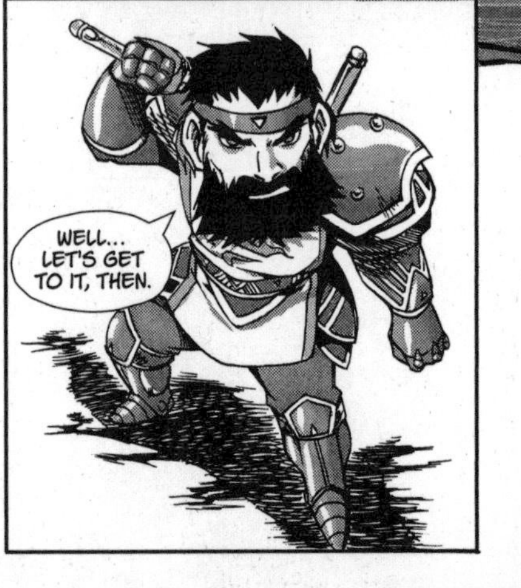
WELL... LET'S GET TO IT, THEN.

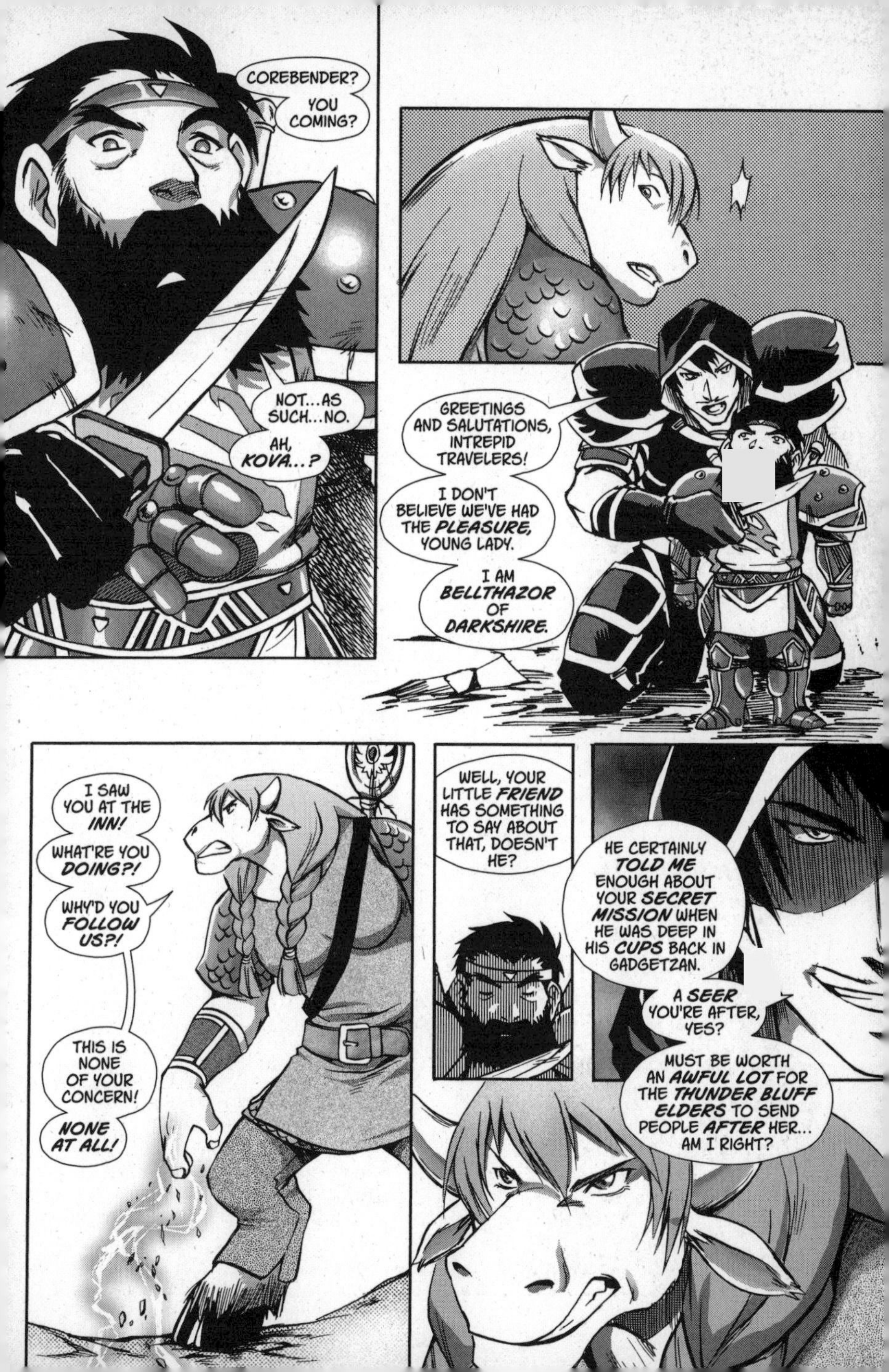
COREBENDER?
YOU COMING?
NOT...AS SUCH...NO.
AH, KOVA...?
GREETINGS AND SALUTATIONS, INTREPID TRAVELERS!
I DON'T BELIEVE WE'VE HAD THE PLEASURE, YOUNG LADY.
I AM BELLTHAZOR OF DARKSHIRE.
I SAW YOU AT THE INN!
WHAT'RE YOU DOING?!
WHY'D YOU FOLLOW US?!
THIS IS NONE OF YOUR CONCERN!
NONE AT ALL!
WELL, YOUR LITTLE FRIEND HAS SOMETHING TO SAY ABOUT THAT, DOESN'T HE?
HE CERTAINLY TOLD ME ENOUGH ABOUT YOUR SECRET MISSION WHEN HE WAS DEEP IN HIS CUPS BACK IN GADGETZAN.
A SEER YOU'RE AFTER, YES?
MUST BE WORTH AN AWFUL LOT FOR THE THUNDER BLUFF ELDERS TO SEND PEOPLE AFTER HER... AM I RIGHT?

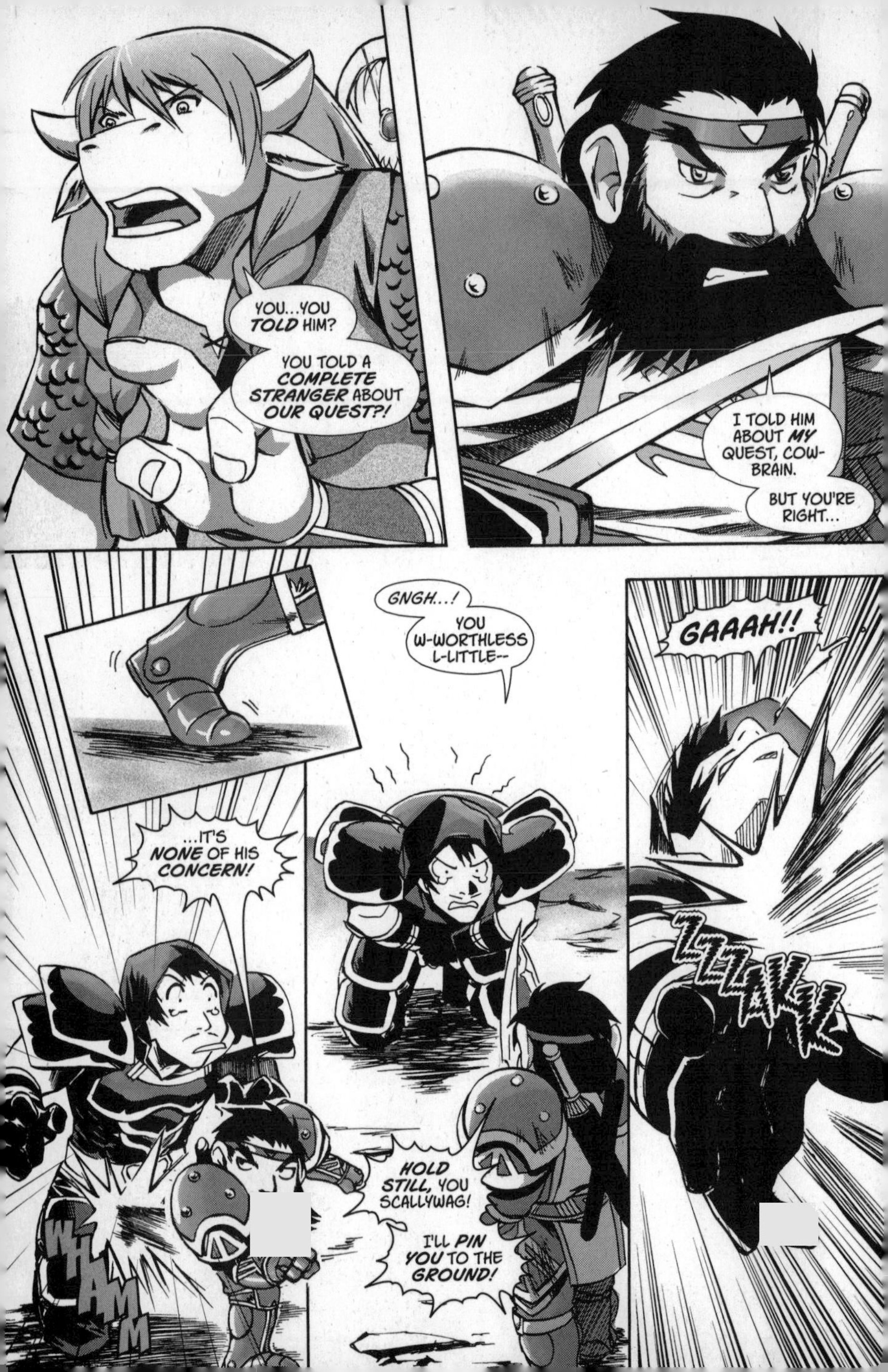
YOU...YOU TOLD HIM?
YOU TOLD A COMPLETE STRANGER ABOUT OUR QUEST?!
I TOLD HIM ABOUT MY QUEST, COW-BRAIN.
BUT YOU'RE RIGHT...
...IT'S NONE OF HIS CONCERN!
WHAMM
GNGH...!
YOU W-WORTHLESS L-LITTLE--
HOLD STILL, YOU SCALLYWAG!
I'LL PIN YOU TO THE GROUND!
GAAAH!!
ZZZAKK

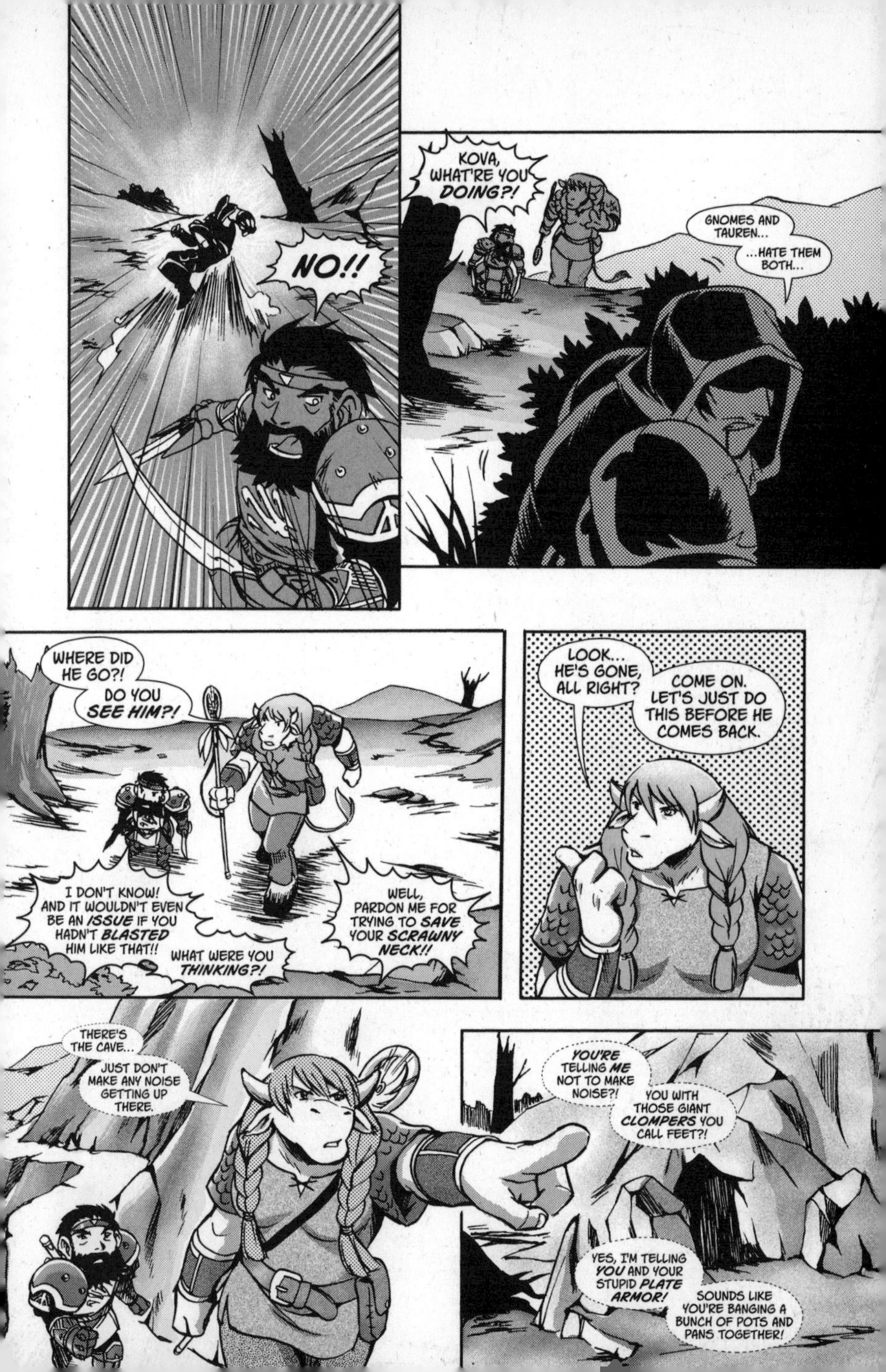
NO!!
KOVA, WHAT'RE YOU DOING?!
GNOMES AND TAUREN...
...HATE THEM BOTH...
WHERE DID HE GO?!
DO YOU SEE HIM?!
I DON'T KNOW! AND IT WOULDN'T EVEN BE AN ISSUE IF YOU HADN'T BLASTED HIM LIKE THAT!!
WHAT WERE YOU THINKING?!
WELL, PARDON ME FOR TRYING TO SAVE YOUR SCRAWNY NECK!!
LOOK... HE'S GONE, ALL RIGHT?
COME ON. LET'S JUST DO THIS BEFORE HE COMES BACK.
THERE'S THE CAVE...
JUST DON'T MAKE ANY NOISE GETTING UP THERE.
YOU'RE TELLING ME NOT TO MAKE NOISE?!
YOU WITH THOSE GIANT CLOMPERS YOU CALL FEET?!
YES, I'M TELLING YOU AND YOUR STUPID PLATE ARMOR!
SOUNDS LIKE YOU'RE BANGING A BUNCH OF POTS AND PANS TOGETHER!

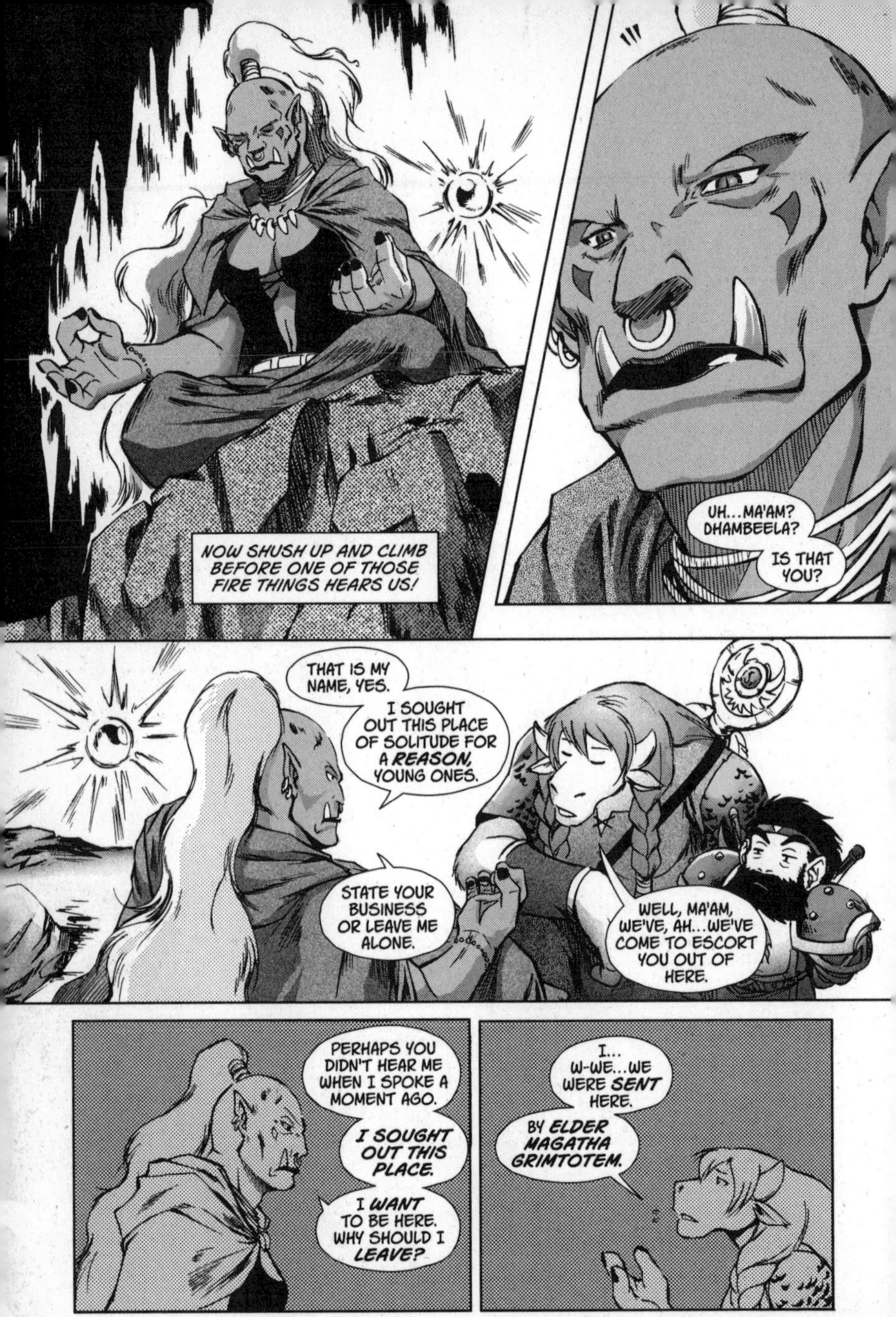
NOW SHUSH UP AND CLIMB BEFORE ONE OF THOSE FIRE THINGS HEARS US!
UH...MA'AM? DHAMBEELA?
IS THAT YOU?
THAT IS MY NAME, YES.
I SOUGHT OUT THIS PLACE OF SOLITUDE FOR A *REASON,* YOUNG ONES.
STATE YOUR BUSINESS OR LEAVE ME ALONE.
WELL, MA'AM, WE'VE, AH...WE'VE COME TO ESCORT YOU OUT OF HERE.
PERHAPS YOU DIDN'T HEAR ME WHEN I SPOKE A MOMENT AGO.
I SOUGHT OUT THIS PLACE.
I *WANT* TO BE HERE. WHY SHOULD I *LEAVE?*
I... W-WE...WE WERE *SENT* HERE.
BY *ELDER MAGATHA GRIMTOTEM.*

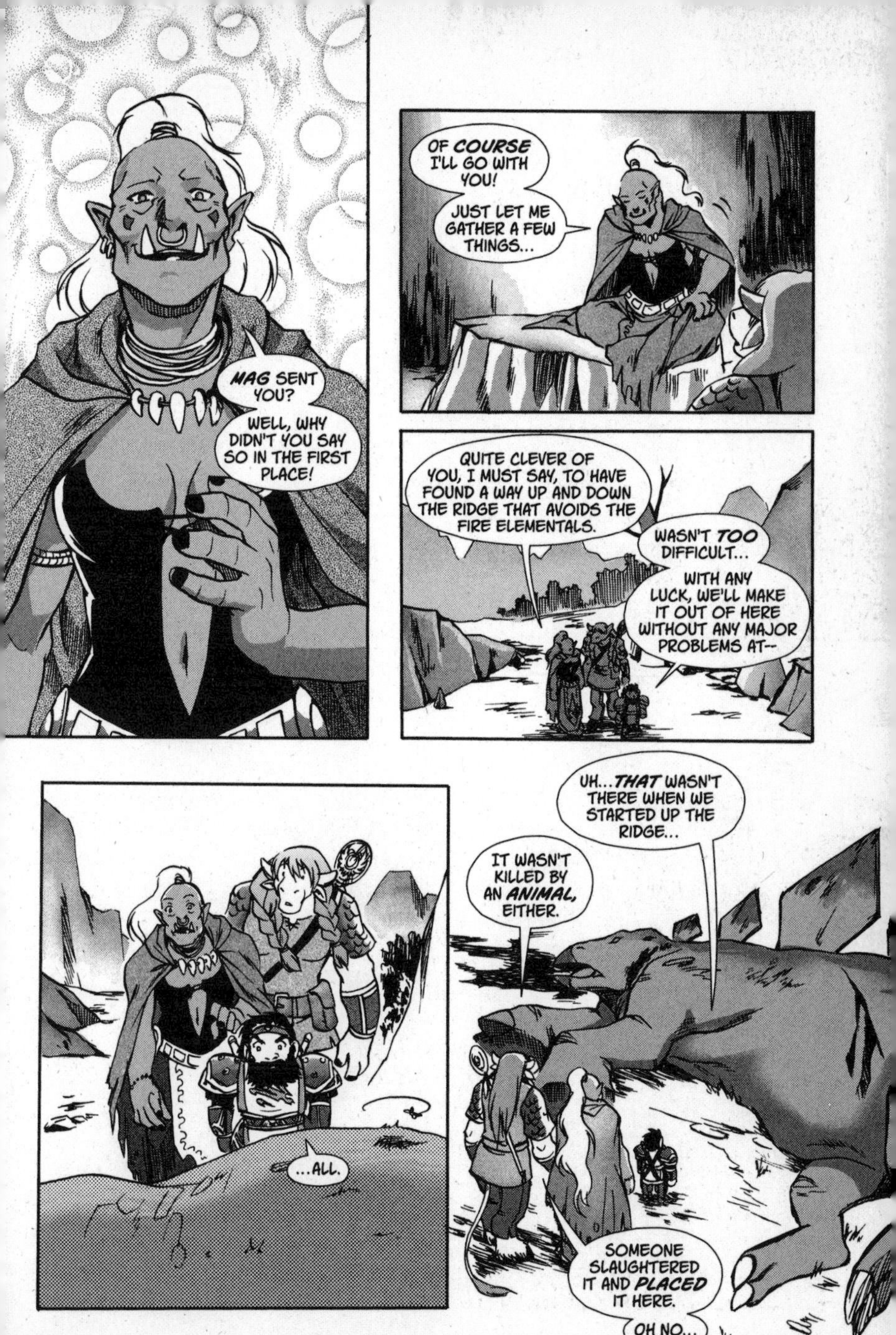
MAG SENT YOU?
WELL, WHY DIDN'T YOU SAY SO IN THE FIRST PLACE!
OF COURSE I'LL GO WITH YOU!
JUST LET ME GATHER A FEW THINGS...
QUITE CLEVER OF YOU, I MUST SAY, TO HAVE FOUND A WAY UP AND DOWN THE RIDGE THAT AVOIDS THE FIRE ELEMENTALS.
WASN'T TOO DIFFICULT...
WITH ANY LUCK, WE'LL MAKE IT OUT OF HERE WITHOUT ANY MAJOR PROBLEMS AT--
...ALL.
UH...THAT WASN'T THERE WHEN WE STARTED UP THE RIDGE...
IT WASN'T KILLED BY AN ANIMAL, EITHER.
SOMEONE SLAUGHTERED IT AND PLACED IT HERE.
OH NO...

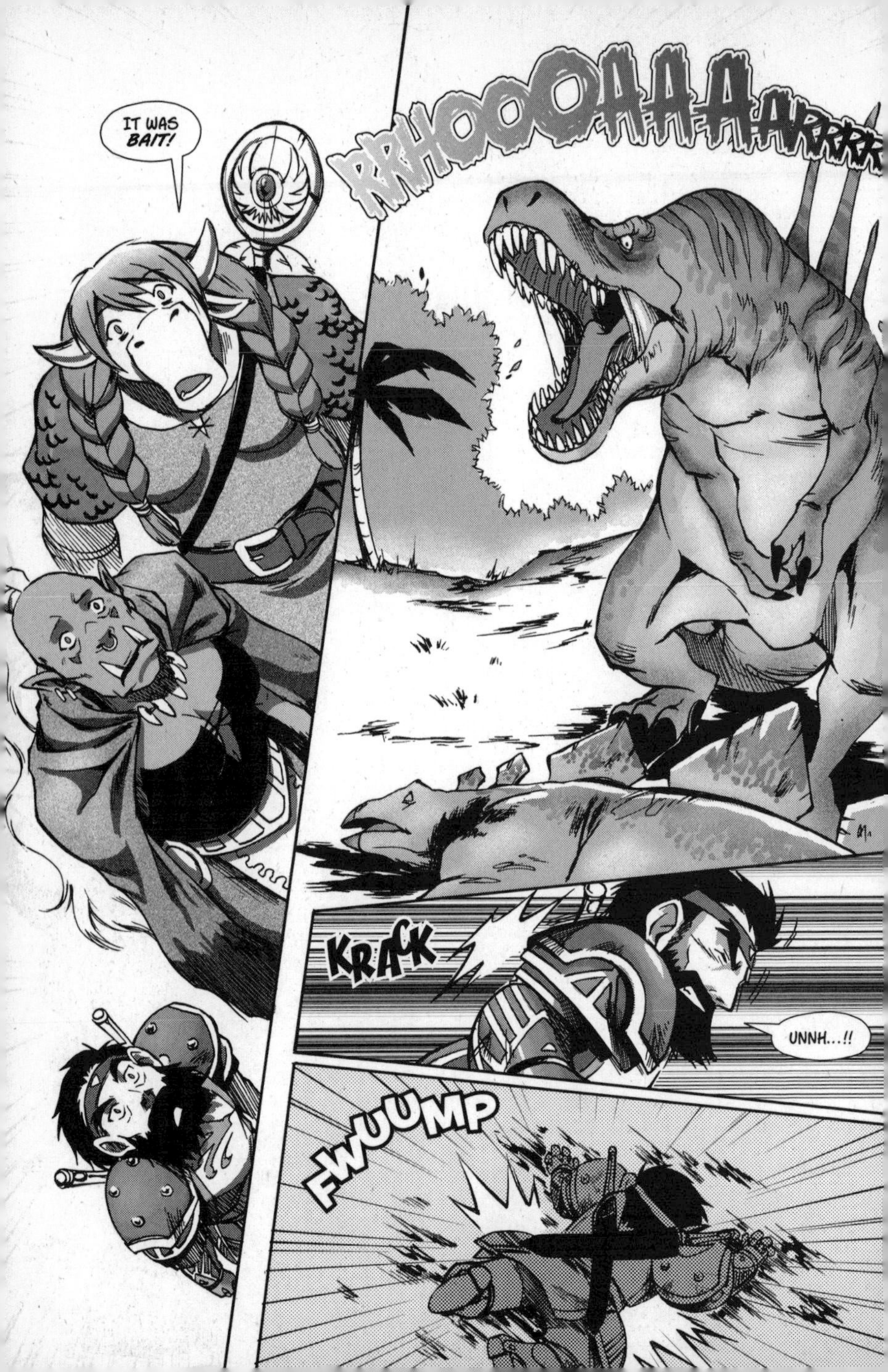
IT WAS BAIT!
RRHOOOAAAARRRRR
KRACK
UNNH...!!
FWUUMP

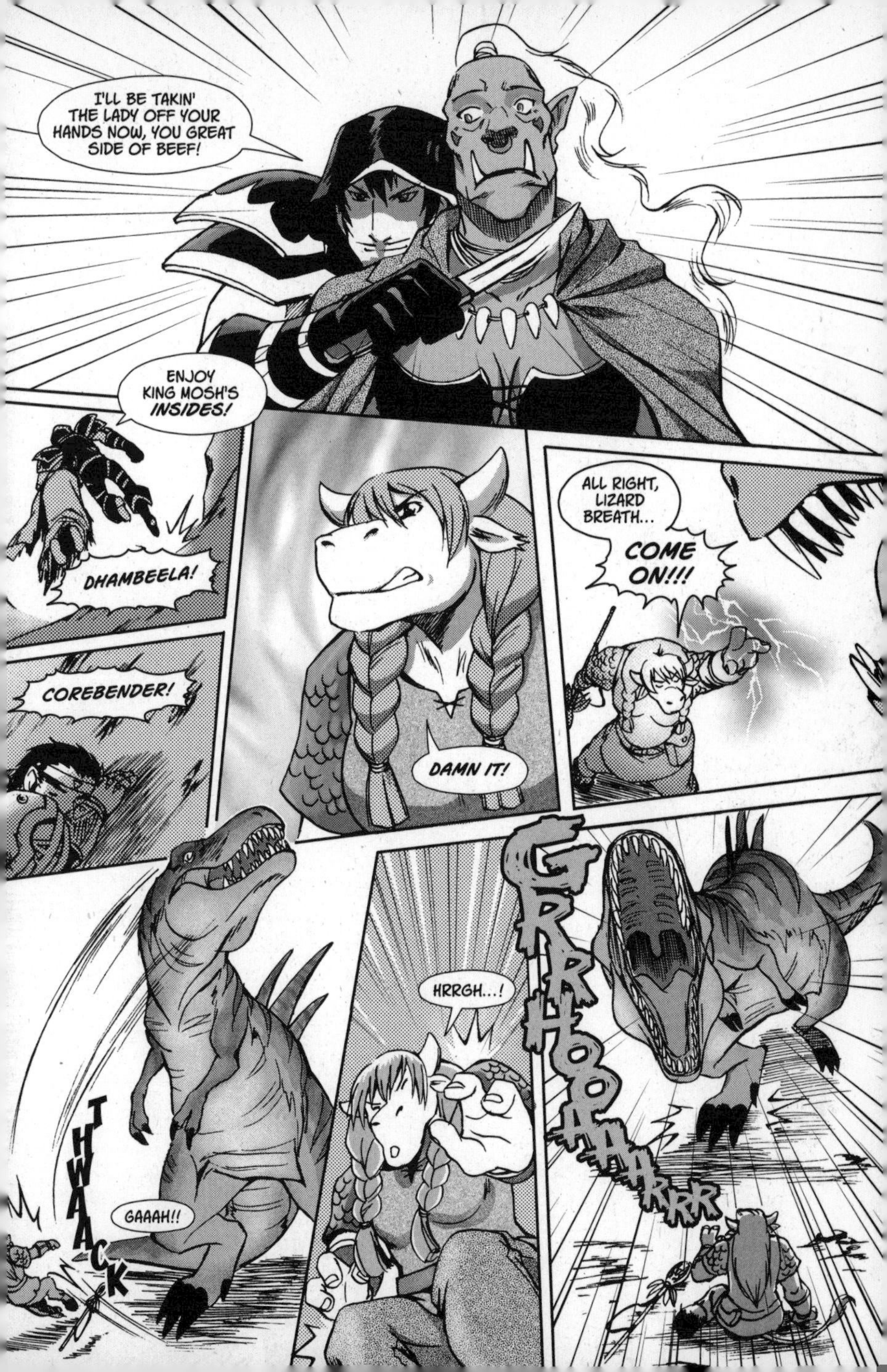
I'LL BE TAKIN' THE LADY OFF YOUR HANDS NOW, YOU GREAT SIDE OF BEEF!
ENJOY KING MOSH'S INSIDES!
DHAMBEELA!
CORECBENDER!
DAMN IT!
ALL RIGHT, LIZARD BREATH...
COME ON!!!
THWAACK
GAAAH!!
HRRGH...!
GRRHOOAAARRRR

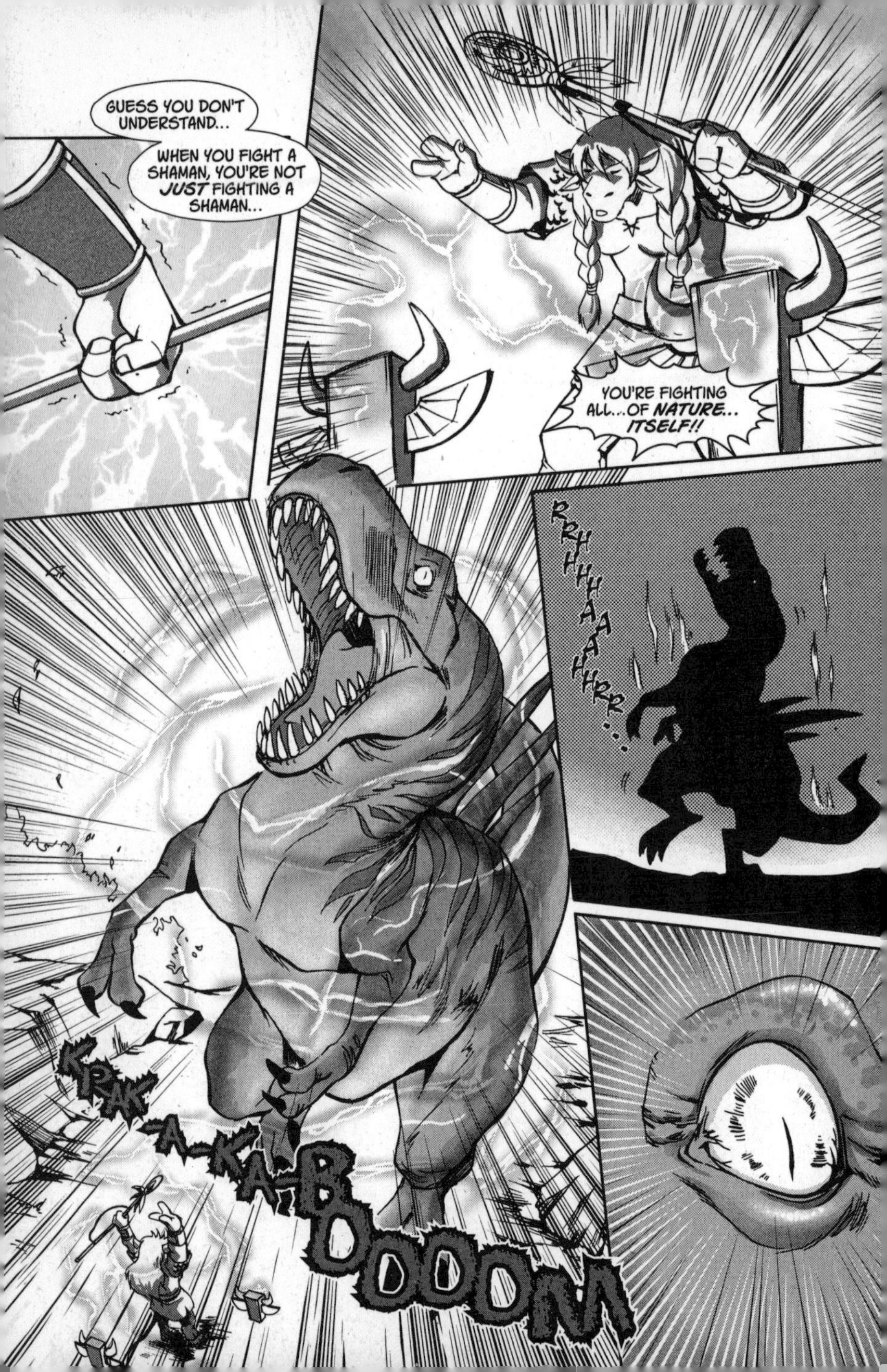
GUESS YOU DON'T UNDERSTAND...
WHEN YOU FIGHT A SHAMAN, YOU'RE NOT *JUST* FIGHTING A SHAMAN...
YOU'RE FIGHTING ALL...OF *NATURE...* *ITSELF!!*
KRAK-A-KA-BOOOOM
RRHHHHAAAHHRR...

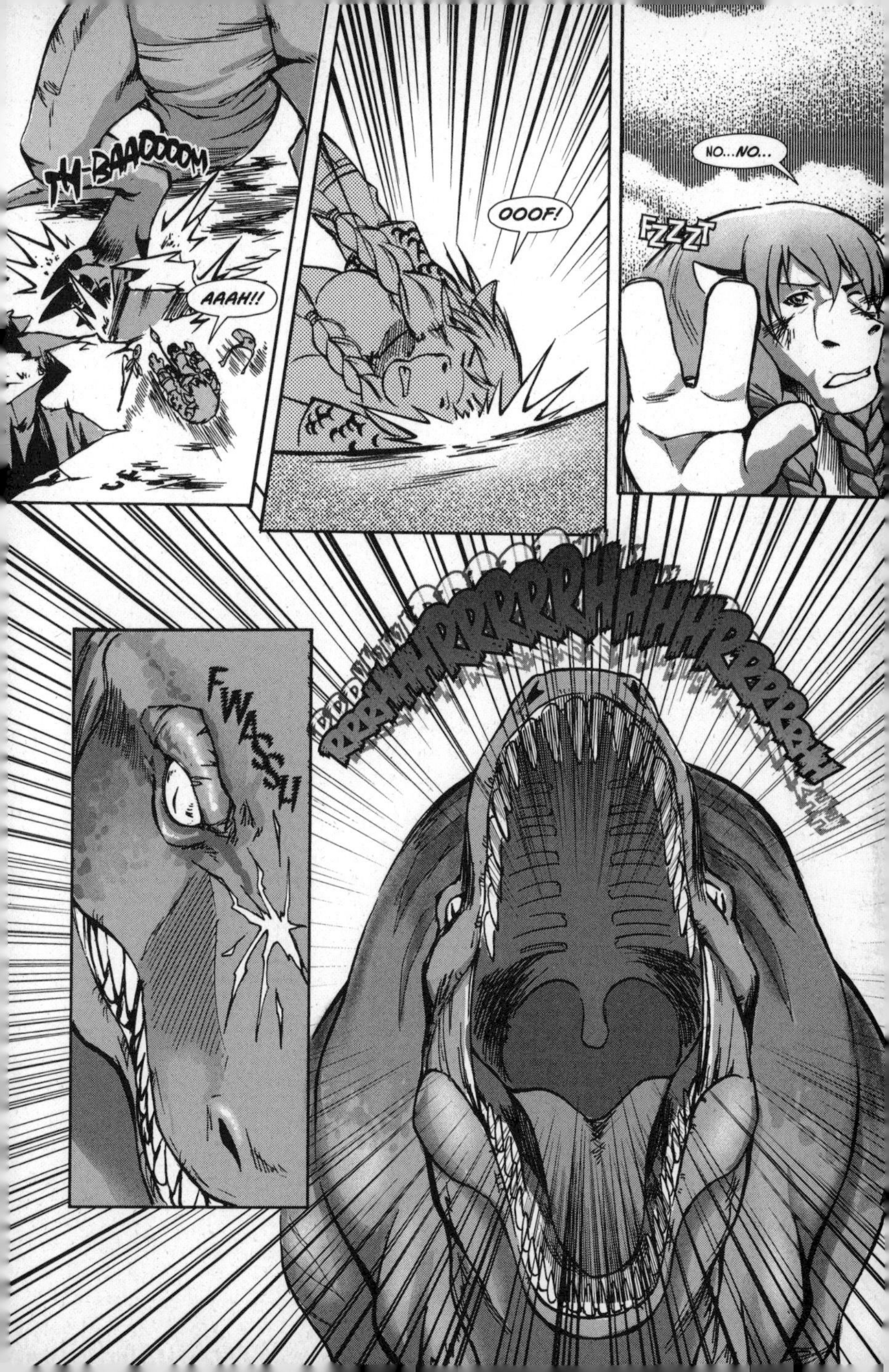
NO...NO...
FZZZT
OOOF!
TH-BAAOOOOM
AAAH!!
FWASSH

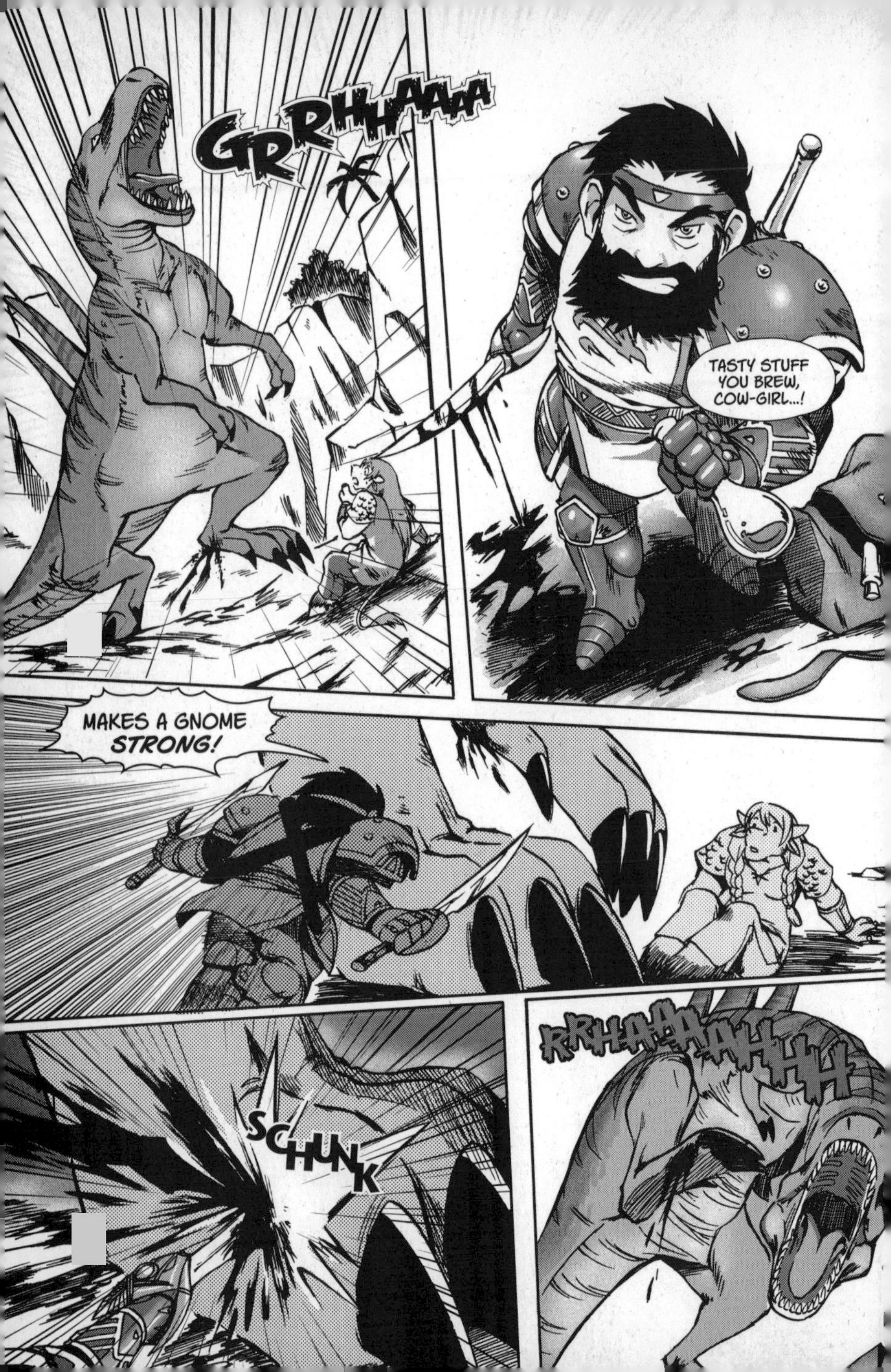
GRRHHAAAA
TASTY STUFF YOU BREW, COW-GIRL...!
MAKES A GNOME STRONG!
SCHUNK
RRHAAAAHHH

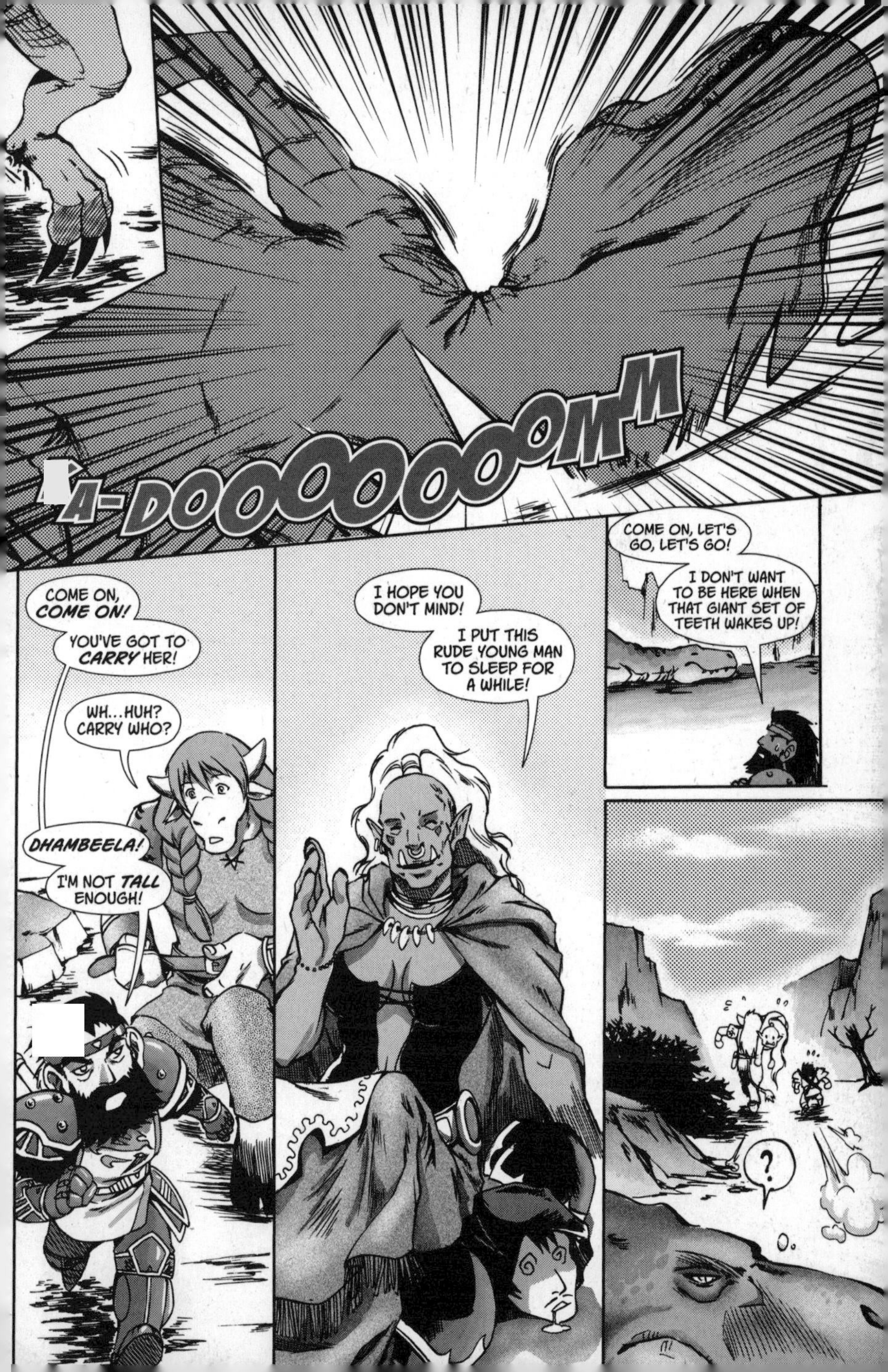

A-DOOOOOOOMM
COME ON, COME ON!
YOU'VE GOT TO CARRY HER!
WH...HUH? CARRY WHO?
DHAMBEELA!
I'M NOT TALL ENOUGH!
I HOPE YOU DON'T MIND!
I PUT THIS RUDE YOUNG MAN TO SLEEP FOR A WHILE!
COME ON, LET'S GO, LET'S GO!
I DON'T WANT TO BE HERE WHEN THAT GIANT SET OF TEETH WAKES UP!
?

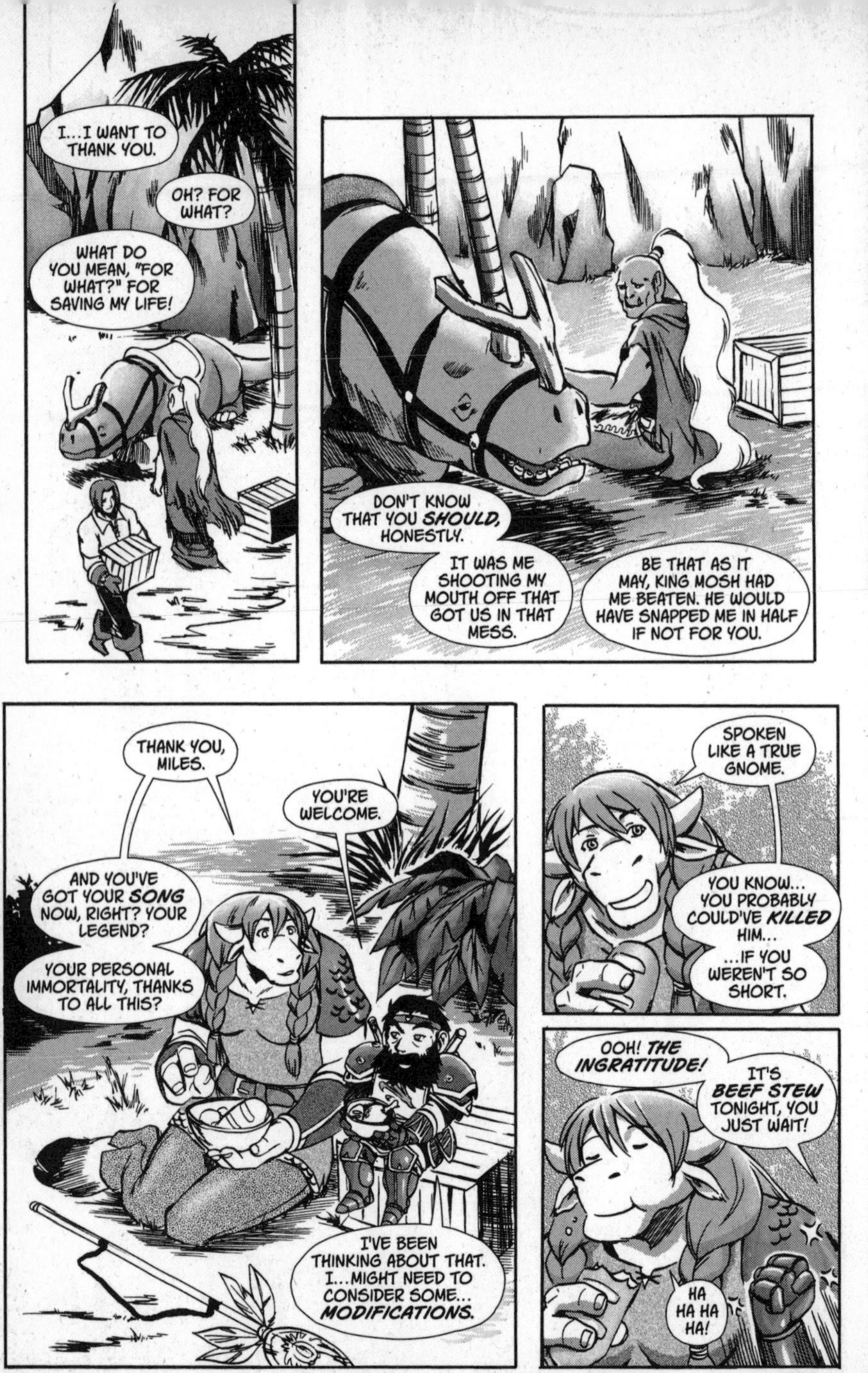
I...I WANT TO THANK YOU.
OH? FOR WHAT?
WHAT DO YOU MEAN, "FOR WHAT?" FOR SAVING MY LIFE!
DON'T KNOW THAT YOU *SHOULD,* HONESTLY.
IT WAS ME SHOOTING MY MOUTH OFF THAT GOT US IN THAT MESS.
BE THAT AS IT MAY, KING MOSH HAD ME BEATEN. HE WOULD HAVE SNAPPED ME IN HALF IF NOT FOR YOU.
THANK YOU, MILES.
YOU'RE WELCOME.
AND YOU'VE GOT YOUR *SONG* NOW, RIGHT? YOUR LEGEND?
YOUR PERSONAL IMMORTALITY, THANKS TO ALL THIS?
I'VE BEEN THINKING ABOUT THAT. I...MIGHT NEED TO CONSIDER SOME... *MODIFICATIONS.*
SPOKEN LIKE A TRUE GNOME.
YOU KNOW... YOU PROBABLY COULD'VE *KILLED* HIM...
...IF YOU WEREN'T SO SHORT.
OOH! *THE INGRATITUDE!*
IT'S *BEEF STEW* TONIGHT, YOU JUST WAIT!
HA HA HA HA!

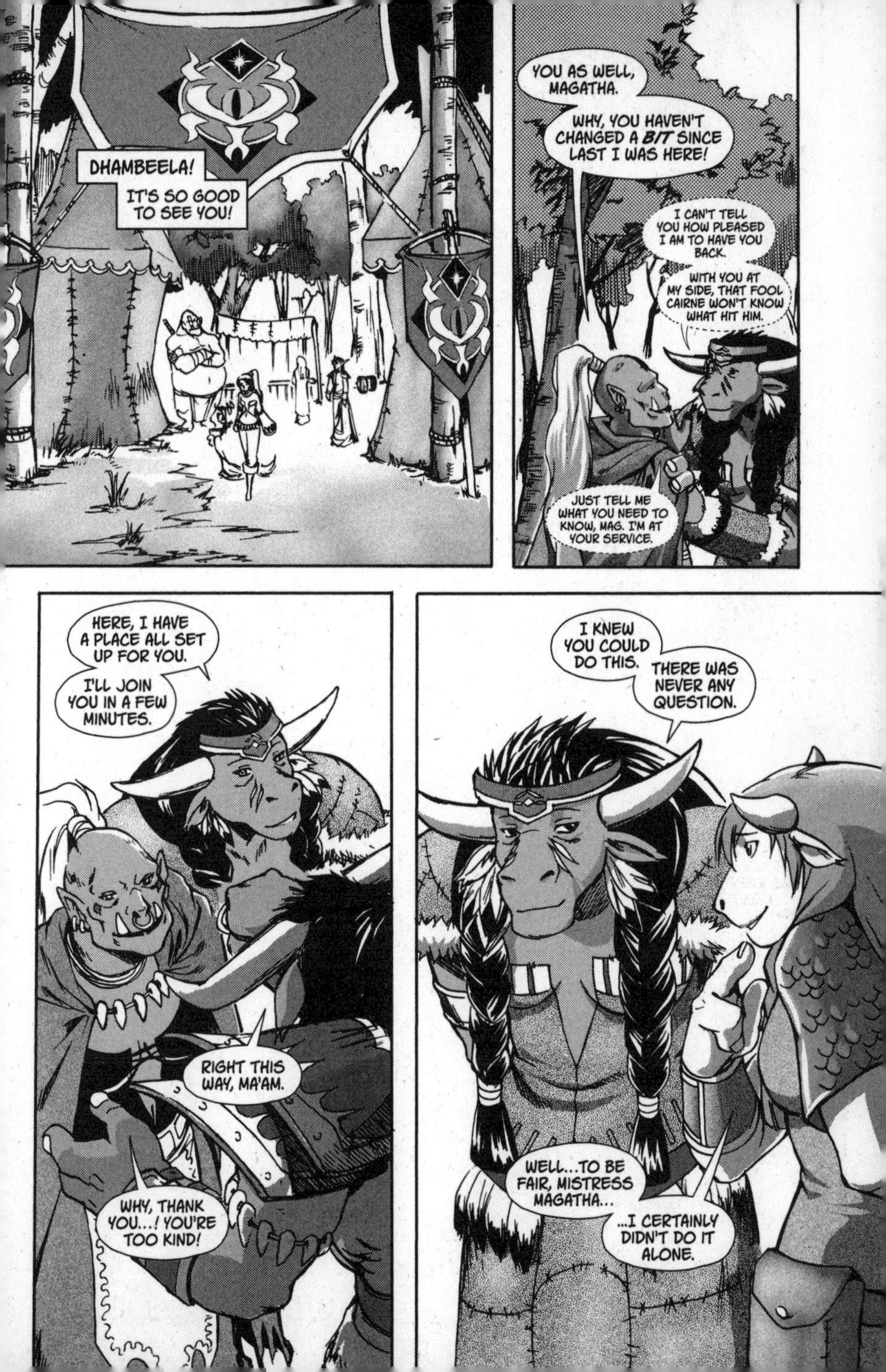
DHAMBEELA!
IT'S SO GOOD TO SEE YOU!
YOU AS WELL, MAGATHA.
WHY, YOU HAVEN'T CHANGED A *BIT* SINCE LAST I WAS HERE!
I CAN'T TELL YOU HOW PLEASED I AM TO HAVE YOU BACK.
WITH YOU AT MY SIDE, THAT FOOL CAIRNE WON'T KNOW WHAT HIT HIM.
JUST TELL ME WHAT YOU NEED TO KNOW, MAG. I'M AT YOUR SERVICE.
HERE, I HAVE A PLACE ALL SET UP FOR YOU.
I'LL JOIN YOU IN A FEW MINUTES.
RIGHT THIS WAY, MA'AM.
WHY, THANK YOU...! YOU'RE TOO KIND!
I KNEW YOU COULD DO THIS.
THERE WAS NEVER ANY QUESTION.
WELL...TO BE FAIR, MISTRESS MAGATHA...
...I CERTAINLY DIDN'T DO IT ALONE.

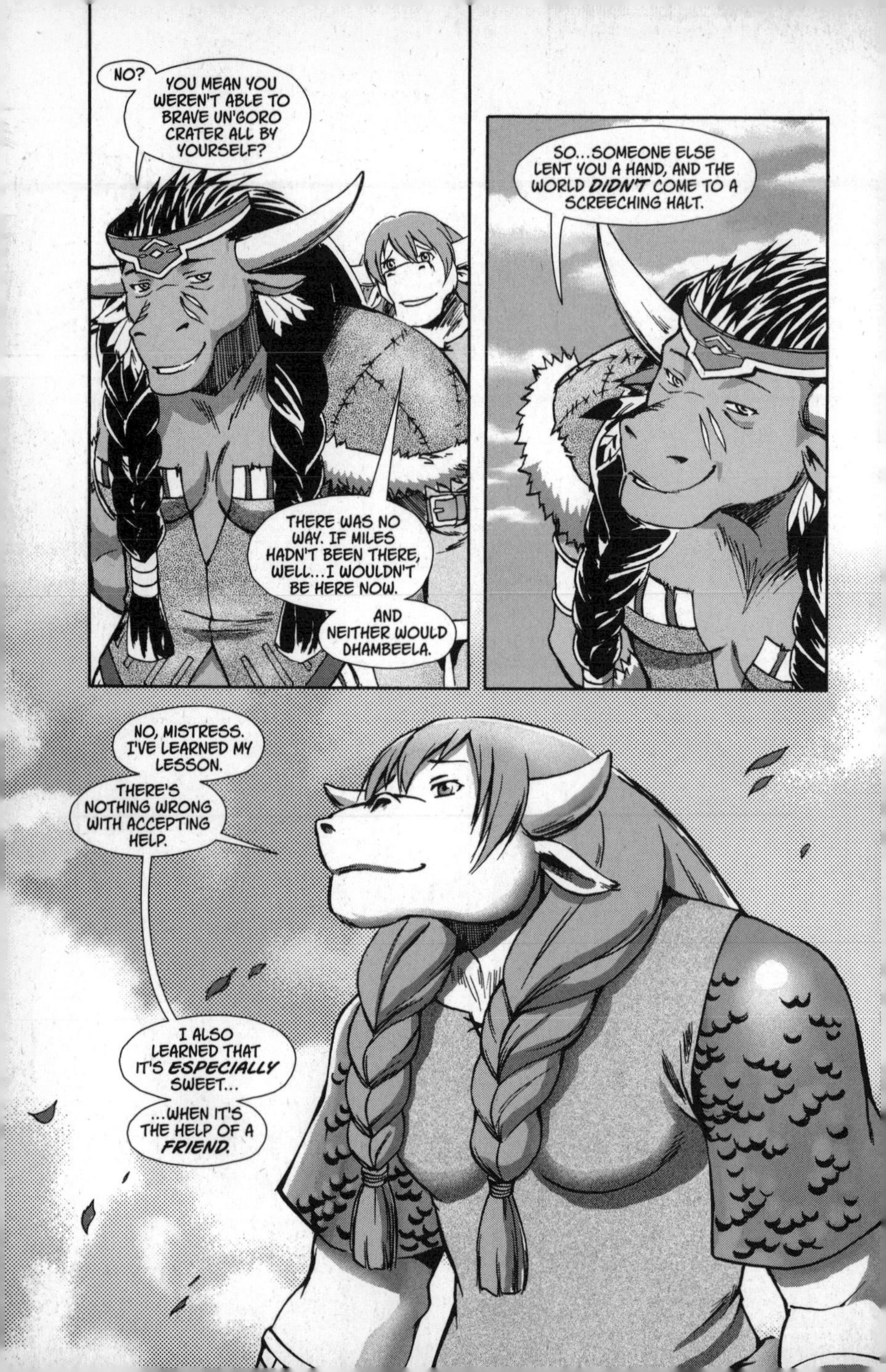
NO?
YOU MEAN YOU WEREN'T ABLE TO BRAVE UN'GORO CRATER ALL BY YOURSELF?
THERE WAS NO WAY. IF MILES HADN'T BEEN THERE, WELL...I WOULDN'T BE HERE NOW.
AND NEITHER WOULD DHAMBEELA.
SO...SOMEONE ELSE LENT YOU A HAND, AND THE WORLD ***DIDN'T*** COME TO A SCREECHING HALT.
NO, MISTRESS. I'VE LEARNED MY LESSON.
THERE'S NOTHING WRONG WITH ACCEPTING HELP.
I ALSO LEARNED THAT IT'S ***ESPECIALLY*** SWEET...
...WHEN IT'S THE HELP OF A ***FRIEND***.

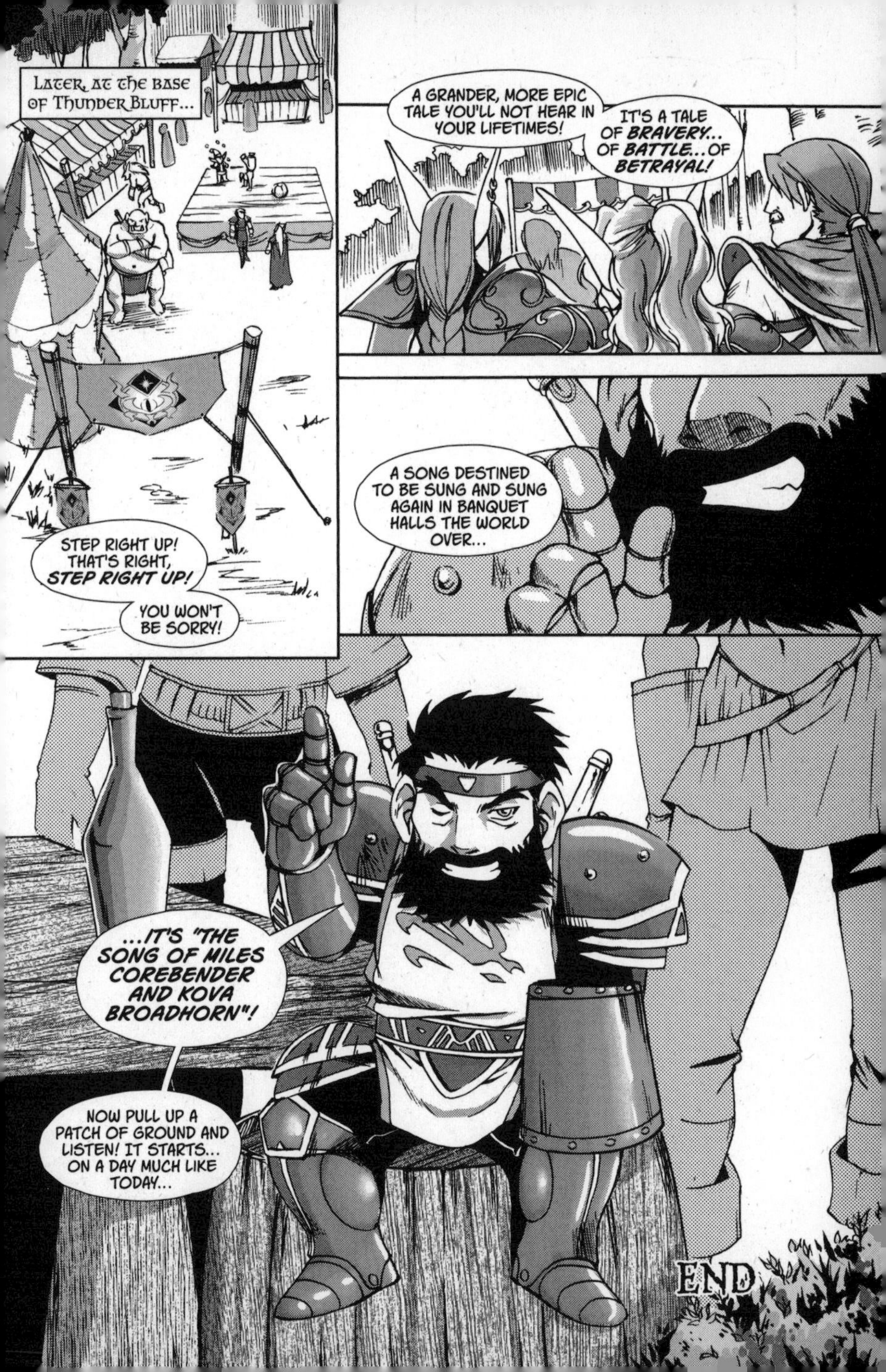
Later, at the base of Thunder Bluff...
STEP RIGHT UP! THAT'S RIGHT, STEP RIGHT UP!
YOU WON'T BE SORRY!
A GRANDER, MORE EPIC TALE YOU'LL NOT HEAR IN YOUR LIFETIMES!
IT'S A TALE OF BRAVERY... OF BATTLE... OF BETRAYAL!
A SONG DESTINED TO BE SUNG AND SUNG AGAIN IN BANQUET HALLS THE WORLD OVER...
...IT'S "THE SONG OF MILES COREBENDER AND KOVA BROADHORN"!
NOW PULL UP A PATCH OF GROUND AND LISTEN! IT STARTS... ON A DAY MUCH LIKE TODAY...
END

LEGENDS
VOLUME TWO

FAMILY VALUES

WRITTEN BY AARON SPARROW

PENCILS BY IN-BAE KIM
INKS BY IN-BAE KIM & MI-JIN BAE
TONES BY JAN MICHAEL ALDEGUER

EDITOR: TROY LEWTER
CONTRIBUTING EDITOR: HYUN JOO KIM
LETTERER: MICHAEL PAOLILLI

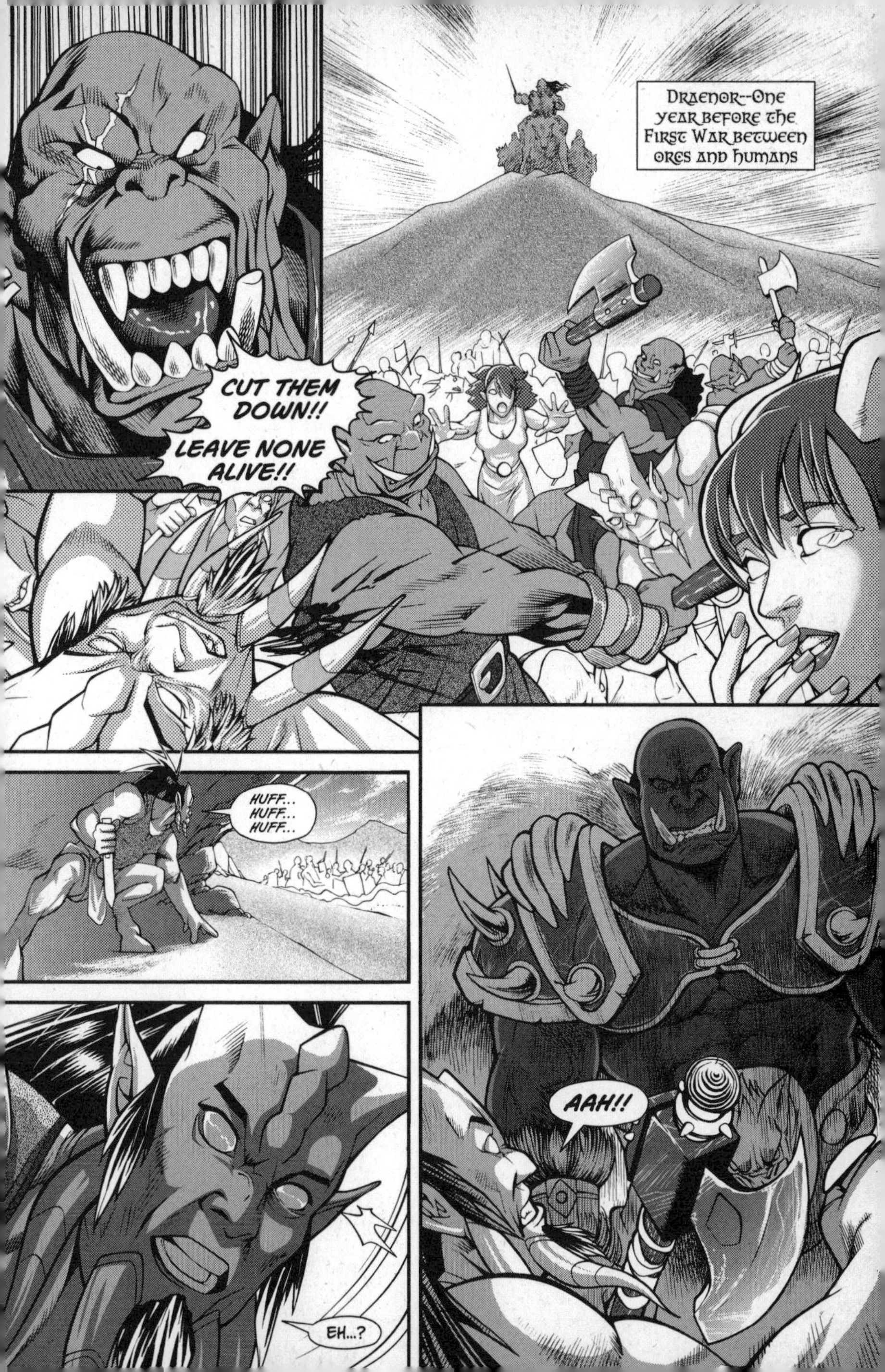
Draenor--One year before the First War between orcs and humans
CUT THEM DOWN!! LEAVE NONE ALIVE!!
HUFF... HUFF... HUFF...
EH...?
AAH!!

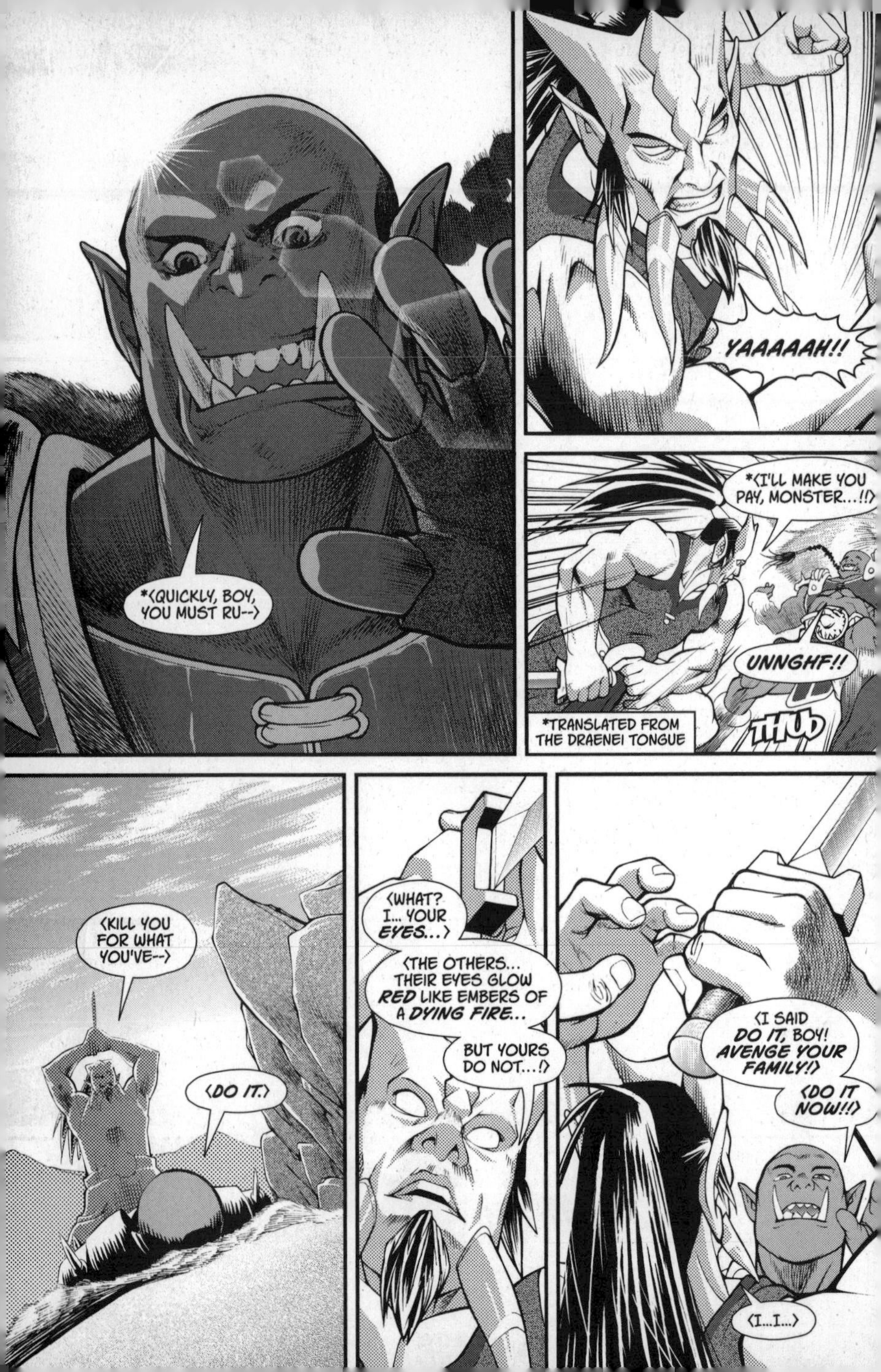
*‹QUICKLY, BOY, YOU MUST RU--›
YAAAAAH!!
*‹I'LL MAKE YOU PAY, MONSTER...!›
UNNGHF!!
*TRANSLATED FROM THE DRAENEI TONGUE
THUD
‹KILL YOU FOR WHAT YOU'VE--›
‹DO IT.›
‹WHAT? I... YOUR EYES...›
‹THE OTHERS... THEIR EYES GLOW RED LIKE EMBERS OF A DYING FIRE...
BUT YOURS DO NOT...!›
‹I SAID DO IT, BOY! AVENGE YOUR FAMILY!›
‹DO IT NOW!!›
‹I...I...›

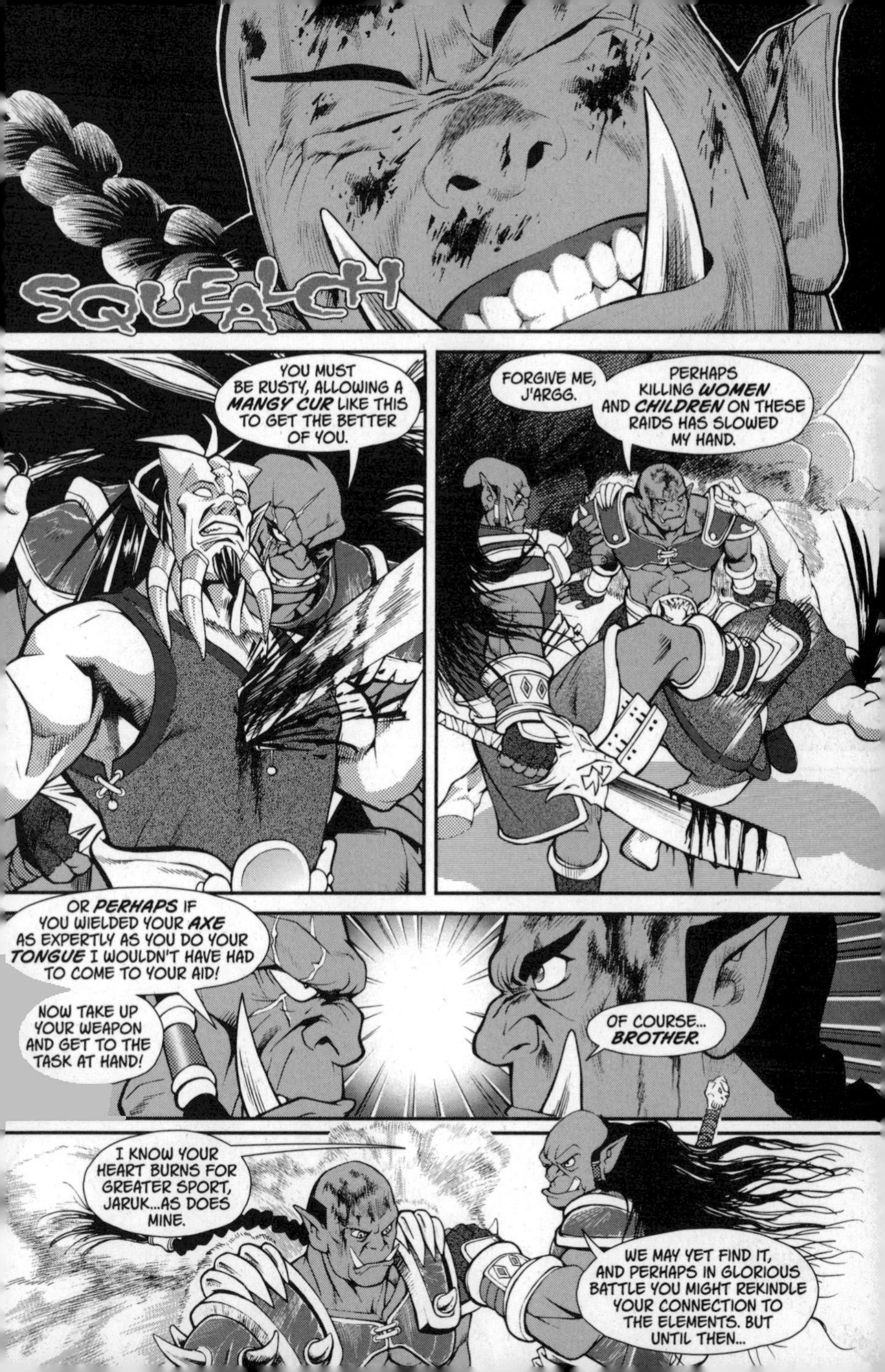
SQUEALCH
YOU MUST BE RUSTY, ALLOWING A MANGY CUR LIKE THIS TO GET THE BETTER OF YOU.
FORGIVE ME, J'ARGG.
PERHAPS KILLING WOMEN AND CHILDREN ON THESE RAIDS HAS SLOWED MY HAND.
OR PERHAPS IF YOU WIELDED YOUR AXE AS EXPERTLY AS YOU DO YOUR TONGUE I WOULDN'T HAVE HAD TO COME TO YOUR AID!
NOW TAKE UP YOUR WEAPON AND GET TO THE TASK AT HAND!
OF COURSE... BROTHER.
I KNOW YOUR HEART BURNS FOR GREATER SPORT, JARUK...AS DOES MINE.
WE MAY YET FIND IT, AND PERHAPS IN GLORIOUS BATTLE YOU MIGHT REKINDLE YOUR CONNECTION TO THE ELEMENTS. BUT UNTIL THEN...

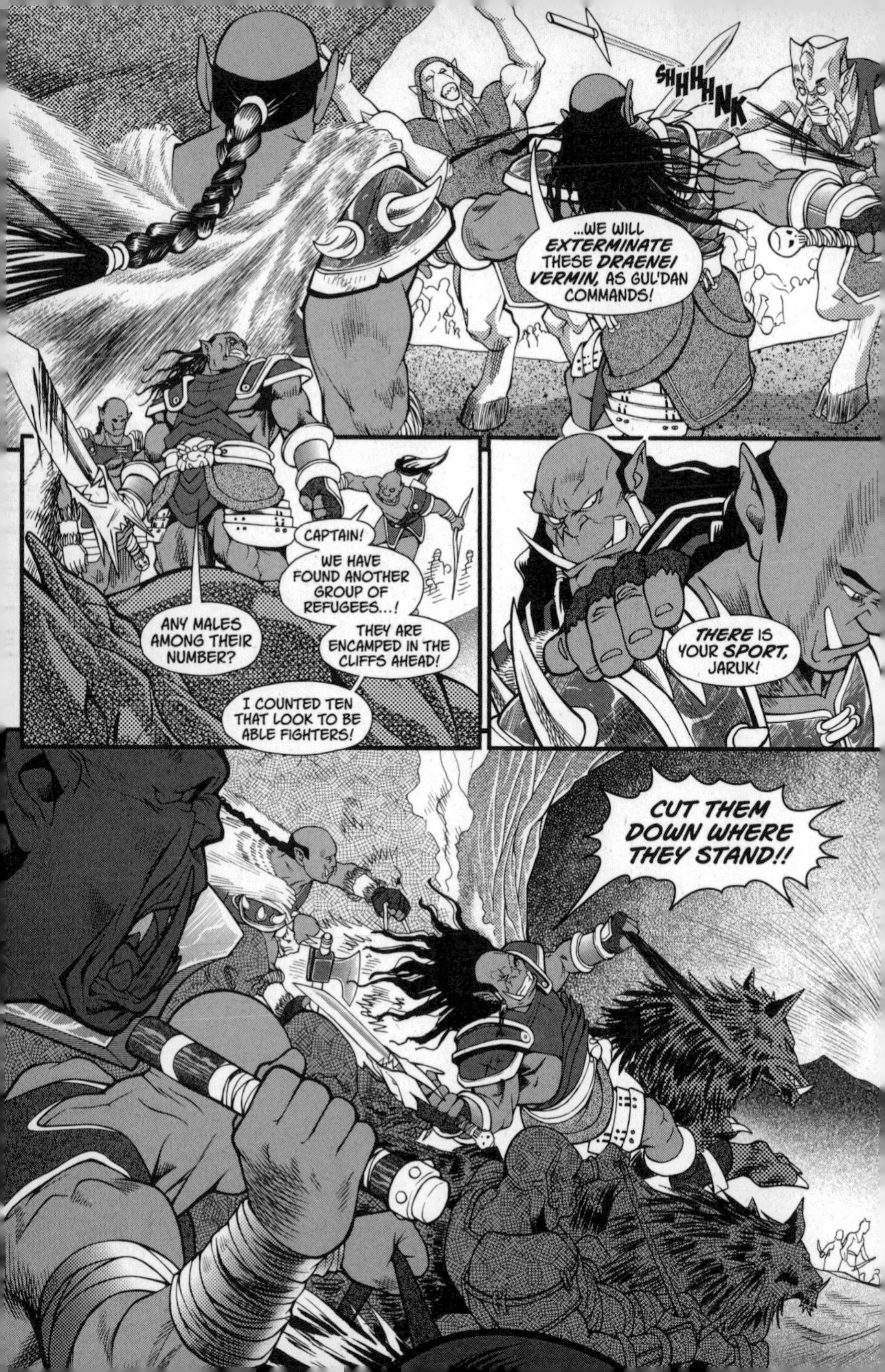
SHHHHNK
...WE WILL EXTERMINATE THESE DRAENEI VERMIN, AS GUL'DAN COMMANDS!
CAPTAIN!
WE HAVE FOUND ANOTHER GROUP OF REFUGEES...!
ANY MALES AMONG THEIR NUMBER?
THEY ARE ENCAMPED IN THE CLIFFS AHEAD!
I COUNTED TEN THAT LOOK TO BE ABLE FIGHTERS!
THERE IS YOUR SPORT, JARUK!
CUT THEM DOWN WHERE THEY STAND!!

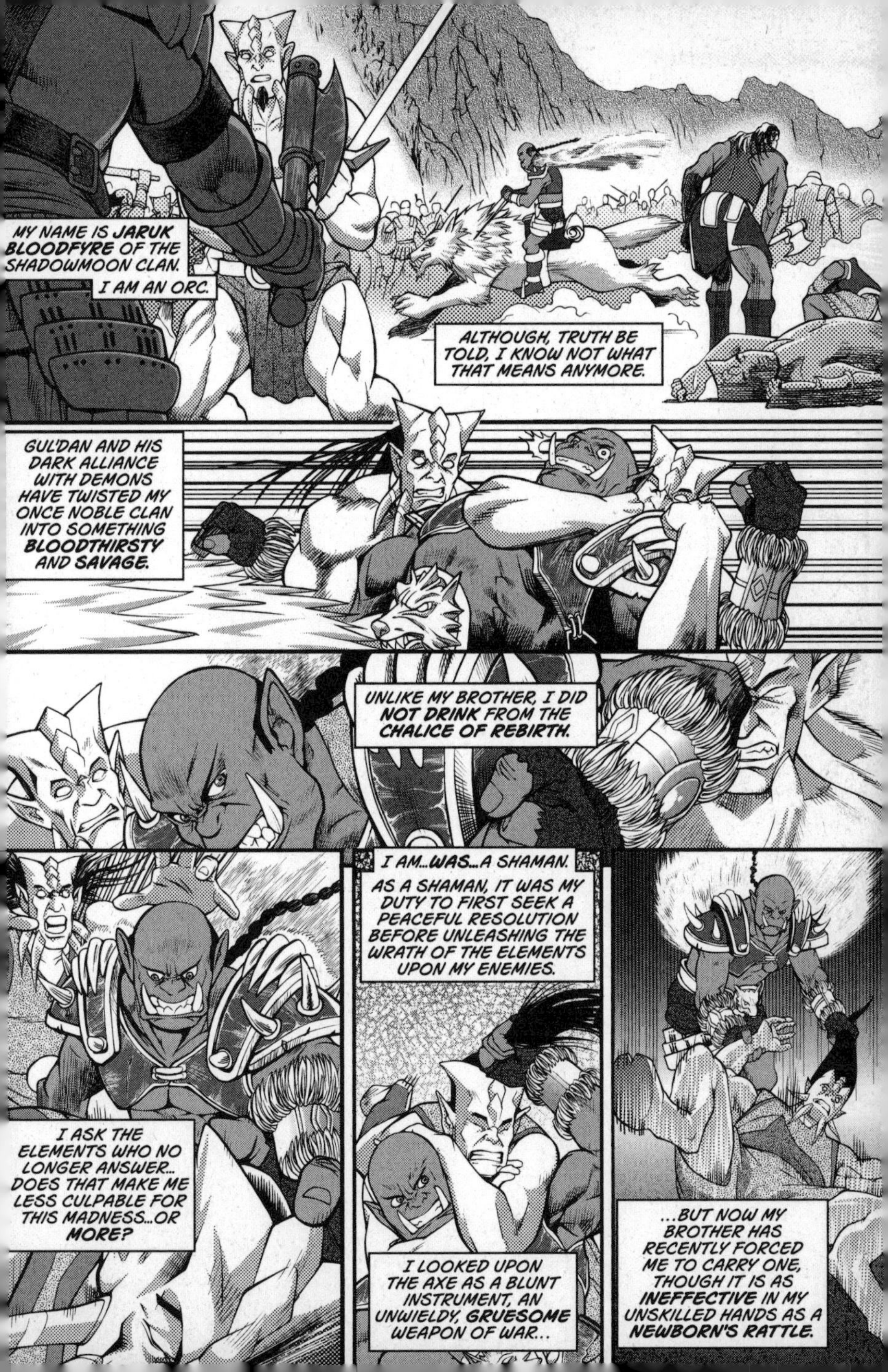
MY NAME IS **JARUK BLOODFYRE** OF THE SHADOWMOON CLAN.
I AM AN ORC.
ALTHOUGH, TRUTH BE TOLD, I KNOW NOT WHAT THAT MEANS ANYMORE.
GUL'DAN AND HIS DARK ALLIANCE WITH DEMONS HAVE TWISTED MY ONCE NOBLE CLAN INTO SOMETHING **BLOODTHIRSTY** AND **SAVAGE.**
UNLIKE MY BROTHER, I DID **NOT DRINK** FROM THE **CHALICE OF REBIRTH.**
I ASK THE ELEMENTS WHO NO LONGER ANSWER... DOES THAT MAKE ME LESS CULPABLE FOR THIS MADNESS...OR **MORE?**
I AM...**WAS**...A SHAMAN.
AS A SHAMAN, IT WAS MY DUTY TO FIRST SEEK A PEACEFUL RESOLUTION BEFORE UNLEASHING THE WRATH OF THE ELEMENTS UPON MY ENEMIES.
I LOOKED UPON THE AXE AS A BLUNT INSTRUMENT, AN UNWIELDY, **GRUESOME** WEAPON OF WAR...
...BUT NOW MY BROTHER HAS RECENTLY FORCED ME TO CARRY ONE, THOUGH IT IS AS **INEFFECTIVE** IN MY UNSKILLED HANDS AS A **NEWBORN'S RATTLE.**

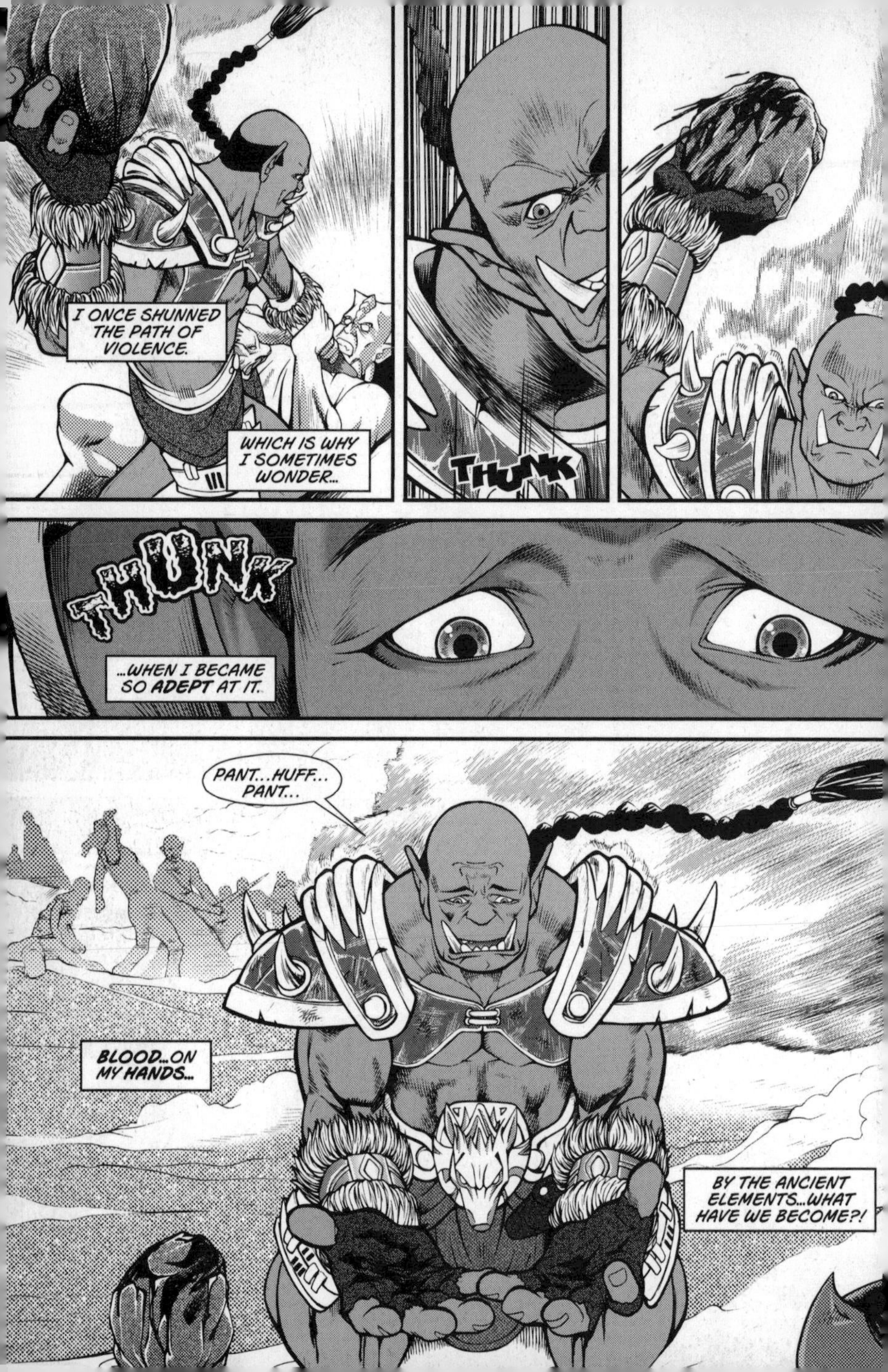
I ONCE SHUNNED THE PATH OF VIOLENCE.
WHICH IS WHY I SOMETIMES WONDER...
THUNK
THUNK
...WHEN I BECAME SO ADEPT AT IT.
PANT...HUFF... PANT...
BLOOD...ON MY HANDS...
BY THE ANCIENT ELEMENTS...WHAT HAVE WE BECOME?!

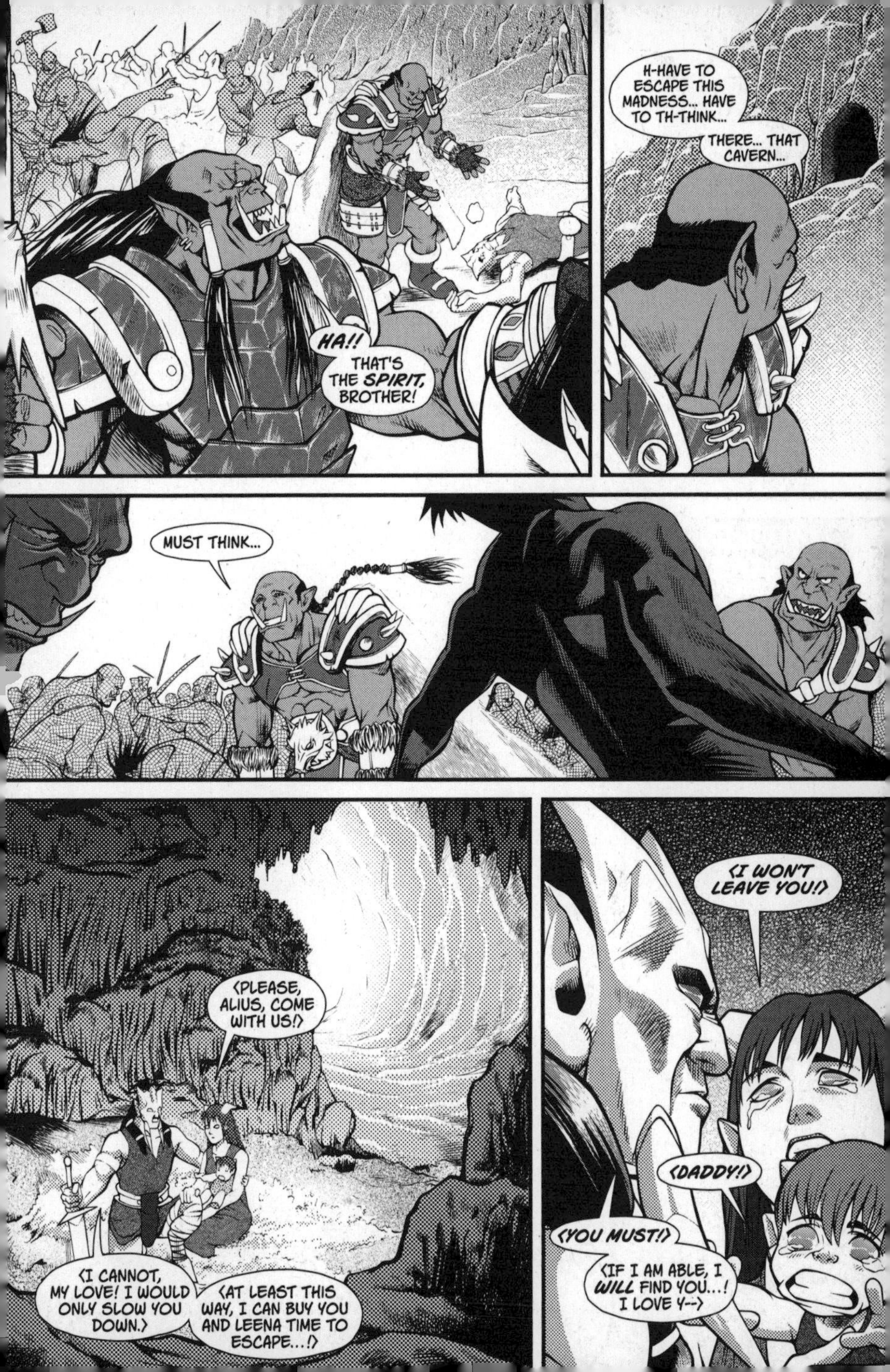
HA!! THAT'S THE SPIRIT, BROTHER!
H-HAVE TO ESCAPE THIS MADNESS... HAVE TO TH-THINK...
THERE... THAT CAVERN...
MUST THINK...
‹PLEASE, ALIUS, COME WITH US!›
‹I CANNOT, MY LOVE! I WOULD ONLY SLOW YOU DOWN.›
‹AT LEAST THIS WAY, I CAN BUY YOU AND LEENA TIME TO ESCAPE...!›
‹I WON'T LEAVE YOU!›
‹DADDY!›
‹YOU MUST!›
‹IF I AM ABLE, I WILL FIND YOU...! I LOVE Y--›

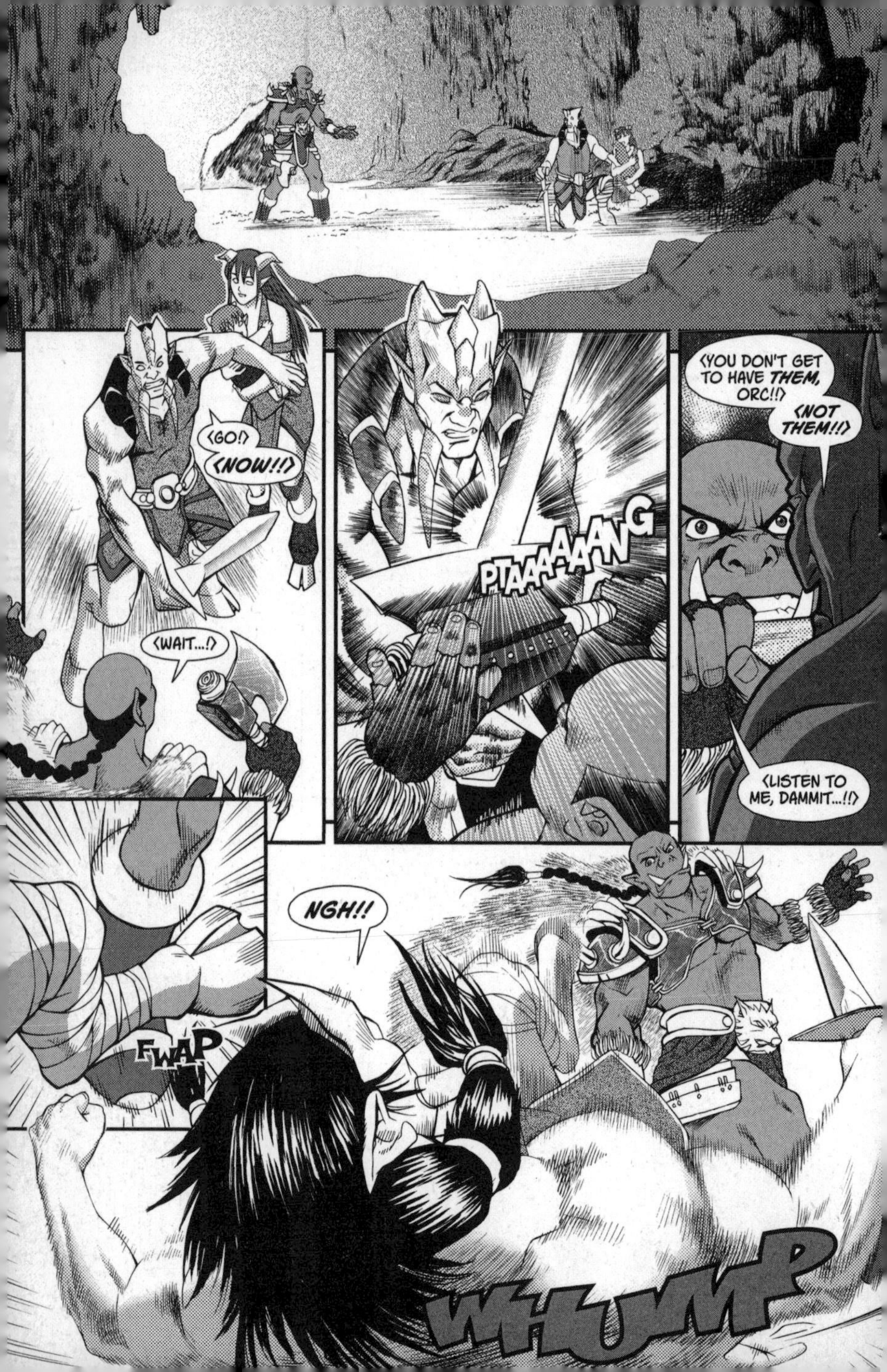

<GO!>
<NOW!!>
<WAIT...!>
PTAAAAAANG
<YOU DON'T GET TO HAVE THEM, ORC!!>
<NOT THEM!!>
<LISTEN TO ME, DAMMIT...!!>
FWAP
NGH!!
WHUMP

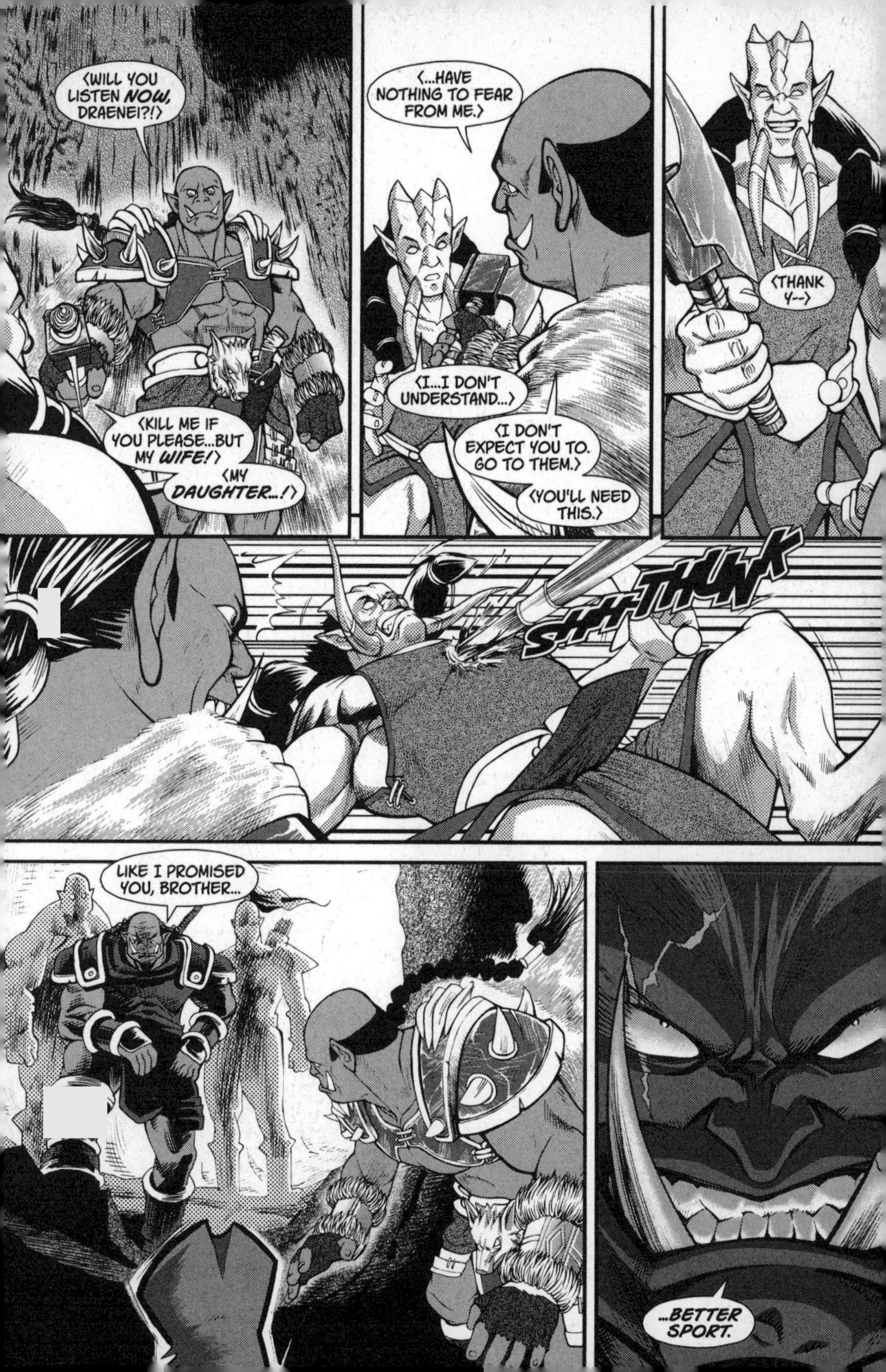

<WILL YOU LISTEN NOW, DRAENEI?!>
<KILL ME IF YOU PLEASE...BUT MY WIFE!>
<MY DAUGHTER...!>
<...HAVE NOTHING TO FEAR FROM ME.>
<I...I DON'T UNDERSTAND...>
<I DON'T EXPECT YOU TO. GO TO THEM.>
<YOU'LL NEED THIS.>
<THANK Y-->
SHHHTHUNK
LIKE I PROMISED YOU, BROTHER...
...BETTER SPORT.

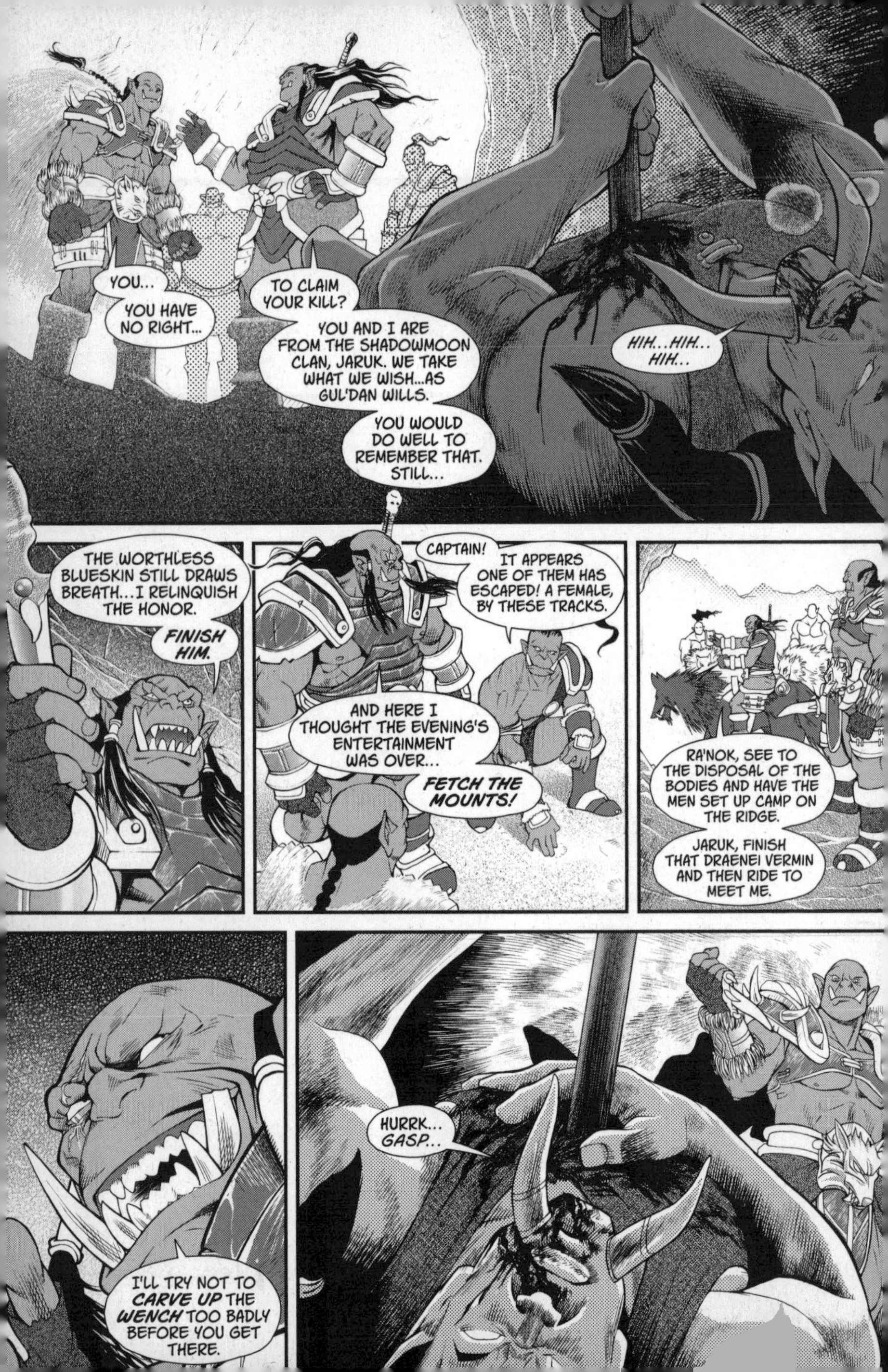
YOU...
YOU HAVE NO RIGHT...
TO CLAIM YOUR KILL?
YOU AND I ARE FROM THE SHADOWMOON CLAN, JARUK. WE TAKE WHAT WE WISH...AS GUL'DAN WILLS.
YOU WOULD DO WELL TO REMEMBER THAT. STILL...
HIH...HIH... HIH...
THE WORTHLESS BLUESKIN STILL DRAWS BREATH...I RELINQUISH THE HONOR.
FINISH HIM.
CAPTAIN!
IT APPEARS ONE OF THEM HAS ESCAPED! A FEMALE, BY THESE TRACKS.
AND HERE I THOUGHT THE EVENING'S ENTERTAINMENT WAS OVER...
FETCH THE MOUNTS!
RA'NOK, SEE TO THE DISPOSAL OF THE BODIES AND HAVE THE MEN SET UP CAMP ON THE RIDGE.
JARUK, FINISH THAT DRAENEI VERMIN AND THEN RIDE TO MEET ME.
I'LL TRY NOT TO CARVE UP THE WENCH TOO BADLY BEFORE YOU GET THERE.
HURRK... GASP...

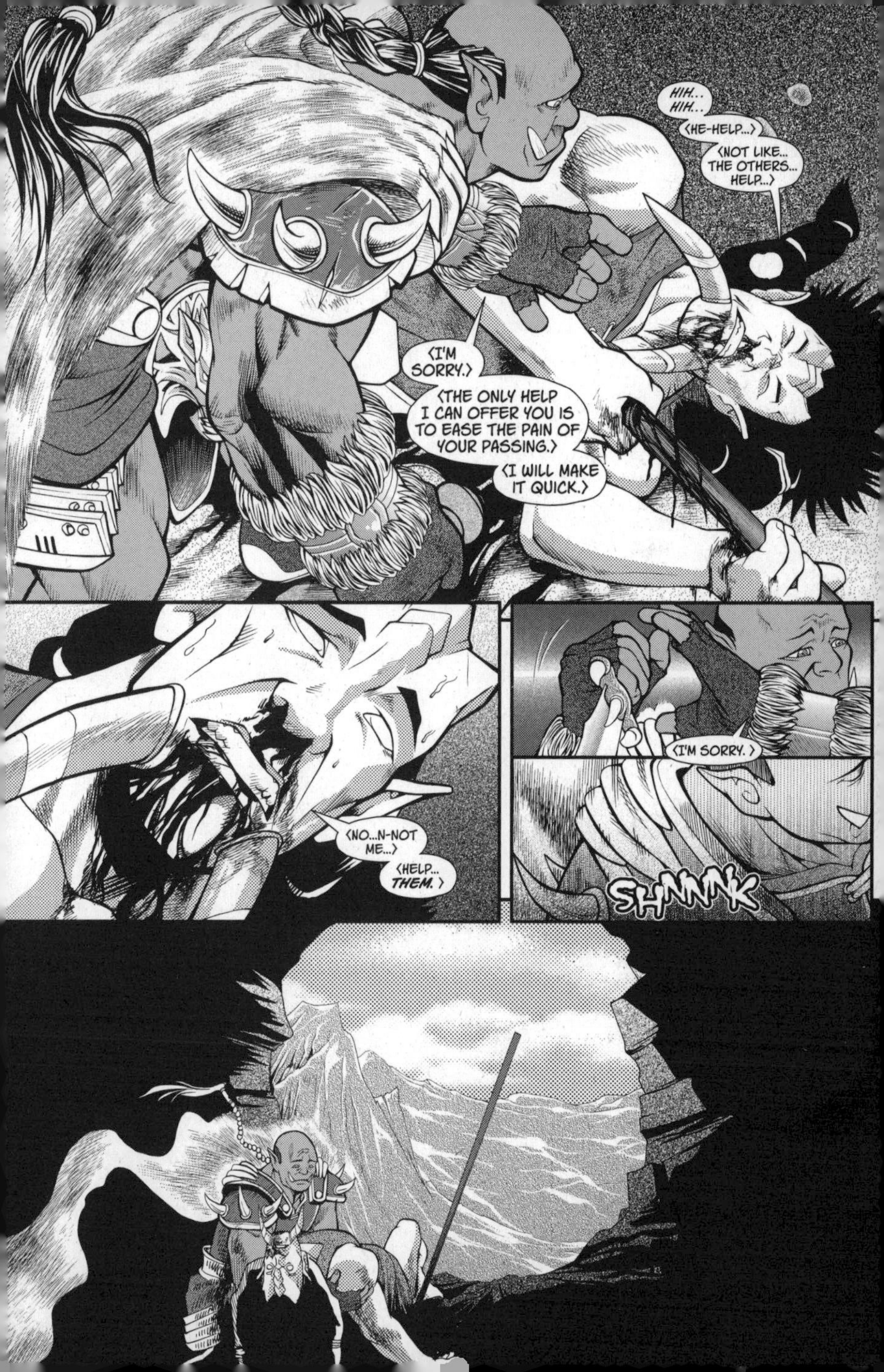

HIH... HIH...
<HE-HELP...>
<NOT LIKE... THE OTHERS... HELP...>
<I'M SORRY.>
<THE ONLY HELP I CAN OFFER YOU IS TO EASE THE PAIN OF YOUR PASSING.>
<I WILL MAKE IT QUICK.>
<NO...N-NOT ME...>
<HELP... *THEM.*>
<I'M SORRY.>
SHNNNK

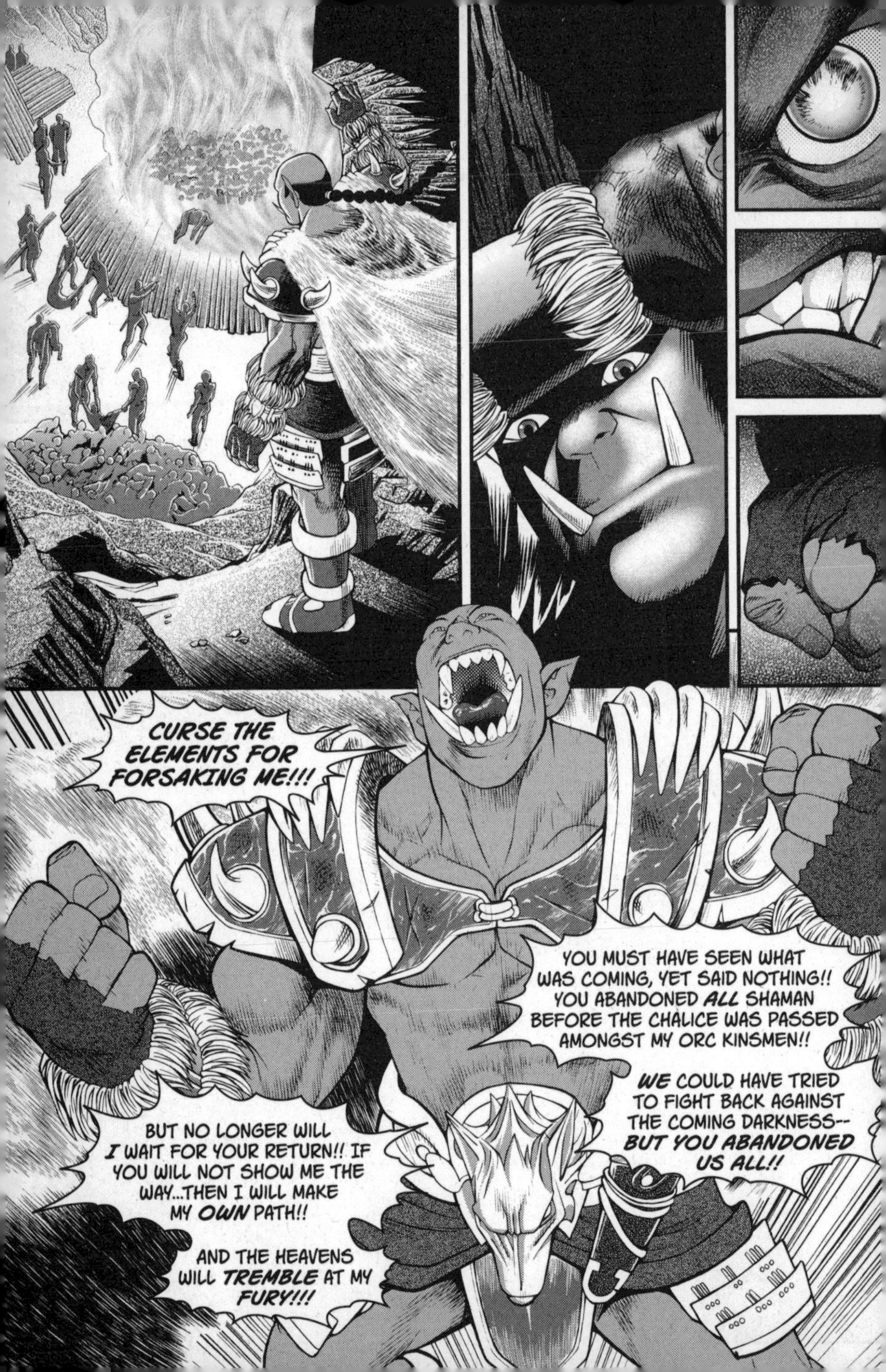
CURSE THE ELEMENTS FOR FORSAKING ME!!!
YOU MUST HAVE SEEN WHAT WAS COMING, YET SAID NOTHING!! YOU ABANDONED ALL SHAMAN BEFORE THE CHALICE WAS PASSED AMONGST MY ORC KINSMEN!!
WE COULD HAVE TRIED TO FIGHT BACK AGAINST THE COMING DARKNESS-- BUT YOU ABANDONED US ALL!!
BUT NO LONGER WILL I WAIT FOR YOUR RETURN!! IF YOU WILL NOT SHOW ME THE WAY...THEN I WILL MAKE MY OWN PATH!!
AND THE HEAVENS WILL TREMBLE AT MY FURY!!!

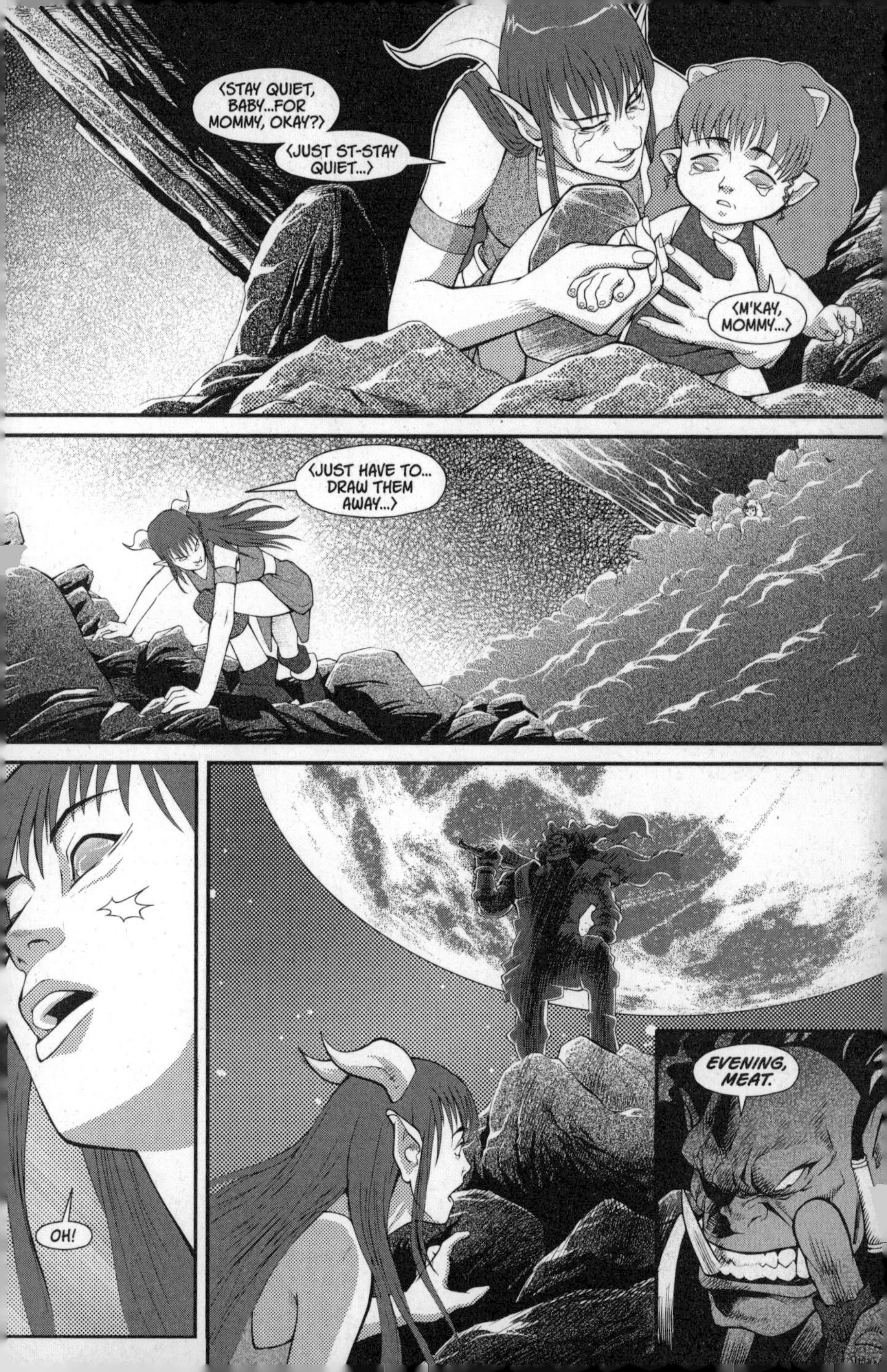

⟨STAY QUIET, BABY...FOR MOMMY, OKAY?⟩
⟨JUST ST-STAY QUIET...⟩
⟨M'KAY, MOMMY...⟩
⟨JUST HAVE TO... DRAW THEM AWAY...⟩
OH!
EVENING, MEAT.

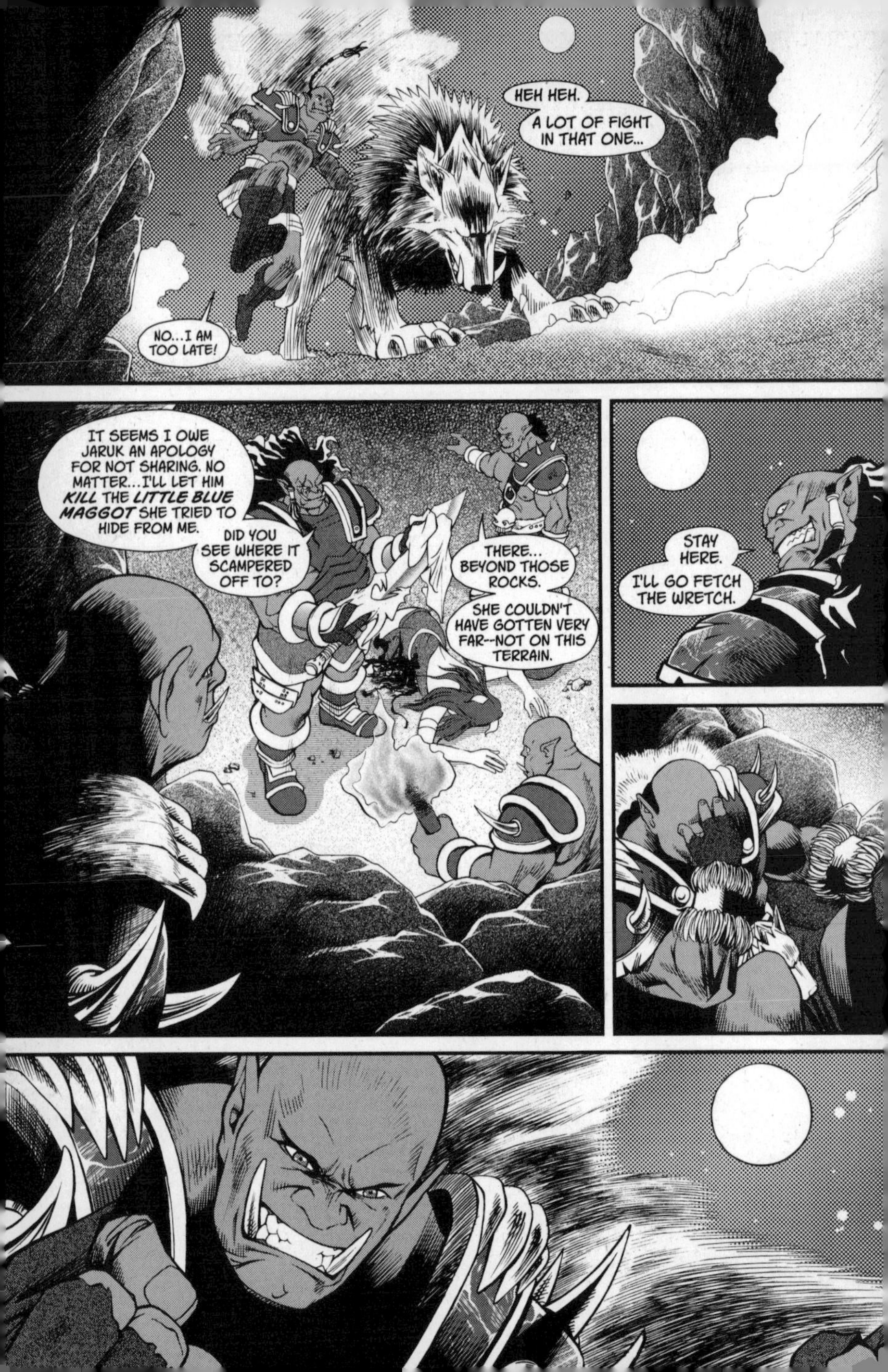
HEH HEH.
A LOT OF FIGHT IN THAT ONE...
NO...I AM TOO LATE!
IT SEEMS I OWE JARUK AN APOLOGY FOR NOT SHARING. NO MATTER...I'LL LET HIM *KILL* THE *LITTLE BLUE MAGGOT* SHE TRIED TO HIDE FROM ME.
DID YOU SEE WHERE IT SCAMPERED OFF TO?
THERE... BEYOND THOSE ROCKS.
SHE COULDN'T HAVE GOTTEN VERY FAR--NOT ON THIS TERRAIN.
STAY HERE.
I'LL GO FETCH THE WRETCH.

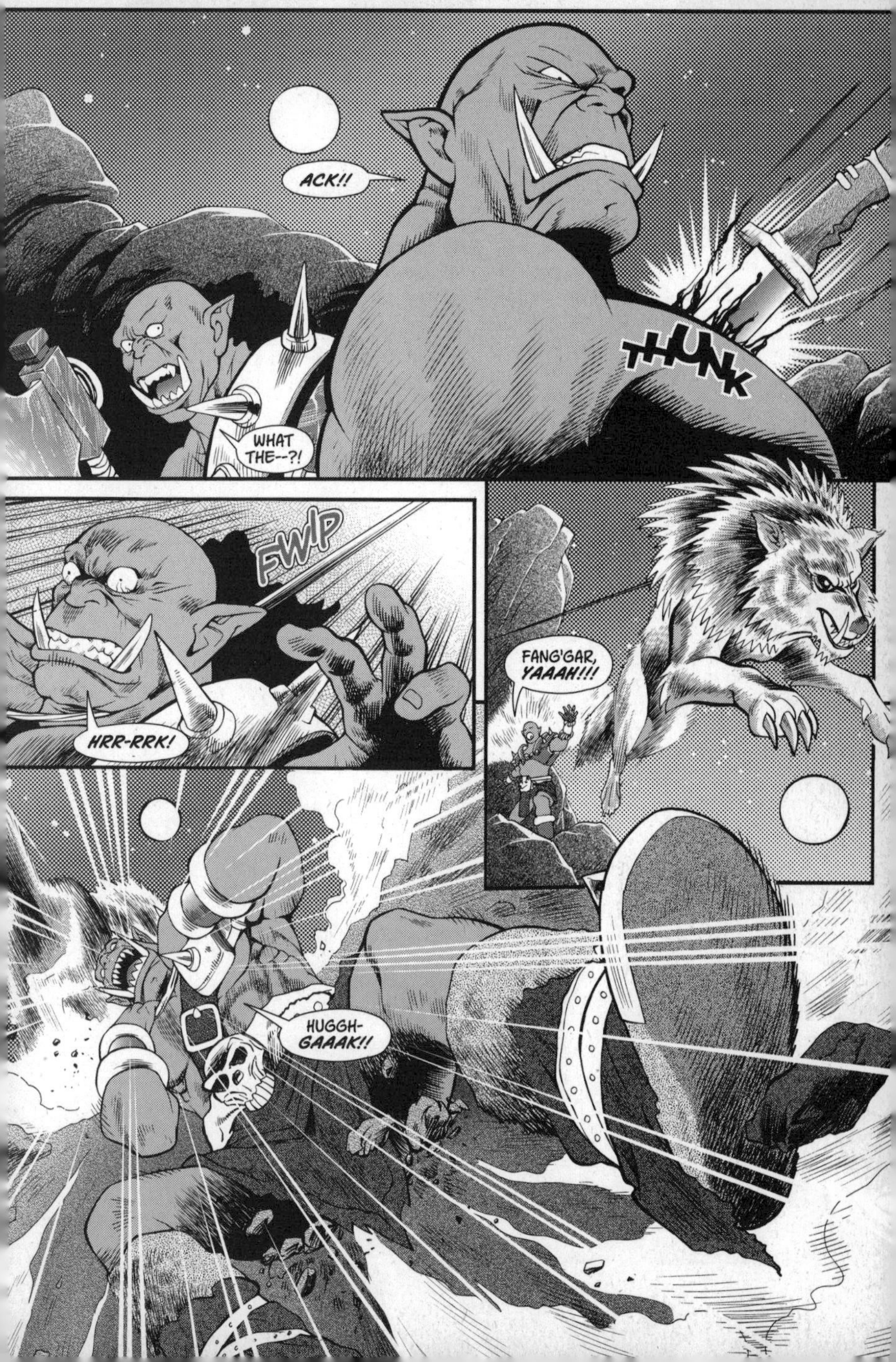
ACK!!
THUNK
WHAT THE--?!
FWIP
HRR-RRK!
FANG'GAR, YAAAH!!!
HUGGH-GAAAK!!

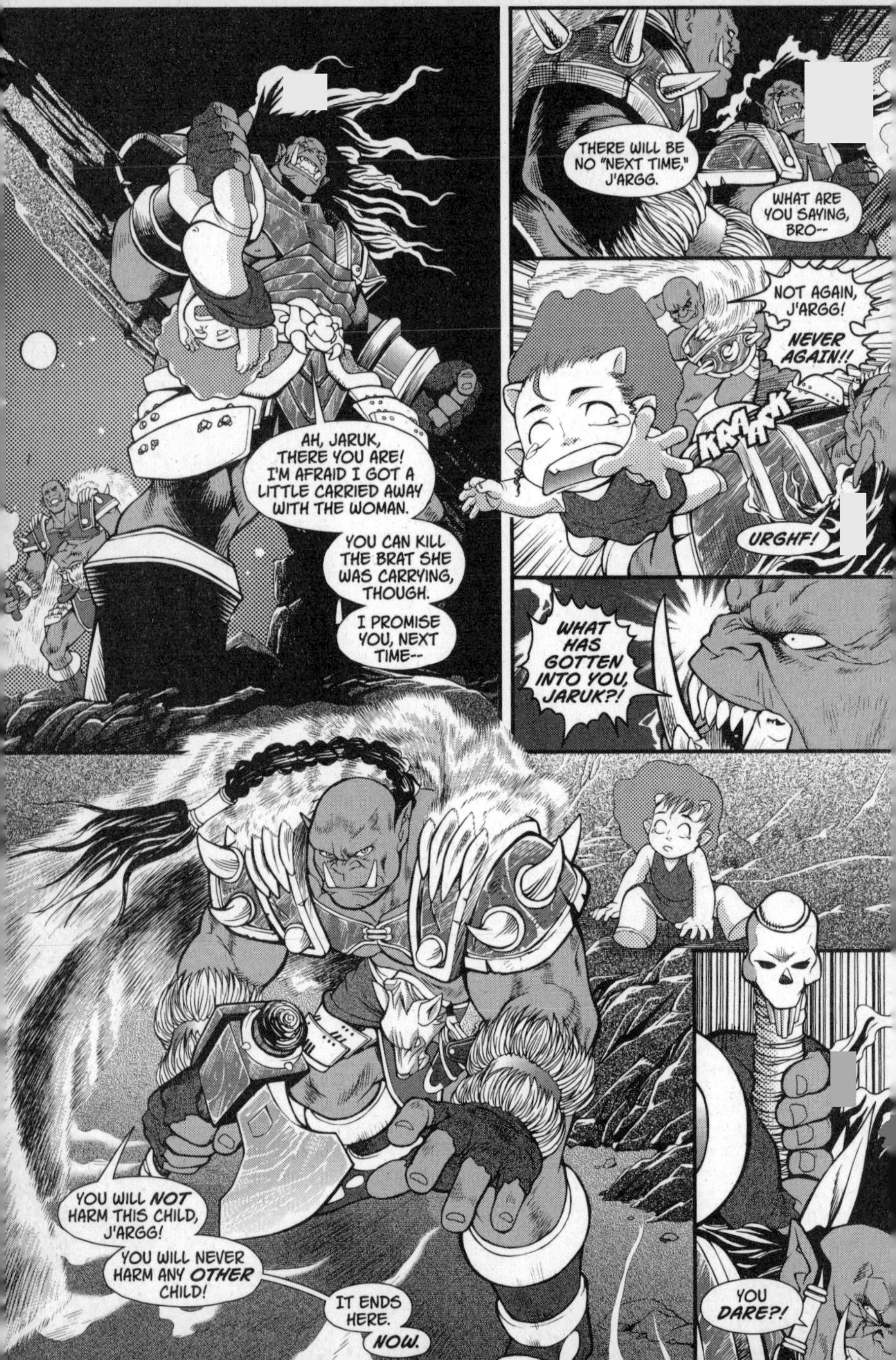
AH, JARUK, THERE YOU ARE! I'M AFRAID I GOT A LITTLE CARRIED AWAY WITH THE WOMAN.
YOU CAN KILL THE BRAT SHE WAS CARRYING, THOUGH.
I PROMISE YOU, NEXT TIME--
THERE WILL BE NO "NEXT TIME," J'ARGG.
WHAT ARE YOU SAYING, BRO--
NOT AGAIN, J'ARGG! NEVER AGAIN!!
KRAAAK
URGHF!
WHAT HAS GOTTEN INTO YOU, JARUK?!
YOU WILL NOT HARM THIS CHILD, J'ARGG!
YOU WILL NEVER HARM ANY OTHER CHILD!
IT ENDS HERE. NOW.
YOU DARE?!

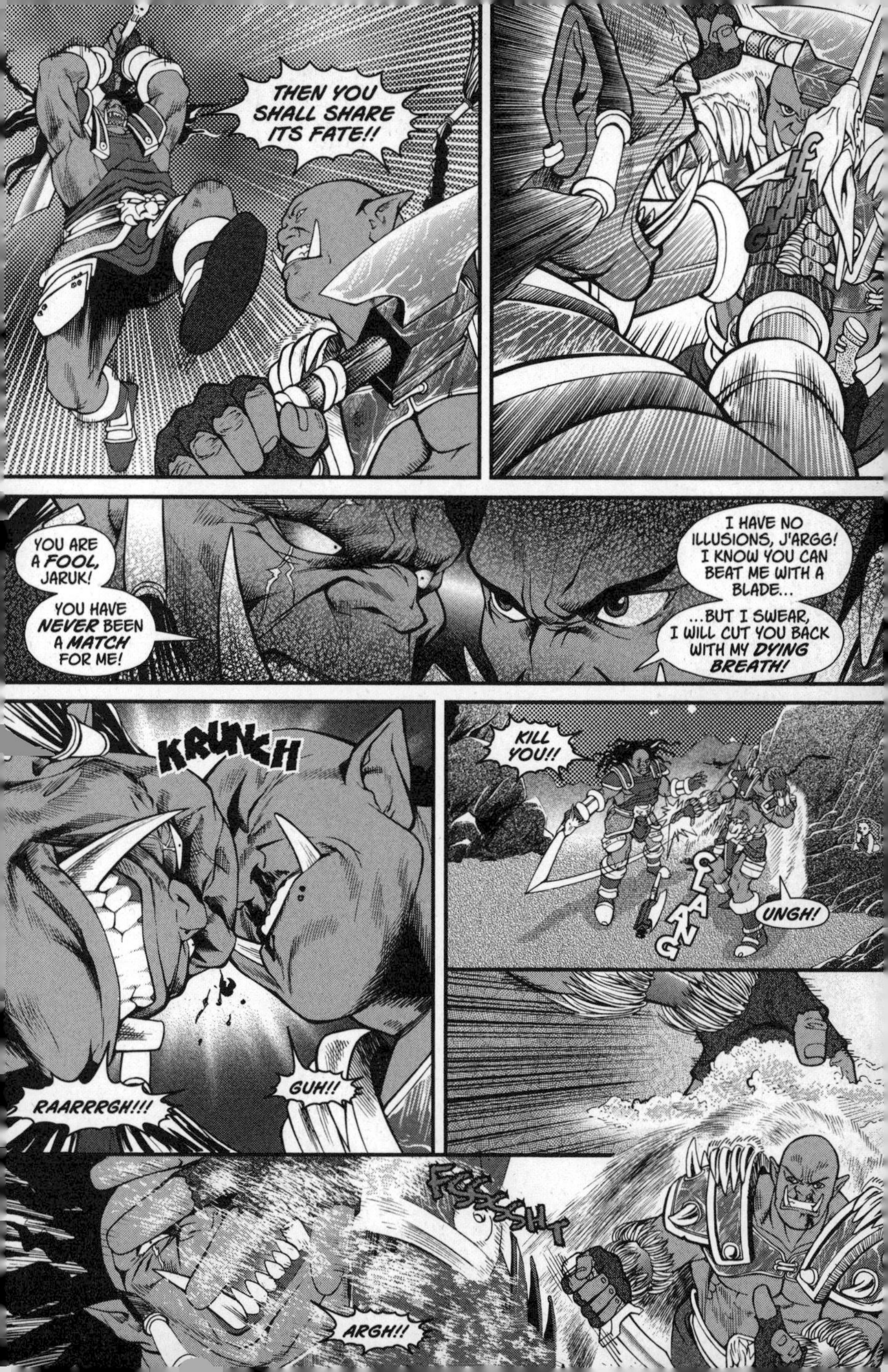
THEN YOU SHALL SHARE ITS FATE!!
YOU ARE A FOOL, JARUK!
YOU HAVE NEVER BEEN A MATCH FOR ME!
I HAVE NO ILLUSIONS, J'ARGG! I KNOW YOU CAN BEAT ME WITH A BLADE...
...BUT I SWEAR, I WILL CUT YOU BACK WITH MY DYING BREATH!
KRUNCH
GUH!!
RAARRRGH!!!
KILL YOU!!
CLANG
UNGH!
ARGH!!

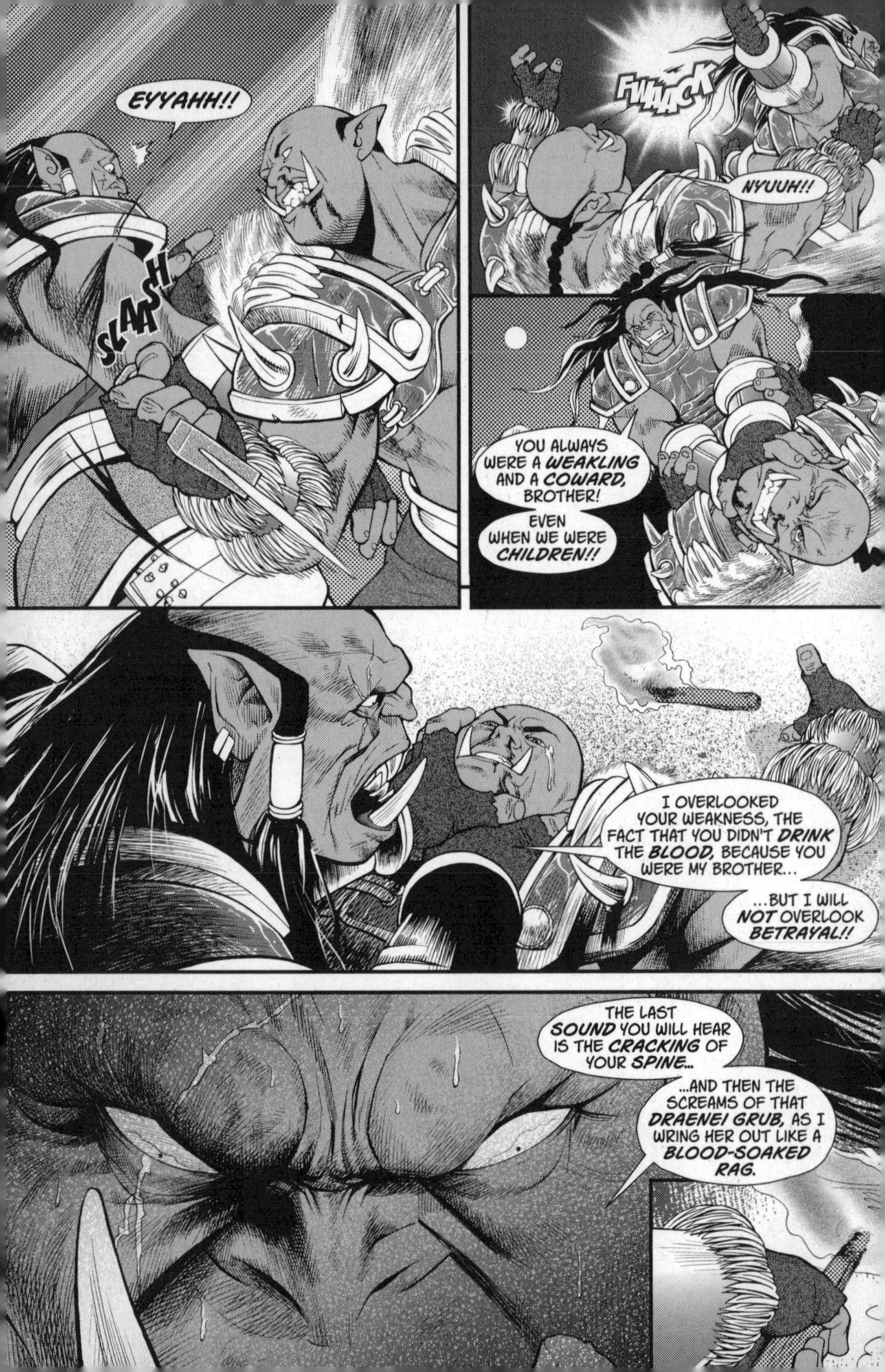
EYYAHH!!
SLAASH
FWAAACK
NYUUH!!
YOU ALWAYS WERE A WEAKLING AND A COWARD, BROTHER!
EVEN WHEN WE WERE CHILDREN!!
I OVERLOOKED YOUR WEAKNESS, THE FACT THAT YOU DIDN'T DRINK THE BLOOD, BECAUSE YOU WERE MY BROTHER...
...BUT I WILL NOT OVERLOOK BETRAYAL!!
THE LAST SOUND YOU WILL HEAR IS THE CRACKING OF YOUR SPINE...
...AND THEN THE SCREAMS OF THAT DRAENEI GRUB, AS I WRING HER OUT LIKE A BLOOD-SOAKED RAG.

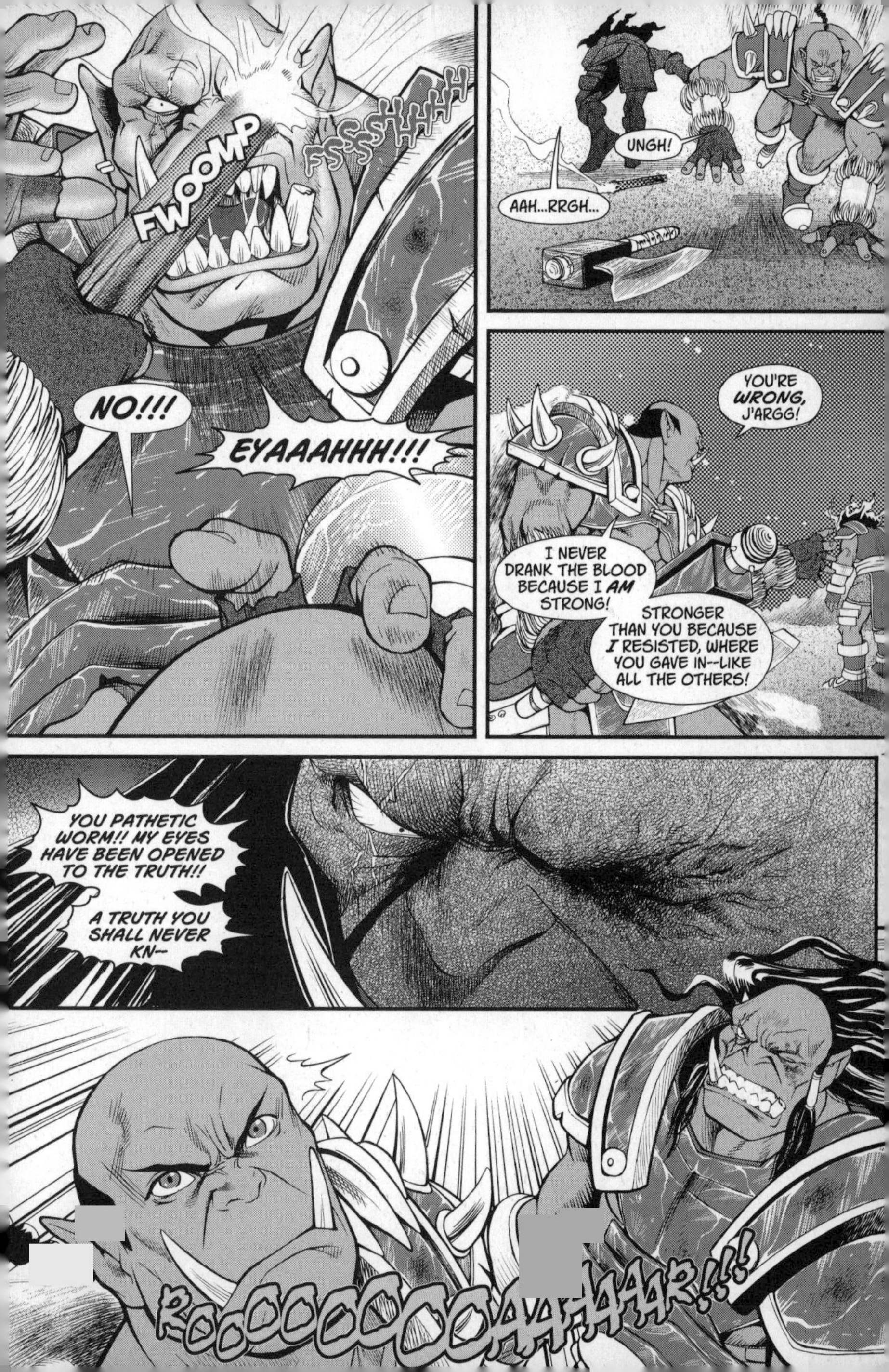
FWOOMP
FSSSHHHH
NO!!!
EYAAAHHH!!!
UNGH!
AAH...RRGH...
YOU'RE WRONG, J'ARGG!
I NEVER DRANK THE BLOOD BECAUSE I AM STRONG!
STRONGER THAN YOU BECAUSE I RESISTED, WHERE YOU GAVE IN--LIKE ALL THE OTHERS!
YOU PATHETIC WORM!! MY EYES HAVE BEEN OPENED TO THE TRUTH!!
A TRUTH YOU SHALL NEVER KN--
ROOOOOOOOOAAAAAAR!!!

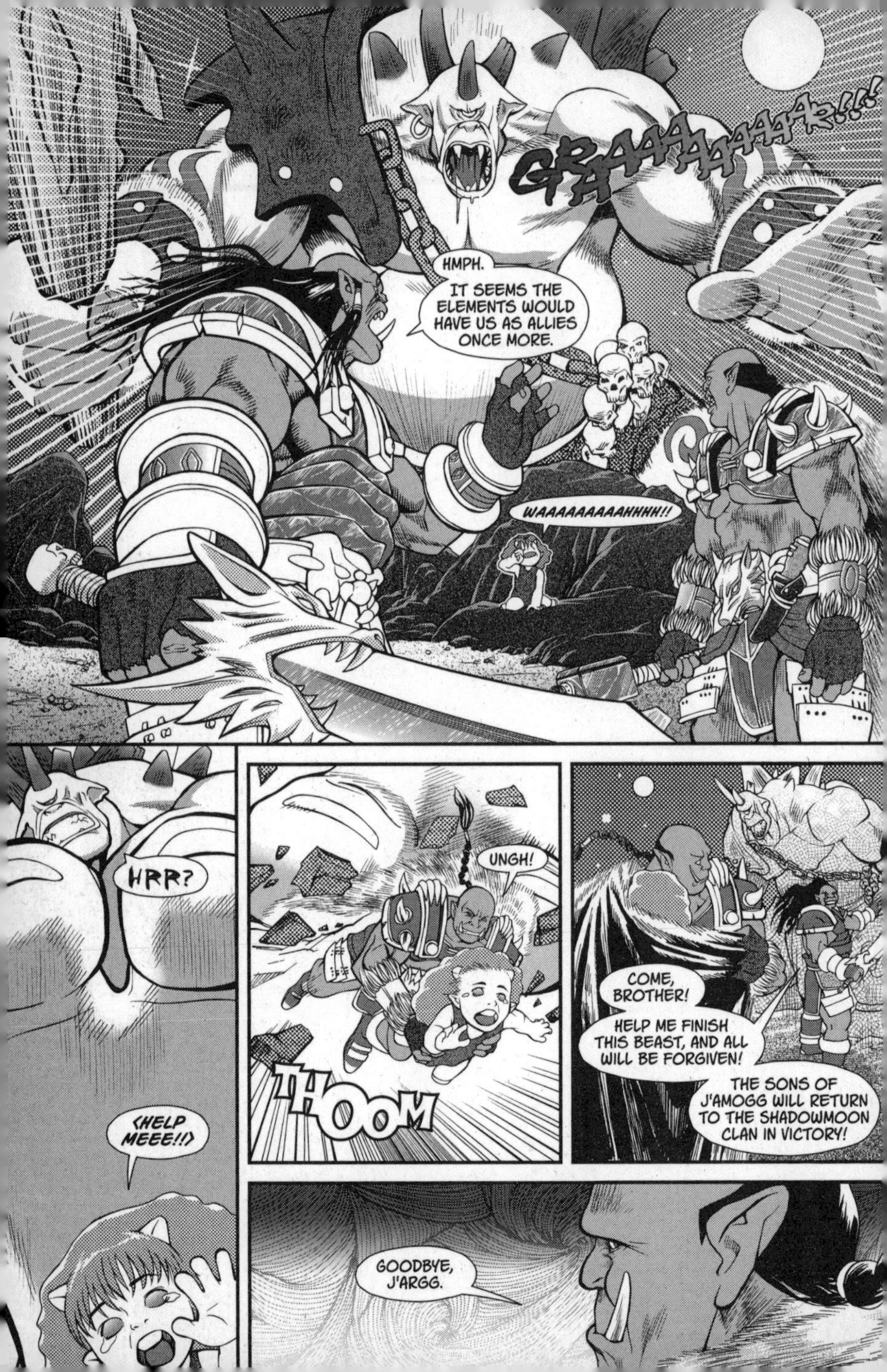
GRAAAAAAAAAR!!!
HMPH.
IT SEEMS THE ELEMENTS WOULD HAVE US AS ALLIES ONCE MORE.
WAAAAAAAAAHHHH!!
HRR?
‹HELP MEEE!!›
UNGH!
THOOM
COME, BROTHER!
HELP ME FINISH THIS BEAST, AND ALL WILL BE FORGIVEN!
THE SONS OF J'AMOGG WILL RETURN TO THE SHADOWMOON CLAN IN VICTORY!
GOODBYE, J'ARGG.

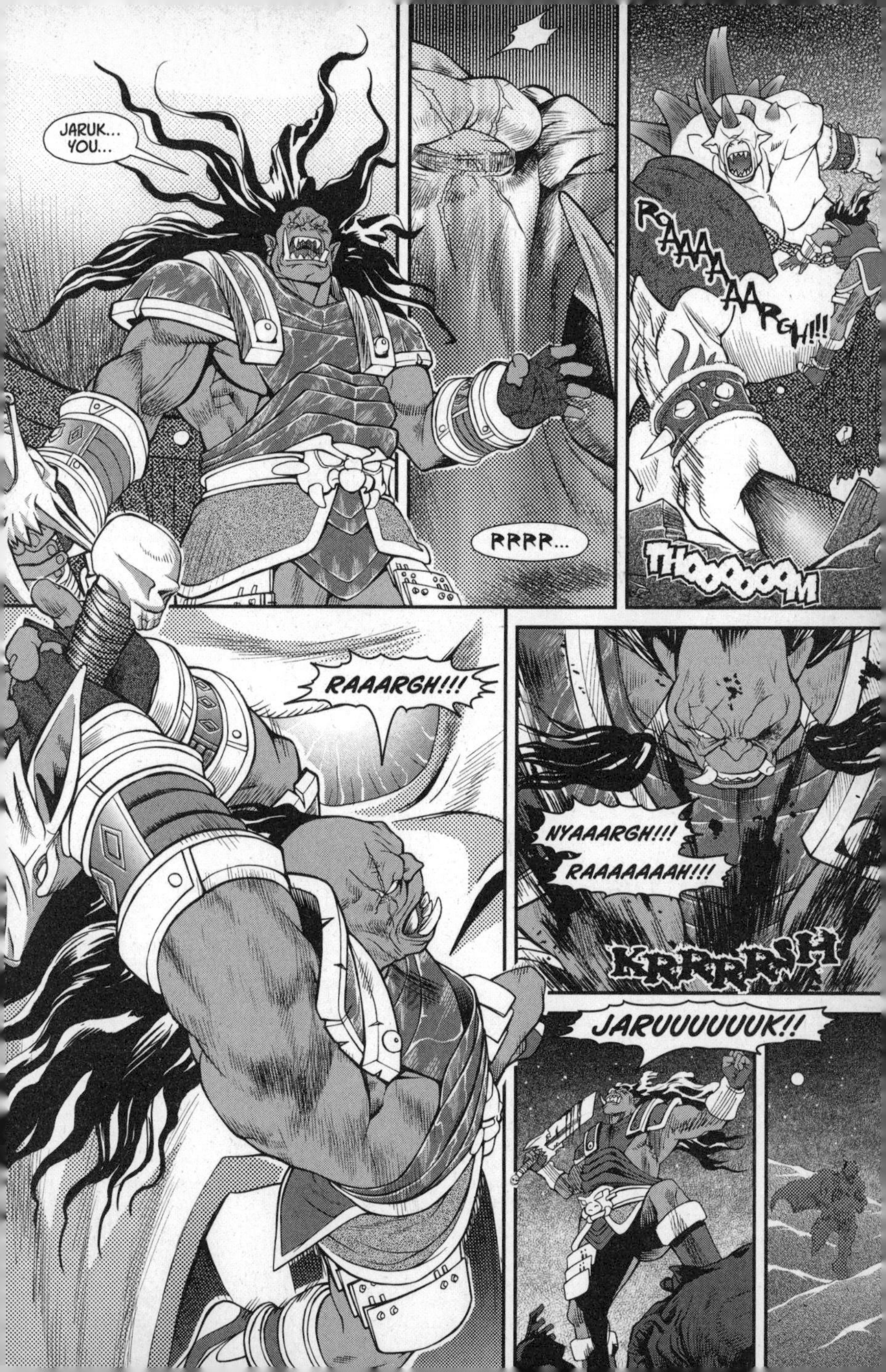
JARUK... YOU...
RRRR...
ROAAAAAAARGH!!!
THOOOOOOM
RAAARGH!!!
NYAAARGH!!!
RAAAAAAAH!!!
KRRRRRSH
JARUUUUUUK!!

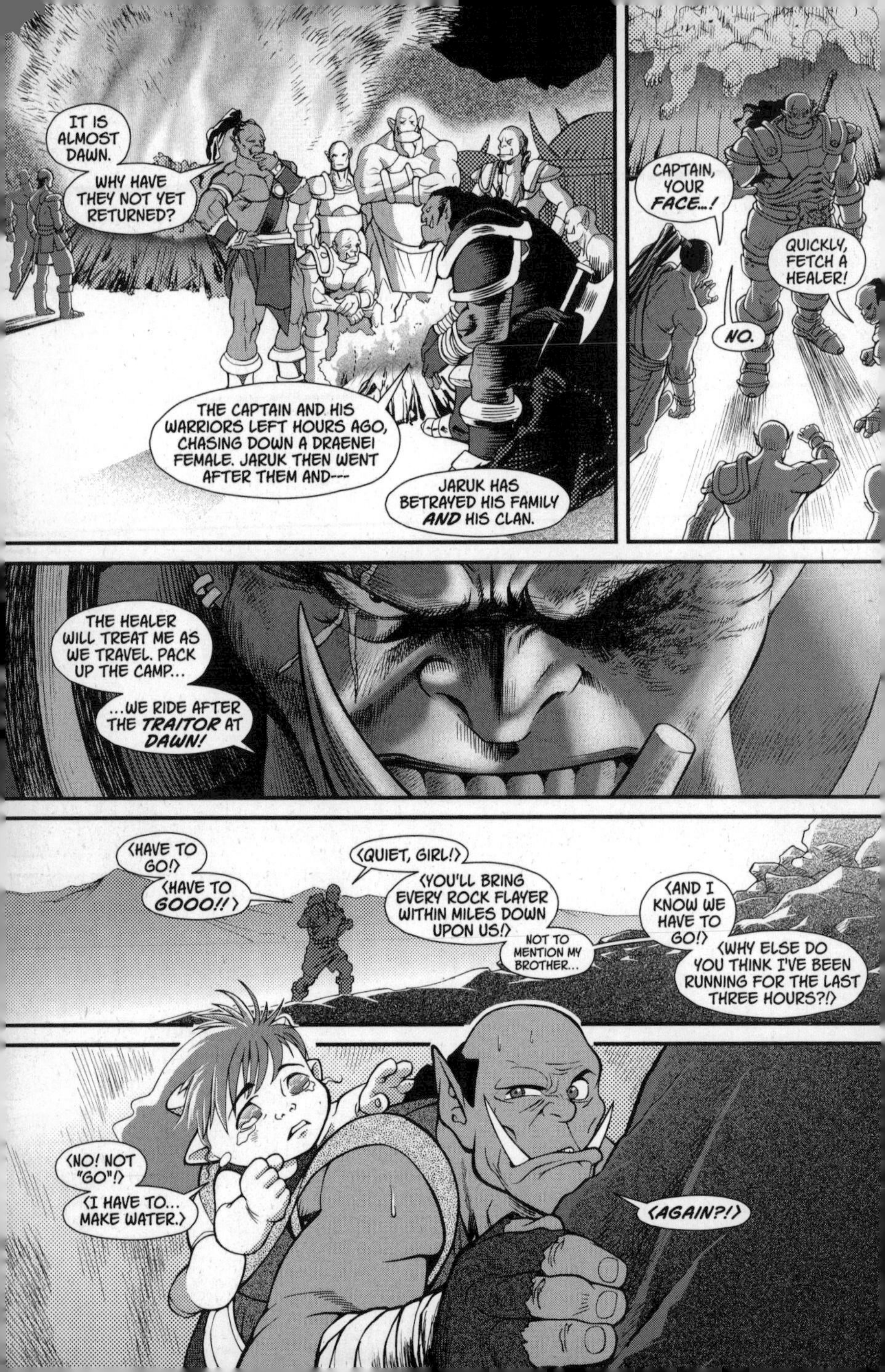
IT IS ALMOST DAWN.
WHY HAVE THEY NOT YET RETURNED?
THE CAPTAIN AND HIS WARRIORS LEFT HOURS AGO, CHASING DOWN A DRAENEI FEMALE. JARUK THEN WENT AFTER THEM AND---
JARUK HAS BETRAYED HIS FAMILY *AND* HIS CLAN.
CAPTAIN, YOUR *FACE*...!
QUICKLY, FETCH A HEALER!
NO.
THE HEALER WILL TREAT ME AS WE TRAVEL. PACK UP THE CAMP...
...WE RIDE AFTER THE *TRAITOR* AT *DAWN!*
‹HAVE TO GO!›
‹HAVE TO *GOOO!!*›
‹QUIET, GIRL!›
‹YOU'LL BRING EVERY ROCK FLAYER WITHIN MILES DOWN UPON US!›
NOT TO MENTION MY BROTHER...
‹AND I KNOW WE HAVE TO GO!›
‹WHY ELSE DO YOU THINK I'VE BEEN RUNNING FOR THE LAST THREE HOURS?!›
‹NO! NOT "GO"!›
‹I HAVE TO... MAKE WATER.›
‹AGAIN?!›

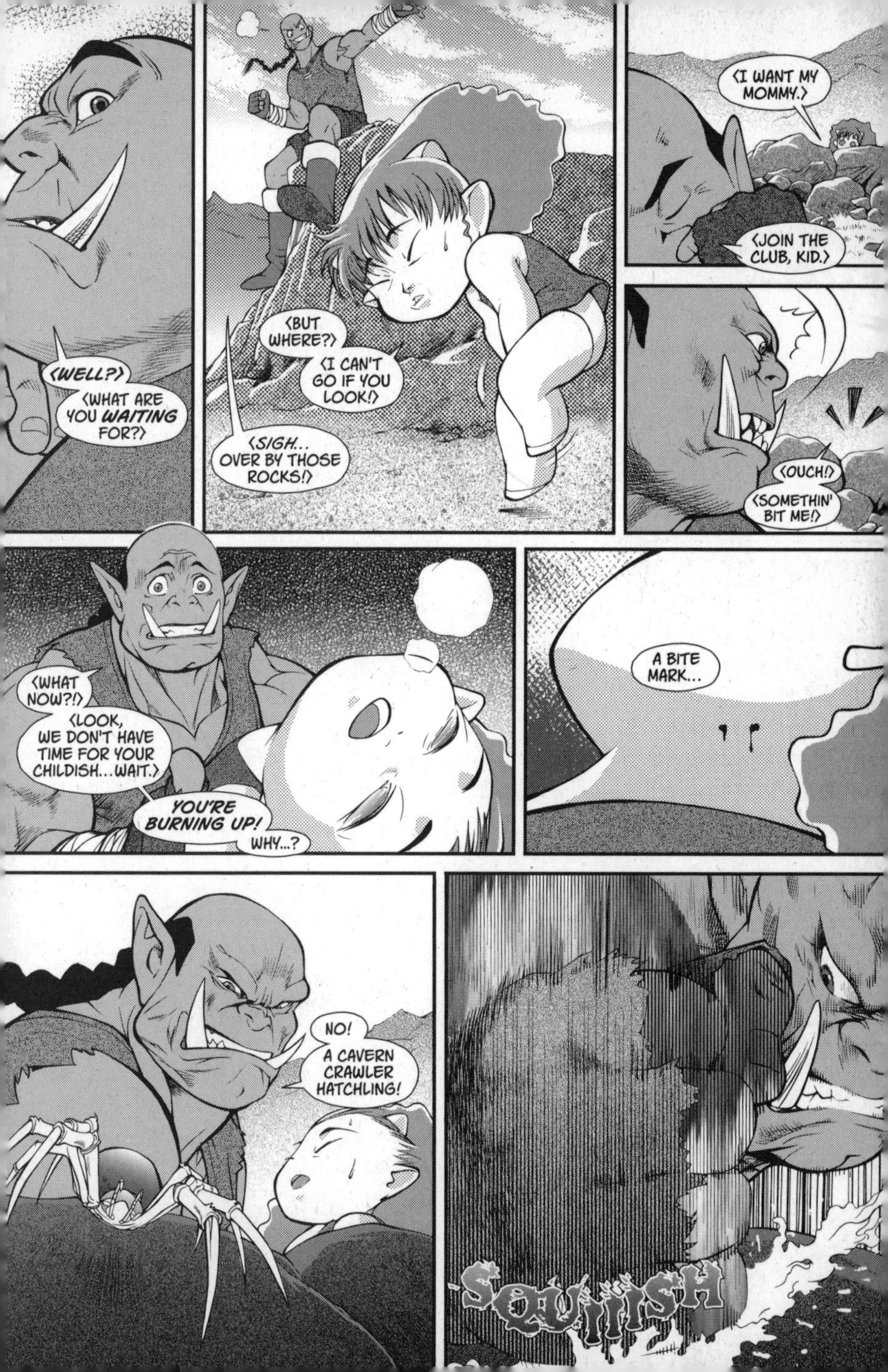

<*WELL?*>
<WHAT ARE YOU *WAITING* FOR?>
<BUT WHERE?>
<I CAN'T GO IF YOU LOOK!>
<*SIGH*... OVER BY THOSE ROCKS!>
<I WANT MY MOMMY.>
<JOIN THE CLUB, KID.>
<OUCH!>
<SOMETHIN' BIT ME!>
<WHAT NOW?!>
<LOOK, WE DON'T HAVE TIME FOR YOUR CHILDISH... WAIT.>
YOU'RE BURNING UP!
WHY...?
A BITE MARK...
NO! A CAVERN CRAWLER HATCHLING!
SQUIIISH

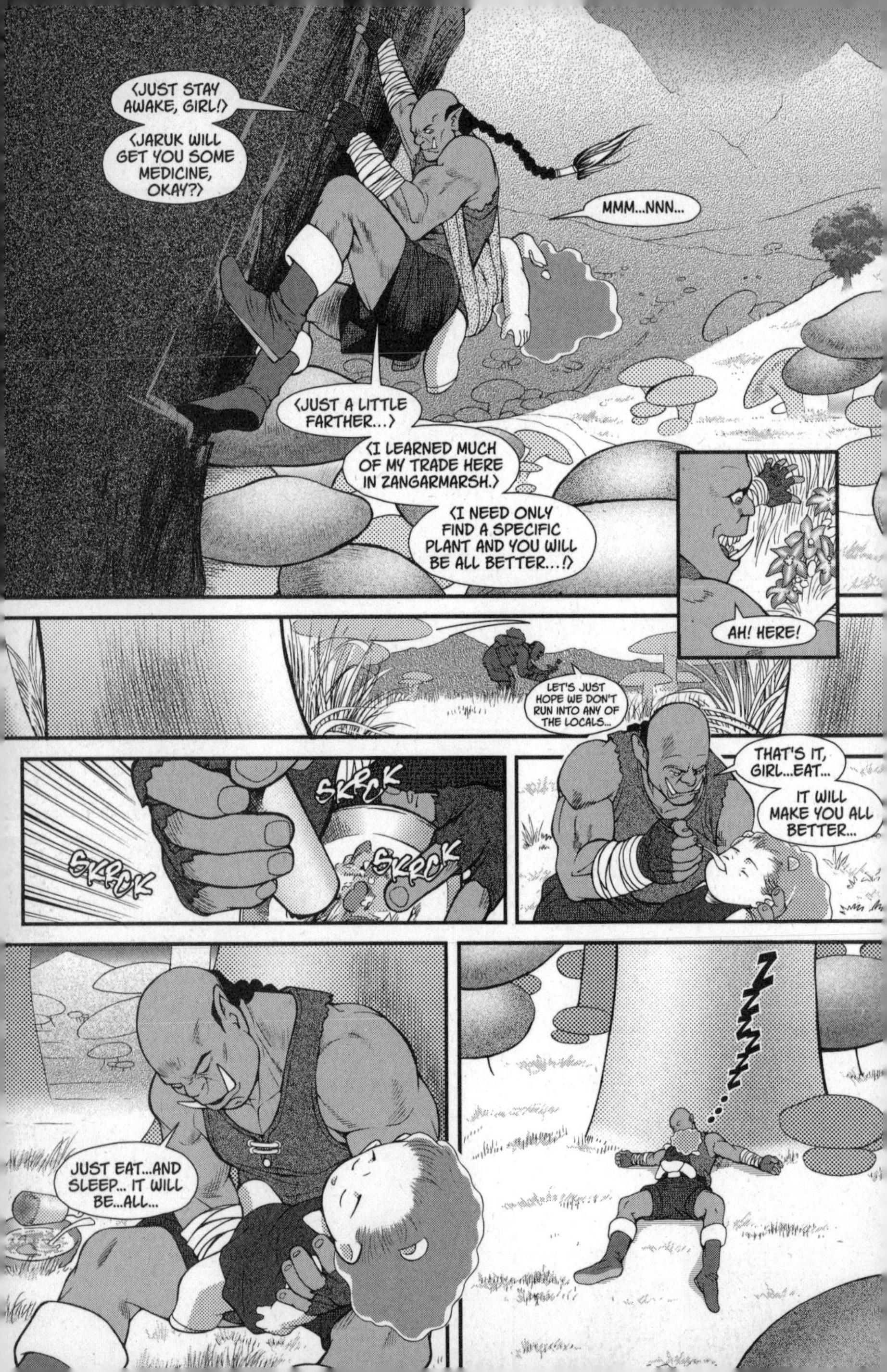

<JUST STAY AWAKE, GIRL!>
<JARUK WILL GET YOU SOME MEDICINE, OKAY?>
MMM...NNN...
<JUST A LITTLE FARTHER...>
<I LEARNED MUCH OF MY TRADE HERE IN ZANGARMARSH.>
<I NEED ONLY FIND A SPECIFIC PLANT AND YOU WILL BE ALL BETTER...!>
AH! HERE!
LET'S JUST HOPE WE DON'T RUN INTO ANY OF THE LOCALS...
SKRCK
SKRCK
SKRCK
THAT'S IT, GIRL...EAT...
IT WILL MAKE YOU ALL BETTER...
JUST EAT...AND SLEEP... IT WILL BE...ALL...
ZZZZZ

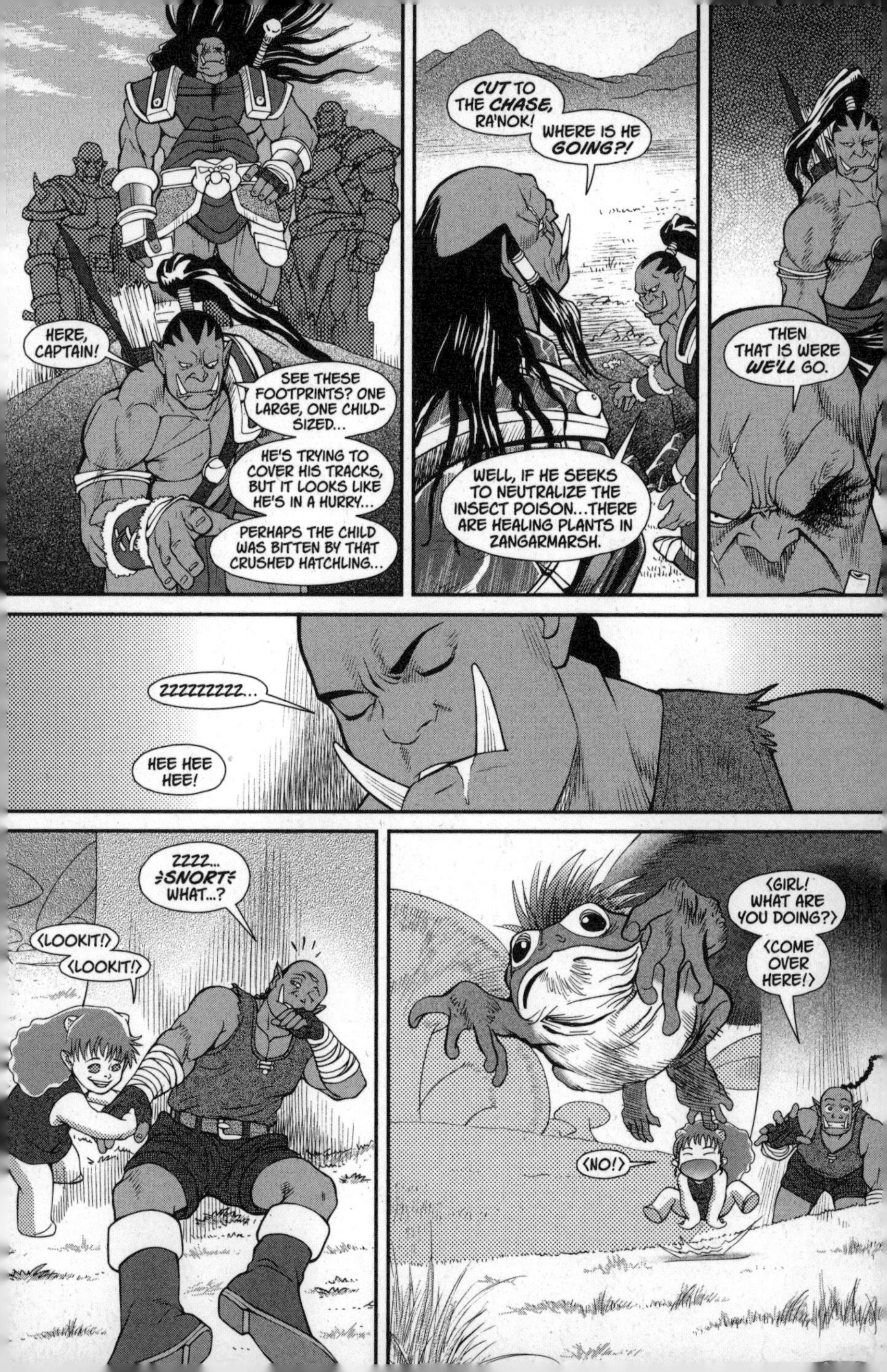
HERE, CAPTAIN!
SEE THESE FOOTPRINTS? ONE LARGE, ONE CHILD-SIZED...
HE'S TRYING TO COVER HIS TRACKS, BUT IT LOOKS LIKE HE'S IN A HURRY...
PERHAPS THE CHILD WAS BITTEN BY THAT CRUSHED HATCHLING...
CUT TO THE CHASE, RA'NOK!
WHERE IS HE GOING?!
WELL, IF HE SEEKS TO NEUTRALIZE THE INSECT POISON...THERE ARE HEALING PLANTS IN ZANGARMARSH.
THEN THAT IS WERE WE'LL GO.
ZZZZZZZZZ...
HEE HEE HEE!
ZZZZ... SNORT WHAT...?
<LOOKIT!>
<LOOKIT!>
<GIRL! WHAT ARE YOU DOING?>
<COME OVER HERE!>
<NO!>

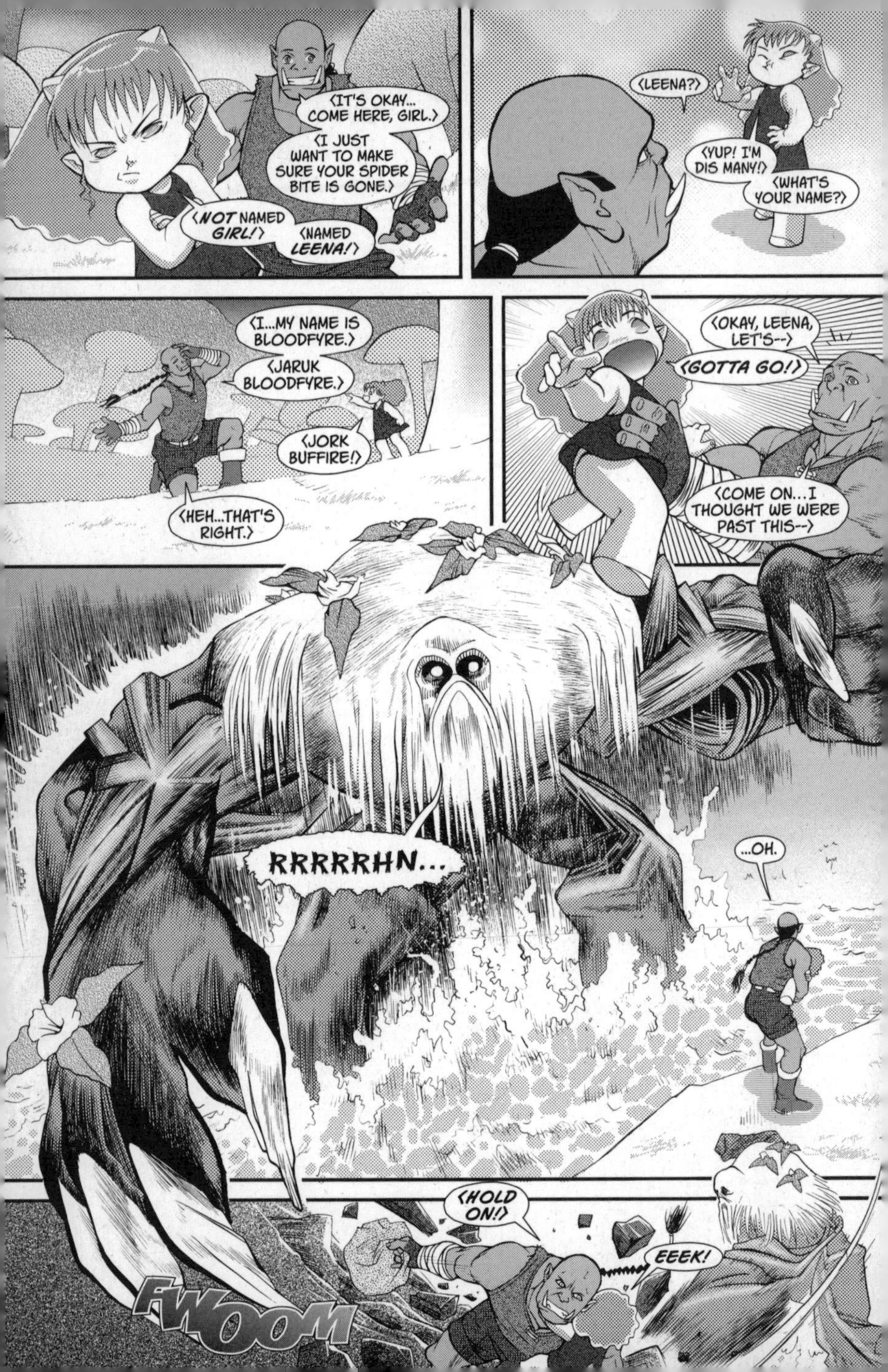

⟨IT'S OKAY... COME HERE, GIRL.⟩
⟨I JUST WANT TO MAKE SURE YOUR SPIDER BITE IS GONE.⟩
⟨NOT NAMED GIRL!⟩
⟨NAMED LEENA!⟩
⟨LEENA?⟩
⟨YUP! I'M DIS MANY!⟩
⟨WHAT'S YOUR NAME?⟩
⟨I...MY NAME IS BLOODFYRE.⟩
⟨JARUK BLOODFYRE.⟩
⟨JORK BUFFIRE!⟩
⟨HEH...THAT'S RIGHT.⟩
⟨OKAY, LEENA, LET'S--⟩
⟨GOTTA GO!⟩
⟨COME ON...I THOUGHT WE WERE PAST THIS--⟩
RRRRRHN...
...OH.
⟨HOLD ON!⟩
EEEK!
FWOOM

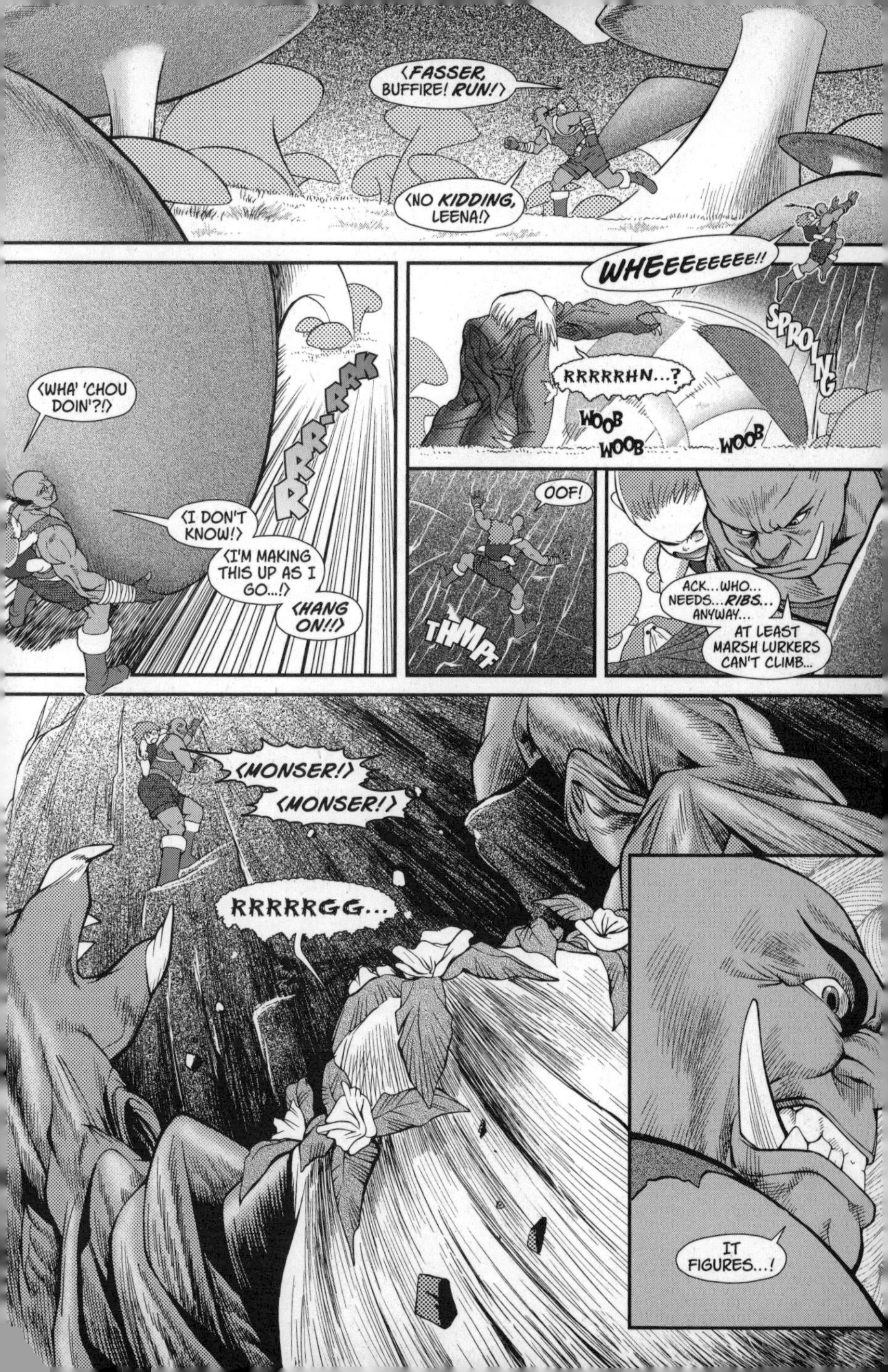
‹FASSER, BUFFIRE! RUN!›
‹NO KIDDING, LEENA!›
‹WHA' 'CHOU DOIN'?!›
‹I DON'T KNOW!›
‹I'M MAKING THIS UP AS I GO...!›
‹HANG ON!!›
RRR-RRK
WHEEEeeeee!!
SPROING
RRRRRHN...?
WOOB
WOOB
WOOB
OOF!
THMPF
ACK...WHO... NEEDS...RIBS... ANYWAY...
AT LEAST MARSH LURKERS CAN'T CLIMB...
‹MONSER!›
‹MONSER!›
RRRRRGG...
IT FIGURES...!

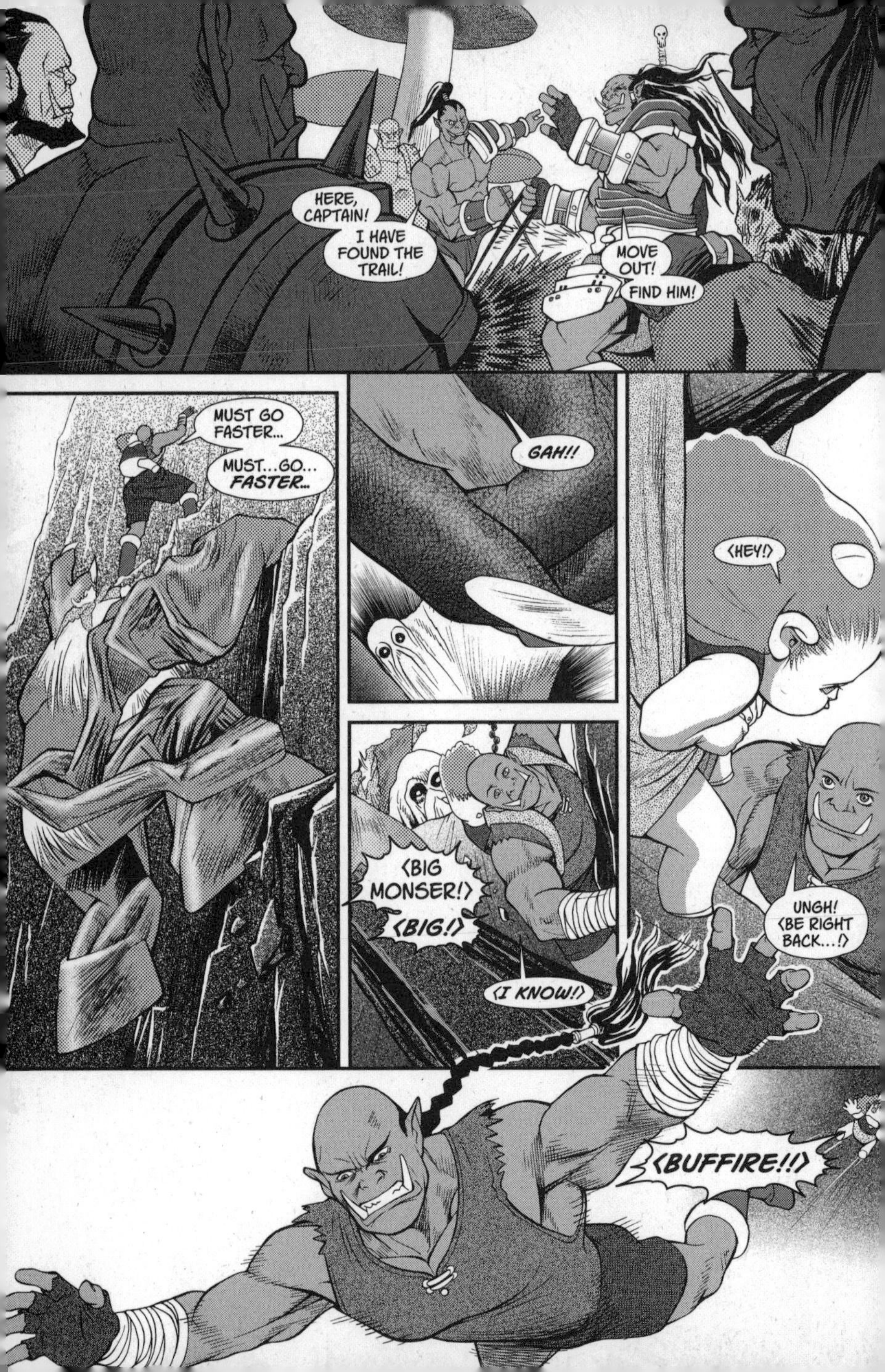
HERE, CAPTAIN!
I HAVE FOUND THE TRAIL!
MOVE OUT!
FIND HIM!
MUST GO FASTER...
MUST...GO... FASTER...
GAH!!
〈BIG MONSER!〉
〈BIG!〉
〈I KNOW!〉
〈HEY!〉
UNGH! 〈BE RIGHT BACK...!〉
〈BUFFIRE!!〉

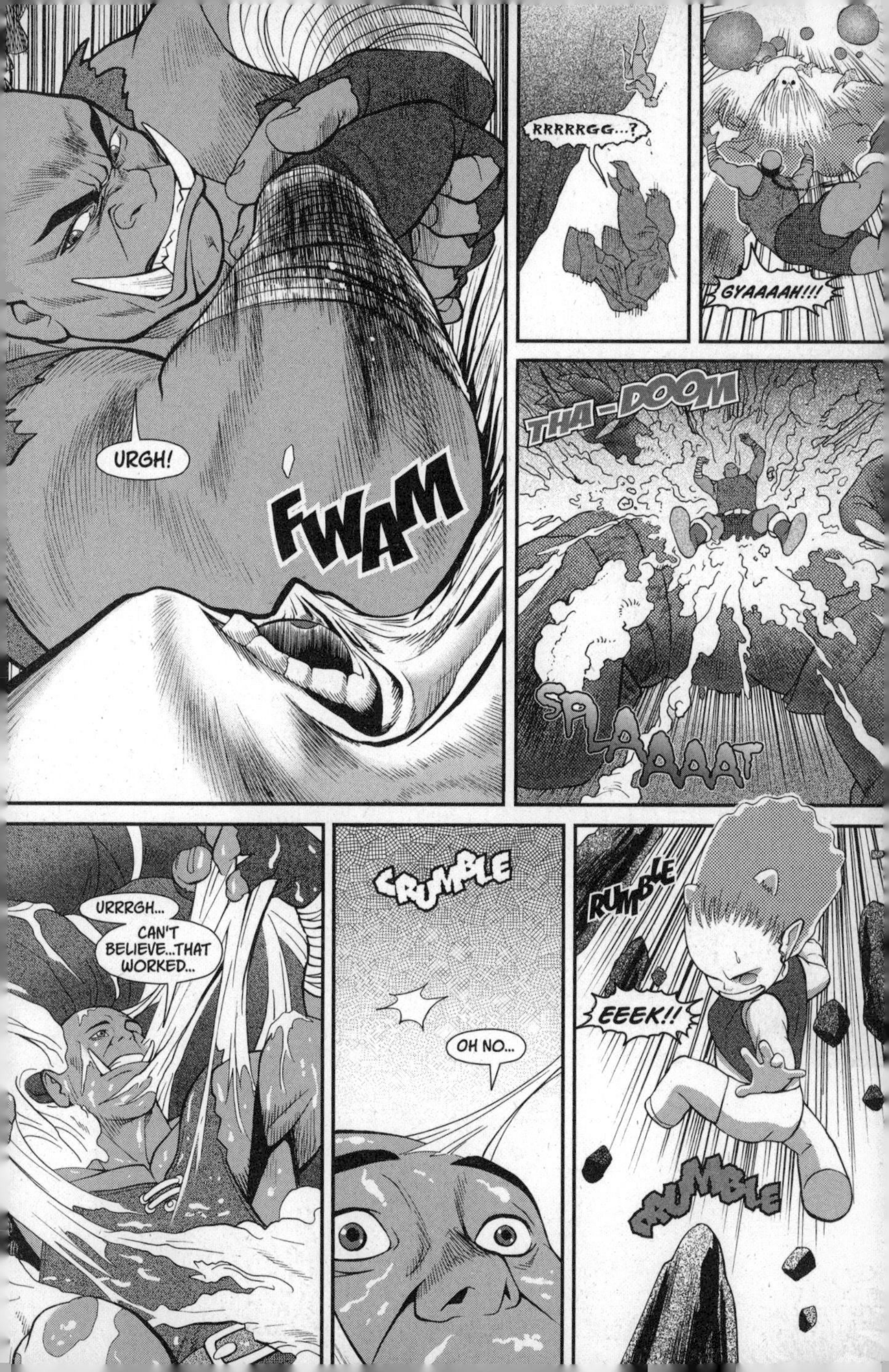
URGH!
FWAM
RRRRRGG...?
GYAAAAH!!!
THA-DOOM
SPLAAAAT
URRRGH... CAN'T BELIEVE...THAT WORKED...
CRUMBLE
OH NO...
RUMBLE
EEEK!!
CRUMBLE

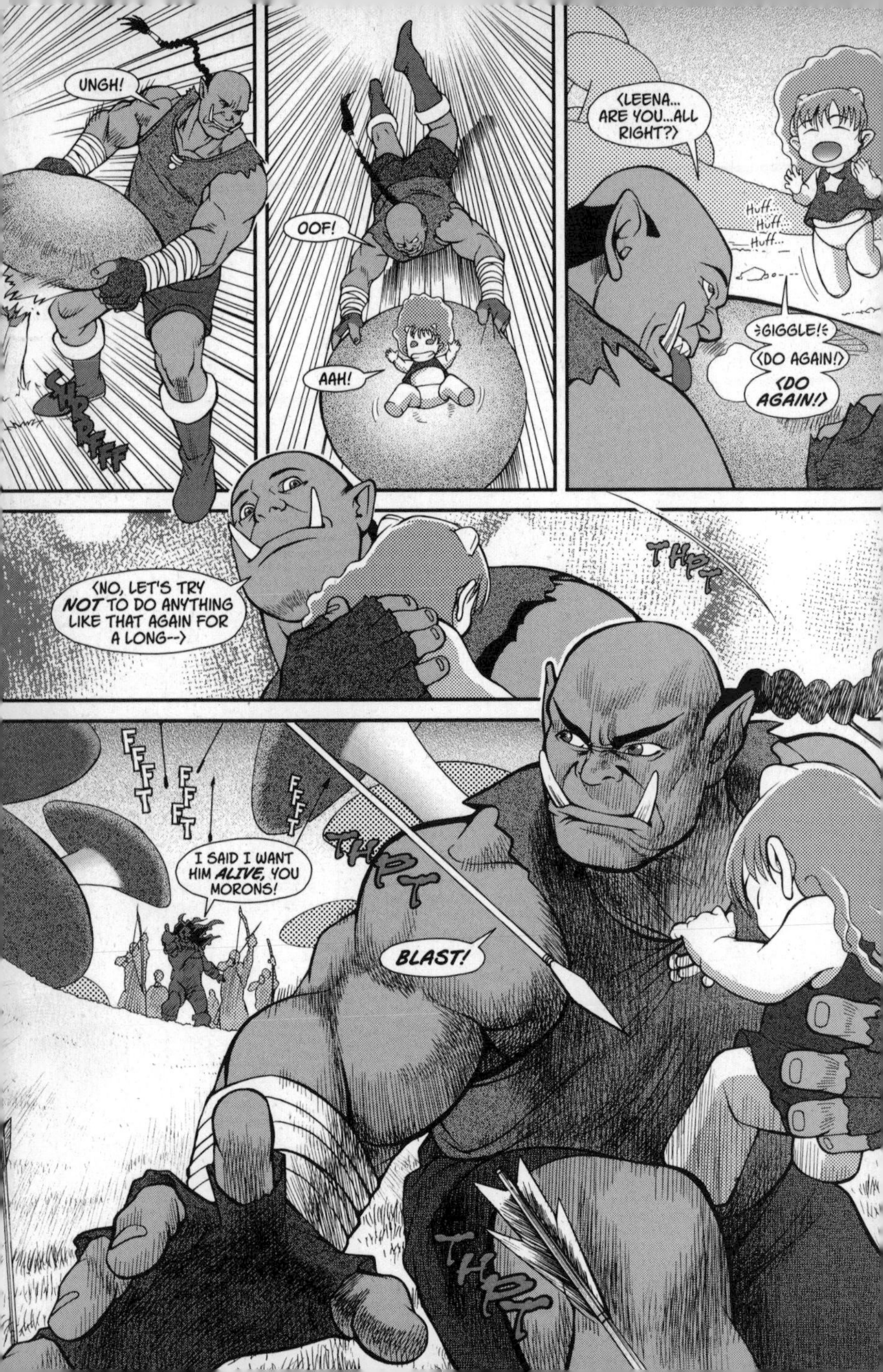
UNGH!
SHPPFFF
OOF!
AAH!
<LEENA... ARE YOU...ALL RIGHT?>
Huff... Huff... Huff...
¡GIGGLE!¡
<DO AGAIN!>
<DO AGAIN!>
<NO, LET'S TRY NOT TO DO ANYTHING LIKE THAT AGAIN FOR A LONG-->
THPT
FFFT
FFFT
FFFT
I SAID I WANT HIM ALIVE, YOU MORONS!
THPT
BLAST!
THPT

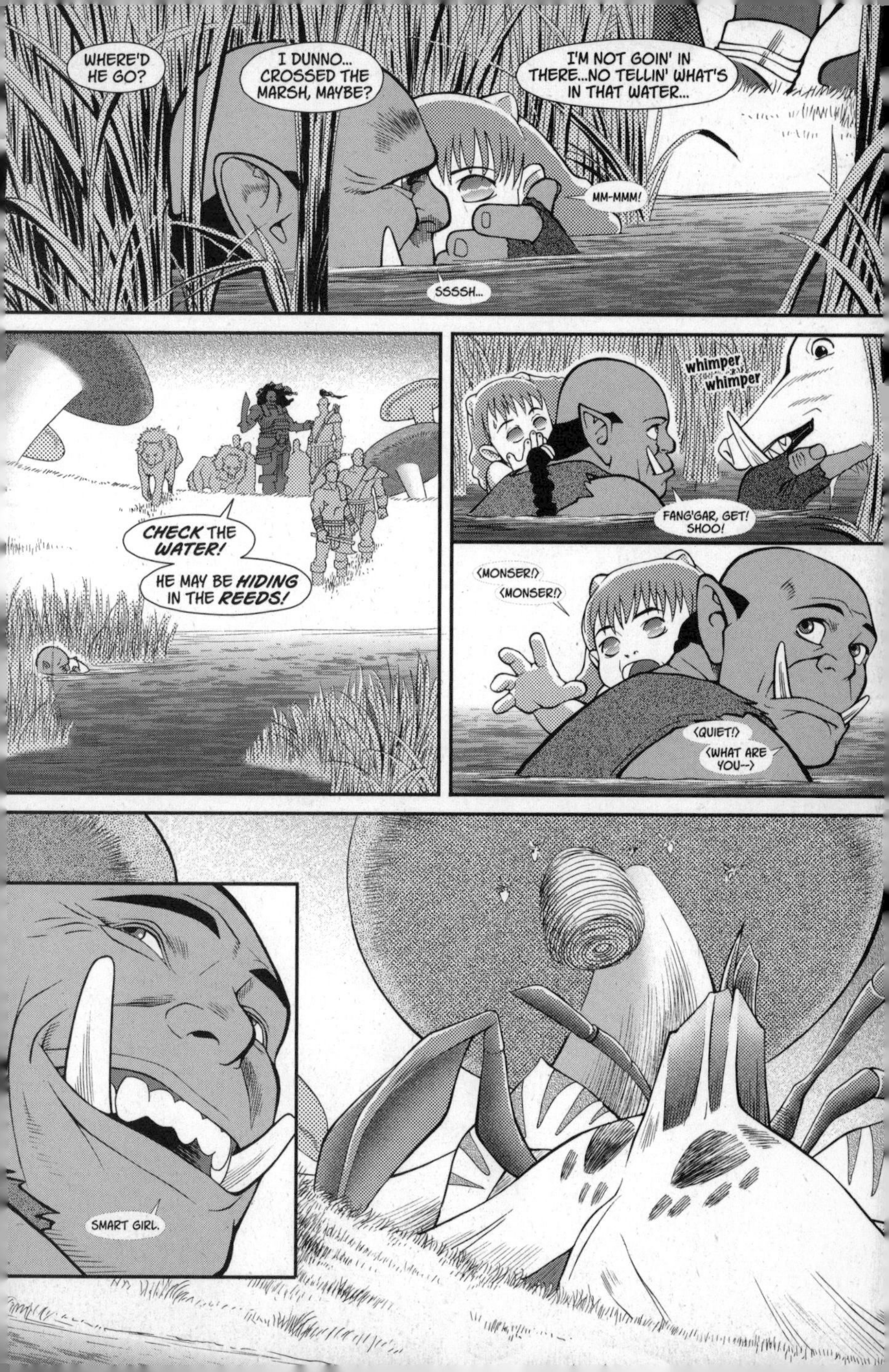
WHERE'D HE GO?
I DUNNO... CROSSED THE MARSH, MAYBE?
I'M NOT GOIN' IN THERE...NO TELLIN' WHAT'S IN THAT WATER...
MM-MMM!
SSSSH...
CHECK THE WATER!
HE MAY BE HIDING IN THE REEDS!
whimper whimper
FANG'GAR, GET! SHOO!
<MONSER!>
<MONSER!>
<QUIET!>
<WHAT ARE YOU-->
SMART GIRL.

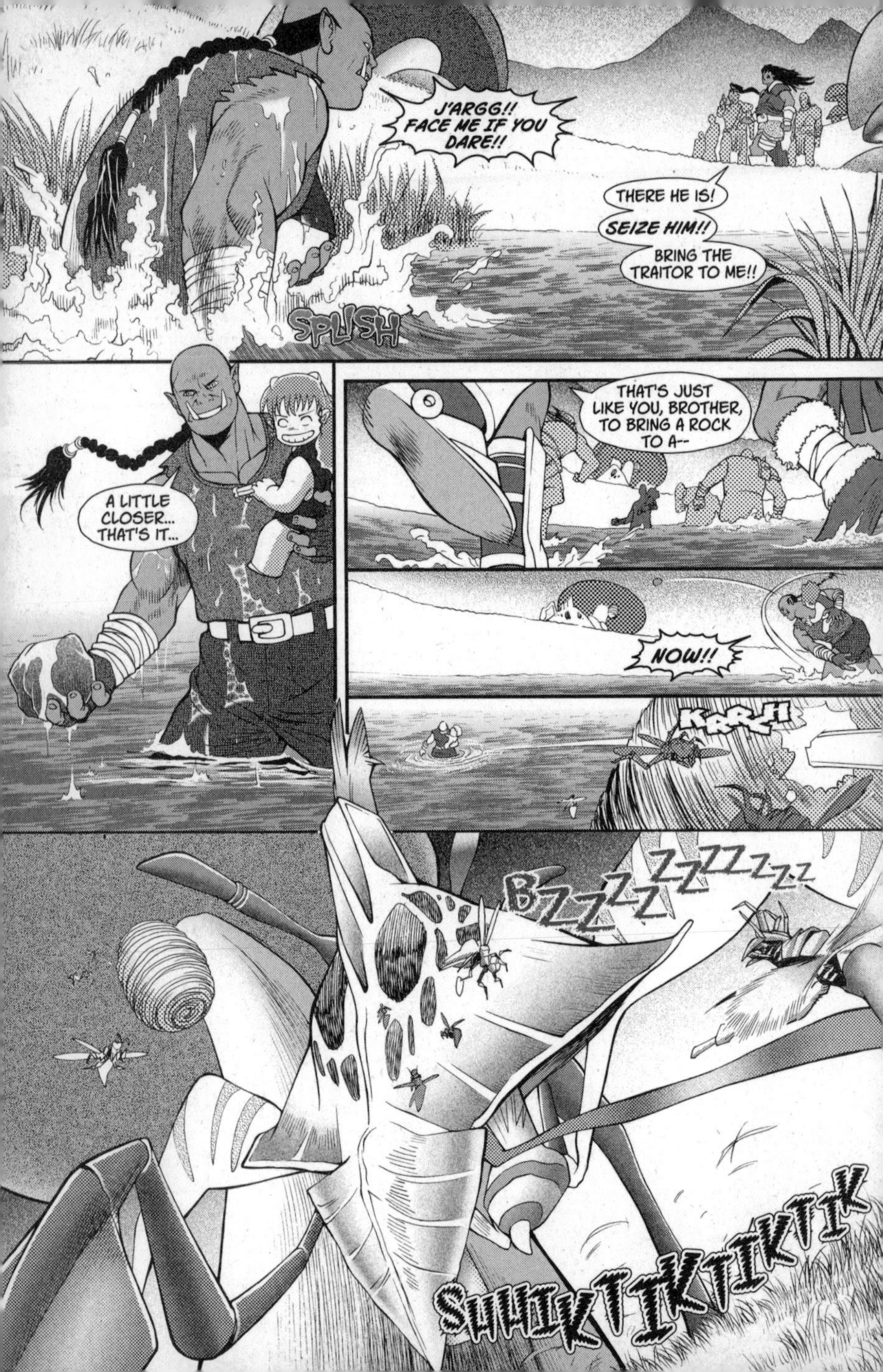
J'ARGG!! FACE ME IF YOU DARE!!
THERE HE IS!
SEIZE HIM!!
BRING THE TRAITOR TO ME!!
SPLISH
A LITTLE CLOSER... THAT'S IT...
THAT'S JUST LIKE YOU, BROTHER, TO BRING A ROCK TO A--
NOW!!
KRRCH
BZZZZZZZZZZZZ
SHHIKTIKTIKTIK

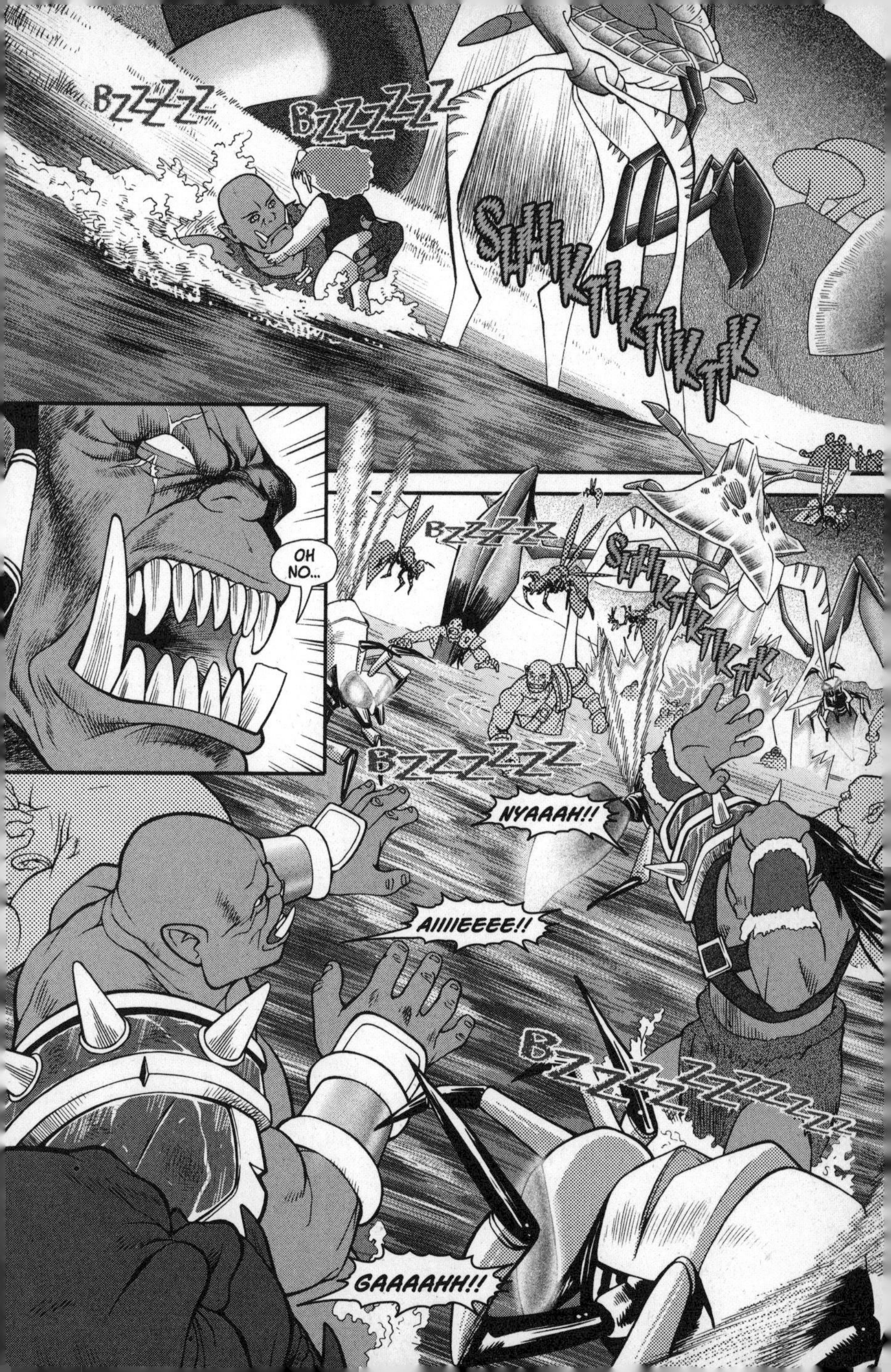
BZZZZZZ
BZZZZZZZ
SHHHKTIKTIKTIK
OH NO...
BZZZZZZ
SHHHKTIKTIKTIK
BZZZZZZZ
NYAAAH!!
AIIIIEEEE!!
BZZZZZZZZZZZZ
GAAAAHH!!

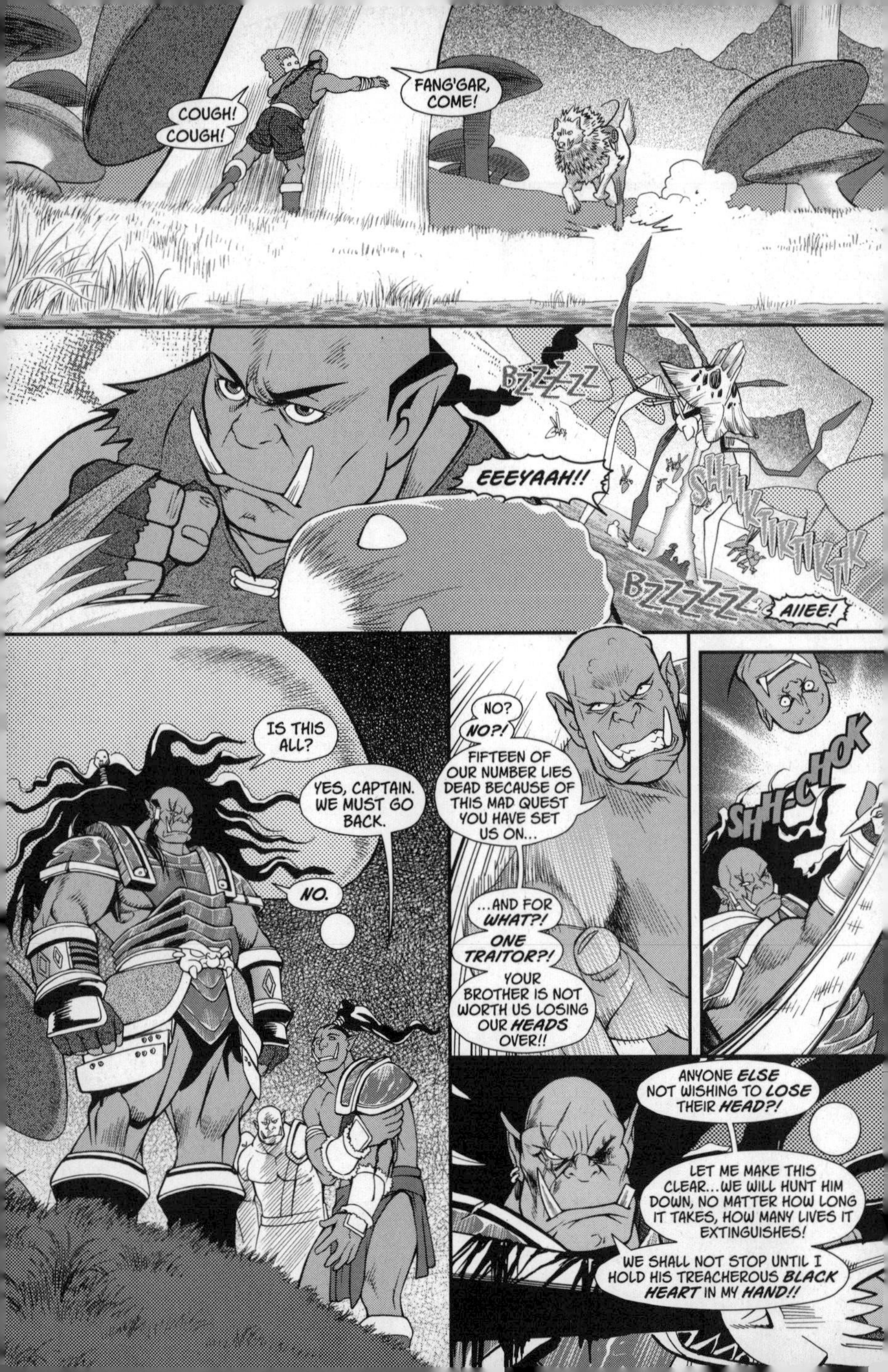
COUGH!
COUGH!
FANG'GAR, COME!
BZZZZZZ
EEEYAAH!!
SHHKTIKTIKTIK
BZZZZZZZ
AIIEE!
IS THIS ALL?
YES, CAPTAIN. WE MUST GO BACK.
NO.
NO?
NO?!
FIFTEEN OF OUR NUMBER LIES DEAD BECAUSE OF THIS MAD QUEST YOU HAVE SET US ON...
...AND FOR WHAT?! ONE TRAITOR?!
YOUR BROTHER IS NOT WORTH US LOSING OUR HEADS OVER!!
SHH-CHOK
ANYONE ELSE NOT WISHING TO LOSE THEIR HEAD?!
LET ME MAKE THIS CLEAR...WE WILL HUNT HIM DOWN, NO MATTER HOW LONG IT TAKES, HOW MANY LIVES IT EXTINGUISHES!
WE SHALL NOT STOP UNTIL I HOLD HIS TREACHEROUS BLACK HEART IN MY HAND!!

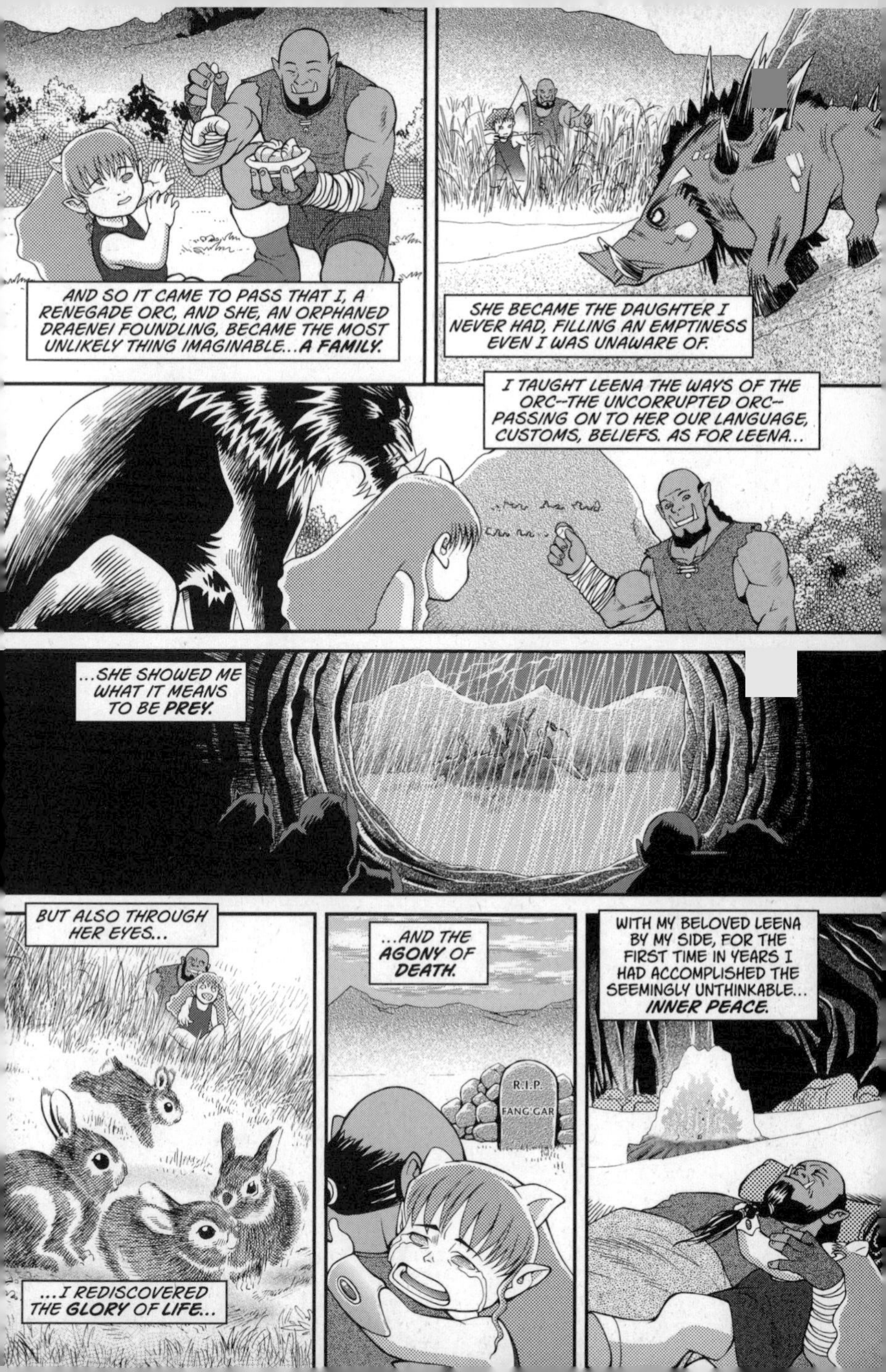
AND SO IT CAME TO PASS THAT I, A RENEGADE ORC, AND SHE, AN ORPHANED DRAENEI FOUNDLING, BECAME THE MOST UNLIKELY THING IMAGINABLE...A FAMILY.
SHE BECAME THE DAUGHTER I NEVER HAD, FILLING AN EMPTINESS EVEN I WAS UNAWARE OF.
I TAUGHT LEENA THE WAYS OF THE ORC--THE UNCORRUPTED ORC--PASSING ON TO HER OUR LANGUAGE, CUSTOMS, BELIEFS. AS FOR LEENA...
...SHE SHOWED ME WHAT IT MEANS TO BE PREY.
BUT ALSO THROUGH HER EYES...
...I REDISCOVERED THE GLORY OF LIFE...
...AND THE AGONY OF DEATH.
R.I.P.
FANG'GAR
WITH MY BELOVED LEENA BY MY SIDE, FOR THE FIRST TIME IN YEARS I HAD ACCOMPLISHED THE SEEMINGLY UNTHINKABLE... INNER PEACE.

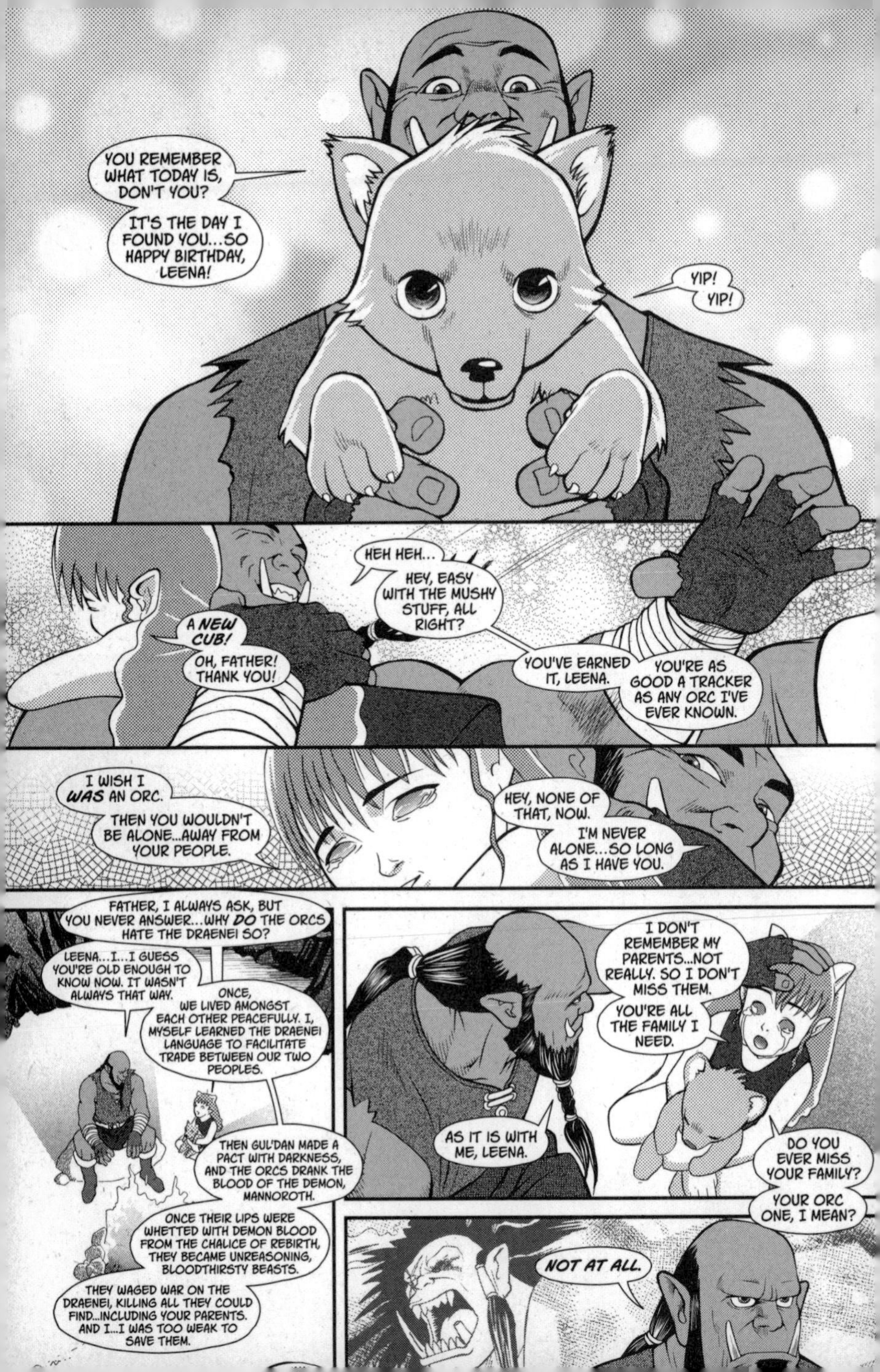
YOU REMEMBER WHAT TODAY IS, DON'T YOU?
IT'S THE DAY I FOUND YOU...SO HAPPY BIRTHDAY, LEENA!
YIP! YIP!
A *NEW CUB!*
OH, FATHER! THANK YOU!
HEH HEH...
HEY, EASY WITH THE MUSHY STUFF, ALL RIGHT?
YOU'VE EARNED IT, LEENA.
YOU'RE AS GOOD A TRACKER AS ANY ORC I'VE EVER KNOWN.
I WISH I *WAS* AN ORC.
THEN YOU WOULDN'T BE ALONE...AWAY FROM YOUR PEOPLE.
HEY, NONE OF THAT, NOW.
I'M NEVER ALONE...SO LONG AS I HAVE YOU.
FATHER, I ALWAYS ASK, BUT YOU NEVER ANSWER...WHY *DO* THE ORCS HATE THE DRAENEI SO?
LEENA...I...I GUESS YOU'RE OLD ENOUGH TO KNOW NOW. IT WASN'T ALWAYS THAT WAY.
ONCE, WE LIVED AMONGST EACH OTHER PEACEFULLY. I, MYSELF LEARNED THE DRAENEI LANGUAGE TO FACILITATE TRADE BETWEEN OUR TWO PEOPLES.
THEN GUL'DAN MADE A PACT WITH DARKNESS, AND THE ORCS DRANK THE BLOOD OF THE DEMON, MANNOROTH.
ONCE THEIR LIPS WERE WHETTED WITH DEMON BLOOD FROM THE CHALICE OF REBIRTH, THEY BECAME UNREASONING, BLOODTHIRSTY BEASTS.
THEY WAGED WAR ON THE DRAENEI, KILLING ALL THEY COULD FIND...INCLUDING YOUR PARENTS. AND I...I WAS TOO WEAK TO SAVE THEM.
I DON'T REMEMBER MY PARENTS...NOT REALLY. SO I DON'T MISS THEM.
YOU'RE ALL THE FAMILY I NEED.
AS IT IS WITH ME, LEENA.
DO YOU EVER MISS YOUR FAMILY?
YOUR ORC ONE, I MEAN?
NOT AT ALL.

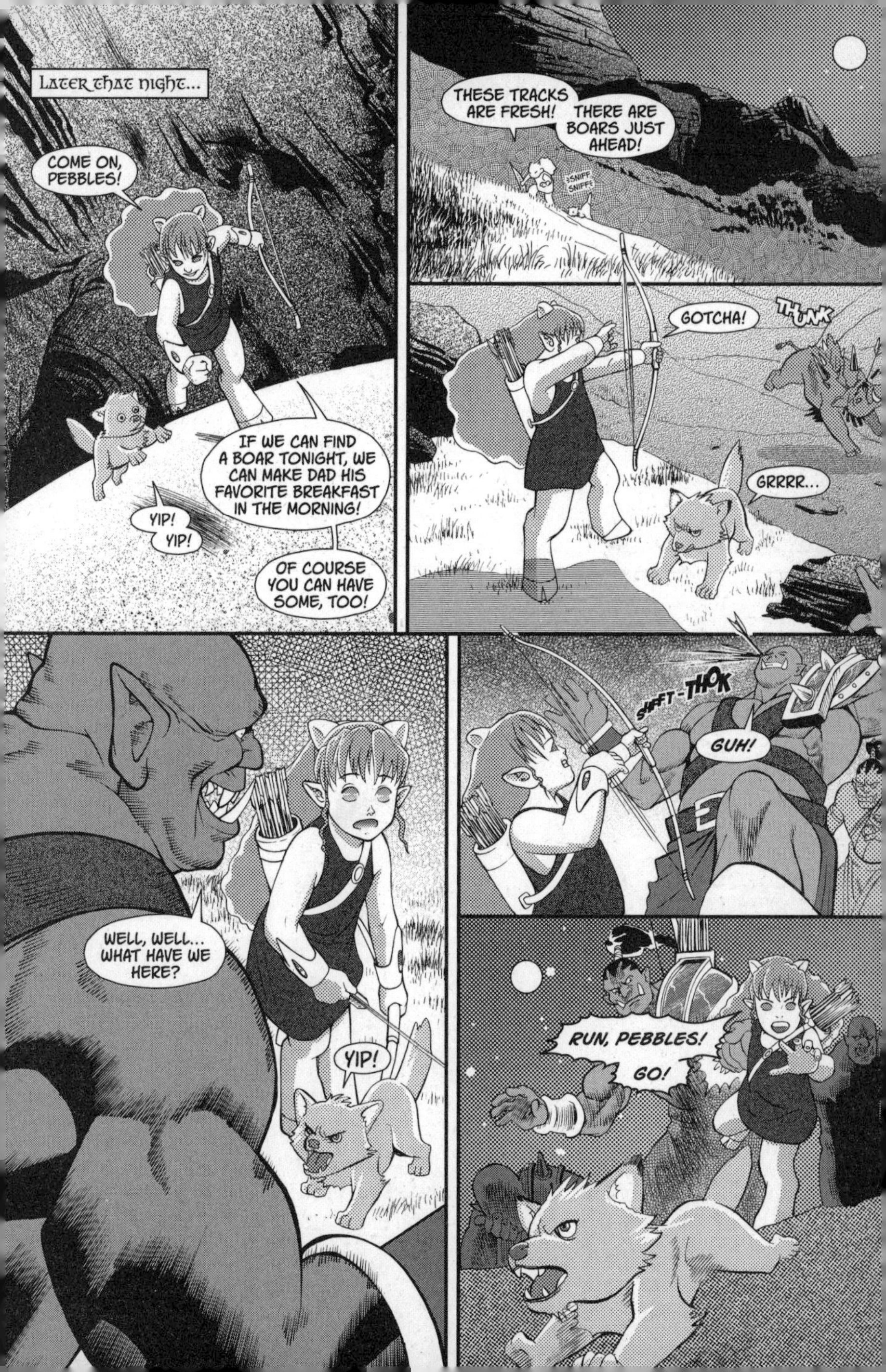
LATER THAT NIGHT...
COME ON, PEBBLES!
IF WE CAN FIND A BOAR TONIGHT, WE CAN MAKE DAD HIS FAVORITE BREAKFAST IN THE MORNING!
YIP! YIP!
OF COURSE YOU CAN HAVE SOME, TOO!
THESE TRACKS ARE FRESH!
THERE ARE BOARS JUST AHEAD!
SNIFF SNIFF
GOTCHA!
THUNK
GRRRR...
WELL, WELL... WHAT HAVE WE HERE?
YIP!
SHFFT-THOK
GUH!
RUN, PEBBLES!
GO!

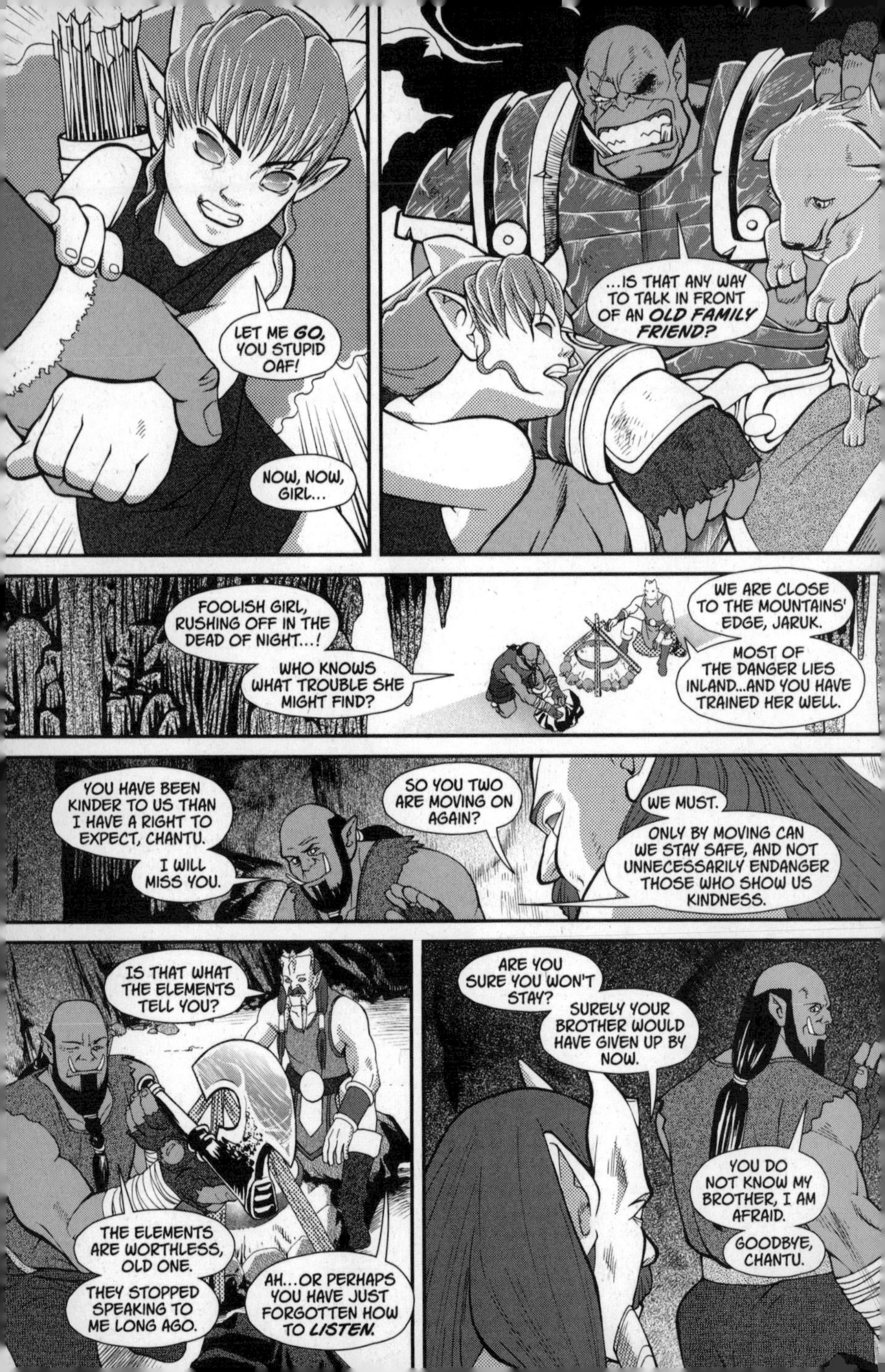
LET ME *GO*, YOU STUPID OAF!
NOW, NOW, GIRL...
...IS THAT ANY WAY TO TALK IN FRONT OF AN *OLD FAMILY FRIEND?*
FOOLISH GIRL, RUSHING OFF IN THE DEAD OF NIGHT...!
WHO KNOWS WHAT TROUBLE SHE MIGHT FIND?
WE ARE CLOSE TO THE MOUNTAINS' EDGE, JARUK.
MOST OF THE DANGER LIES INLAND...AND YOU HAVE TRAINED HER WELL.
YOU HAVE BEEN KINDER TO US THAN I HAVE A RIGHT TO EXPECT, CHANTU.
I WILL MISS YOU.
SO YOU TWO ARE MOVING ON AGAIN?
WE MUST.
ONLY BY MOVING CAN WE STAY SAFE, AND NOT UNNECESSARILY ENDANGER THOSE WHO SHOW US KINDNESS.
IS THAT WHAT THE ELEMENTS TELL YOU?
THE ELEMENTS ARE WORTHLESS, OLD ONE.
THEY STOPPED SPEAKING TO ME LONG AGO.
AH...OR PERHAPS YOU HAVE JUST FORGOTTEN HOW TO *LISTEN.*
ARE YOU SURE YOU WON'T STAY?
SURELY YOUR BROTHER WOULD HAVE GIVEN UP BY NOW.
YOU DO NOT KNOW MY BROTHER, I AM AFRAID.
GOODBYE, CHANTU.

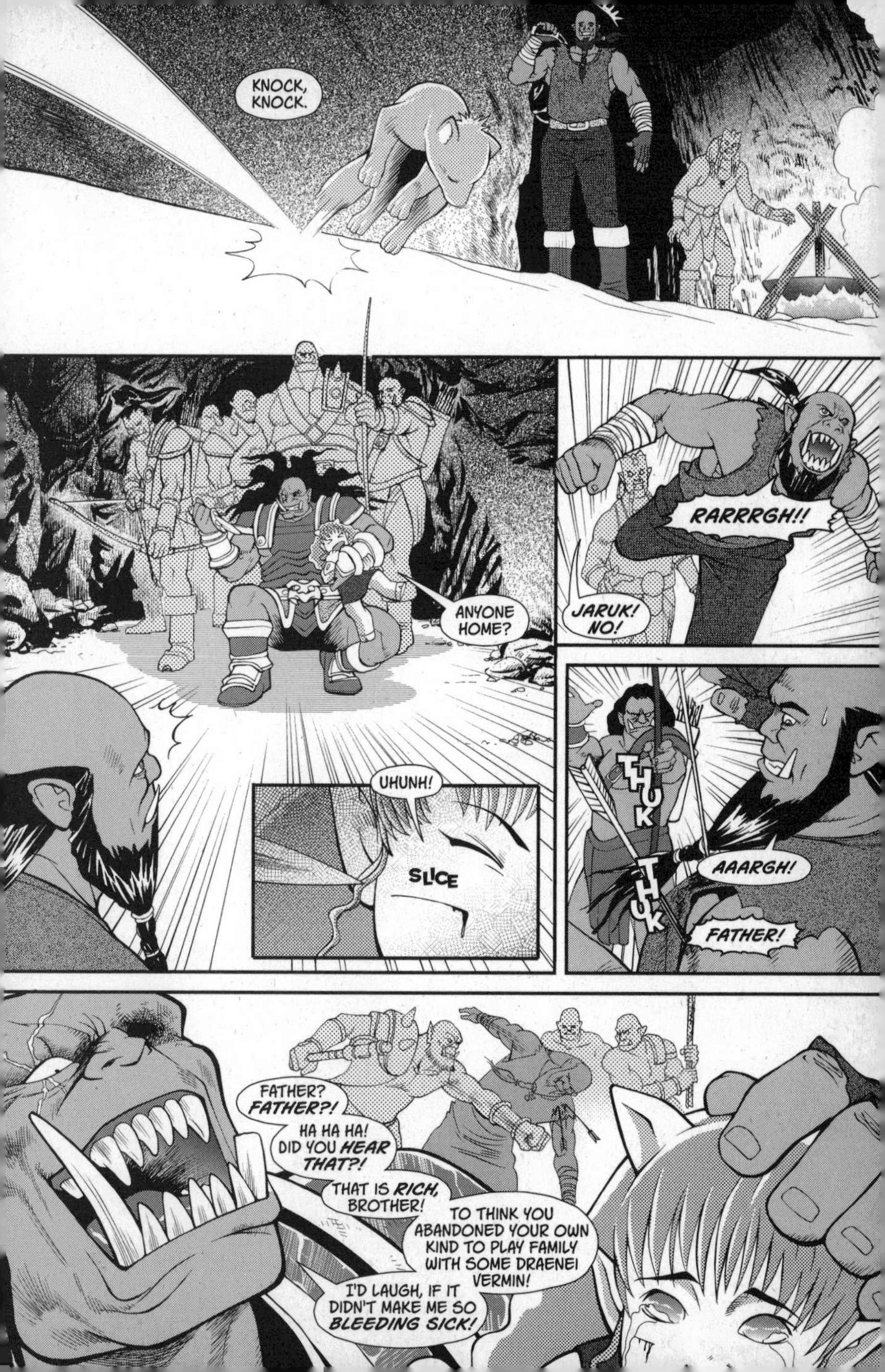
KNOCK, KNOCK.
ANYONE HOME?
RARRRGH!!
JARUK! NO!
UHUNH!
SLICE
THUK
THUK
AAARGH!
FATHER!
FATHER? FATHER?!
HA HA HA! DID YOU HEAR THAT?!
THAT IS RICH, BROTHER!
TO THINK YOU ABANDONED YOUR OWN KIND TO PLAY FAMILY WITH SOME DRAENEI VERMIN!
I'D LAUGH, IF IT DIDN'T MAKE ME SO BLEEDING SICK!

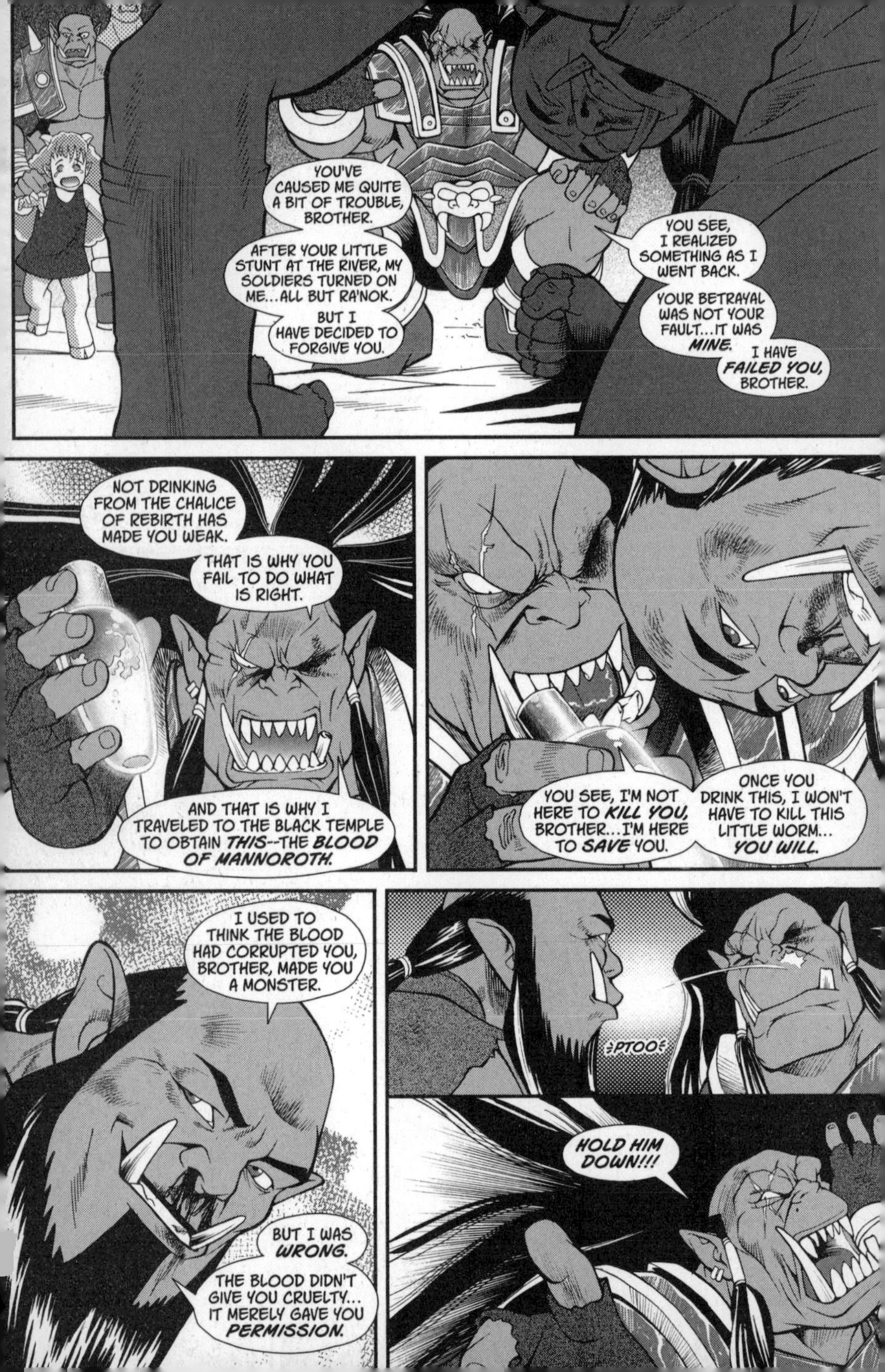
YOU'VE CAUSED ME QUITE A BIT OF TROUBLE, BROTHER.
AFTER YOUR LITTLE STUNT AT THE RIVER, MY SOLDIERS TURNED ON ME...ALL BUT RA'NOK.
BUT I HAVE DECIDED TO FORGIVE YOU.
YOU SEE, I REALIZED SOMETHING AS I WENT BACK.
YOUR BETRAYAL WAS NOT YOUR FAULT...IT WAS *MINE.*
I HAVE *FAILED YOU,* BROTHER.
NOT DRINKING FROM THE CHALICE OF REBIRTH HAS MADE YOU WEAK.
THAT IS WHY YOU FAIL TO DO WHAT IS RIGHT.
AND THAT IS WHY I TRAVELED TO THE BLACK TEMPLE TO OBTAIN *THIS*--THE *BLOOD OF MANNOROTH.*
YOU SEE, I'M NOT HERE TO *KILL YOU,* BROTHER...I'M HERE TO *SAVE* YOU.
ONCE YOU DRINK THIS, I WON'T HAVE TO KILL THIS LITTLE WORM... *YOU WILL.*
I USED TO THINK THE BLOOD HAD CORRUPTED YOU, BROTHER, MADE YOU A MONSTER.
BUT I WAS *WRONG.*
THE BLOOD DIDN'T GIVE YOU CRUELTY... IT MERELY GAVE YOU *PERMISSION.*
PTOO
HOLD HIM DOWN!!!

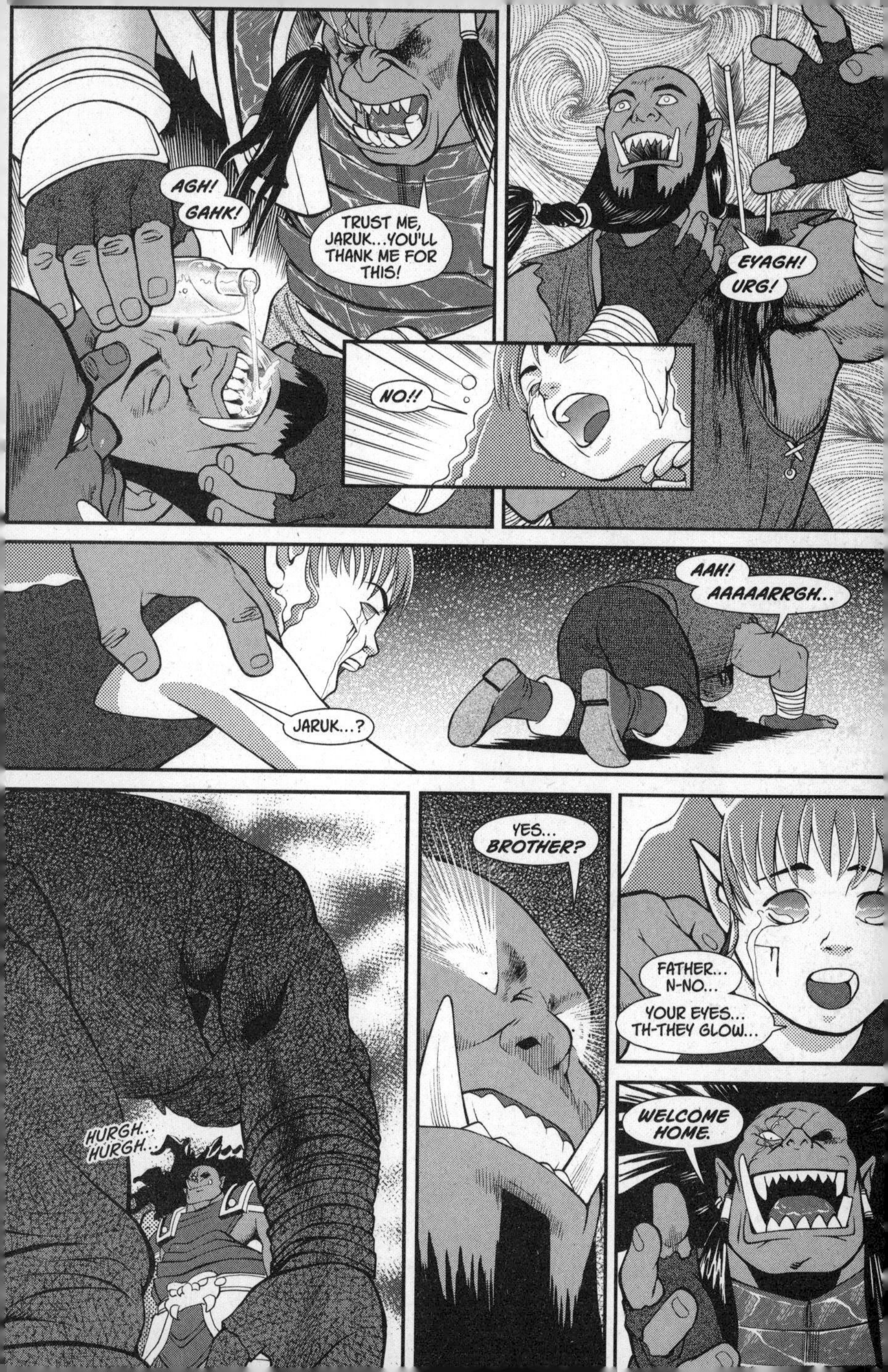
AGH!
GAHK!
TRUST ME, JARUK...YOU'LL THANK ME FOR THIS!
EYAGH!
URG!
NO!!
JARUK...?
AAH!
AAAAARRGH...
HURGH... HURGH...
YES... BROTHER?
FATHER... N-NO...
YOUR EYES... TH-THEY GLOW...
WELCOME HOME.

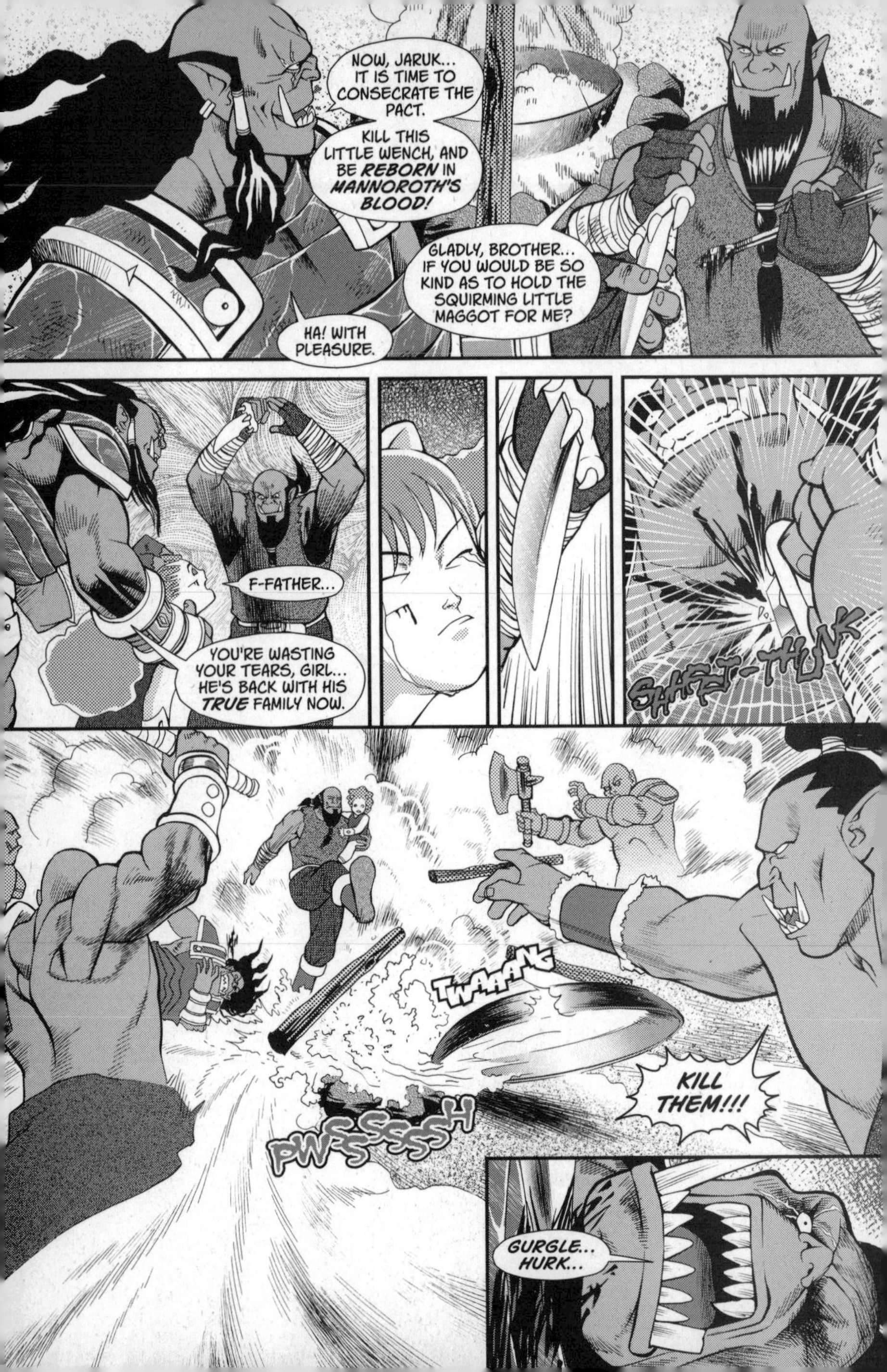
NOW, JARUK... IT IS TIME TO CONSECRATE THE PACT.
KILL THIS LITTLE WENCH, AND BE REBORN IN MANNOROTH'S BLOOD!
GLADLY, BROTHER... IF YOU WOULD BE SO KIND AS TO HOLD THE SQUIRMING LITTLE MAGGOT FOR ME?
HA! WITH PLEASURE.
F-FATHER...
YOU'RE WASTING YOUR TEARS, GIRL... HE'S BACK WITH HIS TRUE FAMILY NOW.
SHHFFT-THUNK
TWAAANG
KILL THEM!!!
PWSSSSSSH
GURGLE... HURK...

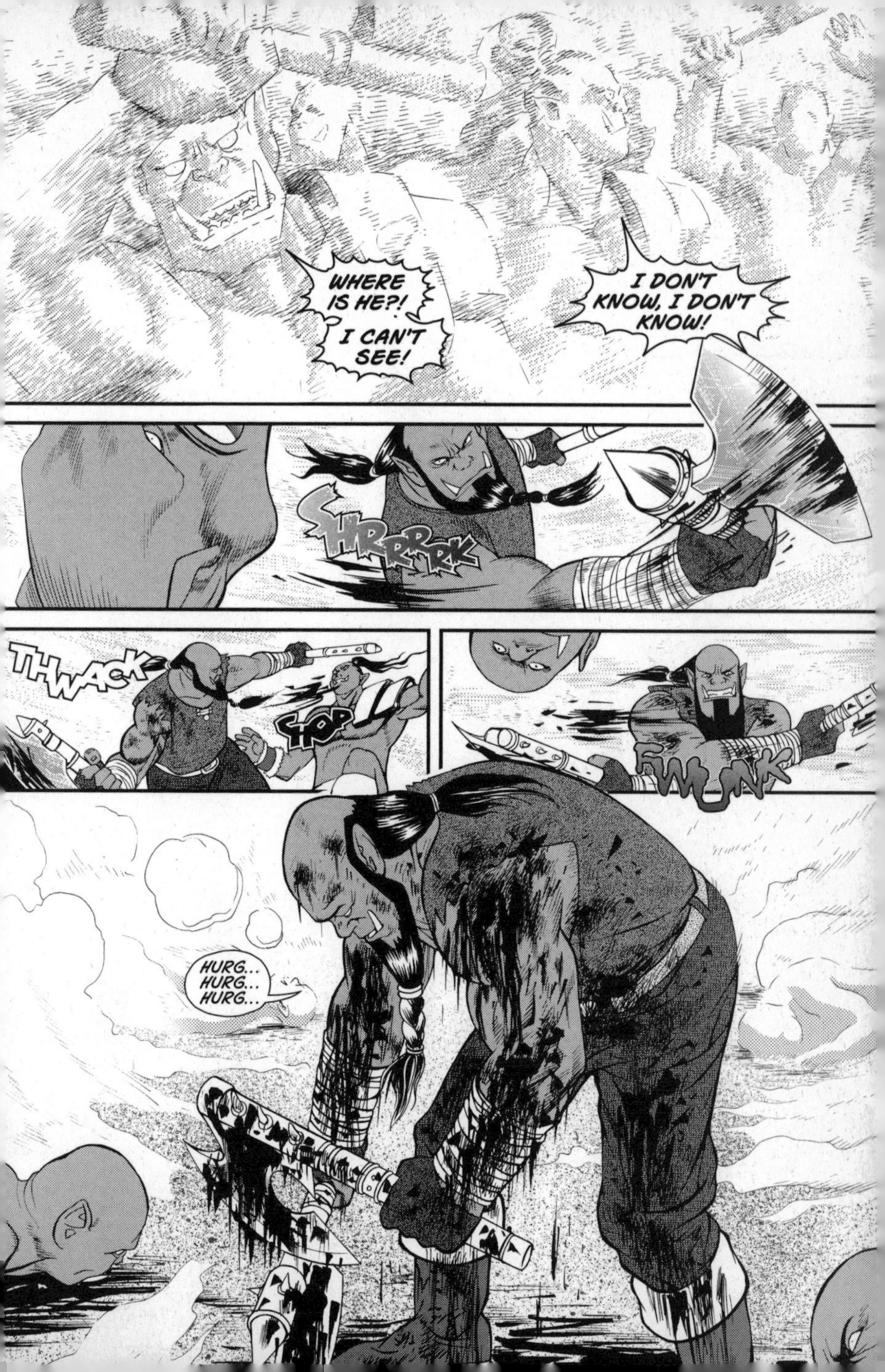
WHERE IS HE?!
I CAN'T SEE!
I DON'T KNOW, I DON'T KNOW!
SHRRRRK
THWACK
FWUNK
HURG... HURG... HURG...

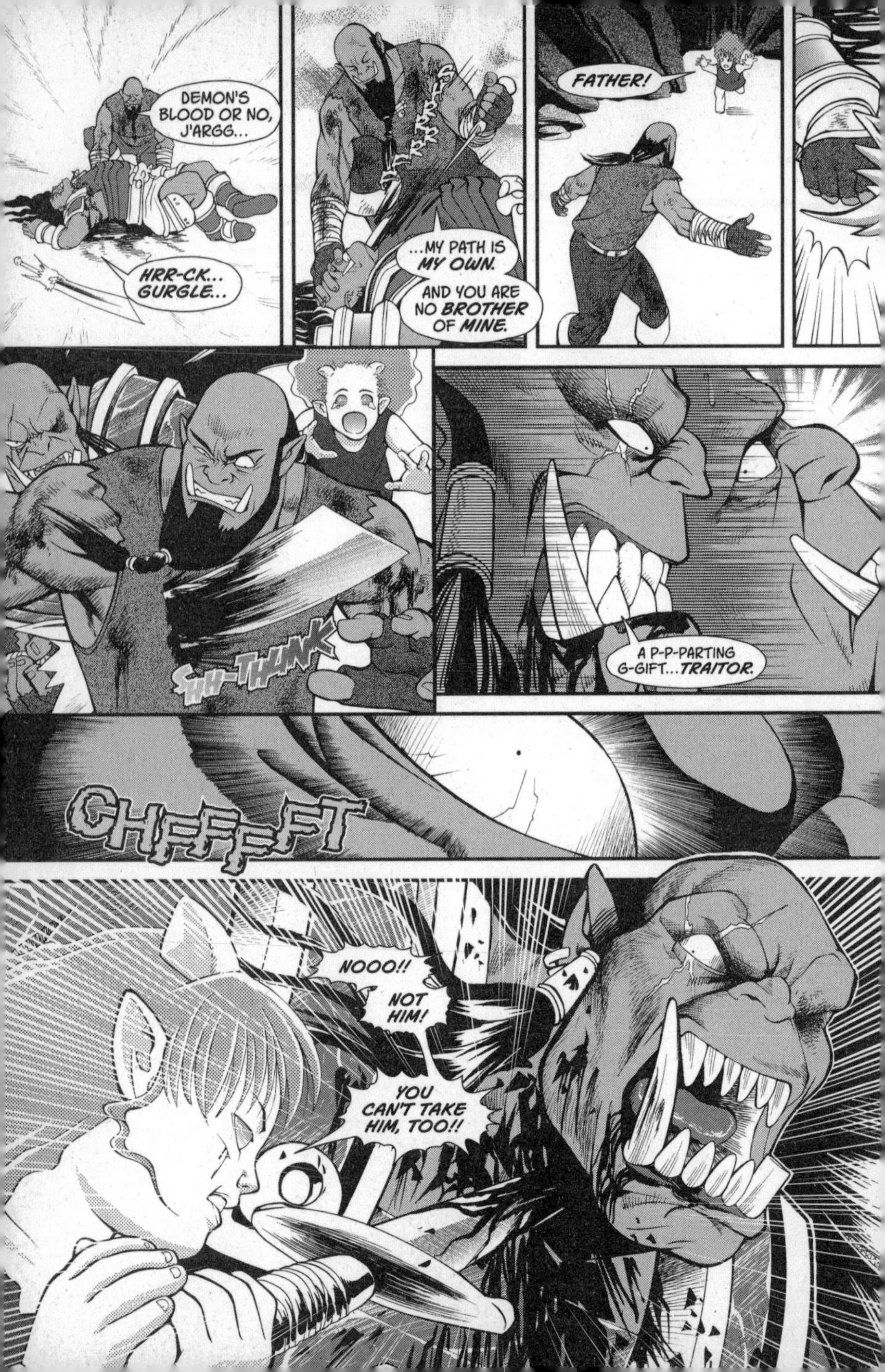
DEMON'S BLOOD OR NO, J'ARGG...
HRR-CK... GURGLE...
...MY PATH IS MY OWN.
AND YOU ARE NO BROTHER OF MINE.
FATHER!
SHH-THUNK
A P-P-PARTING G-GIFT... TRAITOR.
CHFFFFT
NOOO!!
NOT HIM!
YOU CAN'T TAKE HIM, TOO!!

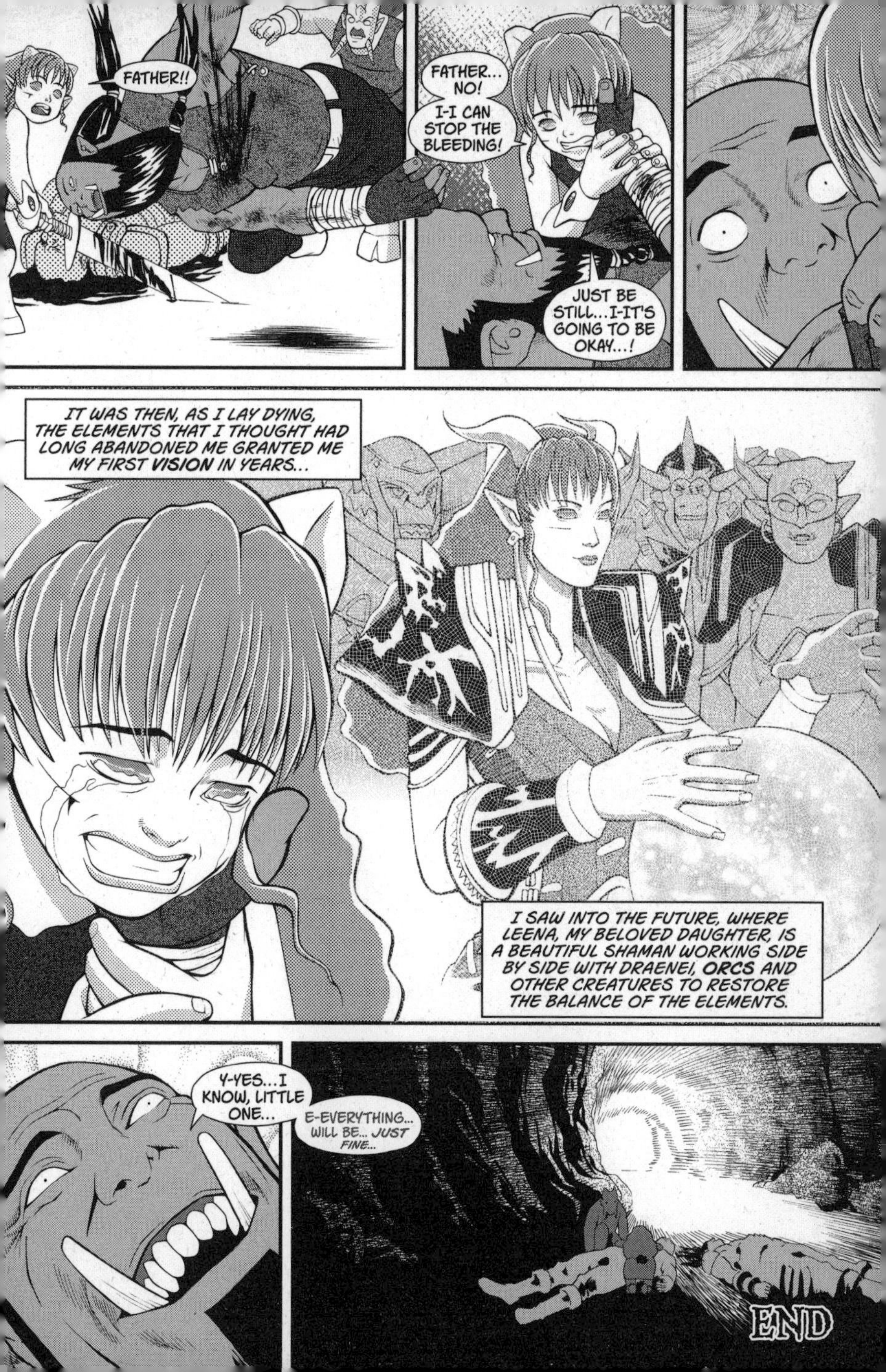
FATHER!!
FATHER... NO!
I-I CAN STOP THE BLEEDING!
JUST BE STILL... I-IT'S GOING TO BE OKAY...!
IT WAS THEN, AS I LAY DYING, THE ELEMENTS THAT I THOUGHT HAD LONG ABANDONED ME GRANTED ME MY FIRST VISION IN YEARS...
I SAW INTO THE FUTURE, WHERE LEENA, MY BELOVED DAUGHTER, IS A BEAUTIFUL SHAMAN WORKING SIDE BY SIDE WITH DRAENEI, ORCS AND OTHER CREATURES TO RESTORE THE BALANCE OF THE ELEMENTS.
Y-YES... I KNOW, LITTLE ONE...
E-EVERYTHING... WILL BE... JUST FINE...
END

ABOUT THE WRITERS

RICHARD A. KNAAK

Richard A. Knaak is the New York Times bestselling fantasy author of 27 novels and over a dozen short pieces, including *The Legend of Huma*, *Night of Blood* for Dragonlance and the *War of the Ancients* trilogy for Warcraft. In addition to the TOKYOPOP series *Warcraft: The Sunwell Trilogy*, he is the author of its forthcoming sequel trilogy, *Warcraft: Dragons of Outland*. To find out more about Richard's projects, visit his website at www.sff.net/people/knaak.

GRACE RANDOLPH

Grace Randolph is a comedic actor and writer born and raised in New York City. Her previous writing credits include *Justice League Unlimited #41* for DC Comics and *Nemesis: Who Me?* for TOKYOPOP's Pilot Program. She also has an upcoming manga adaptation of Meg Cabot's *Jinx*, as well as "Newsworthy," a short story in TOKYOPOP's *StarCraft: Frontline* Volume 2. Outside of comics, Grace is the host/writer/producer of the webshow *RevYOU*, which can be seen on YouTube and NBC/Bravo's *Television Without Pity* website. Grace also studies at the Upright Citizens Brigade Theatre (UCB) where she has written, performed and produced the shows "Situation: Awkward" and "Igor On Strike."

DAN JOLLEY

Dan Jolley is the author of several books for TOKYOPOP, including the young adult novel, *Alex Unlimited*, and the first trilogy of the bestselling Warriors manga, *Warriors: The Lost Warrior*. Dan also authored "How to Win Friends," a short story for *Warcraft: Legends* Volume 1. Much more information about Dan can be found at his website, www.danjolley.com.

AARON SPARROW

When not traveling abroad to explore the dark continent, race Italian sports cars and attend rare fedora conventions, Aaron Sparrow occasionally writes English adaptations for TOKYOPOP, such as *King Of Thorn* and *Devil May Cry 3*. He once killed a man "just to watch him die" but was distracted at the last moment by a pretty butterfly and had to kill a second man shortly thereafter. A senseless waste, really...especially considering the second guy held on so long that Aaron fell asleep and missed his death as well. Aaron is currently looking over applicants for victim #3.

ABOUT THE ARTISTS

JAE-HWAN KIM

Born in 1971 in Korea, Jae-Hwan Kim's best-known manga works include *Rainbow*, *Combat Metal HeMoSoo* and *King of Hell*, an ongoing series currently published by TOKYOPOP. Along with being the creator of *War Angels* for TOKYOPOP, Jae-Hwan is also the artist for TOKYOPOP's *Warcraft: The Sunwell Trilogy*, as well as its sequel trilogy, *Warcraft: Dragons of Outland*, which will be available in 2009. Jae-Hwan is also the artist for Richard Knaak's four-part short story featured in *Warcraft: Legends*, an anthology series also from TOKYOPOP.

ERIE

Erica "Erie" Horita first became an artistic success in Brazil where she lived for several years before joining Glass House Graphics Inc. Erie-chan recently moved back to her native Japan with her family, where she is able to feed her passion for manga, anime and games. *Ethora*, her first comic book mini-series was a resounding success, and led to other career opportunities, such as *Warcraft: Legends* Volume 2 from TOKYOPOP.

ELISA KWON

Elisa Kwon was born in Masan, South Korea and moved to Brazil when she was two years old. She has since graduated from Sao Paulo University with a degree in Visual Arts. Besides creating manga art, Elisa has also worked on 2D animated motion pictures. In Brazil Elisa collaborated with friends on a manga project named *Mercenários*, and in 2007 she joined Glass House Graphics Inc., which led to her inking the manga *Vampire Kisses* Volumes 2 & 3 for TOKYOPOP, as well as being the artist for the TOKYOPOP pilot *Nemesis: Who Me?*. She is a huge Warcraft fan and is honored to have had a role in making the manga.

IN-BAE KIM

In-Bae made his Korean manga debut in 1998 with *Tong-hwa-joong* (On the Phone). He followed that with several webzine manga shorts including "Film Ggengin Nar" (The Day I Blacked Out Drinking) and "Call Me." His serialized manga, "Bbuggoogi" (Cuckoo Bird), has been featured in several newspapers. *Warcraft: Legends* Volume 2 marks his American manga debut.

A manga so fine, we had to do it a second time...

You hold in your hands Volume 2 of *Warcraft: Legends,* the second of many scheduled volumes of Warcraft manga that will be hitting shelves over the next three years from TOKYOPOP and Blizzard Entertainment. They say be careful of success, because it means your next effort not only has to match your first attempt, but best it...but we can say with all confidence that we've definitely pulled it off with this volume by delivering a fantastic manga that any fan of Warcraft or fantasy would be proud to have on their shelves.

As always, these manga are a labor of love for the team here at TOKYOPOP and the really smart and talented people at Blizzard Entertainment. Folks like Jason Bischoff, Cory Jones, Glenn Rane, Micky Neilson, and the man, the myth, the legend, Chris Metzen, all help us make these anthologies the best they could possibly be for you wonderful Warcraft fans! So go on, guys, take a bow (just don't bump your heads on your desks when you do it).

Finally, but no less importantly, we'd like to thank all of the writers, inkers, toners and finishers who sat into the wee hours of the night toiling away at their keyboards and drawing tables in an effort to flee from the Jason Voorhees of the creative mind--the ever-looming deadline. You guys are all *awesome,* because without you we'd have no book! (Seriously, it'd all be white paper and this thank you page.)

That's it for this volume, but don't forget to pick up the first volume of our other Blizzard anthology series, *StarCraft: Frontline,* available in stores now. (You can check out a preview of it when you turn the page.) And be sure to pick up our third volume of *Warcraft: Legends,* available in March 2009!

Troy Lewter
Editor

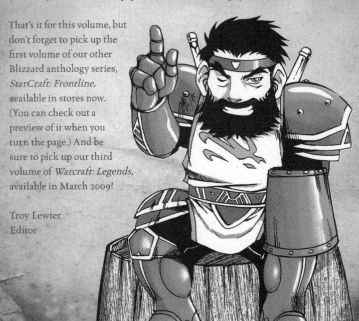

IN THE NEXT VOLUME

What rousing stories of action, comedy and tragedy! But surely we've run out of exciting tales to weave, eh? Well think again, for Azeroth is abundant with secrets and adventures yet to be revealed...

No longer afraid, Trag ventures to the Northrend Dragon Wastes for a weapon to use against the Lich King...

One tragic event places a blood elf mage, a forsaken warrior and a Scarlet Crusade captain on a collision course of vengeance and death...

An ill-tempered goblin becomes the unlikely hero for a little gnome girl when he is thrust into the role of Greatfather Winter...

The greatest hunter in all of Azeroth becomes the unexpected protector of three frostsaber cubs...

The campfire is blazing and the ale flows free, so come back and join us as we spin more yarns of defeat and victory, death and life, infamy... and LEGENDS.

WARCRAFT: LEGENDS VOLUME 3
COMING MARCH 2009

STARCRAFT

FRONTLINE

SNEAK PEEK

NOW THAT YOU HAVE BRAVED THE UNTAMED
LANDS OF AZEROTH, IT'S TIME TO HEAD FOR
THE STARS AND EXPERIENCE THE THRILLING
BLIZZARD SCI-FI FANTASY THAT IS *STARCRAFT:
FRONTLINE*. TOKYOPOP IS PROUD TO PRESENT
THIS SERIES OF ANTHOLOGIES BASED ON
BLIZZARD'S BESTSELLING STARCRAFT REAL-TIME
STRATEGY GAME. LOCKED AND LOADED FOR
YOUR READING PLEASURE IS A SNEAK PEAK AT
"WEAPON OF WAR," ONE OF THE FOUR STORIES
FEATURED IN *STARCRAFT: FRONTLINE* VOLUME 1.

A DARK, ATMOSPHERIC STORY WRITTEN BY PAUL
BENJAMIN & DAVE SHRAMEK AND DRAWN BY
HECTOR SEVILLA, "WEAPON OF WAR" FOLLOWS
A PSIONIC SIX-YEAR-OLD BOY CAUGHT AT THE
CENTER OF A BRUTAL CONFLICT BETWEEN A
TERRAN MINING COLONY AND THE ZERG. AS
TENSIONS ESCALATE, THE MARINES AND MINERS
FIND THEMSELVES IN A MORAL CRISIS THAT
COULD MEAN EITHER LIFE OR DEATH FOR THE
YOUNG BOY...

STARCRAFT: FRONTLINE VOLUME 1
IS AVAILABLE NOW!

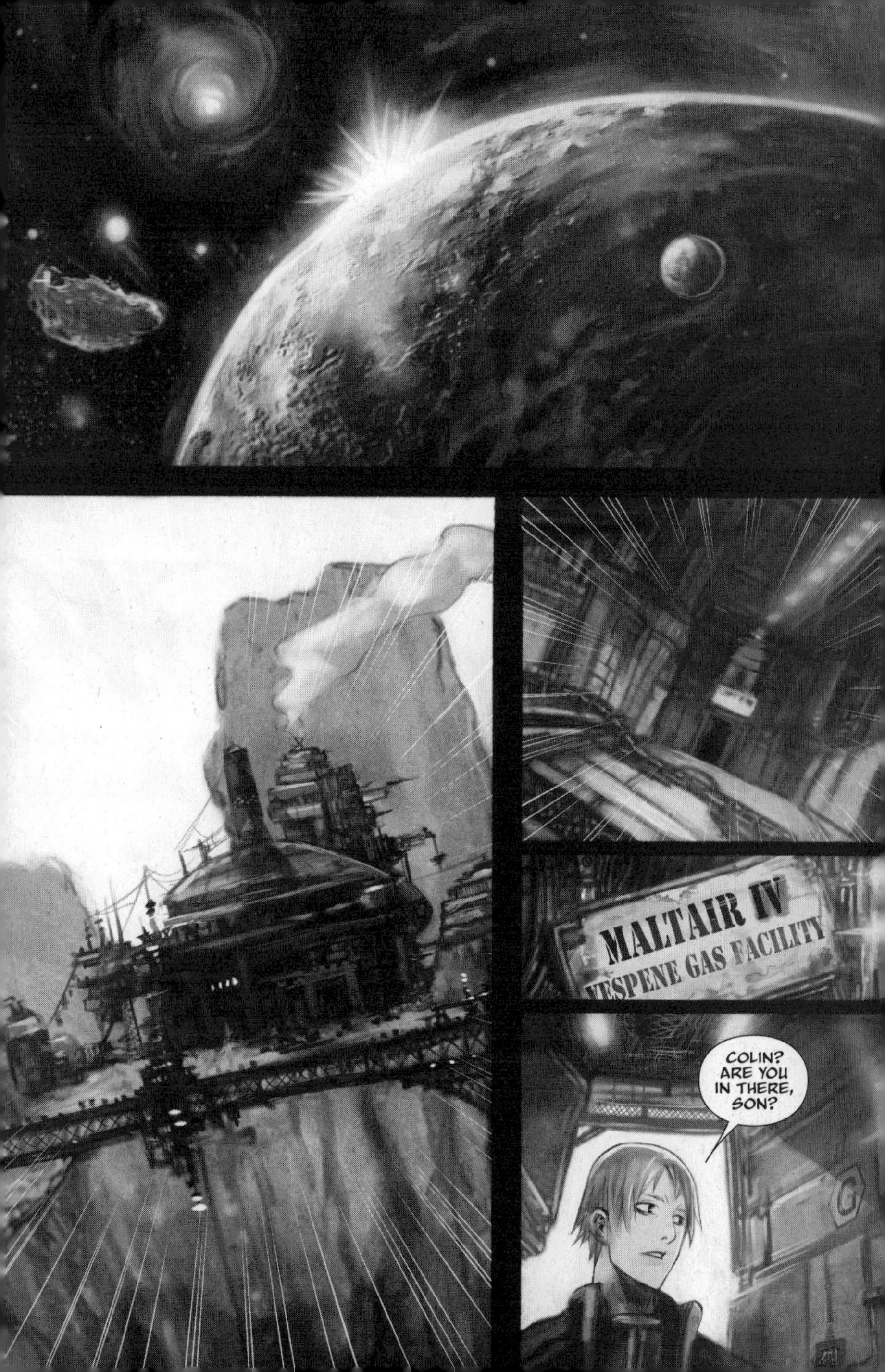
MALTAIR IV
VESPENE GAS FACILITY
COLIN? ARE YOU IN THERE, SON?

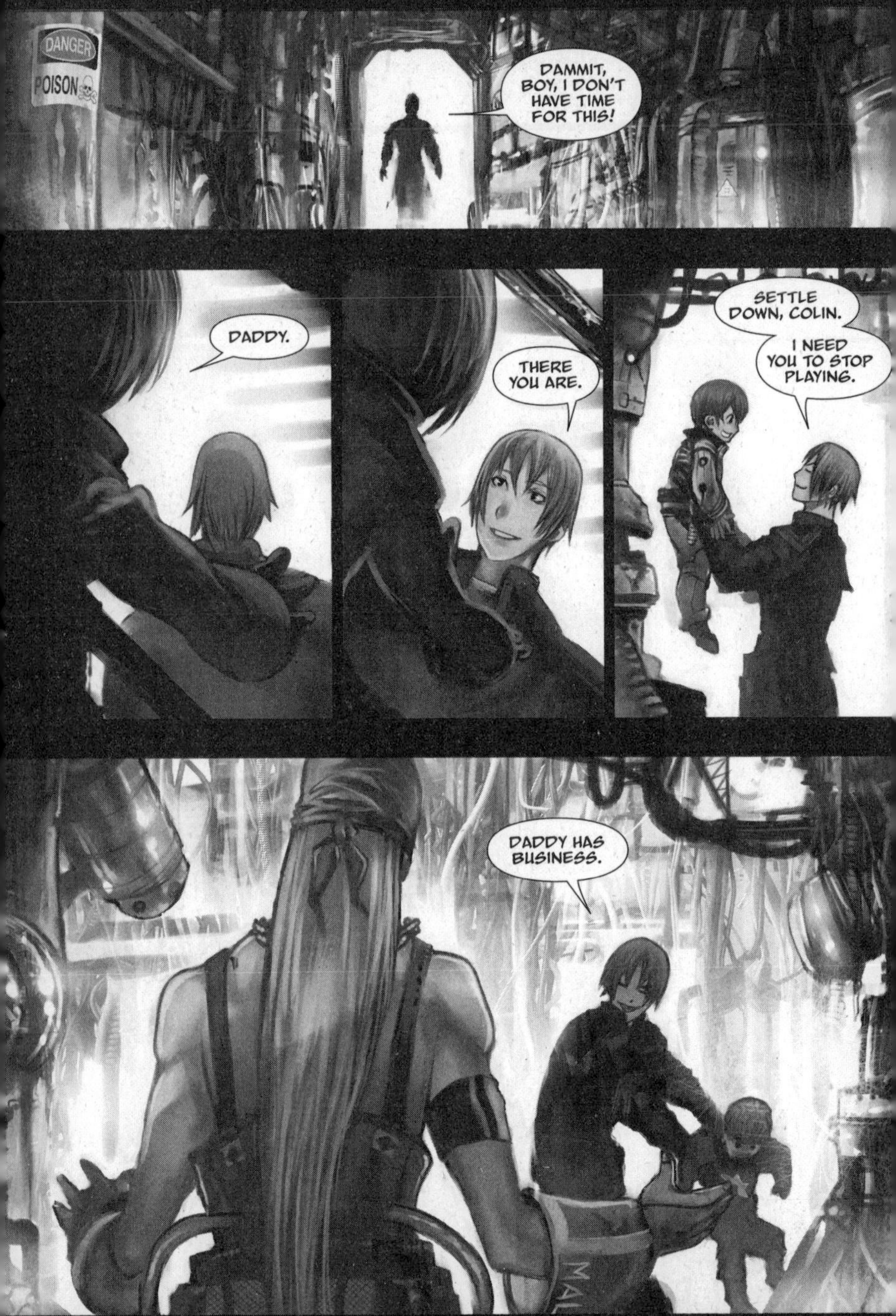
DANGER
POISON
DAMMIT, BOY, I DON'T HAVE TIME FOR THIS!
DADDY.
THERE YOU ARE.
SETTLE DOWN, COLIN.
I NEED YOU TO STOP PLAYING.
DADDY HAS BUSINESS.

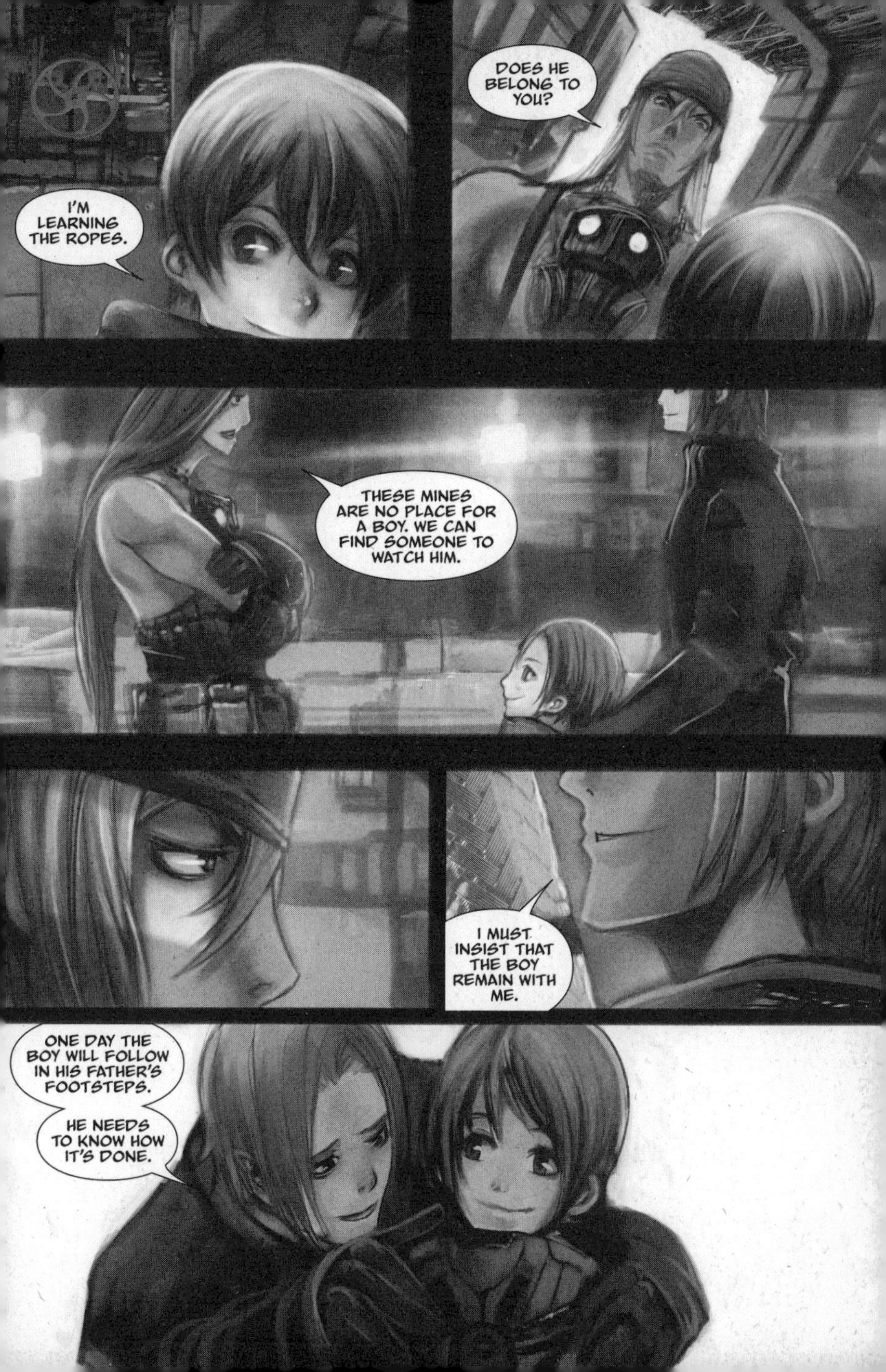
I'M LEARNING THE ROPES.
DOES HE BELONG TO YOU?
THESE MINES ARE NO PLACE FOR A BOY. WE CAN FIND SOMEONE TO WATCH HIM.
I MUST INSIST THAT THE BOY REMAIN WITH ME.
ONE DAY THE BOY WILL FOLLOW IN HIS FATHER'S FOOTSTEPS.
HE NEEDS TO KNOW HOW IT'S DONE.

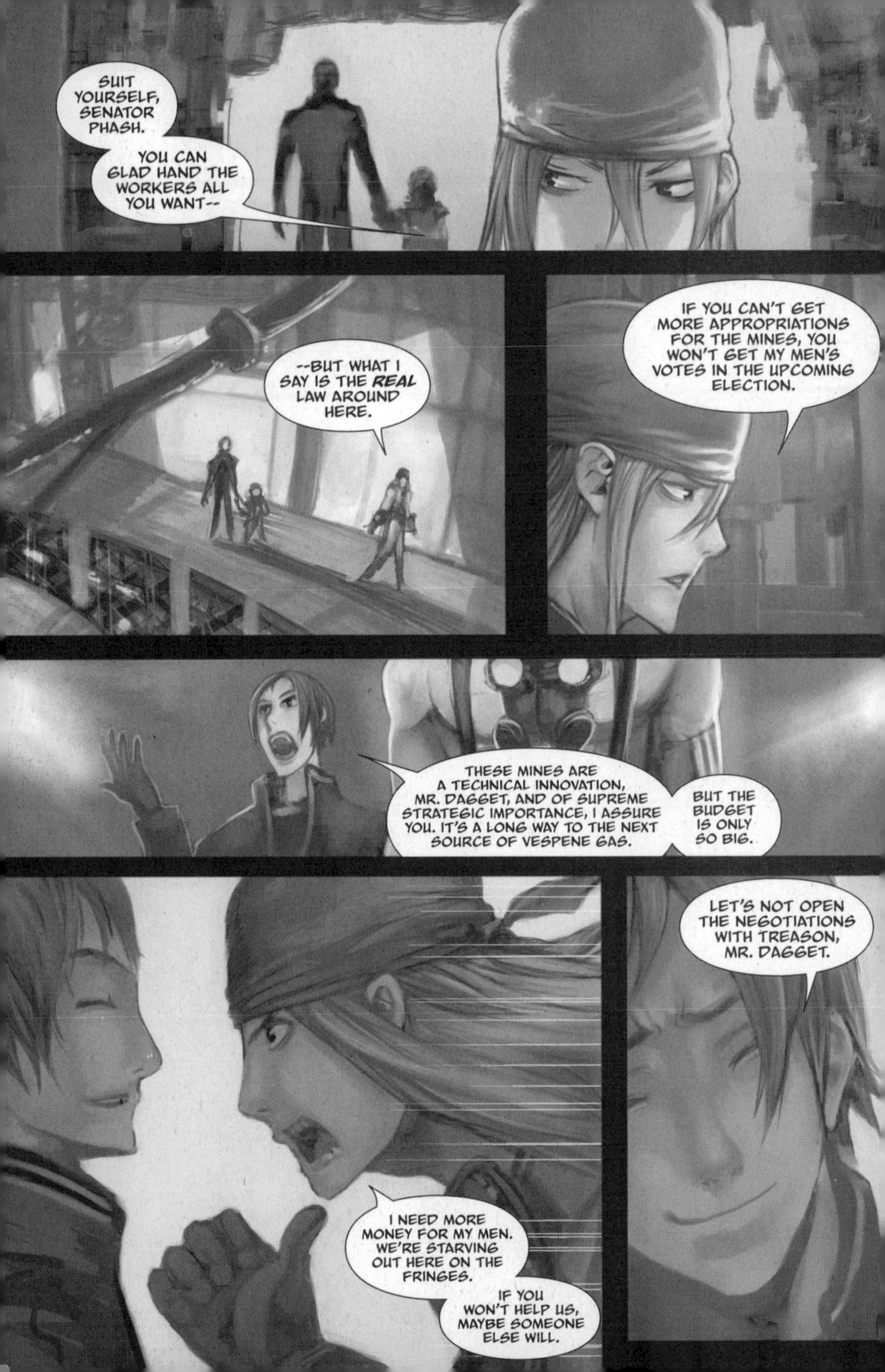

SUIT YOURSELF, SENATOR PHASH.
YOU CAN GLAD HAND THE WORKERS ALL YOU WANT--
--BUT WHAT I SAY IS THE *REAL* LAW AROUND HERE.
IF YOU CAN'T GET MORE APPROPRIATIONS FOR THE MINES, YOU WON'T GET MY MEN'S VOTES IN THE UPCOMING ELECTION.
THESE MINES ARE A TECHNICAL INNOVATION, MR. DAGGET, AND OF SUPREME STRATEGIC IMPORTANCE, I ASSURE YOU. IT'S A LONG WAY TO THE NEXT SOURCE OF VESPENE GAS.
BUT THE BUDGET IS ONLY SO BIG.
I NEED MORE MONEY FOR MY MEN. WE'RE STARVING OUT HERE ON THE FRINGES.
IF YOU WON'T HELP US, MAYBE SOMEONE ELSE WILL.
LET'S NOT OPEN THE NEGOTIATIONS WITH TREASON, MR. DAGGET.

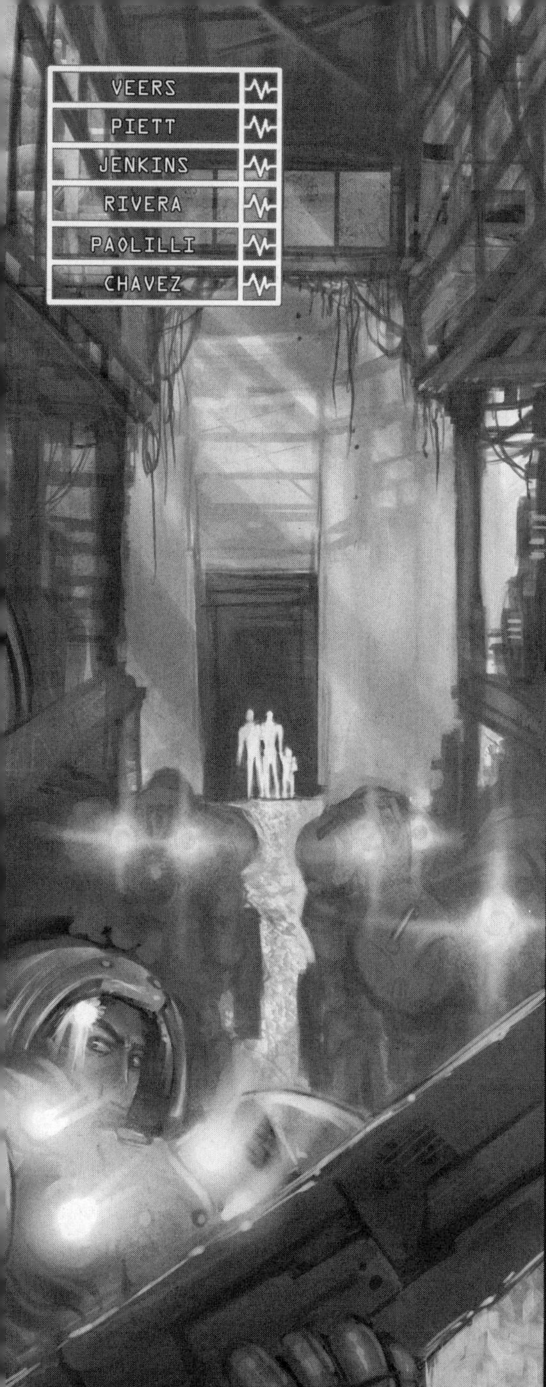
VEERS
PIETT
JENKINS
RIVERA
PAOLILLI
CHAVEZ

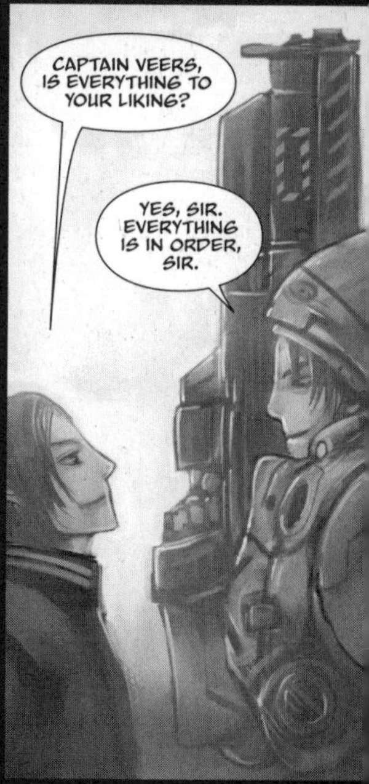
CAPTAIN VEERS, IS EVERYTHING TO YOUR LIKING?
YES, SIR. EVERYTHING IS IN ORDER, SIR.

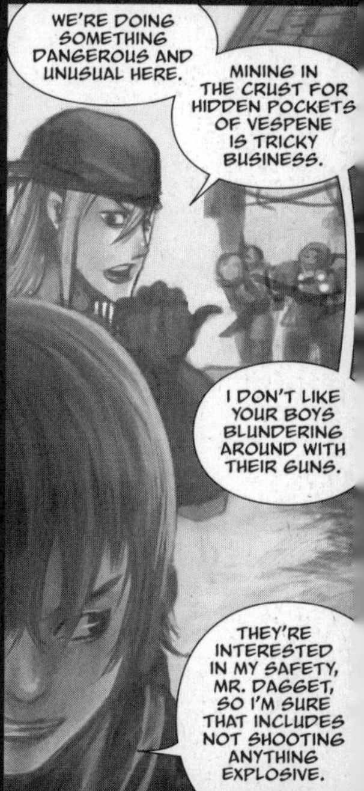
WE'RE DOING SOMETHING DANGEROUS AND UNUSUAL HERE.
MINING IN THE CRUST FOR HIDDEN POCKETS OF VESPENE IS TRICKY BUSINESS.
I DON'T LIKE YOUR BOYS BLUNDERING AROUND WITH THEIR GUNS.
THEY'RE INTERESTED IN MY SAFETY, MR. DAGGET, SO I'M SURE THAT INCLUDES NOT SHOOTING ANYTHING EXPLOSIVE.

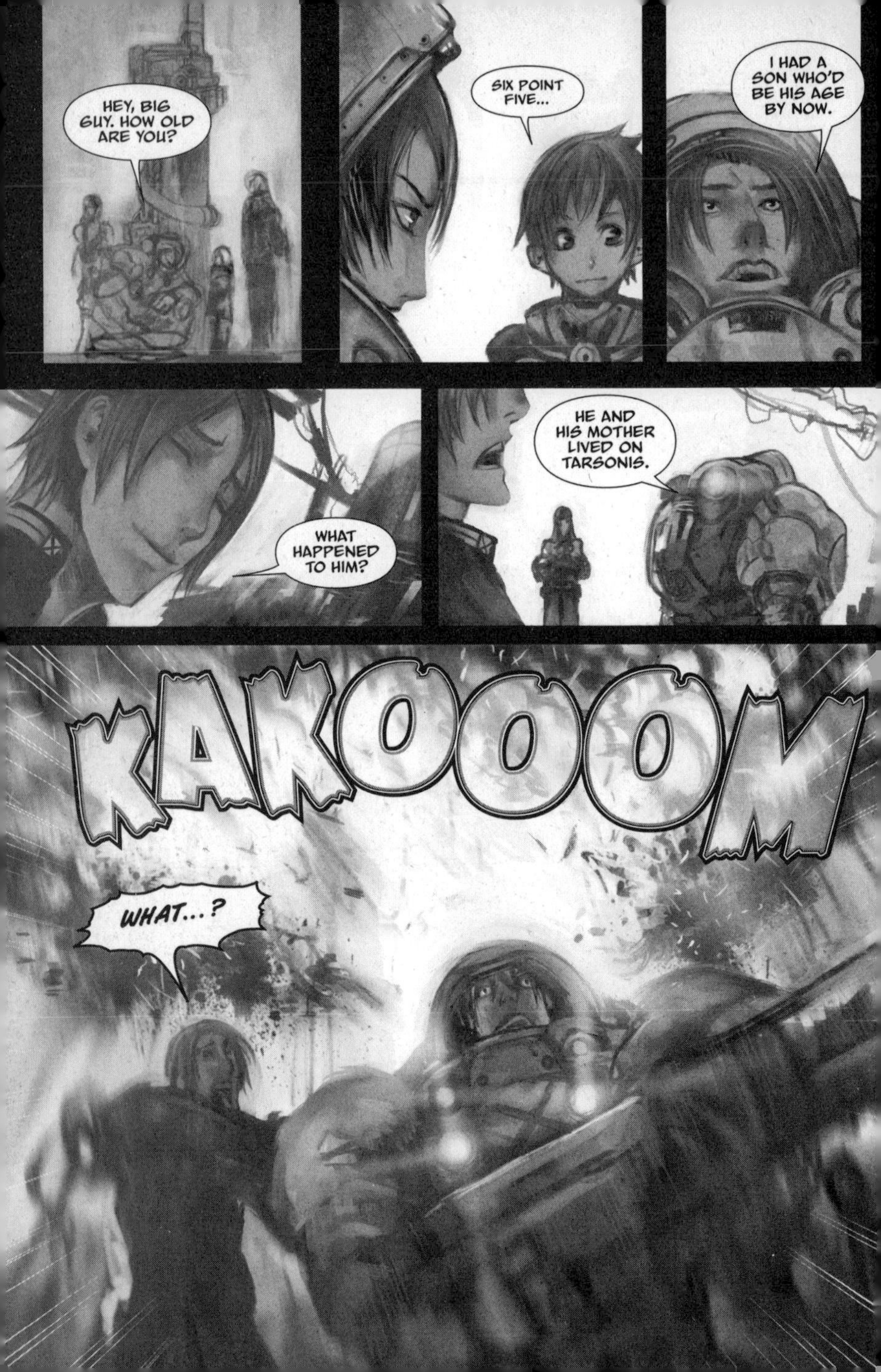
HEY, BIG GUY. HOW OLD ARE YOU?
SIX POINT FIVE...
I HAD A SON WHO'D BE HIS AGE BY NOW.
WHAT HAPPENED TO HIM?
HE AND HIS MOTHER LIVED ON TARSONIS.
KAKOOOM
WHAT...?

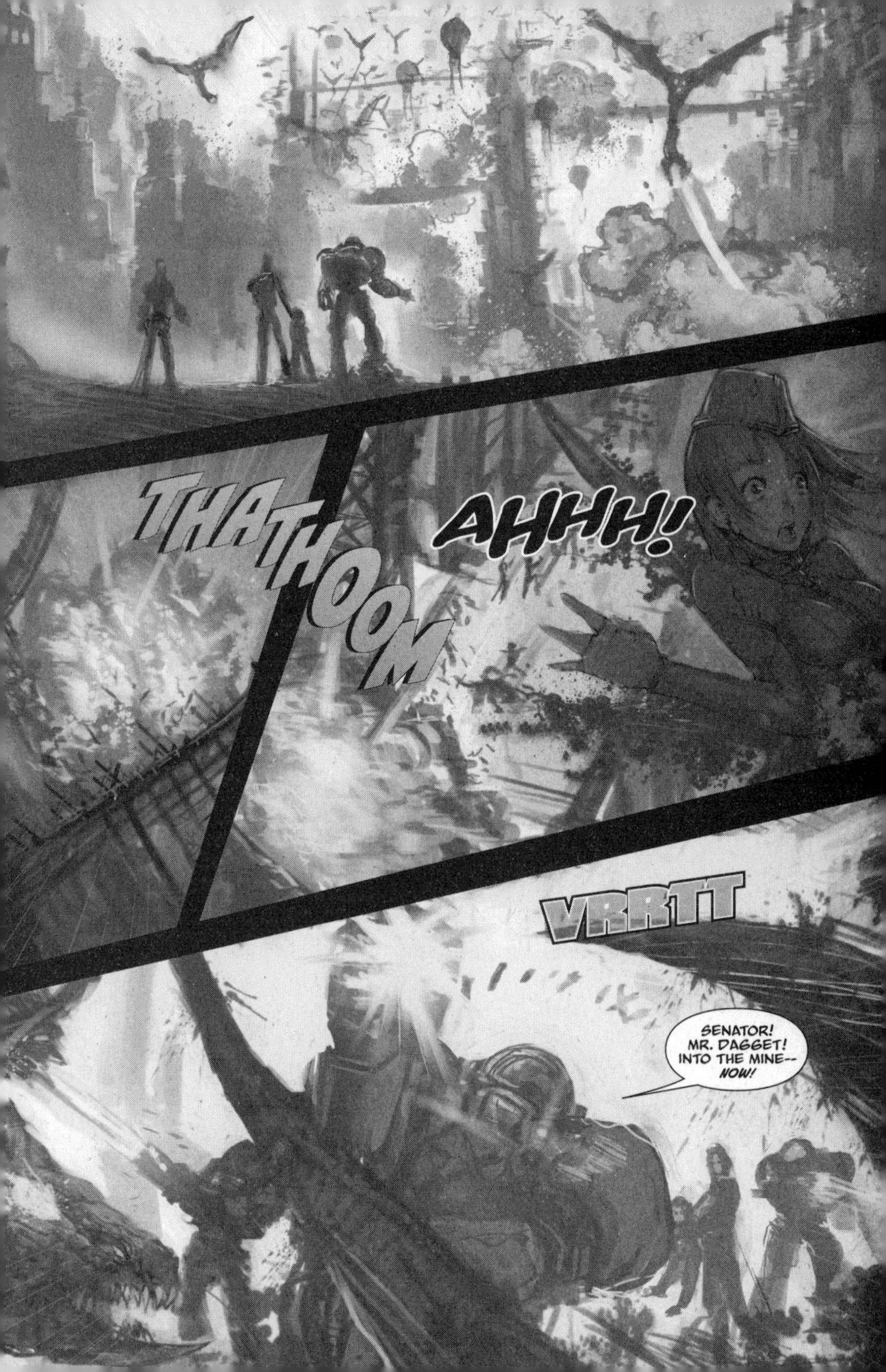
THATHOOM
AHHH!
VRRTT
SENATOR! MR. DAGGET! INTO THE MINE-- NOW!

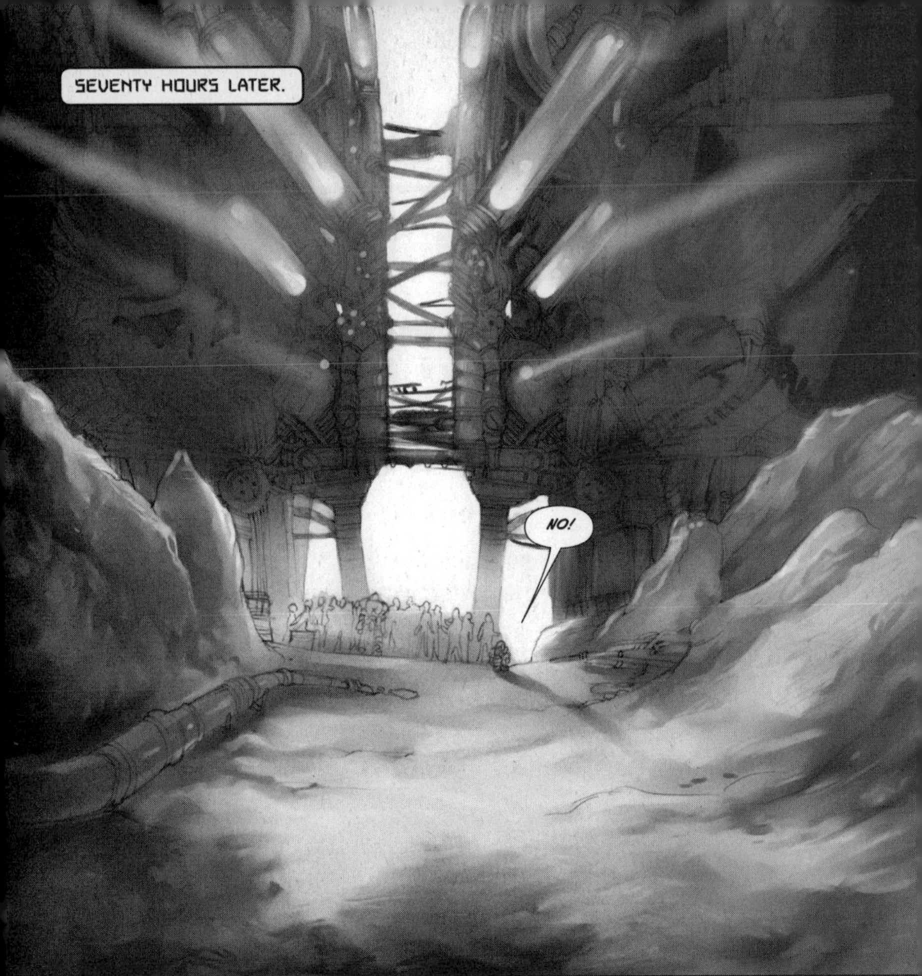
SEVENTY HOURS LATER.
NO!

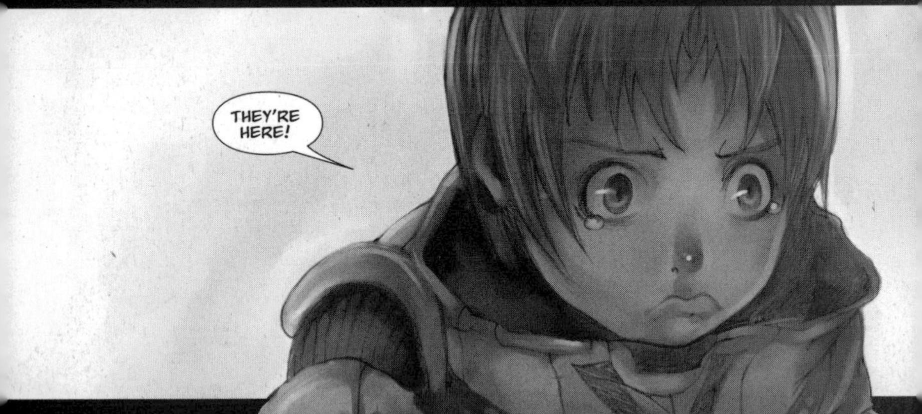
THEY'RE HERE!

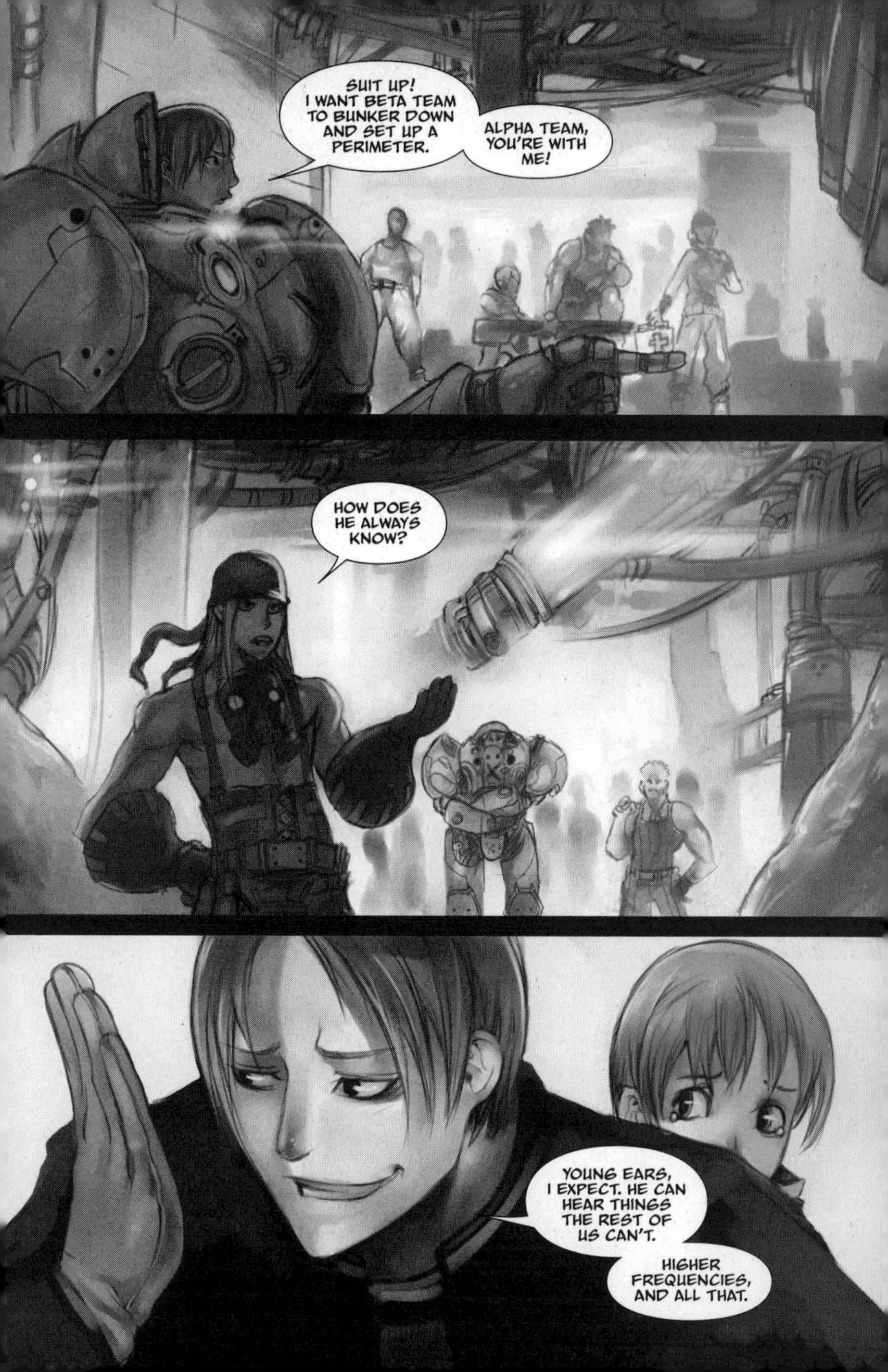
SUIT UP! I WANT BETA TEAM TO BUNKER DOWN AND SET UP A PERIMETER.
ALPHA TEAM, YOU'RE WITH ME!
HOW DOES HE ALWAYS KNOW?
YOUNG EARS, I EXPECT. HE CAN HEAR THINGS THE REST OF US CAN'T.
HIGHER FREQUENCIES, AND ALL THAT.

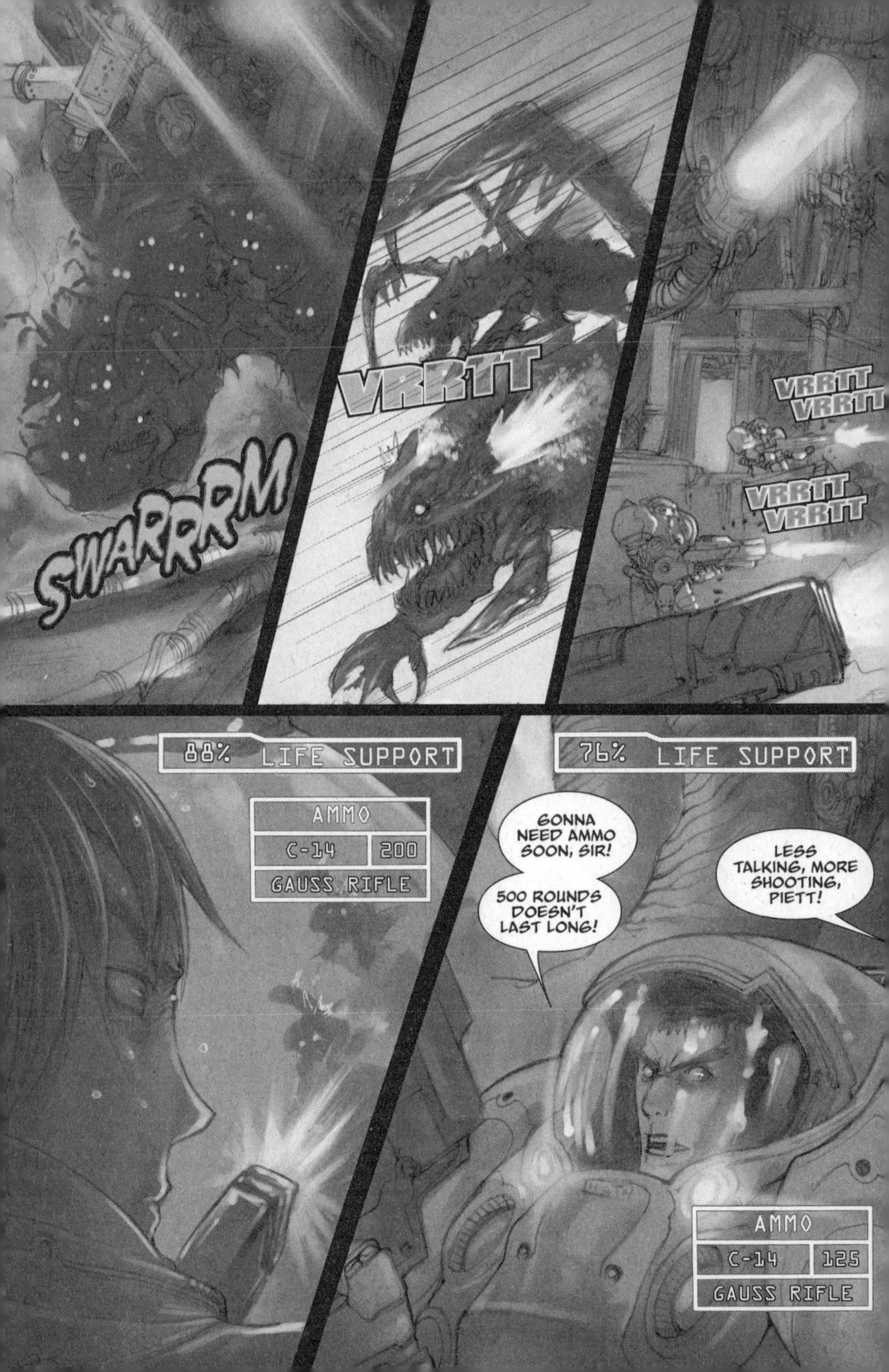
SWARRRM
VRRTT
VRRTT
VRRTT
VRRTT
VRRTT
88% LIFE SUPPORT
AMMO
C-14
200
GAUSS RIFLE
76% LIFE SUPPORT
GONNA NEED AMMO SOON, SIR!
500 ROUNDS DOESN'T LAST LONG!
LESS TALKING, MORE SHOOTING, PIETT!
AMMO
C-14
125
GAUSS RIFLE

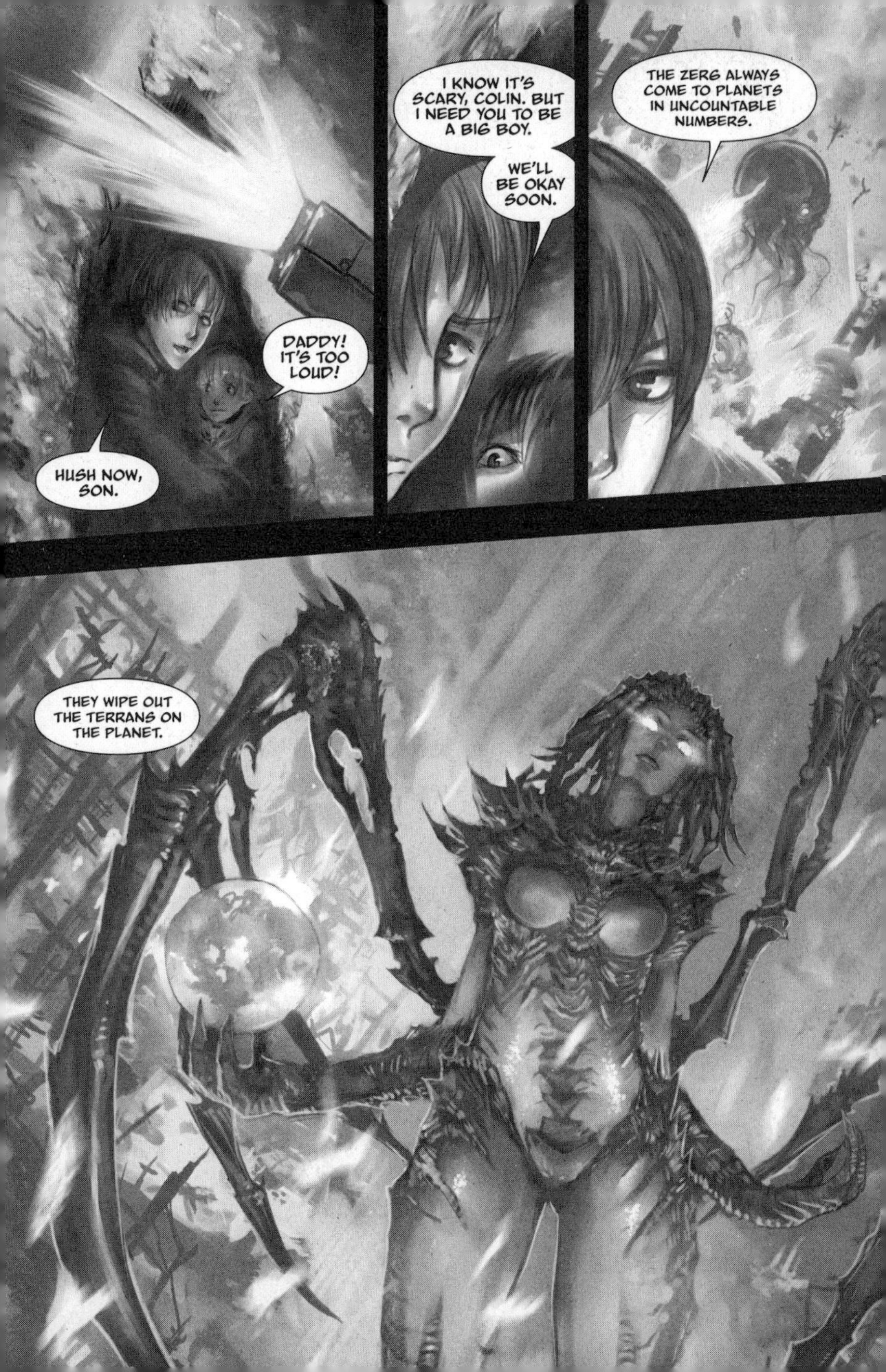
DADDY! IT'S TOO LOUD!
HUSH NOW, SON.
I KNOW IT'S SCARY, COLIN. BUT I NEED YOU TO BE A BIG BOY.
WE'LL BE OKAY SOON.
THE ZERG ALWAYS COME TO PLANETS IN UNCOUNTABLE NUMBERS.
THEY WIPE OUT THE TERRANS ON THE PLANET.

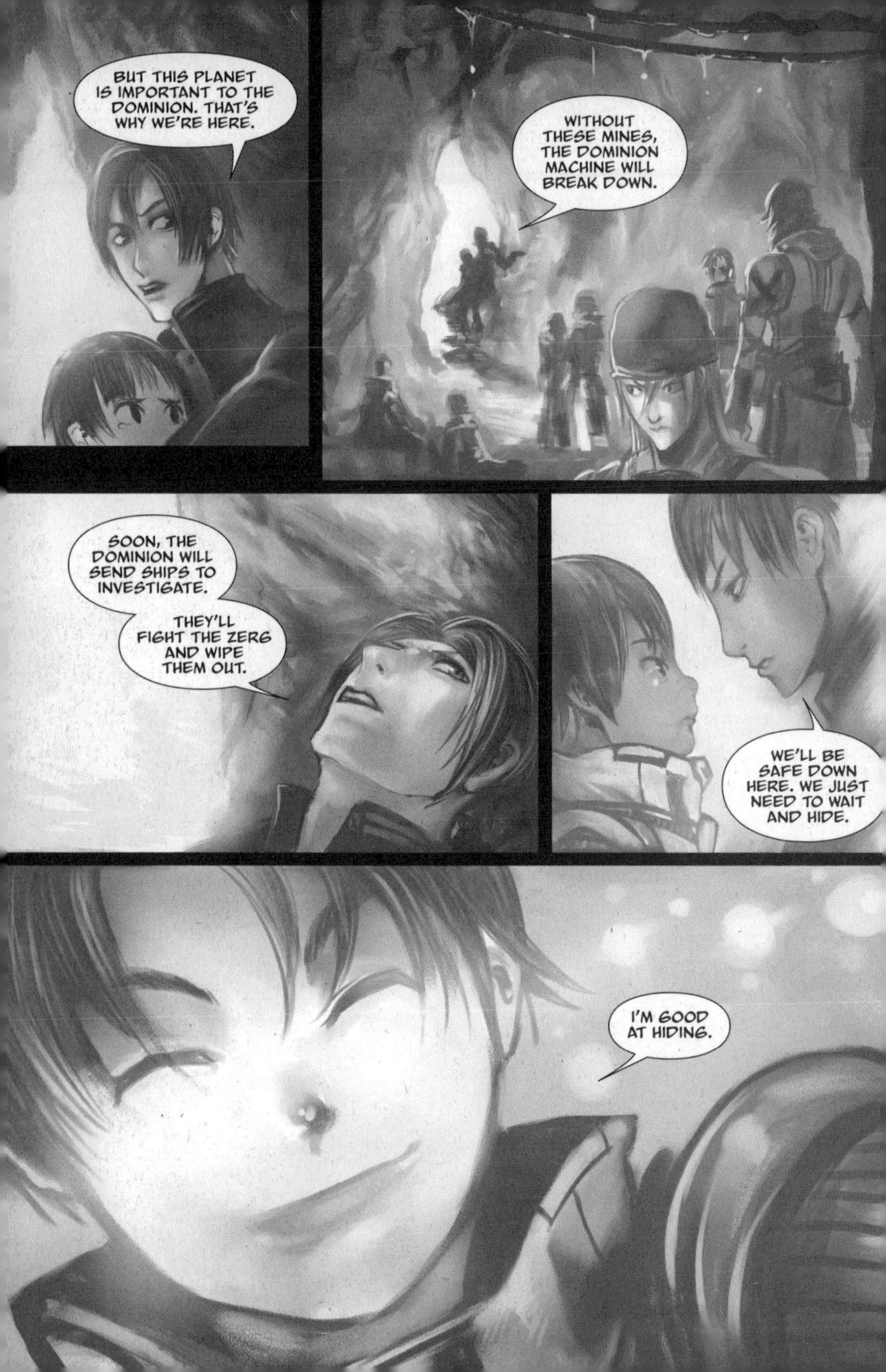
BUT THIS PLANET IS IMPORTANT TO THE DOMINION. THAT'S WHY WE'RE HERE.
WITHOUT THESE MINES, THE DOMINION MACHINE WILL BREAK DOWN.
SOON, THE DOMINION WILL SEND SHIPS TO INVESTIGATE.
THEY'LL FIGHT THE ZERG AND WIPE THEM OUT.
WE'LL BE SAFE DOWN HERE. WE JUST NEED TO WAIT AND HIDE.
I'M GOOD AT HIDING.

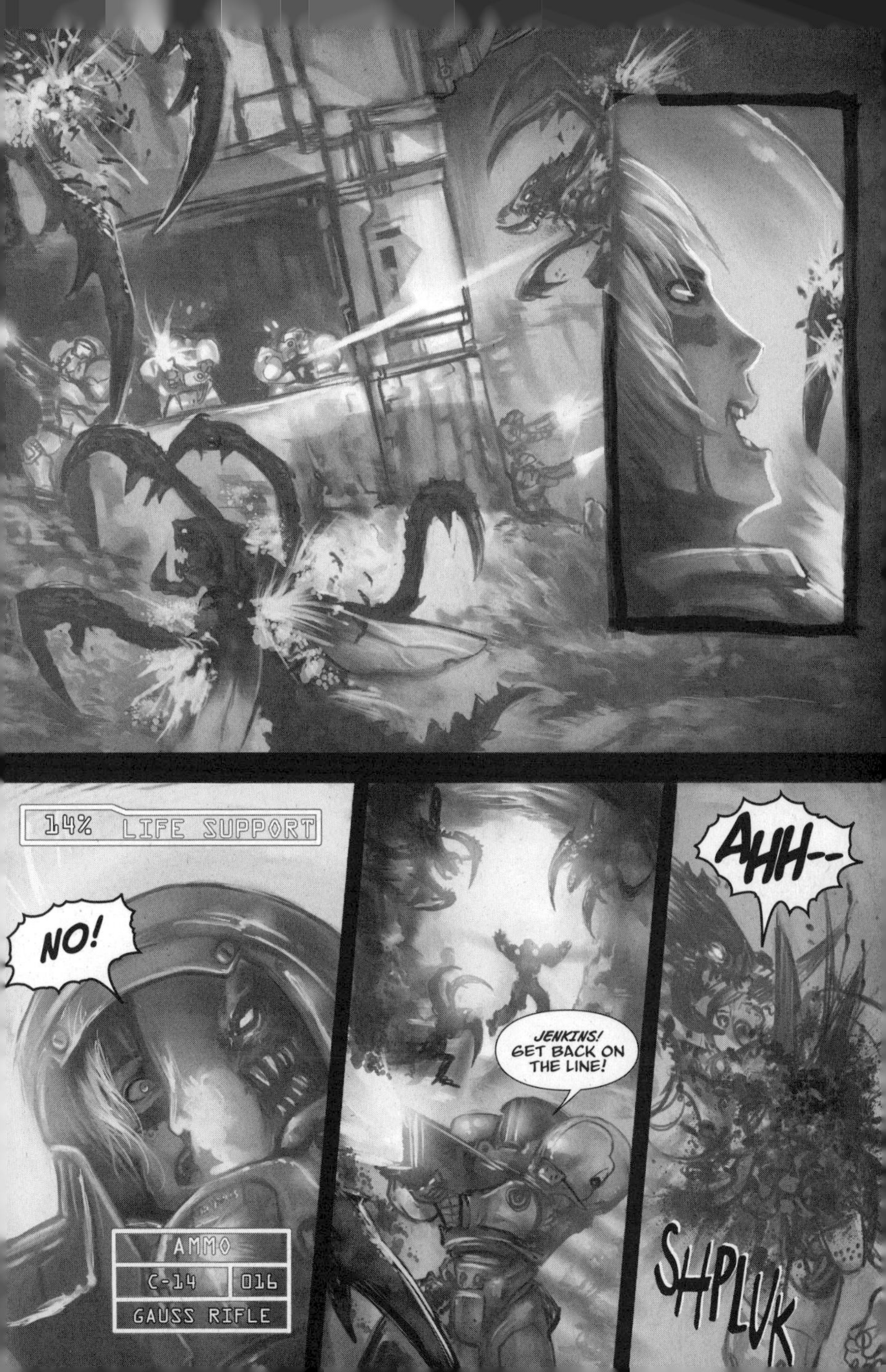
14% LIFE SUPPORT
NO!
AMMO
C-14
016
GAUSS RIFLE
JENKINS! GET BACK ON THE LINE!
AHH--
SHPLUK

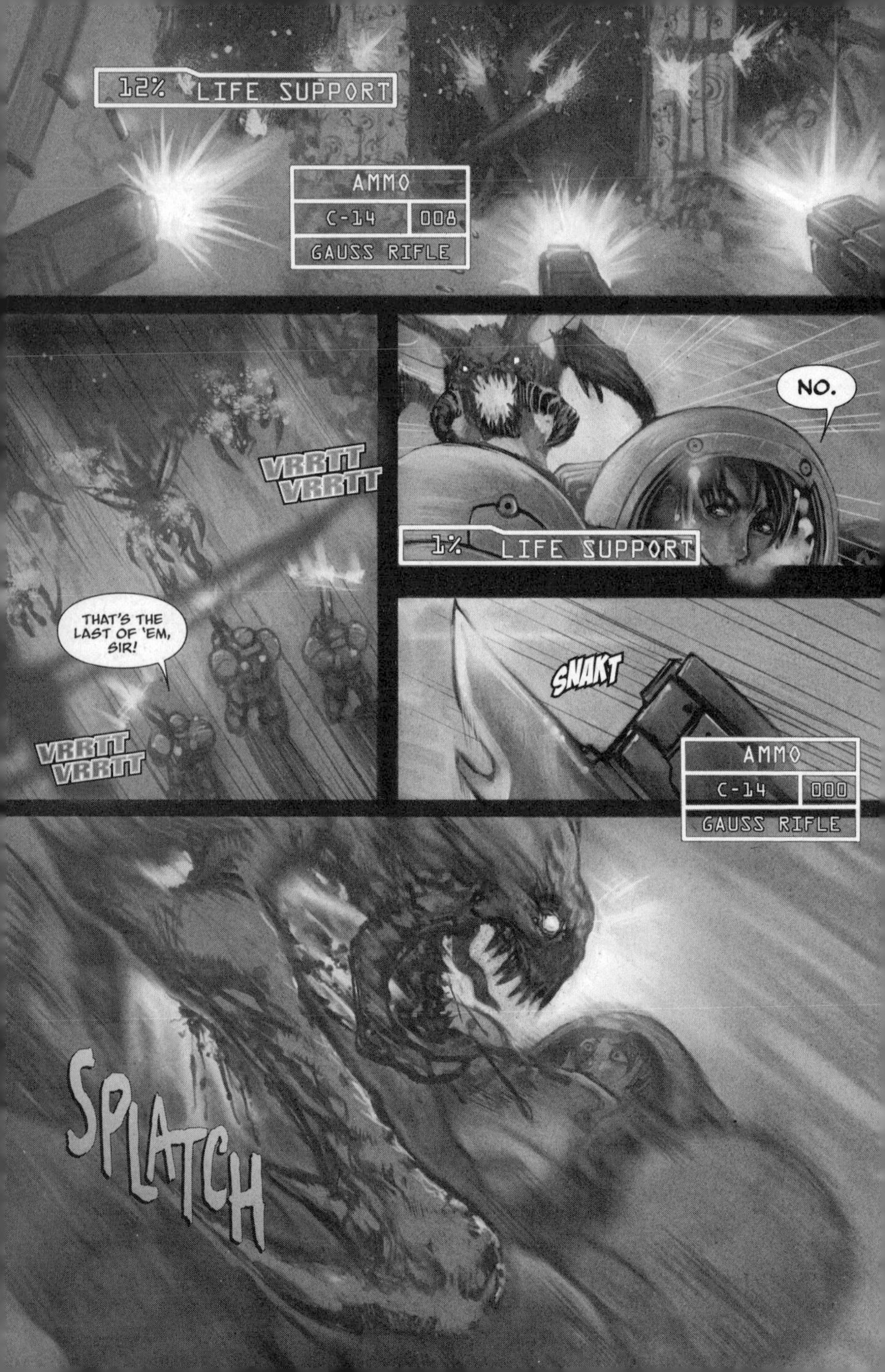
12% LIFE SUPPORT
AMMO
C-14
008
GAUSS RIFLE
VRRTT VRRTT
THAT'S THE LAST OF 'EM, SIR!
VRRTT VRRTT
NO.
1% LIFE SUPPORT
SNAKT
AMMO
C-14
000
GAUSS RIFLE
SPLATCH

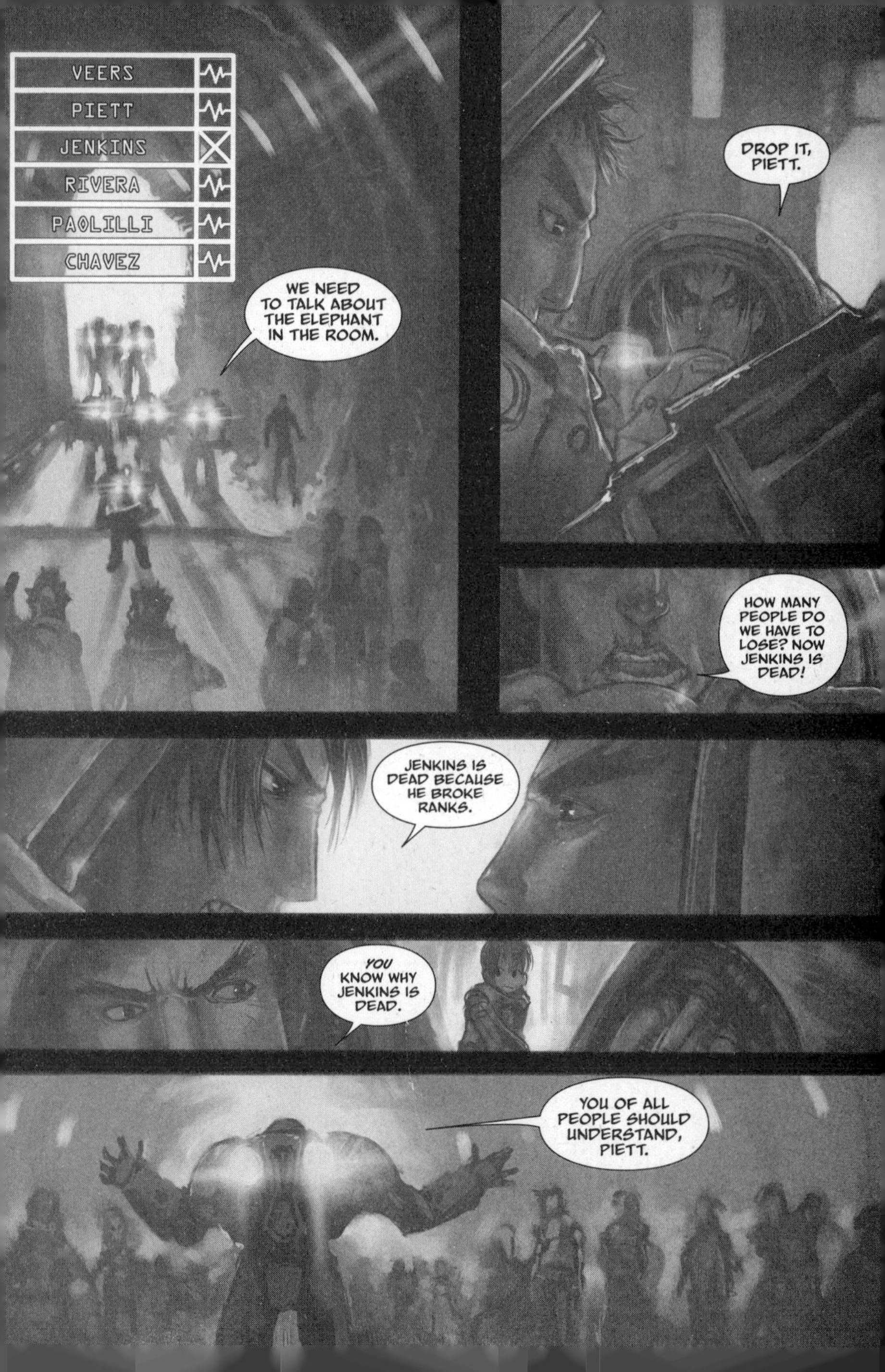
VEERS
PIETT
JENKINS
RIVERA
PAOLILLI
CHAVEZ
WE NEED TO TALK ABOUT THE ELEPHANT IN THE ROOM.
DROP IT, PIETT.
HOW MANY PEOPLE DO WE HAVE TO LOSE? NOW JENKINS IS DEAD!
JENKINS IS DEAD BECAUSE HE BROKE RANKS.
YOU KNOW WHY JENKINS IS DEAD.
YOU OF ALL PEOPLE SHOULD UNDERSTAND, PIETT.

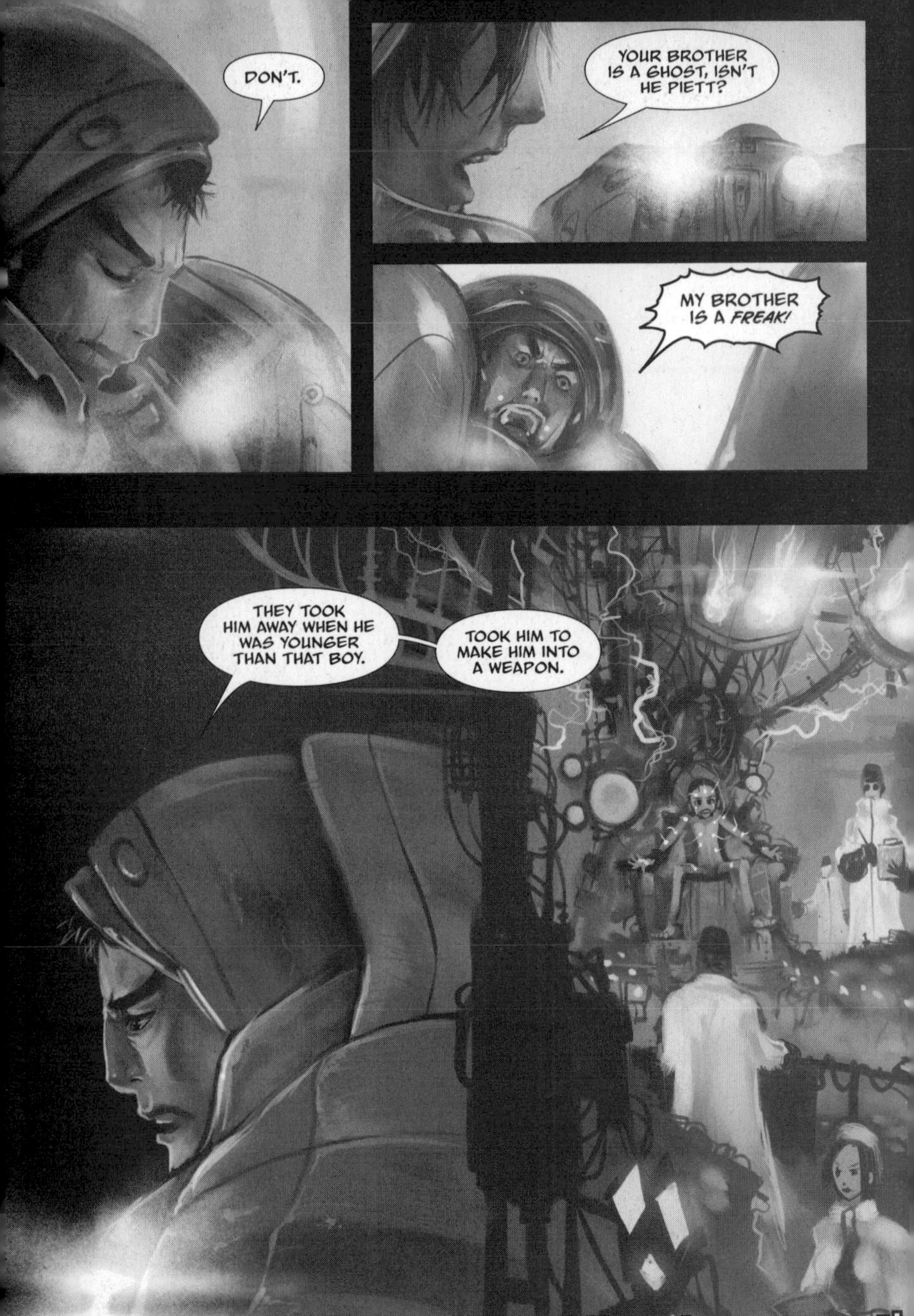
DON'T.
YOUR BROTHER IS A GHOST, ISN'T HE PIETT?
MY BROTHER IS A *FREAK!*
THEY TOOK HIM AWAY WHEN HE WAS YOUNGER THAN THAT BOY.
TOOK HIM TO MAKE HIM INTO A WEAPON.

CONTINUED IN STARCRAFT: FRONTLINE VOLUME 1!

MMO GAMING MOUSE

World's first
gaming mouse
designed exclusively
for World of Warcraft®

Incredible customization options:

- 6 million illumination choices
- 15 programmable buttons
- Custom macro creation

Intuitive, ergonomic design and
premium components ensure superior
performance, comfort and control

Available Q4 2008

⚫steelseries

Actual Gameplay.

NO. I'D RATHER KILL RATS.

With millions of players online, World of Warcraft has made gaming
history — and now's it's never been easier to join the adventure.
Simply visit **www.warcraft.com**, download the FREE TRIAL and join
thousands of mighty heroes for ten days of bold online adventure.

WORLD OF WARCRAFT®

MASSIVELY EPIC ONLINE

Stop Poking Me!

Lazy Peons

Quest

Orc Hero Required

Lazy Peons enters play exhausted.

Exhaust Lazy Peons to complete this quest.

Reward: Draw a card.

"Stop poking me!"

DARK PORTAL 303/319

Art by: Steve Ellis

©2007 UDC ©2007 Blizzard Entertainment, Inc.

- Each set contains new Loot™ cards to enhance your online character.
- Today's premier fantasy artists present an exciting new look at the World of Warcraft®.
- Compete in tournaments for exclusive World of Warcraft® prizes!

For more info and events, visit:
WOWTCG.COM

EPIC BATTLES
IN THE PALM OF YOUR HAND

WORLD of WARCRAFT MINIATURES GAME

World of Warcraft® Collectible Miniatures Game

· Premium miniatures with detailed paints designed by Studio McVey

· Standard and deluxe starter sets plus three-figure boosters

· Innovative game play utilizing the unique detachable UBase

Coming Fall 2008!

For more information, visit

WOWMINIS.COM

Legends Forged Dail

WORLD OF WARCRAFT
The ADVENTURE GAME

Grab your sword, ready your spells, and set off for adventure in the World of Warcraft! Vanquish diabolical monsters (as well as your fellow heroes) through intrigue and in open battle!

Play one of four unique characters, each with their own abilities and style of play. Ultimately, only one hero can be the best – will it be you?